HIGH CRIMES

HIGH CRIMES

THE CORRUPTION, IMPUNITY, AND IMPEACHMENT
OF DONALD TRUMP

MICHAEL D'ANTONIO

AND

PETER EISNER

THOMAS DUNNE
BOOKS
NEW YORK

First published in the United States by Thomas Dunne Books, an imprint of St. Martin's Publishing Group

www.thomasdunnebooks.com

Designed by Omar Chapa

Library of Congress Cataloging-in-Publication Data

Names: D'Antonio, Michael, author. | Eisner, Peter, author.
Title: High crimes : the corruption, impunity, and impeachment of Donald Trump / Michael D'Antonio and Peter Eisner.
Description: First edition. | New York : St. Martin's Press 2020. | Includes bibliographical references and index. |
Identifiers: LCCN 2020031672 | ISBN 9781250766670 (hardcover) | ISBN 9781250766687 (ebook)
Subjects: LCSH: Trump, Donald, 1946-—Impeachment. | Misconduct in office—United States. | Political corruption—United States. | United States—Politics and government—2017- | United States—Foreign relations—Ukraine. | Ukraine—Foreign relations—United States.
Classification: LCC E912 .D37 2020 | DDC 973.933092—dc23
LC record available at https://lccn.loc.gov/2020031672

First Edition: 2020

10 9 8 7 6 5 4 3 2 1

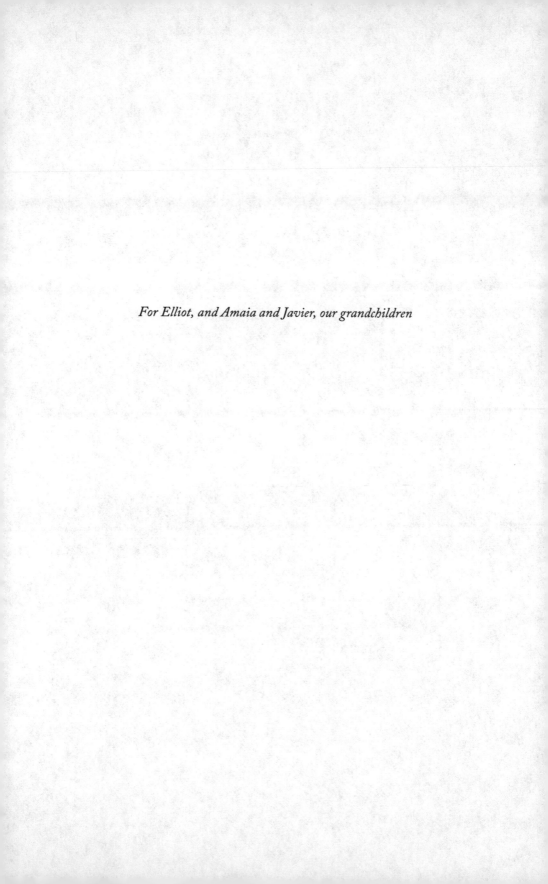

For Elliot, and Amaia and Javier, our grandchildren

"Many of us, indeed, have a feeling that we are living in a country where lunatics, hooligans, and eccentrics have got the upper hand."

BRITISH AMBASSADOR TO GERMANY,
WRITING FROM BERLIN, JUNE 30, 1933

CONTENTS

PART THREE: HIGH CRIMES

HIGH CRIMES

INTRODUCTION

Just another Witch Hunt by Nancy Pelosi and the Do Nothing Democrats!

—Donald Trump, president of the United States, via Twitter,
September 29, 2019

As Virginia congressman Gerald Connolly walked a private corridor to a conference room hidden inside the Capitol, his mind was divided. This wasn't a new condition. A decade in Congress had taught Connolly, a white-haired sixty-nine-year-old with a brushy mustache, to deal with the fact that issues constantly competed for his attention. Also, members of Congress were always occupied, simultaneously, by the business of governing—legislation, hearings, constituent concerns—and by the game of election politics. If you couldn't juggle it all, you didn't belong in the House.

Speaker Nancy Pelosi had agreed to spend a little time listening to a few House Democrats who wanted more vigorous support for a two-state solution to the Israeli-Palestinian conflict. Connolly had worked on this issue since the 1980s, when he was an aide to the Senate Committee on Foreign Relations. It mattered to him. But in this moment, on the morning of September 26, 2019, an immediate crisis was overwhelming Washington and pushing aside every other concern.

President Donald Trump had tried to extort an ally—Ukraine—by withholding promised military aid for its war against Russia until he received help in his campaign for reelection. This scheme involved him in a variation on the scandal of the 2016 campaign, when Russia made a sweeping online effort to boost him, harm his opponent, and sow confusion among voters. The outlines of the new plot, revealed by a whistleblower, indicated an abuse of power unparalleled in the history of the presidency. For House Democrats like Connolly, the Ukraine ploy capped a long list of offenses, including obstruction of justice and accepting emoluments—money from foreign and domestic sources—that had already qualified Trump for impeachment. For months, they had pushed Pelosi to support a vigorous impeachment process, but she had resisted. Obstruction and emoluments are difficult things to explain. Impeachment is the most profound action Congress can take against a wayward president. Pelosi didn't want to pursue it unless the path was clear-cut, so, even as two hundred members of her caucus had called for action, she had resisted to the point where it seemed she would move only in the event that Trump was caught during a crime in progress. Then he was.

In the very moment when Trump had seemed to escape accountability for all his other apparent crimes, he had recklessly engaged directly in this obvious and blatant corruption. He had done so during a phone call with Ukraine's president, Volodymyr Zelensky, which had been monitored in real time, and then reviewed later, by dozens of White House national security experts. Many of these men and women were career officials who had sworn to protect the United States of America, not the person of Donald Trump. At least one had been so alarmed by what had transpired on the call that he or she had used a formal process for reporting executive branch national security breaches to a small group of senators and representatives with the clearances and authority to investigate. The investigation, and press reports about the call, had led to this point where impeachment was more likely than ever.

Inside the Speaker's conference room, Connolly noted the clear autumn sunlight that streamed through the windows that overlooked the National Mall. Water tumblers and glass bowls filled with foil-wrapped Ghirardelli chocolates were set on the wooden table that filled much of the space. (Ghirardelli was based in Pelosi's district, and as a chocolate lover, she always kept them at hand.) Connolly also noted an oil portrait of Abraham Lincoln as he would have looked when he served in the House. One of just a few presidents who had served first in the House, Lincoln enjoyed an extra measure of respect on Capitol Hill. A few feet away, on the other side of a thick wall, tourists milled about Statuary Hall, where a plaque marked the spot once occupied by Lincoln's desk. Ethan Allen, Daniel Webster, and thirty-six other stone and metal figures stood in the hall. Enrico Causici's *Liberty and the Eagle* statue, which featured the lone woman in the rotunda, gazed down from above a doorway where she has stood for two centuries.

Although the artworks and architecture reliably inspired visitors, they were little noticed by those who inhabited the House, except at history-making moments. Connolly felt the connection to history as Speaker Pelosi entered the room wearing a white dress and a blue-and-red necklace. The Democratic women in Congress had taken to wearing white in an homage to the suffragists of the previous century and to signal their stand against what they regarded as Trump's immorality. Connolly detected that Pelosi, too, seemed distracted. As the group took their places at the table, he reached for the nearest bowl of chocolates and took one. He unwrapped it as his colleague Alan Lowenthal, who represented Long Beach, California, started to explain why it was time for the House to pass a new resolution on the two-state concept. Connolly liked him, but, boy, could he talk, and for a moment, Connolly lost focus as Lowenthal started to drone. Then Connolly heard Pelosi say something that showed she wasn't focused on Lowenthal either.

"I just got a call from the president."

As he glanced at Pelosi, Connolly could see that she was wrestling with whether to say more.

Lowenthal didn't seem to notice what had happened and returned to the matter of Israel. Inside his own mind, Connolly screamed in the fuzzy staccato voice, the one that still betrayed he was a son of Boston and that cable news addicts would recognize in an instant. He imagined himself saying: *Shut up, Alan! This is history happening. She's talking about impeachment!*

Lowenthal paused. Pelosi spoke again. Connolly would later recall that she said, "We're going to be in a whole new ball game here soon, with much tougher things to worry about."

With a little encouragement, Pelosi then told the small group that the Democratic Caucus would meet at 4:00 p.m. to discuss impeachment, and then she would have a press conference at 5:00. What this meant was obvious. Less than ten months into her term as Speaker of the House, Pelosi was going to drop the block she had placed on impeachment.

Before noon, rumors flew around Capitol Hill. One that proved true was that in his call, Trump had told Pelosi that he wanted to "work something out." All year long, Pelosi had done everything to spare the country, if not the president, this trauma. But it was too late. Now, a reality the president had courted so recklessly was coming to pass.

Impeachment wouldn't mean Trump's removal, since his partisan en-ablers in the Senate would guarantee the result of his trial *in advance*. But even if the fix was in, the process of investigation and debate over the president's high crimes and misdemeanors would be a necessary institutional response to both his abuse of power in the Ukraine scandal and his obstructions of Congress as it attempted to fulfill its role of overseeing the executive. Claiming a nonexistent right to refuse every request for documents and testimony, Trump had made oversight almost impossible. But this Ukraine incident meant that at least one part of the government, the unruly House of Representatives, could take action despite the Trump cult of personality.[1]

• • •

At 12:30 p.m., after the House of Representatives was gaveled into session and two colleagues had offered routine remarks about National Recovery Month, Representative John Lewis of Georgia walked across the thick blue carpet of the well of the chamber and placed some papers on the wooden lectern where members stood to speak. An original Freedom Rider who had been beaten many times as he marched for civil rights in the 1960s, Lewis was regarded as a voice of conscience in Congress. Trained as a Baptist preacher, he was also known for stirring oratory, but he struck a somber tone as he began: "Today, I come with a heavy heart, deeply concerned about the future of our democracy."

A steadfast ally of Speaker Pelosi, Lewis had previously refrained from taking a public stand on impeachment—even though he had been pressured to do so—out of respect for her. Now he would voice the fear that "our country is descending into darkness" under the leadership of a president who seemed, to him, unconstrained by the law and the Constitution.

"The people have a right to inquire," said Lewis. "The people have a right to know whether they can put their faith and trust in the outcome of our election. They have a right to know whether the cornerstone of our democracy was undermined by people sitting in the White House today. They have a right to know whether a foreign power was asked to intervene in the 2020 election. They have a right to know whether the president is using his office to line his pockets."

In referencing election security, disdain for the law, and the kind of self-dealing the Founders feared as they prohibited presidential emoluments, Lewis hit every note that his colleagues stressed when they discussed the possible misconduct that made Donald Trump worthy of impeachment. As he concluded—"I truly believe the time to begin impeachment proceedings against this president has come"—all of Congress, as well as the White House and the Capitol press corps, knew that the biggest of the day's rumors was true. Pelosi had finally concluded that impeachment would be pursued in earnest.

• • •

The Speaker of the House had made her choice after a month of startling revelations and remarkable reactions. The revelations in the whistleblower complaint had actually been withheld from Congress. Federal law, in fact, a law Pelosi had helped write, required that when intelligence officials lodge serious misconduct complaints—those judged to have raised an "urgent concern"—they must be forwarded directly to the House and Senate committees that oversee intelligence matters. On September 9, the inspector general who oversaw the U.S. Intelligence Community, Michael Atkinson, reported to Congress that he had reviewed the whistleblower's report and deemed it credible enough to meet the "urgent concern" threshold.

No one in the know failed to understand the implications of the whistleblower complaint. For months, the press had reported on a campaign being waged by the president's personal lawyer, Rudy Giuliani, and others who wanted to draw officials in Ukraine into helping Trump in his bid for reelection in 2020. Their target was his potential 2020 rival, former vice president Joe Biden, whom they hoped Ukraine would smear by announcing a bogus criminal investigation of his family. Then, in midsummer, the news outlet *Politico* reported that the administration was "slow-walking" hundreds of millions of dollars in military aid promised to aid Kiev's defense in a war against Russian proxies.

The whistleblower had connected the delay and the demand for election help to the president himself.[2]

With the truth emerging, the administration suddenly released the funds Ukraine needed on Wednesday, September 11. Besides confirming a consciousness of guilt, this move was too little too late to affect the tide of controversy. A flood of news reports, which Trump dismissed as "fake" but which were, in fact, accurate, indicated that he had actively sought a foreign power's interference in an American election. Remarkably, Trump had done this even though the 2016 election interference case had brought about a series of official investigations, which had caused him to complain ad nauseam for more than two years. The most important of these, carried out by Special Counsel Robert Mueller, had uncovered nearly a dozen instances in which the president and his people appeared to have obstructed justice but stopped short of confirming that they had invited Russia's email thefts and other forms of interference.

Now the president was involved in this kind of activity, violating both the law and the sanctity of the election system.

So much of what Trump did as president violated basic norms, if not legal strictures, that by September of 2019, it was hard to imagine something he *wouldn't* do, if only to prove his contempt for boundaries and limits. Faced with his unique kind of deviance, official Washington had found ways to maintain its equilibrium without the president's attendance at many of the kinds of occasions, whether solemn or celebratory, his predecessors attended. The White House Correspondents' Association annual dinner? Not for Trump. The same was true for the 2017 gala at the Kennedy Center for the Performing Arts. When the much-admired senator John S. McCain died in 2018, Trump was pointedly not invited to any of the events that honored him. The president had repeatedly insulted McCain when he was alive and resumed this behavior after the senator's death.

It was best for all concerned that Trump had stayed away on Saturday, September 21, 2019, when Republicans, Democrats, and members of the press came together at the Cathedral of St. Matthew the Apostle in downtown Washington. The funeral of journalist Mary "Cokie" Roberts attracted a throng in part because she had a long and celebrated career but also because she had been the daughter of two members of Congress who served in the days when bipartisanship still happened. This earned her a eulogy from the Speaker of the House, who declared her a "national treasure" and said, "Cokie was raised in a family that believed that public service was a noble calling. Cokie acted upon those values throughout her entire life."

As with so many other normal acts in the time of Trump, the Roberts funeral and Pelosi's eulogy were rebukes to a president who couldn't abide criticism or sharing the spotlight and disdained the happy warrior dynamic that might find weekday adversaries becoming weekend friends. In Trump's Washington, journalists like Roberts were not public servants but, as he termed them, "enemies of the people." Likewise, long-serving members of Congress were denizens of a "swamp," and a peaceful compromise was worse than a bloody defeat. So it was that on Sunday the president would proclaim that his call with Ukrainian president Volodymyr Zelensky had been "perfect." Without offering any specifics, he also accused Joe Biden of doing something "very dishonest" and contributing to "corruption" overseas. Having flung political mud and admitted he was dragging a foreign power into a U.S. election, he then jetted off on official business in Texas and Ohio.[3]

With the facts of the Ukraine scandal becoming plain for all to see and the president fully committed to his usual blustery deflections, Speaker Pelosi had devoted much of her weekend to reflecting on whether the time for impeachment had arrived. House Intelligence Committee Chairman Adam Schiff noted, for the first time on national television, that impeachment might be the only proper response to Trump's behavior.

On Monday, while in New York City, Pelosi spoke by telephone with several of the House members whom she had been protecting from the impeachment issue. For nine months, this group of military and intelligence service veterans, all freshmen in districts where Trump enjoyed much support, had not supported impeachment. However, they had been put off by the Trump administration's refusal to comply with House subpoenas. For many, the frustration turned to anger as former Trump campaign manager Corey Lewandowski had used his time before a House committee to dodge questions while denigrating and demeaning their colleagues. At one point, he had even admonished the committee, saying, "Don't ask me a question I won't answer." When his class-clown performance ended, it seemed the House effort to discover whether Trump had tried to obstruct the Mueller investigation ended, too. *Beautiful* was the word Trump used to describe the performance as he watched it on television.[4]

A week later, with this performance still fresh in their minds, the Security Seven, as they were called, concluded that the way Trump had held up aid to Ukraine in anticipation of election help had betrayed American strategic interests. Writing in *The Washington Post*, they said, "These new allegations are a threat to all we have sworn to protect. We must preserve the checks and balances envisioned by the Founders and restore the trust of the American people in our government. And that is what we intend to do."

After talking with the freshmen, Pelosi called her second in command in the House, majority leader Steny Hoyer. A year older than Pelosi, Hoyer was already a three-term representative from Maryland when she arrived in Washington to represent a San Francisco district in 1987. They had been rivals of a sort over the years—he called himself her "partner," not her "lieutenant"—but they managed the caucus well together. Though regarded as old-school, Hoyer went out of his way to be helpful to younger members who may have expected him to be resistant to their ideas. This made him valuable when it came time to herd these same members into a majority. Hoyer would recall that when Pelosi informed him that she had decided to move forward on impeachment, he had already reached the same conclusion.[5]

On her late Monday-night flight from New York back to Washington, Pelosi began to handwrite the speech she would give to the nation, announcing her decision. After more than thirty years in Congress, much of it in leadership, this would be her most fateful choice, and she wanted to express herself well. Her main points would be about the sanctity of the Constitution, the notion that no American stands above the law, and the way the president betrayed national security for political gain. By the time the airplane landed, she had made a good start on a draft. As the plane reached the gate and the door to the jetway was opened, she pulled her things together and departed. She left the speech behind.

•   •   •

On Tuesday, after Nancy Pelosi hinted at what was afoot in her meeting with Connolly and his colleagues, she met privately with the heads of six committees that had been working on impeachment issues. Despite claims of unity, Democrats had fought some intramural contests over the impeachment process. The Lewandowski debacle had soured some House members on Jerrold Nadler and his Judiciary Committee. However, Nadler's team had rallied to his defense, and Pelosi decided that his committee would stay in the process, charged with collecting reports from the others and ultimately writing articles of impeachment. However, the bulk of the impeachment work would be done by the House Intelligence Committee, which was led by a rising star of the party, Representative Adam Schiff.

Part of what other Democrats called the "California mafia," as well as a graduate of Harvard University and Stanford Law School, Schiff had worked as a federal prosecutor, and this experience made him a precise and energetic investigator. He was six feet tall, fit enough to compete in triathlons, and looked much younger than his fifty-nine years. Under another circumstance, the logical choice for the impeachment job might have been Nadler, who led the Judiciary Committee. Impeachment is a constitutional process, which is Judiciary's bailiwick. It was the committee that led the process against Bill Clinton in 1998. However, during spring and summer, Nadler and his committee had been unable to make a solid case for impeachment. By most accounts, they had lost the Speaker's confidence.

In her talks with her leadership group, Pelosi revealed more of the substance of her call with the president. He had deviated from the stated purpose of the call, which was to discuss gun violence, and broached the matter of impeachment. He had said something like, "Hey, can we do something about this whistleblower complaint? Can we work something out?" Pelosi, keenly aware that the administration had defied the statute on handing over the complaint, told him he could order that the law be followed. "Mr. President, you have come into my wheelhouse," she told him, referencing the fact that she had spent twenty-five years on the Intelligence Committee. She knew what had been required of the president and that he had failed to meet his duty. He didn't seem to grasp that this was going to be the worst day of his presidency thus far.[6]

In the afternoon, when the Democratic Caucus met to hear about the Speaker's decision, the members already knew she would have the votes she needed to create the process to examine evidence and write articles of impeachment for the House to consider. They were almost as certain that should the process lead to a full House vote on whether to impeach Trump and remand him to trial in the Senate, she would have a majority there, too. It was true that the Speaker had previously said she wanted some Republicans to join in the effort should impeachment be considered, but that was before the Ukraine issue arose. If the facts supported the contention that Trump had sought political help from Kiev and held up aid to get it, and Republicans remained 100 percent behind him, Pelosi wouldn't be deterred.

It wasn't just the impeachment issues that had changed. As the Congress that was elected in 2018 took shape in 2019, it had shown itself to be more divided than ever and less capable of bipartisanship. Indeed, every one of the traditional Republicans who had been there in 2018—the ones who just might consider standing against Trump now and then—was gone. Many had considered the prospect of a primary challenge from an ardent, pro-Trump challenger and retired. Others had been defeated in the general election. In their places stood Republican newcomers who acted as extensions of the president's ego. Add the sense of alienation many Republicans experienced as they lost majority control of the House, and it was obvious that if any check were going to be placed on the abuses of the president, it would have to be imposed by the Democrats. "We have to strike while the iron is hot," Pelosi would explain. "This is a national security issue and we cannot let him think that this is a casual thing, so that's where I'm at."[7]

As Pelosi explained her thinking and shared the gist of her morning call with Trump, she recalled that he had claimed to be unaware of the steps his own administration had taken to block the whistleblower report. "He said, 'You know, I don't have anything to do with that,'" she told her caucus. "I said,

'Well, then undo it.' Undo it. Because you are asking the DNI [Director of National Intelligence] to break the law. I mean, it's just outrageous."[8]

No one inside the caucus room challenged Pelosi's decision. The members also aligned with her demeanor, which was gravely serious. In recent weeks, she had begun referencing prayer and faith as if to signal her feelings about this moment. Yes, Trump had abused the Constitution and insulted Democrats in ways ranging from the petty to the dangerous. But the answer was not to join him in the gutter, and as the caucus meeting ended, there were no emotional displays. This was a political tragedy, and the group united in this attitude.

However, in this group of more than two hundred, divisions could be found. Some who served on the House Judiciary Committee and who knew the breadth of Trump's crimes against the law and the Constitution were not yet persuaded that the Ukraine scandal should be the sole focus of impeachment efforts. They looked at Special Counsel Mueller's findings, Trump's obstructive acts, and the money flowing into his businesses and saw egregious behavior that should not be ignored. In the liberal wing of the caucus were members who saw impeachable offenses in Trump's punitive immigration policy, his diversion of military budget funds to build a largely symbolic wall on the border with Mexico, and in his broad effort to evade the Senate confirmation powers by appointing "acting" officials to key posts. Defenders of press freedom thought Trump should be impeached for trying to use the Espionage Act to prosecute those who published information leaked from within the government.

The split between those who wanted to investigate and possibly present many impeachment articles highlighted a more general division between rank-and-file Democrats and "frontline" representatives from districts where Trump was popular and whom Pelosi had favored by holding back on impeachment until this moment. In siding with them, the Speaker had been trying to protect her hard-won House majority. Without it, no branch of government would possess the power to investigate the administration. As bad as Trump may be, Pelosi believed he would be that much worse in a Washington where his party controlled both houses of Congress. If she was moving cautiously, it was because the only thing worse than an emboldened Trump was an emboldened Trump unencumbered by an empowered opposition.

•   •   •

At 5:00 p.m., Nancy Pelosi stood at a lectern set before a bank of American flags and faced television cameras ready to broadcast remarks she had begun to shape on her Monday-night flight from New York to Washington. In contrast with the president, who often struggled with U.S. history and didn't seem to identify with any institutional continuum, Pelosi was keenly aware of her role in a centuries-long experiment in democracy. She began speaking by recalling that one week prior, the country had marked the anniversary of the Constitution and restated the often-used quote from Benjamin Franklin at the end of the convention that produced it. It's worth noting here that the question asked of Benjamin Franklin was posed by one of the first American women to be recognized as an influential political figure. Though Elizabeth Willing Powel's husband was the mayor of Philadelphia, *she* was regarded as the political thinker in the family, and throughout the convention, her home was where the framers and their wives met in the evenings to debate the document as it was being written. As the first female Speaker of the House reached for the Franklin quote, she left out Powel, perhaps for brevity's sake, and paraphrased the exchange, saying, "'What do we have, a republic or monarchy?' Franklin replied, 'A Republic if you keep it.'

"Our responsibility is to keep it," continued Pelosi. "The wisdom of our Constitution enshrined in three co-equal branches of government serving as checks and balances on each other. The actions taken by the president have seriously violated the Constitution, when the president says 'Article 2 says I can do whatever I want.'"

In fact, the president had often exaggerated his powers under the Constitution, saying things like, "I have an Article 2, where I have the right to do whatever I want as president." No scholarship is required to understand that presidents are bound by laws and that other branches of government—the courts and Congress—hold countervailing powers that limit a president's authority. But what mattered here was not Donald Trump's misreading of the American system but his identification with the monarchical rule the Founders deliberately rejected. Trump's way of thinking, and governing, reflected the sensibilities of a man who, after being born into one of the nation's richest families, isolated himself in that wealth and used it to gain power. Taught that some families are just superior, he had never worked outside the family businesses and never practiced the kind of retail politics that would have challenged the idea that government authority might reside within him personally. The Ukraine affair, with all its implications for the integrity of American democracy, illustrated how much danger could arise from this point of view.[9]

"This week, the president has admitted to asking the president of Ukraine to take actions which would benefit him politically," continued Pelosi. "The actions of the Trump presidency revealed dishonorable facts of betrayal of his oath of office and betrayal of our national security and betrayal of the integrity of our elections. Therefore, today I'm announcing the House of Representatives is moving forward with an official impeachment inquiry and directing our six committees to proceed with their investigation under that umbrella of impeachment inquiry."

After Pelosi announced her decision, Trump took to the social media platform Twitter to offer a true-to-form response that affirmed the difference between these two powerful leaders. "A total witch hunt!" he declared at 5:14 p.m. Not satisfied, three minutes later, he raised his voice, writing in capital letters, "PRESIDENTIAL HARASSMENT." Less than a half hour later came, "A total Witch Hunt Scam." And at 10:37 p.m., he declared, "IT'S A DISGRACE."

With the juxtaposition of serious action by Speaker Pelosi and juvenile rants from the White House, the country began its journey toward only the third presidential impeachment in its history. In the months to come, the House and Senate would determine the president's future and the future of the American experiment in democracy. In Trump, the presidency was represented by a man with an insatiable appetite for power and little regard for norms honored by even the most imperious of his predecessors. In Pelosi, the House of Representatives was led by a champion of traditional checks on the power of the presidency and a high standard for public service. Although the leader of the Republican-controlled Senate, where Trump would be tried on the impeachment charges, declared Trump would never be convicted, the Speaker and her colleagues acted as a matter of principle and in order to establish a record of official sanction.

No matter what Senate Republicans might say, Trump had clearly violated the Constitution and deserved to be removed. Unfortunately, decades of increasing partisanship had all but destroyed the ability for many Republicans to trust the Democrats' motives. They considered themselves to be in a continuous state of political warfare in which the only thing that mattered was winning the current skirmish. More recently, Donald Trump's presidential campaign, and his conduct in office, had replaced verifiable facts with what one of his advisors called "alternative facts" that had destroyed the sense that Americans shared the same reality. This made it possible to believe anything, and nothing.

In truth, a vast record would show that for years Trump associates had pursued power and wealth in Russia and Ukraine and that the immediate arms-for-dirt scandal was the product of shady activities that should have rung alarms in Washington long ago. Trump's own financial ties to Russians and other Eastern Europeans demanded deep investigation, and his family's ongoing receipt of monies from foreign governments fit the textbook definition of the emoluments prohibited by the Constitution. In his report, Special Counsel Robert Mueller had offered sweeping proof that Trump had obstructed Congress, and Mueller had invited Congress to take up this issue in a serious way. Similarly, Trump had defied Congress's every effort to investigate his impeachable offense, and in this defiance could be found additional crimes.

In another era, a Congress dealing with a less deviant president might have taken up the entire scope of wrongdoing. Less value would have been attached to the need for an easy-to-grasp narrative of a discrete crime that could be examined and debated quickly. But in this case, the House was dealing with a president who created such a powerful blizzard of distortion and corruption that investigators operated in near-zero-visibility conditions. Those who had managed to find their way to clarity through a painstaking process, like Robert Mueller's team, saw their work spun into fiction by administration officials like Attorney General William Barr, who turned their serious findings into game-show entertainment. As the Trump team made it all but impossible for anyone to see the truth, even when it was reported, it seemed obvious that the House should only proceed with a case that was simple, straightforward, and irrefutable. This approach would also demonstrate that House Democrats were not just swinging wildly at a president they didn't like.

But as Speaker Pelosi seized on Trump's call with Zelensky—which was itself set in a tangled web of intrigue—she necessarily abandoned the sweeping tale of corruption of which it was a small part. But it is the context of the long-running and varied schemes of Trump and his minions that gives true meaning to the president's attempted extortion. Long before Americans heard of Volodymyr Zelensky or Lev Parnas, Trump and the key players in the scandal had schemed to get their hands on some of the billions of dirty dollars that were gushing out of former Soviet countries. It is this corruption, hidden in secretive shell corporations and conducted according to gangster rules, that explains Trump's high crimes.

$$\bullet \quad \bullet \quad \bullet$$

After the impeachment of the president and a sham trial—no witnesses were called—that produced a predetermined result, the larger story remained untold.

Several members of the House, including those in Pelosi's leadership circle, told us that even the Speaker didn't see the breadth and depth of the Trump team's misconduct. The dense record established by the House suggested it, but as facts were piled upon facts, the task of understanding it all became a challenge that could only be resolved by recognizing that there were three related narratives.

The main story of Donald Trump's impeachment, and the one history will stress first, features the president's attempt to extort an embattled ally—Ukraine—for the purpose of making the American people believe lies about his rival in the 2020 election. This plot grew out of his associate Paul Manafort's many years of work in Ukraine on behalf of oligarchs and politicians who drained the national economy and provoked deadly violence. We cover this part of the epic in part 1, "The Call."

In addition to the Ukraine scandal, Trump's impeachment was informed by Special Counsel Robert Mueller's account of Russia's criminal effort to help Trump win election in 2016 and the president's many obvious attempts to obstruct his investigation. Mueller's end product, a two-volume report, establishes a convincing record of the crimes Russia committed to help Trump gain office and the president's efforts to create a false narrative to aggrandize himself and deceive the American people. The part of the story is detailed here in part 2, "Mueller and His Report."

Finally, the impeachment of Donald Trump depended on the president's inexplicably reckless actions, which energized the House to act at the precise moment when, thanks to the deceptions practiced by his attorney general, he seemed to have prevailed over Mueller. Like the third act in a theatrical tragedy, this final series of events relied on the elements of character revealed in the first and second acts—the Ukraine scheme and the Mueller report—to produce a dramatic resolution. Here it is described in part 3, "High Crimes."

We have told the story in three parts so that we can indicate the sweep of the abuses that led to just the third impeachment of an American president. The most remarkable—perhaps unique—aspect of this spectacle is its complexity, which can be seen as a reflection of Donald Trump's mind. Throughout his long life, Trump has labored intensely and spent lavishly on schemes intended to make the world accept his conception of himself as brilliant, beautiful, and fearsomely powerful. This effort involved the construction of mythic tales in which he accomplished great things while battling an endless supply of enemies whom he created with provocations and declarations. In the beginning, he turned federal civil rights lawyers enforcing antidiscrimination laws into jackbooted thugs. Next came public feuds with the mayor of New York and his first wife, whom he divorced amid lurid tabloid headlines he helped to write. In time, hundreds of orchestrated episodes obscured the truth and demonstrated Donald Trump's endless capacity for deceiving even himself.

Analysis of Trump's impeachment requires some application of social psychology, because this moment in history grew out of his extraordinary need to create a fantasy self who occupies the center of a fantastical story that he demands that others accept. His impeachment can best be understood as the moment when this Trump phenomenon was exposed—by the Ukraine scandal and the Mueller report—in a way that saw him held to account. Though not removed from office, he was exposed, and his presidency was permanently marked by ignominy. Then, in an extraordinary development that even his theatrical mind could not have conjured, nature itself revealed his incompetence as the United States became the country most affected by a global pandemic. (Epidemiologists generally agreed that because of the administration's slow response, the chance to prevent 90 percent of the eventual U.S. deaths was lost.)[10]

As Trump's failure at preparedness, rejection of science, and pitches for snake oil cures—malaria drugs, exposure to light, ingestion of household cleaners—added to a toll that included more than one hundred thousand dead and a paralyzed national economy, the scandal of impeachment was eclipsed. Yet they were not fully distinct and separate episodes. Both depended on Donald Trump's rejection of objective reality, impulsive mythmaking, and abuse of his authority. By comprehending the first, we see how the second, more tragic one was, in fact, inevitable.[11]

PART I

THE CALL

1

INTERNATIONAL MAN OF MYSTERY

Who was treated worse, Alfonse Capone, legendary mob boss, killer and "Public Enemy Number One," or Paul Manafort, political operative & Reagan/Dole darling, now serving solitary confinement—although convicted of nothing.

—Donald Trump, president of the United States, via Twitter,
August 1, 2018[1]

In the early-morning hours of July 20, 2016, three men and one woman wandered separately in the alleys of a neighborhood in Kiev called Shevchenkivs'kyi. An enclave of the upper middle class, Shevchenkivs'kyi is a place of quiet residential blocks and commercial areas with cafés, restaurants, and shops. In the predawn darkness, the streets were deserted but for these walkers and a band of young musicians lugging instruments. At 2:30, two of the walkers met on the same block of Ivana Franka Street. After taking a dozen or so steps, they stopped. The man acted as a lookout while the woman appeared to place a package under a red Subaru that was parked at the curb. They separated and within minutes had left the neighborhood.

Well after sunrise, a forty-four-year-old investigative journalist named Pavel Sheremet left his home and walked to the red Subaru, which he usually drove to a radio station where he worked. With his blue eyes, white hair, and a stubble of beard, Sheremet was a familiar figure to those who watched the live-stream video of the studio where he was part of the morning show team. On this sunny, seventy-degree morning, he found the car parked on Ivana Franka Street. He used his key remote to unlock the door, got behind the wheel, started the engine, and pulled away.

Pavel Sheremet drove about a hundred yards and stopped in a busy intersection to make a left turn. As he waited to clear approaching traffic, a remote-controlled bomb that had been planted on the underside of the car was detonated. The explosion filled the air with a brief, concussive roar. Crows and pigeons flew into the air. Alarms on parked cars blared. The car, immediately engulfed in flame and smoke, rolled backward for a few feet as the blast popped open the rear door on the driver's side. Sheremet died almost instantly.

At the radio station, as Sheremet's cohosts worked at a big desk outfitted with computers and microphones, they told the audience that their colleague was likely rushing to the studio. Moments later, a reporter joined the broadcast to say Sheremet had been killed by a bomb planted in his car. The shocked announcer, who had just noted Sheremet's absence, put her hands over her mouth. Later, Ukrainian officials would say the killing was likely a political act. Among the evidence was a package sent anonymously to the website of *Ukrainska Pravda*, which published Sheremet's writing. Inside had been notes describing phone calls of many local journalists, including Sheremet. Someone with the means to wiretap phones had been tracking them.

Journalists in Kiev wouldn't need much time to connect Sheremet's death with their country's struggle against Russia, which had annexed its territory in Crimea and backed a separatist uprising. For more than a decade, Russia had sown chaos in Ukraine, seeking to block its turn toward America and Western Europe. The country was a hotbed of intrigue, where violence was a political tool and the pro-Russia president, Viktor Yanukovych, had recently fled in the middle of the night after his security forces had killed more than one hundred protesters. In this place, events were assumed to be connected to struggles within, and between, nations with far greater resources and might. In this context, Ukraine was a place to be exploited and people like Pavel Sheremet were expendable.[2]

•   •   •

On the morning when Pavel Sheremet was killed, a former power player in Ukrainian politics awakened in Cleveland, Ohio. He washed and shaved and styled his thick hair, which was carefully dyed to a glossy auburn hue, into the Elvis Presley pompadour he had worn his entire adult life. He put on a crisp white shirt with a fashionable wide-spread collar and selected a blue suit with a soft pinstripe that came from his million-dollar wardrobe. A yellow silk tie, looped into a perfect Windsor, completed a look that communicated cool, moneyed success.[3]

Paul Manafort had departed Kiev for good in 2015. Considering the trouble he left behind, including at least one bill collector and lots of angry Ukrainian citizens, you might say that he fled. Once back in America, where it was almost impossible to imagine a connection between gritty Kiev and a major-party candidate for president, Manafort had lobbied hard to get a high position with the Donald Trump campaign.

For a sixty-seven-year-old who hadn't worked in U.S. politics in more than a decade, the leap to the top of a campaign for president might seem improbable, but Manafort had exploited certain connections to reach this spot. He owned an apartment in Trump Tower in Manhattan. His former business partner, dirty trickster Roger Stone, was a longtime Trump confidant. A mutual friend, billionaire Thomas Barrack, was a senior campaign advisor. A letter to Barrack led to a meeting at the Montage Beverly Hills. Afterward, Barrack told Trump that Manafort was "the most experienced and lethal of managers" and "a killer." He forwarded memos in which Manafort pitched himself as a man who knew how the game was played. The clincher may have been the price Manafort placed on his services to the campaign: zero. First hired in March, by May, he was chairman. Now, on July 20, Donald Trump was thirty-six hours away from accepting the Republican Party nomination for president.

On this morning, conditions in Cleveland were remarkably similar to what Pavel Sheremet had discovered as he had walked from his apartment building to his car in Kiev. The sun shone brightly. Humidity was low, and the temperature—in the high sixties—was perfectly comfortable. When Paul Manafort reached the arena where the GOP convention was under way, he went inside to find the studio ABC News had set up to handle its coverage of the four-day festival of speeches and cheers. The day's sessions wouldn't begin for hours so the great hall was almost empty of people, which made it easy for Manafort to glide past security officers and into the studio. Thanks to his bespoke suit, his dark hair, and the TV makeup, the chief of the Trump campaign looked elegant and refreshed when he sat for a live interview with George Stephanopoulos. In a deep, relaxed voice, he spoke with pride of how convention speakers had "scored points" for his man and against rival Hillary Clinton.

Stephanopoulos noted the boisterous chants of "Lock her up!" that had followed mentions of Clinton's name. (Perhaps the most enthusiastic leader of this cheer had been retired army lieutenant general and Trump advisor Michael Flynn, who had barked into a microphone, "Lock her up! Damn right! Exactly right! There is nothing wrong with that!") Stephanopoulos asked if delegates really thought she should be imprisoned. Manafort paused for a beat and then said, with his voice rising to suggest the question was absurd, "Uh . . . yeah?" He then offered a gasping little laugh and let a cosmetically perfect white smile light up his face. Crow's-feet made his eyes seem to twinkle.

"Is that what *you* think?" asked Stephanopoulos.

Here, Manafort's voice tightened a bit as he said, "I think what the people, uh, the p-people in this, uh, this hall feel, is that she should be pruh-prosecuted for alleged crimes."

Manafort was vague about the nature of Clinton's crimes but clear that he believed the chants, which represented a new low in American presidential politics, called attention to a valid concern. He then offered a confident prediction that by the end of the convention, the country would know Donald Trump not just as a candidate but "as a father, a compassionate human being, and a successful businessman."[4]

Although it was belied by his many bankruptcies, Trump's claim to great success as a businessman was a key element of his appeal to voters. Manafort, too, seemed every bit the success as he had replaced Trump's first campaign head, Corey Lewandowski, who had been caught on camera in a couple of physical altercations. First, he had roughed up a female reporter. The next incident involved a protester at a Trump rally. Having shown himself to be an actual thug and not just a man with a thuggish personality, Lewandowski could not be trusted with the sensitive work of managing the upcoming party convention under ever-increasing scrutiny from the national press.[5]

When he joined the Trump team, those who didn't know Manafort were assured that he was such an expert at managing national conventions and corralling delegates that his nickname—"the Count"—was a reference to his ability to keep track of them. However, political veterans told a different story in which "the Count" was a reference to the fictional Count of Monte Cristo, international man of mystery. In this truer version, Manafort had turned from domestic campaigns to the more lucrative and shadowy business of aiding dictators around the world. Indeed, Manafort served so many violent strongmen that when the Washington-based Center for Public Integrity published its 1992 report, *The Torturers' Lobby*, it ranked his small firm fourth in revenues from countries renowned for human rights abuses.[6]

·   ·   ·

At the convention, delegates and reporters buzzed about the recent publication of embarrassing emails Russian hackers had stolen from computer systems of the Democratic Party. Moscow was clearly intervening on Trump's behalf. The only hint of a return favor, and at Manafort's controversial past, arose when delegates altered the party platform to favor Russia in its military conflict with Ukraine. A call to give Kiev "lethal defensive weapons" was replaced with a recommendation for "appropriate assistance." Delegates named the campaign workers who pushed for the change, and Trump himself acknowledged he wanted to go easy on Russia. But when Manafort was asked, he seemed to lie about it, saying that "no one" on Trump's team favored the shift.[7]

Trump, whose personal brand was all about his perfect judgment, reflexively defended whatever his team did in Ukraine. To do otherwise only allowed for cracks in the veneer of perfection. Manafort saw some advantage in denying that he or the candidate had requested the shift on Ukraine. Only later, as scandals involving Russia and Ukraine defined the Trump presidency, would all the reasons for Manafort's deception come into focus. Understanding them would require recognizing that in addition to the normal realm of global affairs, where diplomats and intelligence agents pursue U.S. national interests, there exists another, secret world of American political mercenaries who will aid just about anyone's will to power provided that the checks don't bounce.

• • •

Readers of history and, for that matter, spy novels have long known that during the Cold War, America meddled in the domestic political affairs of other countries. By one count, in the years 1946–1989, the United States intervened in more than sixty foreign elections. In recent decades, as the U.S. government pulled back from this activity, a private industry of consultants and strategists—detached from national interests—replaced it. As this occurred, Paul Manafort and others turned what they had learned manipulating American voters with advertising and stagecraft into techniques that could be tailored to fit any political figure in any country. Manafort's specialty, informed by the successful race-baiting he had used to win in the United States, involved searching for the ethnic, regional, or class divisions latent in a given society and then amplifying them to favor a client. With this method, he weaponized fear, hatred, and resentments to drive voters to the polls.

New opportunities for political mercenaries arose with the collapse of the former Soviet Union.

The end of Communism set off a frenzied competition for power as state-held assets were privatized and experiments in democracy began. Former New York mayor Rudy Giuliani, who would one day be a leading spokesman for Trump, got to Moscow ahead of Manafort and was immediately welcomed by Vladimir Putin's foreign minister, Sergey Lavrov. He soon built a network of clients and contacts in Russia and Ukraine. Another future Trump campaign aide, Michael Caputo, followed the same path, but unlike Giuliani, he actually lived in Moscow for years. When Manafort got there in 2004, he discovered a landscape where a kind of ruthlessness known as *proizvol* added an element of danger to every transaction and relationship. The Putin-allied moneyed men—loosely called *oligarchs*—who would pay Manafort for years to come had direct ties to mobsters known to use violence to enforce agreements. Proof of this arrangement appeared, from time to time, in the form of bloodied corpses.[8]

In Russia, Manafort first courted the richest of the oligarchs, Oleg Deripaska. As the last man standing in Russia's so-called Aluminum Wars, which saw dozens of businessmen killed in the battle for control of mines and smelters once owned by the state, Deripaska was widely feared. By 2005, he was trying to cultivate an image of more civilized worldliness. He bought a 240-foot superyacht named *Queen K* that was, in turn, served by a support yacht named *Sputnik*. In 2006, when he and Manafort began collaborating in earnest, he was about to close on the purchase of a mansion on Embassy Row in Washington. It featured a chandelier from the Paris Opera House.

Deripaska sent Manafort to work in Montenegro, where he owned an aluminum mill and favored a nationalist campaign for independence from Serbia. (The Kremlin favored this movement, too.)

After Manafort helped the independence movement win a voter referendum, he moved on to Ukraine, where pro-Russia political efforts were funded by other oligarchs, including Dmytro Firtash. Close to both Deripaska and Putin, Firtash had accumulated a vast fortune in the corrupt business of selling Russian natural gas to Ukraine, which relied on it for 65 percent of its supply.

Long the fulcrum of Ukrainian political corruption, the energy business was controlled by paperwork entities that were granted state-authorized contracts to buy the supply in Russia and sell it at home. Political leaders in both countries gave these contracts to favored individuals who were assumed to pay kickbacks to their patrons. Many Ukrainians credited a strange and compelling political character named Yulia Tymoshenko with establishing their country's side of this corrupt game. Thanks to her shrewd maneuvering, she and her husband seized early control of all imports of Russian gas. Nicknamed "the Gas Princess," Tymoshenko often dressed in provocative outfits and wore her dyed-blond hair in a peasant braid that encircled her head like a halo.

Advised by astrologers and psychics, she came to believe herself to be the reincarnation of Evita Perón. In her theatrical public appearances, she often threw herself to the floor while crying out, "Forgive us! People of Ukraine, forgive us!" In private, she was known to veer from flirtation to rage in a moment.[9]

More typical of the energy oligarchs, Firtash operated quietly and depended on the respect his wealth and power commanded. His initial patron, Vladimir Putin, enabled him to purchase Russian gas for the Ukrainian market and helped him get financing for the purchases from a state-controlled Russian bank. All this activity produced hundreds of millions of dollars in excess profits. Firtash shared his take with several partners, including the mobster Semion Mogilevich. Mogilevich had been a mainstay on the FBI's Ten Most Wanted list, but absent an extradition treaty with Russia, he was beyond America's reach. By 2014, Firtash would also be wanted by the United States for his part in an alleged international bribery scheme.

At home, Firtash had sought political protection by funneling millions into Ukraine's Party of Regions and doing what he could to persuade American officials that it really wasn't a pro-Russia front. As far back as 2008, Firtash had gone to make this case at the American embassy, which occupied the former headquarters of the Communist Party. In meetings with then ambassador William Taylor, Firtash described himself as an anti-Communist from humble beginnings, whose rise had nothing to do with Putin. After Firtash came Party of Regions consultant Manafort, who wanted to convince the embassy staff that the party's candidate for president, former Communist apparatchik Viktor Yanukovych, wasn't a Putin puppet (he was) but a Ukrainian patriot who favored capitalism and the rule of law.[10]

• • •

With its strategic location and long history under Russian domination, Ukraine was of vital interest to the United States, but in the hall of mirrors that was Ukrainian politics, American officials in Kiev had no way of knowing where Yanukovych's loyalties, or for that matter Manafort's, resided. Manafort's background as a Republican operative would suggest a skepticism toward Russia, but Manafort had not been known by embassy staff, and he was, in his current incarnation, a political mercenary. Indeed, the trail of money that could be followed from him to the Party of Regions, Firtash, and Russian gas would have been a big warning, but at the time, these connections were not well understood. Another clue would have been discovered at Manafort's Kiev office, which had been opened so he could fulfill his Party of Regions contract. It was run by a former Russian security agent named Konstantin Kilimnik, who had traded a modest life in suburban Moscow for a Manafort-esque existence in Kiev, where he rode in chauffeured cars and lived in a mansion.

Kilimnik was fluent in English and experienced in information warfare. Although he was Ukrainian by birth, he had chosen Russian citizenship as the USSR collapsed. He had used a Russian diplomatic passport to visit the United States in 1996 and for a time was known in Moscow as "the guy from the [Russian intelligence agency] GRU." At various times, he had worked for Russian, Ukrainian, and American sponsors. His projects had been as varied as arms deals and political campaigns. To some, like the oil executives who turned down his bid for a job, Kilimnik was too passive for high-level responsibilities. To others, he was a cynic whose loyalties depended on the sources of his income. Manafort valued him as a guide through the maze of political affairs in a region where intrigue was the norm. He came to call Kilimnik his "Russian brain."[11]

While Kilimnik minded everyday business in Kiev, Manafort played Henry Higgins to his client's Eliza Doolittle, teaching him how to dress, act, and speak like a modern politician. (Thanks to a new grooming regimen, Yanukovych even came to look remarkably like Manafort.) In addition to sanding down Yanukovych's rough edges, Manafort helped put together a vague but super-patriotic message that would distract from the many blemishes in his man's record. The worst was the scandal that arose in a previous election, when Yanukovych's opponent was nearly killed by a poison attack that had all the earmarks of a classic Russian hit. The opponent survived and won with the help of the sympathy vote.[12]

When Yanukovych was finally elected president in 2010, he set about plundering the national economy, repressing political rivals, and favoring Russia over the West in trade and diplomacy. These policies and reports of corruption led to mass protests. By early 2014, the crowds gathered to demand Yanukovych step down reached eight hundred thousand. In various clashes, more than one hundred were killed by security forces. Manafort continued offering counsel until his man fled, in the middle of the night, aboard Russian aircraft that brought him to the safety of Belarus. Yanukovych left behind a $1 billion palace complete with a zoo and a golf course, built with state funds but transferred to his possession. Searchers eager for evidence of corruption fished files out of a nearby river and set them out to dry in a helicopter hangar. Other incriminating documents were discovered at the Party of Regions office.[13]

Though largely invisible to outsiders, Manafort's role in Ukraine's trauma was known to every Ukrainian who paid close attention to national political affairs. His activities were never secret. In Kiev, his company had operated from a ground-floor office in a prominent location just a few doors down from the central square where the anti-Yanukovych protesters built a tent city surrounded by barricades. Everyone knew it had been Manafort who outfitted Party of Regions spokesmen in fancy rented suits and taught them to wear makeup for public appearances. As his business partner Rick Gates would eventually explain, after Yanukovych won, Manafort established "a whole separate shadow government structure," which he used to grant favors. "In every ministry," Gates explained, "he has a guy."

Locals who dealt with the Yanukovych regime understood that Manafort wielded such great influence that they often went to his offices prior to visiting government officials. This power meant he bore some responsibility for the corruption they opposed and for the security forces' deadly attacks on their encampment. However, in the funhouse media landscape that was Eastern Europe, alternative facts abounded. Pro-Russian Ukrainians would be able to cite an alternative theory, soon proffered by the Kremlin-run media outlet Russia Today, which said that Hillary Clinton was to blame for Ukraine's problems and her campaign for president of the United States was being directed by oligarchs.[14]

In the United States, where news from Eastern Europe was given short shrift, only experts would know that a private American citizen like Manafort had been so deeply involved in Ukraine's political trauma. As he fled Kiev in 2015, leaving behind bill collectors, dissatisfied oligarchs, and angry Ukrainian citizens, Manafort was a man under extraordinary pressure. The man he had helped rise to power had become a pariah under investigation for crimes against his country. This turn of events meant that Manafort had failed his powerful oligarch patrons, Firtash and Deripaska, and ultimately disappointed their sponsor, Vladimir Putin. Manafort had also gotten into trouble playing at oligarch himself. In this scheme, he tried to use Deripaska's money—$18.9 million to be precise—to buy a company called Black Sea Cable from some Yanukovych cronies. The purchase was never made, and Deripaska wanted his $18.9 million back. He also wanted a refund on the $7.3 million in management fees he had paid. Add enormous personal debts and potential legal troubles lurking in his offshore companies, and Manafort returned to the United States with so many problems, he might have used a spreadsheet to track them.[15]

Determined to keep up appearances, Manafort continued to flit between homes in New York City, Virginia, the Hamptons, and Florida. But even as he flashed his familiar bright smile and piloted his Range Rovers around posh neighborhoods, he was descending further into a kind of personal hell. Millions invested in his daughter Jessica's filmmaking career and her husband's real estate deals appeared to be going down the drain. A young mistress whom he maintained in high style in Manhattan posted incriminating photos on social media, which his wife and daughters discovered. Though he pledged to break it off and committed to marriage counseling, Manafort was caught again with his mistress. Though he admitted himself to a treatment center in Arizona, his life continued to unravel. Text messages that were hacked and anonymously leaked to the press would reveal that Manafort's daughters were appalled by his treatment of their mother. They became painfully aware of their father's connection to Yanukovych's brutality and of the fact that the family's wealth and status had depended on it.

"You know he has killed people in Ukraine? Knowingly," wrote Andrea Manafort to her sister, Jessica, in March 2015. In fact, no evidence showed Manafort issuing orders. However, Andrea may have known that the forces controlled by her father's man, Yanukovych, did kill protesters during street-level battles and from sniper positions. Two positions they used were atop buildings next to Manafort's office, on the northwest corner of the central square.[16]

After some back-and-forth about the details of the Ukraine crisis, Andrea Manafort made it clear she didn't exempt herself from moral responsibility. "Don't fool yourself," she wrote. "That money we have is blood money." She also said she had been in Ukraine when some of the violence occurred and "I saw him on his shady email." As the trouble deepened, Andrea would write about the complicity of those around her father, including herself. "We keep showing up and eating the lobster," she wrote. "Nothing changes." Other text message exchanges dwelled on evidence of forged signatures on real estate documents and concern about their mother's well-being. In time, Jessica would even change her last name. She would be a Manafort no more.[17]

• • •

Paul Manafort's daughters couldn't have imagined the depth of the crisis their father faced. Yes, he had maintained the illusion that he was successful and returned to the domestic political game. However, he still had no income, and on the other side of the Atlantic, his troubles had continued to mount. In

February 2016, as Thomas Barrack had been advancing Manafort's cause with the Trump campaign, a Ukrainian journalist named Sergii Leshchenko had received twenty-two pages from what appeared to be a ledger showing payments made by the Party of Regions. Then in May 2016, as Manafort was promoted to chairman of the Trump campaign, a former Ukrainian prosecutor named Viktor Trepak opened the door of his home and saw, on the step, a package containing the entire Black Ledger book. In roughly four hundred pages were recorded more than $2 billion worth of transactions. Some of it seemed to have been paid to Paul Manafort.

Trepak handed his package over to authorities, who announced they would carry out an investigation into what appeared to be evidence of corruption in the Party of Regions. As word spread, Leshchenko, realizing that his pages were related to Trepak's, went public with what he knew. Suddenly, reporters from as far away as the United States—*The New York Times* was among them—began looking into the story. Manafort had to know his name was recorded in the ledger and that this fact would soon mean bad news for him.[18]

The Black Ledger story—soon to be the Black Ledger *scandal*—ticked like a time bomb heard only by Paul Manafort as he organized the Republican National Convention and watched as it proceeded toward the moment when Donald Trump accepted the GOP nomination. Reporters for *The New York Times* were on to the story, which meant it would soon break in the United States. All the while, Deripaska and his very dangerous friends still expected him to make good on the failed cable company takeover.

Realizing that as a Trump campaign insider he might have something of value to offer to Deripaska, Manafort raised the idea with Konstantin Kilimnik, who remained in contact with the oligarch. "If he needs private briefings," said Manafort in an email, "we can accommodate." At the end of July, Kilimnik wrote back saying that he wanted to meet Manafort face-to-face to discuss his contact with "the guy who gave you your biggest black caviar jar several years ago." *Black caviar* was code for money, and the guy in question was either Deripaska or one of his key men, an arms dealer named Viktor Boyarkin. A former Russian spy who had served in Washington, Boyarkin had been leaning hard on Manafort, who, in turn, had been looking for ways he might pay his debt.[19]

Four days after he sent his coy message about caviar, Kilimnik was in Manhattan, where he made his way to a wood-paneled private cigar club—the Grand Havana Room—on the top floor of 666 Fifth Avenue. The skyscraper was owned by the family of Donald Trump's son-in-law, Jared Kushner. In the interconnected realm that was Trumpworld, Kushner was both Ivanka Trump's husband and a top campaign official. He was also eagerly trying to resolve the mess created when he acquired 666 at a price higher than had ever been paid for a Manhattan building just prior to the real estate bust of 2007. Burdened with enormous debt, the property purchased to announce Kushner's arrival to the big time threatened the survival of the family firm. (Trump friend Tom Barrack had helped by investing in the building, but it was still not on firm financial footing.)[20]

The Grand Havana is the type of place where smoke-puffing masters of the universe preen and scheme while taking in a view that makes the world below look like a board game. Attendants quietly deliver food and drink while members fetch expensive smokes from a vault-like humidor. The riffraff is kept at a distance by a steep initiation fee and annual dues. Regulars go, in part, to be noticed by other masters, which made the club a strange setting for a man like Kilimnik to meet Manafort and his colleague Rick Gates, who had come from campaign headquarters at Trump Tower.[21]

Manafort, Gates, and Kilimnik talked about the fighting between Russian-backed separatists and Ukrainian forces in the Donbass region and about the prospects for ending the economic sanctions the United States had imposed on Russia after the annexation of Crimea. The sanctions were hurting Russia generally and Deripaska specifically. It's safe to assume that they also chatted about the Black Ledger mess and about Manafort's proposal to offer briefings on the election campaign to Deripaska. This would be something of value to post against his debt to the oligarch.

At the time of the Grand Havana meeting, Manafort began to float with others the notion that Ukraine—not Russia—was responsible for the recent theft and public release of embarrassing emails hacked from accounts of officials of the Democratic National Committee and the Hillary Clinton presidential campaign. This narrative, pinning the crimes on Ukraine, had no basis in evidence, but it was favored by Kilimnik and anyone else with an interest in protecting Russia and driving a wedge between Ukraine and its allies in the West.[22]

The cigar bar conference ended with a bit of amateur spy craft as the men split up so they wouldn't be seen exiting the building together. They took this precaution after sitting together in a place just four blocks from Trump's campaign headquarters, where Manafort would be recognized and their conversation could be overheard. Precisely when did Kilimnik return to Eastern

Europe? This would remain a mystery, although Deripaska's Gulfstream G550 jet touched down in Newark the next day, remained there for a few hours, and then departed for Moscow. Although discrepancies in paperwork obscured which part of Kilimnik's travel had been aboard the G550, logs did indicate he had used the jet during his mission to New York.[23]

2

WORLDS COLLIDE

Funny how the failing @nytimes is pushing Dems narrative that Russia is working for me because Putin said "Trump is a genius." America 1st!

—Donald Trump, GOP nominee for president, via Twitter,
July 27, 2016

On Sunday, August 14, 2016, Paul Manafort invited the Trump campaign's chief propagandist, Steve Bannon, to his home in Trump Tower. As he arrived, Bannon wondered if Manafort had acquired the swanky apartment as part of his no-paycheck deal to work in the campaign. Subterfuge and misdirection were so common in Trumpworld that Bannon's suspicion was well founded, even if it was slightly off the mark. Trump hadn't given the place to Manafort in lieu of a salary. Manafort had bought it during his Ukraine days. However, the property was key to Manafort's quiet but rather desperate effort to keep up appearances. In fact, he was in the middle of a borrowing spree, taking out $16 million in mortgages against the apartment and other holdings. The money, which may have exceeded the equity in the real estate, was coming from an Illinois bank headed by a major donor to the Trump election effort who hoped for a big job in a Trump administration.[1]

Shady real estate maneuvers were not on the agenda that August Sunday. What Manafort had summoned Bannon to discuss was an imminent *New York Times* story that would reveal some of the facts in the Party of Regions' Black Ledger. Having pored over the records, *Times* reporters had concluded that Manafort had received $12.7 million in off-the-books payments for his political work in Ukraine. The money almost certainly came from pro-Russia oligarchs, including Dmytro Firtash. Given the opportunity to respond to a list of written questions, Manafort had declined.[2]

Manafort had a printout of the article, which had just been posted to the *Times'* website but wouldn't be in the physical paper until the morning. As he handed it to Bannon, Manafort sloughed the piece off as a hatchet job. He said most of the money he had been paid by the party went to pay expenses, which the article didn't note. He also explained that he had declined the chance to answer questions from the reporters based on his lawyer's advice. Bannon, who believed in dealing with controversies head-on, thought Manafort had a fool for a lawyer. He told him to speak to Donald Trump immediately. Trump considered himself a master of gossip and insider information and truly hated being surprised by bad news.[3]

On Monday the fifteenth, *The New York Times* appeared on newsstands with the headline SECRET LEDGER IN UKRAINE LISTS CASH FOR DONALD TRUMP'S CAMPAIGN CHIEF. Far from a hatchet job, the story read as a well-sourced article, which, by its third paragraph, noted that the cash payments to Manafort—twenty-two in all—were being investigated by Ukraine's new National Anti-Corruption Bureau. The *Times* report also said that Ukrainian officials were checking into offshore companies used by Yanukovych and his cronies to make secret deals, including the one involving Manafort, the oligarchs, and Black Sea Cable. On television, online, and in print, journalists at other outlets laid out in detail the Trump campaign chairman's work on behalf of Yanukovych and against Ukraine's current pro-Western government. Many also noted Yanukovych's corruption, which was represented symbolically by his $1 billion palace.

The story brought Manafort's hidden-away past and his very public present into a devastating collision. On the day after its release, Donald Trump elevated his pollster Kellyanne Conway to the position of campaign manager. The next day, Trump announced that Bannon would become the campaign's chief executive. Although it was obvious that these two promotions made his job as chairman redundant, Manafort responded with a chirpy memo to the staff that said, "This is an exciting day for Team Trump. I remain the campaign chairman and chief strategist, providing the big-picture, long-range campaign vision." Trump had begun to talk about him as "low energy." Coming from a candidate who had dispatched GOP rival Jeb Bush with the same epithet, it was the kiss of death. On Friday, Manafort resigned.

Without access to the candidate, Manafort couldn't offer himself as an agent of influence or as a source of inside information that the likes of Oleg Deripaska might value. And outside of those who remained active since the

Bob Dole campaign of 1996, Manafort had few connections to the GOP. Even among these friends, Manafort would have been seen as so encumbered by controversy that he was unemployable. Worse were the hints of future trouble embedded in the reports about Manafort's activity in Ukraine. Mentions of cash payments, offshore companies, and what appeared to be work as a lobbyist for a foreign government raised obvious questions. Had Manafort declared the cash as income in his tax returns? Were his offshore companies operated in an above-board fashion? Had he run afoul of the law requiring Americans who lobby for foreign governments to register as foreign agents?[4]

Manafort may have believed he was on the right side of the tax code and the law, but one of the keys to staying out of trouble with the government is avoiding the kind of publicity that would invite investigation. (Tax officials are so over-burdened most fraud goes undetected.) Another option, for those inclined to depend on corruption, might involve helping friends reach positions of power where they could render a few favors. If President Nixon could order the Internal Revenue Service to investigate his enemies, why couldn't President Trump order it to ignore a friend's transgressions? Trump was so transactional in his relationships and so devoted to the use of raw power, he might even intervene in a Department of Justice criminal investigation. And then there was the president's pardon power, which was limited only by propriety, and Trump never let that interfere with something he wanted to do.

Unfortunately for Manafort, few things bothered Trump more than surprises and being made to look bad by an underling. The Black Ledger scandal checked both of these boxes. However, Trump would let the fallen back into his good graces, especially if they offered something of value along with their apology. With the press and the Democrats asking why Russian hackers and trolls were so busy aiding him, Trump needed an effective response. Russia Today, the Kremlin "news" service, had pointed in the right direction when, in 2015, it published its baseless claims about Hillary Clinton and oligarchs. More recently, Konstantin Kilimnik had talked about how Ukraine and not Russia was the bad actor, and this meant that instead of Trump being the *beneficiary* of interference, he was the *victim*. No evidence supported this idea, but evidence was not required if the goal was to obscure the truth and give Trump and Putin cover.

The Ukraine-did-it narrative could not be refuted with absolute certainty. Indeed, just as a handful of doubting voices permitted Trump to reject the overwhelming scientific consensus on climate change, the mere mention of an alternative theory on election interference would allow him to cast doubt on the obvious truth. This move also fit nicely with Trump's preference for reversing roles whenever he met trouble. He used this method in his very first public controversy when, in the 1970s, the Justice Department sued the Trump family firm for housing discrimination. He promptly filed a countersuit alleging harassment by authorities; his lawyer accused the feds of using "gestapo tactics." The suit failed, but it distracted from the evidence that the Trumps used race to exclude applicants for apartments. Forevermore, Donald Trump would answer accusations with his own charges, no matter how flimsy the evidence.

With Manafort providing the spark of inspiration, others in the campaign began talking up the Russia-derived theory about Clinton and Ukraine. The candidate's chief national security advisor, retired lieutenant general Michael Flynn, told others in the campaign that he did not accept U.S. government intelligence reports that the Russians were responsible for the email hacking and a massive effort to influence American public opinion via social media. Weeks before Election Day, Trump advisor Erik Prince, who founded a company that provided private military fighters to the United States and governments in the Middle East and worked for the CIA, urged Bannon to promote an "alternative narrative" that was even more far-fetched than the Ukraine theory. "Consider this response," he told Bannon in an email. "It's unclear to me if Russia is directly involved in attempting to influence the US election. That said, it's safe to say they are keenly interested, and likely using surrogates to poke in the US election. Who does the Kremlin want to see in the White House? Ms. Clinton."[5]

With Donald Trump promising to pursue closer ties with Moscow and Clinton's record of icy regard for Vladimir Putin, Prince's suggestion was nothing more than a propaganda fantasy offered by a fringe figure. Lieutenant General Flynn's insistent claim that Russia wasn't interfering with an American election was more significant because it came from a source with greater authority. Flynn had built a successful career capped by a brief stint as the Pentagon's top intelligence advisor. He abruptly retired amid concerns that he may have been compromised by a personal relationship. He became a civilian security consultant, and in late 2015, as he advised Trump, he accepted more than $30,000 from Russia Today to speak at a conference in Moscow, where he dined with Vladimir Putin.

As a former intelligence chief, Flynn surely knew that Russia Today, which was being rebranded as simply RT, was controlled by Putin and was a creature of the state. RT's mission wasn't the dissemination of factual information but, rather, the constant production of media that would boost Russia while degrading the United States and other Western societies. RT's top staffers were rewarded with military medals. It was quite possible that whoever got Flynn to sit with Putin at an RT gala, and thus exploited his status as a retired American general, received a medal as a reward.[6]

As Flynn developed his foreign business, at home, he fumed about the Obama administration and moved steadily away from the defense establishment. Always a man of intense opinions, he became more eager for the spotlight and more devoted to arguments laced with the kind of untruths that his former colleagues called "Flynn facts." For example, Flynn was inclined to say that Iran had killed more Americans than the terror group al-Queda and that Africans purchased 75 percent of the cell phones sold in the world. Neither claim was true, but he continued to make them both even after aides informed him of the facts. Hence, Flynn facts.[7]

Colleagues who had been dismayed by Flynn facts and appalled by the spectacle of a retired general leading televised "Lock her up!" chants about a presidential candidate would have been at a loss to explain the kind of counsel he was offering Trump. But those who understood how the candidate operated may have seen that it was, actually, quite effective. If the general had his own facts and showed a heedless disregard for norms, then so did the candidate.

Trump's habit was not the pursuit of expertise or understanding but rather the search for a useful story, which he could convert into a slogan and repeat ad nauseam. As scientific studies had shown, beliefs are not dependent on facts. This is what Joseph Goebbels meant when he said, "Repeat a lie often enough and it becomes the truth." The method takes advantage of the fact that people tend to give credence to statements that echo something they've heard previously. Today's cries of "Crooked Hillary" prepare people to accept tomorrow's "Lock her up!" without asking why. The method works best with complex subjects and worst when used against well-established and widely known facts. Thus, it's a waste of time to say the Yankees didn't win the 2009 World Series. But if you want to argue that they won by cheating, you'll be able to build a following.

Anyone who had ever talked with Trump about, say, his insistent suggestion that Barack Obama had been born abroad and was thus an illegitimate president, understood how he wielded arguments. In this case, the power of Trump's disinformation campaign could be seen in polls that showed doubts about Obama's birthplace rising over time until, by August 2016, just 27 percent of Republicans said they believed Obama was born in the United States. When it came to Russia's attack on the U.S. election, which obviously benefited him, Trump would be most interested in counterarguments that might be packaged into slogans. *Ukraine is meddling in the election. Russia prefers Clinton.* If these phrases came courtesy of a retired U.S. Army officer whose credentialed credibility Trump could borrow, all the better.[8]

As the Russia problem loomed, Team Trump would use Flynn's bona fides to discredit the evidence and denigrate the entire U.S. Intelligence Community, because, it seemed, it was easier to denounce the source of the evidence than to refute it. The game began when, just *before* his first classified briefing, Trump announced that he was going to bring Flynn along because he didn't really trust intelligence findings "from the people that have been doing it for our country." They were suspect, he inferred, because they were *mainstream* experts and part of the government *establishment*. This sentiment was echoed by Trump's man Giuliani, who said, "The reality is, our intelligence has been terrible." Coming from another candidate or campaign, a categorical rejection of America's spy agencies would have been big news. Coming from Trump, it was just the latest development in his effort to create doubt about any information coming from sources he did not control. The expertise, technology, and effort of those who monitored Russian aggression should be dismissed in favor of whatever Trump and Company might say.[9]

When Trump and Flynn attended their first briefing, they brought along their attitude. As nonpartisan career experts reviewed their concerns about Russia's criminal email hacking and online anti-Clinton campaign, Flynn interrupted with pointed questions. He was so unruly that according to one press account, another Trump advisor, former New Jersey governor Chris Christie, grabbed his arm and told him to calm down. (Though the story was told by reliable sources, Christie denied this happened.) Afterward, Trump breached protocol to politicize the meeting. He announced that he had learned that the intelligence experts were dissatisfied with President Obama. How did he know this? "I could tell—I'm pretty good with body language—I could tell they were not happy," he said.

Two former CIA directors noted that no precedent existed for Trump's abuse of a process that had always been respected by candidates of both major parties. Michael Morell, who had regularly briefed George W. Bush, noted Trump crossed "a long-standing red line." Former CIA director Michael

Hayden observed that intelligence experts don't communicate with "body language" and that in almost four decades in intelligence work, "I have never seen anything like this before."

News reports suggested a short-term political purpose in Trump's remarks and Flynn's behavior but did not consider the full context of events and how they might contribute to a larger project. For years, Trump, and many in his orbit, had voiced dark suspicions about government in general and security agencies in particular. Their shorthand for the intelligence community—they called it the "Deep State"—communicated a sense of fear and distrust that would permit paranoia to bloom in Trump-friendly media environments. Steve Bannon spoke of it often. One of Trump's favorite online media stars, Alex Jones, made it a staple of the programs he broadcast daily to millions of viewers and listeners. According to the true believers, the Deep State was a cabal of analysts, spies, and bureaucrats who used their positions in government offices to determine the course of events. Voters and elected officials might imagine they had some say, but in fact, they were thwarted by Deep State conspiracies.

Jones, who hosted Trump on his program early in the 2016 campaign, rose to fame voicing claims about satanic cults taking over America and the military controlling the weather. He had announced that a variety of tragic events, including the 9/11 terror attacks and mass shootings at schools, were "false flag" operations staged by government officials to justify imposing restrictions on civil rights. The fact that these restrictions never came didn't stop him from spinning new conspiracy theories and winning new fans. Similarly, Jones's extremism hardly disqualified him from the candidate's orbit. By the time Trump was nominated, Jones was so entwined with the campaign that he had been given special high-level credentials to attend the convention. Afterward, Jones would marvel at how his ideas, among them strange claims that Hillary Clinton and Barack Obama were actually helping terrorist organizations, found their way into the candidate's pronouncements. Jones said it had been "surreal to talk about issues here on air and then word-for-word hear [Donald] Trump say it two days later."

As they endorsed each other, Jones could tap into Trump's large base of voter support and Trump could access the devoted audience that tuned in to part or all of Jones's programs. Both men were leaders in what might be called modern political entertainment, where the payoff came in the form of votes, campaign donations, broadcast ratings, and advertising dollars. The two realms—politics and entertainment—had long mixed, but with the advent of conservative talk radio, which spawned Jones, and then reality TV, which Trump had helped pioneer as host of *The Apprentice,* the lines between the two had disappeared. Voters had become more like fans who accepted that their candidate might distort facts in order to make a point, but that's what made Trump's rallies and Jones's rants exciting.

The difference between Trump and Jones was that Trump was one step away from the presidency. Whatever the candidate might gain by attacking the parts of the government responsible for national security hardly seemed worth the damage he was doing. The agencies that used spy craft to protect the nation could not function without the trust of the public, and this trust could not be maintained if elected officials, who oversee their activities, no longer vouched for them. Of course, a candidate who imagined a presidency in which he would be the source of facts and information for the American people might prefer to delegitimize the CIA, FBI, and all other competing authorities. Given the secrecy required for the agencies to operate, officials were rarely able to say much at all about their activities. Add the paranoia seeded by countless movies and TV shows about fictional conspiracies, and it would be relatively easy for Trump to persuade millions that they should trust him and him alone.

Winning the trust of voters has always been the ultimate goal for anyone seeking to win an election and then govern. Traditionally the news media played the role of fact-checker in this process, helping citizens sort through campaign claims. However, the rise of a more partisan press and the growth of social media had made this fact-checking process less reliable. In the election of 2016, Trump overwhelmed the old process with false claims and distortions that came at such volume that they could not be debunked fast enough. A tidal wave of fake Russian social media posts added to the chaos and drove many voters to simply choose a candidate and stay loyal come what may.[10]

The big test for Trump and his loyalists came when the press revealed a video in which the candidate was heard bragging to the host of a TV show called *Access Hollywood* about how his celebrity status permitted him to sexually assault women—"grab 'em by the pussy" was how he put it—because "when you are a star, they let you do it." For a moment, it seemed the old standards might apply as many establishment Republicans refrained from contributing to the nominee's campaign and some GOP senators said they hoped Trump would resign and let his running mate, Mike Pence, take the top spot. The tape silenced every campaign spokesperson except for former New York mayor Rudy Giuliani, who took to television to defend what he termed "locker room talk." True to his candidate's style, he defended Trump with audacity and false equivalence, saying that somehow Hillary Clinton had committed similar offenses. (He cited the Bible's admonition about those without sin casting the first stone.) At a debate held two days after the video was made public, the Trump campaign used some of its ticket allotment to give prominent seats to a few women who had claimed to have sexual affairs with his opponent's husband, former president Bill Clinton.

The gamesmanship altered conversations about the debate but did not resolve Trump's problem with prominent supporters. Here, a Giuliani friend named Lev Parnas came through, promptly donating $50,000 to keep the Trump effort going. Parnas and his business partner Igor Fruman were both middle-aged immigrants from, of all places, the former Soviet Union. Parnas had been born in Ukraine but immigrated to the United States as a child. He spoke English with a slight accent, moved around his South Florida haunts in a Rolls-Royce driven by a white-gloved chauffeur, and regularly bragged about his connection to billionaire Dmytro Firtash. Although Parnas claimed business interests in real estate, technology, and investments, he was dogged by legal troubles. As with many hustlers who work Florida's playgrounds for the rich selling penny stocks and precious metals, he had a court record built on run-ins with angry clients and lawsuits filed by landlords seeking back rent on lavish homes. He had worked for three brokerage firms that had been shut down by regulators.[11]

Fruman had grown up in Belarus and started in business in Ukraine before coming to America as an adult. His résumé included the controversial bankruptcy of a major Ukrainian food company, which devastated a local community, and associations with organized crime figures. As chief executive of a firm called Otrada, he was nominally responsible for running a hotel, luxury retail operations, and an upscale bar/restaurant in Kiev. However, in Odessa, where he owned a nightclub called Mafia Rave, he somehow managed to gain control of a prized seaside property once operated as a municipal lifesaving station. All this made Fruman something of a mini Donald Trump, whose connections had led to a level of wealth and power that found him settling in South Florida. This was where many of the newly rich from the former Soviet Union had put their money, some of it ill gotten as state assets were privatized, into American real estate. Among them were mobsters who resumed their trade in greater Miami and soon eclipsed both the old Italian Mafia and gangs from Latin America.

Many Russians who settled in South Florida bought apartments in a Trump-branded development in a community called Sunny Isles. United in the three forty-five-story buildings, which overlooked the Atlantic Ocean, the development was marketed by brokers who spoke Russian and advertised their services on Russian-language websites. Russian was so commonly heard on the white-sand beach that residents gave Sunny Isles the nickname "Little Moscow." Trump didn't construct or own the Sunny Isles buildings but, rather, he collected a fee for the use of his name. The name was prized by buyers who assumed it represented quality and luxury—Igor Fruman bought a home there—and it only increased in prestige as Trump moved into politics.[12]

In any other campaign, the arrival of newcomers like Parnas and Fruman would have prompted some sort of background checks if only to protect the candidate from rubbing elbows with the wrong kind of persons. A basic internet search would have shown that Parnas had posted photos of himself at a 2014 Trump-hosted golf tournament, where he attended a fashion show hosted by the future president's daughter Ivanka. More recently, he and Fruman had begun looking for investors for a security company they called Fraud Guarantee. The company's service would have something to do with scrubbing derogatory information about its clients from the internet. Given that a federal court on Long Island had recently ordered Parnas to pay $510,000 to a family trust that had alleged he had previously *committed* fraud, the name was exceedingly ironic. (The fraud involved Parnas soliciting money for a Jack Nicholson movie—*Anatomy of an Assassin*—that never went into production. An introduction to Nicholson himself helped seal the deal.) Further suspicion might have been raised by the fact that Fraud Guarantee had no clients and no workforce, and a Florida court had recently issued a judgment against the company for failing to pay rent.[13]

In light of the record, it was reasonable to wonder if Parnas may have jumped into the Trump campaign with something more in mind than donating time and money to a cause he believed in. Parnas had been circling Trump for years. With his donation, he had bought himself proximity and a ticket to high-level events for supporters of the Republican Party's presidential candidate. Where else could an ambitious, obscure entrepreneur be welcomed so readily into rooms filled with rich and powerful people?[14]

The new guys may have avoided close scrutiny because at a moment when others stopped writing checks, Lev Parnas stepped up. By acting as a friend in the moment of Trump's acute need, Parnas raised his status in Trumpworld to a high level. When FBI director James Comey revived Trump's chances by briefly reopening an investigation into Hillary Clinton's use of a private email system when she was secretary of state, Parnas saw the tide turn in Trump's favor. He couldn't know the outcome as he received an invitation to New York for the campaign's election-night party, but suddenly, a Trump victory was possible.

Fifteen months before, Parnas paid little attention to politics and wasn't registered with any party. Now on election night, he was being interviewed at the entrance to the hotel ballroom by the French newspaper *Le Figaro,* and he predicted Trump would win because "America wants a change."

As the vagaries of the Electoral College gave Trump the presidency despite a three-million-vote deficit in the popular vote, Parnas joined a crowd that erupted when TV news networks declared Trump the winner. Moments later, the president-elect appeared with his family to offer thanks to luminaries like Rudy Giuliani—"That Rudy never changes!"—and Lieutenant General Mike Flynn, both of whom were expected to assume top positions in a new administration. Indeed, many who crowded into the victory party would find ways to continue as part of what Trump described as "not a campaign but rather an incredible and great movement." As he joined the celebration, Lev Parnas stood as living proof that America still offered immigrants the chance to contribute. He was not a household name, like Giuliani or Flynn, but he was in the room, and he was going to find a way to continue to help his man, and perhaps himself, as America became great once more.

3

WHY NOT GET ALONG WITH RUSSIA?

Russia just said the unverified report paid for by political opponent is "A COMPLETE AND TOTAL FABRICATION, UTTER NONSENSE." Very unfair!

—Donald Trump, president-elect of the United States, via Twitter,
January 11, 2017

Donald Trump was about to become the most powerful political leader on earth, and yet, he seemed sorely aggrieved. The press was continuing to report evidence that a Russian campaign of document theft and disinformation aided his election. Given his popular-vote loss, and that fewer than one hundred thousand ballots in three states allowed him to win the Electoral College, it was likely that Russia did get him elected. In response to this idea, he exaggerated this win as a "landslide" and repeatedly raised the false claim that millions of people had voted "illegally" for his opponent. When he sat with *Time* magazine journalists for a Person of the Year interview, he was, at least initially, adamant about the Russia matter.

"I don't believe they interfered. That became a laughing point, not a talking point, a laughing point. Any time I do something, they say 'oh, Russia interfered.' Why not get along with Russia? And they can help us fight ISIS, which is both costly in lives and costly in money. And they're effective and smart."

This was classic Trump; a strong statement followed by a change in direction. Then he added the kind of touches, also common to his rhetorical method, that both confused the issue and gave him the chance to claim, later on, that he had never actually made a definitive statement.

"It could be Russia," he said. "And it could be China. And it could be some guy in his home in New Jersey. I believe that it could have been Russia and it could have been any one of many other people. Sources or even individuals."[1]

The only certain conclusion that could be reached by a *Time* reader was that the president-elect was unhappy about the pall cast over his election but also determined to stay committed to his idiosyncratic position on America's relationship with Russia. This second point was reinforced as he selected Mike Flynn to be his national security advisor and chose ExxonMobil executive Rex Tillerson for secretary of state.

Flynn was known for his good working relationships with Russian military officers. Tillerson was said to have closer ties with Vladimir Putin than any American save Henry Kissinger. Putin had given Tillerson a medal for his work with Russia's gas and oil industries, which supposedly brought the two countries closer together. Tillerson had, in turn, opposed the sanctions Barack Obama had imposed on Russia after its invasion of Ukraine. In choosing Tillerson, the president-elect passed over his friend Rudy Giuliani, who wanted the job but lacked the background for it. Giuliani would have to find some other way to be of service to the president.[2]

Tillerson did not share Trump's skepticism about the Kremlin's election attack. He believed U.S. intelligence reports about what had happened and considered it a kind of political warfare. In contrast, Michael Flynn actually encouraged Trump's denial and began pursuing his own secret diplomacy with Russia. While still a private citizen, barred by law from conducting foreign policy, he talked with Russia's long-serving ambassador to the United States, Sergey Kislyak, about freezing a United Nations resolution condemning Israel's expansion of settlements in the Palestinian West Bank territory. A freeze would align with Trump's hawkish views on Israel and the territories but conflict with the policy being advanced by the American government, which was still directed by Barack Obama.

Obama considered Russia's election interference an attack not on a candidate or a political party but on the integrity of the election system that sustains America's democracy. It didn't matter which side gained or lost due to Russia's cyber warfare, because Moscow was always free to choose a different side. What mattered was that such attacks could destroy public faith in the system and turn skeptical citizens into paranoid cynics who might conclude that democracy was impossible. On December 29, Obama ordered sanctions on certain Russians and Russian companies that were involved in the attacks. He also ordered thirty-five Russians working in the United States to leave and shut down two Russian embassy retreat houses, in Maryland and on Long Island.

The new sanctions were announced as Flynn and his wife vacationed at a beach resort in the Dominican Republic. A man of action, Flynn responded with a flurry of calls to Donald Trump's Mar-a-Lago resort in Florida, where the president-elect and a retinue were camped for the holidays. After Flynn spoke to his deputy, K. T. McFarland, she wrote an email to another security advisor, Thomas Bossert, arguing that Obama was acting to discredit Trump's election win "by saying it was due to Russian interference." She said she hoped Russia would refrain from a tit-for-tat response. On the same day, Flynn spoke with Kislyak five times to persuade him that Russia should stand pat. When it became clear that Moscow was not going to expel Americans, Trump himself took to Twitter saying, "Great move on delay (by V. Putin)—I always knew he was very smart."[3]

Putin's cool response to the eviction of Russia's embassy personnel was so out of character that it raised red flags in American intelligence agencies. It was an easy matter for them to check Kislyak's phone calls, which were routinely monitored, and discover his discussions with Flynn. This communication didn't just violate the law. Conducted over unsecure telephone lines, which were sure to be monitored by both Russian and U.S. spy agencies, the calls also exposed Flynn to being blackmailed at some future date. It was possible that Flynn was ignorant of best practices followed by intelligence officials or he was sure that as president, Trump would be so eager to break with Obama and the intelligence community that he wouldn't care about the risk Flynn had undertaken.[4]

Flynn's confidence would have been informed by Trump's response to the evidence of Russia's election attack. For months, before and after the election, Trump had rejected what he had heard in the high-level briefings he received. He was especially dismissive of intelligence concerns U.S. officials had seen in a document written by a former British intelligence agent named Christopher Steele. While working for MI6, the United Kingdom's version of the CIA, Steele had been posted in Moscow and ran the Russia desk in London. He had left the agency after two decades of service to work as a private analyst. In 2015, he had been hired by a prominent Republican opponent of Trump's bid for the GOP nomination who wanted to know all about Trump's Russia connections. Democrats later paid him to do the same. He had compiled a dossier based on information supplied to him mainly by Russian sources. Steele's long experience in Russia had taught him the pitfalls of this work, but his sources had been accurate in the past and he knew how to accommodate their motivations and possible conflicts.

In the fall of 2016, when Steele gave his dossier to U.S. officials, they noted his report that Russian operatives had cultivated relationships with Trump and his associates beginning in 2011. At that time, Trump was publicly challenging President Obama's citizenship status and becoming more outspoken about political issues. The dossier suggested that the Kremlin and Trump's team had exchanged information. Steele also told a salacious tale of Trump's involvement with prostitutes in Moscow, which was supposedly caught on videotape, and suggested cooperation between the Trump campaign and Moscow.

Hints of the dossier's existence appeared in the press just prior to Election Day. But only after the election, on January 6, were the contents fully described to Trump himself. FBI director James Comey performed this uncomfortable duty and got the impression that Trump was not surprised by what he heard. Days after the briefing, the TV network CNN reported that Russia possessed compromising information about Trump.

On January 10, the news website *BuzzFeed* published thirty-five pages of the raw information that had informed the Steele report. The documents showed that Vladimir Putin had ordered Russian intelligence agencies to hack the computers of the Democratic National Committee and intervene in U.S. elections in favor of Trump. They described a web of contacts between Russians and Trump advisors and loyalists who were already under investigation by U.S. government agencies. The main points in the dossier included:

- Putin had directed Russian efforts in "cultivating and supporting" Trump. "Its aim was to sow discord and disunity."

- The Kremlin had been "feeding Trump and his team valuable intelligence on his political opponents," especially Hillary Clinton.

- "Russia has [an] extensive programme of state-sponsored offensive cyber operations."

- The Russians used the website WikiLeaks to pass along information on Hillary Clinton to people connected to the Trump campaign.

- Ex-Ukrainian president Yanukovych told Putin that he authorized improper payments to Paul Manafort. Putin was worried that Yanukovych didn't cover his tracks.

As the allegations in Steele's report became public, Trump denied them all. He even said that he had no interest in big real estate deals in Russia. In fact, Trump had long talked about building a Trump Tower Moscow, and in a 2016 version of this concept, eventually revealed by his associates Michael Cohen and Felix Sater, Vladimir Putin was to receive the gift of a $50 million penthouse suite.

On the day after *BuzzFeed* published the Steele dossier, its competitor *Politico* posted its own report, which would fuel a counter-narrative embraced by the president, titled "Ukrainian Efforts to Sabotage Trump Backfire." The piece reported that some Ukrainian officials in Washington had spoken with a Clinton campaign consultant about Paul Manafort's work for Viktor Yanukovych. The most important source cited was a young man who was identified as a "political officer" in the Ukrainian embassy. At the time, Andriy Telizhenko's entire diplomatic career consisted of a six-month stint at the embassy, but thanks to the notoriety he received, he would soon become a celebrated figure in Trumpworld who parlayed the attention into a consulting business.[5]

Politico gave Team Trump a "Ukraine did it, too" argument to use whenever anyone mentioned how Russia helped them win the election. It also brightened the mood at celebrations of the incoming president's inauguration. On January 19, an upbeat Trump attended a number of pre-inaugural events, including two attended by Lev Parnas. At one, a GOP leadership luncheon, Parnas was photographed with Donald Trump Jr. At a later black-tie party at Washington's Union Station, he was caught on camera five feet from the president-elect. On the day Trump took the oath, Parnas joined the crowd gazing upon Trump as he placed his hand on a Bible and then listened to a speech in which he spoke ominously of the "American carnage" that, presumably, his predecessors enabled. He promised action against a nonexistent crime wave, the restoration of middle-class wealth, top-notch schools, and vast improvements in public infrastructure.[6]

Two days after Trump's inauguration, as Mike Flynn assumed command of a four-hundred-person National Security Council staff, *The Wall Street Journal* reported that U.S. counterintelligence agencies were looking into his contacts with the Russians. The agencies, among them the FBI and the CIA, were tracing Russia's effort to influence both the election and Trump policy makers. Four days later, on January 26, acting attorney general Sally Yates went to the White House to tell the president's counsel, Don McGahn, that Flynn had been lying to top officials, including Vice President Mike Pence, about his contacts with Ambassador Kislyak.[7]

McGahn took no immediate action on Flynn, but on January 27, he asked Yates to return to the White House. In this second meeting, he asked, "Why does it matter to D.O.J. [the Department of Justice] if one White House official lies to another White House official?" Yates answered that Russia knew the truth about Flynn's deception and could use it against him. More generally, Flynn's dishonesty was a bad omen for a man entrusted with a highly sensitive job. And then there was a pattern of behavior for the White House to consider. While a campaign advisor, Flynn had taken $500,000 from Turkey and then consulted with Ankara on the possible kidnapping, from his home in Pennsylvania, of a dissident Turkish cleric named Fethullah Gülen.

Flynn's poor judgment had been displayed on Election Day, when he published a meandering essay that attacked Gülen as a "radical Islamist" in heated terms Recep Erdoğan would have used. Published by a Washington-based website called *The Hill*, Flynn's essay linked Gülen to Egyptian clerics who had been dead for half a century to declare him "shady" and equivalent to "Turkey's Osama bin Laden." In fact, Gülen was a former Erdoğan ally who had come to oppose a regime that was becoming more autocratic every day. That Flynn would focus on him, of all people, for an article to be published as he assumed his official post was strange indeed.[8]

• • •

For two weeks, Flynn's troubles were contained inside the White House. Then *The Washington Post* made public that he had discussed the sanctions issue with Kislyak. This account, which directly contradicted a version Pence had offered to the press in defense of Flynn, put the director of national intelligence in an untenable position. He tried to quell the controversy by letting an aide say that while he had no recollection of discussing sanctions with Kislyak, he "couldn't be certain that the topic never came up." This didn't work.

On February 10, Andrew McCabe, deputy director of the FBI, brought transcripts of the Flynn/Kislyak calls to the White House. McCabe, Vice President Pence, Chief of Staff Reince Priebus, and counsel Donald McGahn met in the spy-proof Situation Room, where they read that Flynn had raised the topic of delaying Putin's response to Obama's sanctions and done so in a direct and purposeful way. Flynn had obviously lied about this, and it was this deception that they cited when they went to the president and said he had to go. To their surprise, Trump would not agree to do it.

Trump's reticence would prompt the kinds of questions that would be raised over and over again. Chief among them was whether the president was secretly vulnerable to the other players in the drama. Had he personally authorized or even planned Flynn's illegal outreach to Kislyak? Was there evidence of this in Flynn's possession, which posed a threat to Trump? Was the president compromised in some other way that would make him vulnerable to blackmail by any of the parties in this scheme?

Whatever the reason for Flynn's indecision, someone in the administration decided to give him a push by leaking to *The Washington Post* that White House officials were regarding Flynn with suspicion. On the morning the article about Flynn appeared, he resigned. He had not served even a full month. Flynn's public statement included a perfectly Trumpian evaluation of his own career: "I am tendering my resignation, honored to have served our nation and the American people in such a distinguished way." In the years to come, Flynn would spend much of his time dealing with the legal fallout from his many deceptions and trying to stay out of federal prison.[9]

On the day after Flynn quit, Trump hosted FBI director James Comey and a few others for an Oval Office intelligence briefing. Trump had already ambushed Comey with a request for his personal loyalty, which Comey deflected. This time, he dismissed the others in the room in order to speak to Comey alone. The director, wary of what was to come, strained to commit every detail to memory. As he later recalled, after the Oval Office door closed, Trump had said, "I want to talk about Mike Flynn." Comey had personally sent two agents to interview Flynn, so he knew all about his controversies. Trump said he believed Flynn had done nothing wrong but had been dismissed because he misled the vice president. Comey quoted Trump as then saying, "I hope you can see your way clear to letting this go, to letting Flynn go. He is a good guy. I hope you can let this go."[10]

What Trump clearly meant was that he hoped that Comey and the Justice Department would decline to prosecute Flynn. The FBI director offered some mild agreement about the general being a good guy but did not commit to dropping any investigation. Indeed, Flynn had involved himself in so many potential crimes, including his engagements with the Russian ambassador, that a small army of investigators and prosecutors would be required to sort it all out.

In many ways, the president did himself no favors as he put the squeeze on Comey. First, his request could be seen as attempted obstruction of justice, since the FBI was obviously looking into Flynn's behavior. Second, it flouted the spirit of a 1976 law that established a ten-year term for the FBI director—two years more than any president might serve—in order to shield him or her from politics. This law and a tradition that grew up around it was a response to revelations of the political activities of longtime director J. Edgar Hoover, who did political favors for presidents of both parties. A month after Hoover died, Richard Nixon tried to order the FBI to cease investigating the Watergate scandal. Instead, the bureau gathered much of the evidence that drove Nixon to resign rather than face impeachment. Trump's clumsy attempt to manipulate the bureau showed he was ignorant of history, unaware of Comey's devotion to the FBI's independence, and reckless to the point of self-destructiveness.[11]

If the Flynn case proved anything, it was that the big problem, which Trump would call "this Russia thing," was extremely dangerous to his presidency. And yet, in the moment when he could have moved away from it, thanks to Flynn's resignation, Trump plunged right back in. Three explanations for this behavior come readily to mind. The simplest would hold that the president was a kind of adrenaline junkie who thrived on risk. The second involved his commitment to proving that he truly believed that as president, he could do whatever he wanted. (This was a notion he would assert more strongly over time.) The third would suggest that Trump understood the threat he faced from the Russia election controversy and believed he needed to do more to counter it, even if it included trying to corrupt the FBI.

Countering the U.S. Intelligence Community's assessment of the Russia threat would be a tall order, especially without Flynn, who had been one of the president's main defenders against the intelligence establishment, and without Paul Manafort, who had been an advocate for the alternative, Ukraine-did-it theory. Beyond losing their assistance, Trump had to worry about what damage these men could do as, under the threat of prosecution, they might feel tempted to seek leniency in exchange for testimony that could hurt him. In March 2017, Flynn's lawyer announced, ominously, that if granted immunity, his client would testify, because he "certainly has a story to tell." Manafort showed no signs of becoming a cooperator but would come under great pressure as investigators abroad and at home dug into the payments he received and whether he had paid taxes due in various jurisdictions.[12]

• • •

After Trump's inauguration, Manafort jetted off to Madrid to meet Konstantin Kilimnik. His former partner arrived at Manafort's hotel where, for ninety minutes, the men reviewed, among other issues, the state of a Ukrainian investigation of the Black Ledger. Kilimnik assured Manafort that the probe had stalled. It was true that the investigators with the Ukrainian anti-corruption bureau were making little progress, but this didn't mean that the matter was going away. In fact, as Kilimnik and Manafort were trying to understand the state of play in Kiev, the new tenant in the center-city office space once occupied by Manafort contacted the anti-corruption journalist Sergii Leshchenko to say he had found a safe in the office and the landlord had given him permission to open it. He wanted Leshchenko to see the contents, meager as they were.

After rushing across the city, Leshchenko sat in Manafort's old office and inspected credit cards in the names of two Manafort employees and an application for a German boarding school that had educated European royalty. The forms seemed to have been filled out for one of Kilimnik's children, whose report card was also in the safe. The only documents of real interest to Leshchenko were records related to a $750,000 payment sent to an account controlled by Manafort at a bank in Virginia.[13]

The bank papers showed that after Manafort had received the money, it was transferred to an account in the former Soviet republic of Kyrgyzstan, which belonged to a firm called Neocom Systems, which in turn listed an address in Belize, where banking laws shielded corporations from scrutiny. (One of the officers of the company turned out to be a hairdresser from Kiev whose passport had been stolen.) As Leshchenko would later report, the $750,000 was also recorded in the Black Ledger, and $2.5 million more had been sent directly to Neocom by the Party of Regions. The money had been related to a contract for computer equipment that was never delivered and which Leshchenko considered to be part of a fraud intended to facilitate tax evasion. At the very least, the record would provide U.S. investigators with another lead to pursue as they tried to trace Manafort's earnings and match them with his tax returns.[14]

Like Flynn, Manafort faced the kind of legal jeopardy that could lead to a prison cell. However, he was also a man who understood the value of information. Present during the Russian hacking attacks of the 2016 campaign, he might know things that investigators would like to learn about the campaign's engagement with Russians of various stripes and whether anyone around Donald Trump had helped with the release of the information stolen from the Democrats. This made him a potential threat to the president and one of two men, alongside Mike Flynn, who should have paid close attention when Trump published a Twitter post that reminded the world that "the U.S. President has the complete power to pardon."[15]

4

ALTERNATIVE FACTS AND DEZINFORMATSIYA

I call my own shots, largely based on an accumulation of data, and every-
one knows it. Some FAKE NEWS media, in order to marginalize, lies!

—Donald Trump, president of the United States, via Twitter,
February 6, 2017

At the start of Donald Trump's presidency, no one who maintained even a
passing interest in American politics could have been unaware of the fact that
he remained eager to get past the Russia imbroglio and would be willing to
take help with this problem from just about anyone. A more avid student of
Trump's methods would also know that Trump would not require this assistance to be based on any verifiable facts. Indeed, by the third day of the Trump
presidency, the White House was so fully committed to his aggressive style
of distortion that Press Secretary Sean Spicer devoted all his time at the press
room podium defending Trump's obviously false claims that a record-setting
crowd attended his inauguration and to scold reporters who told the truth.
"We're going to hold the press accountable," said Spicer.

The issue was a petty one, but it proved telling as administration officials
dug in their heels against photographic evidence showing vast empty areas of
the National Mall that had been filled when Barack Obama took the oath of
office in 2009. Spicer was caught playing with subway ridership figures to back
up Trump's claims, but the absurdity didn't reach a crescendo until the president's counselor Kellyanne Conway declared the false claims were actually
"alternative facts" and complained about "the way we're treated by the press."[1]

The crowd-size controversy demonstrated that even as president, Trump
would not abandon the techniques he'd adopted as a young man. After college,

he had been nurtured in the art of manipulation by the notorious Roy Cohn, chief inquisitor for Senator Joe McCarthy. Cohn taught him to be pugnacious and insistent, no matter the facts. So it was that when authorities found Trump discriminating against minority applicants for apartments, he responded by claiming he was the victim of government discrimination. Later, he and Roger Stone, another Cohn mentee, developed political schemes governed by Stone's rules, which were summarized as "Attack, attack, attack. Admit nothing, deny everything, launch counterattack."[2]

The Cohn, Trump, and Stone way to gain and wield power wasn't so different from the information warfare practiced by Soviet intelligence officers as Vladimir Putin rose through the ranks of the KGB. Before the demise of the USSR, Soviet agents conducted thousands of these propaganda attacks against Western governments, using forged government documents and "witnesses" trained to offer alternative "facts" to dupe journalists, opinion makers, and societies at large. For example, after the assassination of President Kennedy, the Soviets played a key role in spreading conspiracy theories about his murder, which eroded public faith in the government and fueled political paranoia. A more recent *dezinformatsiya* (disinformation) campaign planted the harebrained idea that the AIDS virus was created by the U.S. government to kill minority citizens. By 1993, when pollsters asked black Americans whether "AIDS was produced in a government laboratory" over 30 percent of men and 24 percent of women said that it was.[3]

Putin had revived information warfare with three missions in mind. The first called for strengthening his grip on power at home. The second involved destabilizing neighboring countries—Georgia, Ukraine, Moldova, Latvia—to restore Russian dominance in the post-Soviet era. (A special case, because of its strategic value, Ukraine received the brunt of this effort.) The third was to avenge the collapse of the Soviet Union and gain strategic advantage by wreaking havoc in Western Europe and America. With planted false stories, staged events, and fake organizations, citizens would be turned against citizens and allies against allies. All of this could be accomplished at costs that declined markedly year by year, thanks to the online technologies that made it possible to deliver propaganda at minimal cost.

Eventually, history may show that Russia's greatest *dezinformatsiya* victory came with Donald Trump's election in 2016, but early in the new president's first term, Putin was not resting on this success. What good was there in helping elect a U.S. president if his presence couldn't be turned to Russia's advantage? To succeed, the Kremlin would have to follow a strategy that would benefit both parties—Trump *and* Russia—whenever possible. Here, Moscow's favorite target, Ukraine, would be especially handy.

In February 2017, as Washington focused on the Mike Flynn debacle and Donald Trump's struggle to assume the presidency, a buoyant Vladimir Putin arrived in Budapest for talks with his counterpart Viktor Orbán. A nationalist with an autocratic streak, Orbán was systematically attacking the Hungarian courts, co-opting the national assembly, and destroying the free press. He also trafficked in conspiracy theories—among them were anti-Semitic attacks on philanthropist George Soros, whom the American Right also reviled—and demonized immigrants. His soft version of autocracy led to one-party rule and became a model for others who would degrade democracy in favor of strongman rule.

At a joint press conference, Orbán and Putin said they had worked on agreements to ensure Russian energy supplies to Hungary and on improving relations overall. When asked about Ukraine, Putin ignored the facts of Russia's annexation of Ukrainian territory and military action in eastern Ukraine and instead said Ukraine was playing the victim to gain international aid. He then seamlessly offered the false accusation that during the U.S. elections, Kiev had tried to help Hillary Clinton get elected. He said:

> As we all know, during the presidential campaign in the United States, the Ukrainian government adopted a unilateral position in favor of one candidate. More than that, certain oligarchs, certainly with the approval of the political leadership, funded this candidate, or female candidate, to be more precise. Now they need to improve relations with the current administration, and using a conflict to do so is always a better, easier way to draw the incumbent administration into addressing Ukrainian problems and thus establish a dialogue.

With his first phrase—"As we all know"—Putin used a Trump-like sales technique to open his listeners' minds and invite agreement to his lie. In fact, no Ukrainian government campaign had been created to influence the 2016 election, and no oligarchs had given money to Hillary Clinton. But as Putin voiced these fictions, he planted ideas that would benefit Russia, harm Ukraine, and please the new American president, with whom he was building a close relationship. The news reports that followed the press conference would place this propaganda in the public record, where it would be picked up by fringe media and then, eventually, more mainstream outlets. With nothing more than words, Putin could change what people believed had occurred and how they might act in the future based on this understanding. All that was required was a willingness to lie and deceive, which would come naturally to a well-trained agent.[4]

•   •   •

In Washington, Donald Trump was confronted by two problems that mere words would not resolve. Under pressure from federal investigators, Mike Flynn could choose to seek leniency by sharing information that would damage the president. Meanwhile, by asking the FBI director to go easy on Flynn, the president may have committed the crime of obstruction of justice. At the very least, he had violated the post-Nixon norms that separate the president from the Department of Justice. In the past, Trump had solved problems with the help of employees who were loyal to him. Guided by his own sense of what his duties required, James Comey was, for Trump, a wild card. And since the president held the power to fire the FBI director, Trump watched for an opportunity. It came in early May as Comey addressed a Senate Judiciary Committee hearing on his brief reopening of the bureau's investigation into the Clinton email server.

Many postmortem reviews of the election had cited Comey's announcement that he would reopen the email probe as a key factor in the election outcome. At the time when Comey made his announcement, so many inside the FBI were opposed to Clinton that one agent described the agency as "Trumpland." In this environment, Comey had faced pressure to act in a way that violated a long-standing tradition against taking acts that might affect an election. Although the new material was quickly determined to be unimportant and Clinton was cleared, the damage was done.[5]

When Comey addressed the Senate committee, he said he felt "mildly nauseous to think we might have had some impact on the election." He also confirmed Russia's interference in American politics and described it as "the greatest threat [to America] of any nation on earth given their intention and their capability." He said the FBI was continuing to investigate Russia's past and ongoing assaults on American democracy. This work meant the feds would continue to focus on Trump campaign operatives who had been involved in the Russia controversies, including figures as disparate as former general Mike Flynn and Trump's longtime political advisor Roger Stone. (A grand jury had already been impaneled in the Flynn case, and the general would soon be called before it.) Comey did not say that President Trump had been fully cleared of wrongdoing and was therefore not the subject of investigation. Anyone who wanted to know how the president felt about this could learn it from Rudy Giuliani, who was advising the president on legal matters. "He's entitled to that," Giuliani would say. "Hillary Clinton got that and he couldn't get that."[6]

Days after Comey testified, Trump met with Attorney General Jeff Sessions and his number two at the Justice Department, Rod Rosenstein. Sessions had been the first United States senator to endorse candidate Trump and therefore enjoyed the president's confidence. Trump ordered the men to develop a rationale for Comey's dismissal. Within twenty-four hours, Sessions sent the White House a memo Rosenstein had written to explain how Comey's handling of the Clinton matter justified his firing. As Comey visited the FBI field office in Los Angeles, Trump had his longtime private bodyguard, a former New York City police detective named Keith Schiller, deliver the letter firing Comey to FBI headquarters in Washington. After the White House announced the dismissal, Comey's supporters expressed shock. Roger Stone turned to Twitter to post a picture of Trump and the words *You're fired.*[7]

The bravado that would prompt Roger Stone to taunt James Comey was an essential element of the way Trump and his partners did business. Gloating signaled power and expressed a sense of confidence that your side was in the right. The president practiced this same kind of gamesmanship on the day after the firing, May 10, when he hosted Russian ambassador Kislyak and foreign minister Sergey Lavrov in the Oval Office and said of Comey, "He was crazy, a real nut job. I faced great pressure because of Russia. That's taken off." In this same meeting, Trump shared classified intelligence information provided by a U.S. ally, without that ally's permission. Any other official could be prosecuted for this action, but as president, Trump was legally free to declassify anything at any moment.[8]

Trump continued with his brazen, do-it-in-the-open method on May 12 in an interview with NBC's Lester Holt. He told Holt that he was going to fire Comey no matter what Rosenstein recommended in his memo. As Trump put it, he believed that "this Russia thing, with Trump and Russia, is a made-up story." Since he believed Comey was responsible for keeping the story alive, it was only natural that Trump fired him. As if to rub it in, Trump also took the time on the day he spoke with Holt to send out a tweet that said Comey "better hope there are no 'tapes' of our conversations before he starts leaking to the press."

If the president had any hope of quelling the obstruction controversy, it expired with the May 12 interview. In this time before the president had tightened his grip on congressional Republicans, a number were willing to join Democrats to raise concern about Trump's obvious effort to influence prosecutors, who should be impartial. Attorney General Sessions, who had been part of the Trump campaign, recognized he had conflicts of interest that required him to recuse himself. On May 17, he appointed former FBI director Robert Mueller, a lifelong Republican, to the position of special counsel empowered to investigate any links between Trump and his people and Russian interference in the 2016 election. The mandate also gave Mueller authority to investigate "any matters that arose or may arise from that investigation." Although it read like a bit of boilerplate, the bit about other "matters" meant that Mueller could look into anything from tax evasion to obstruction of justice if he came upon it in the course of his work.

When the special counsel was named, no one knew more about what Mueller might find as he turned over rocks than Donald Trump. Some of his campaign aides *had* been in contact with various Russian figures, and talk about the release of hacked emails had swirled around the campaign for many months. Who knew what might be discovered by an independent federal investigator with the money, the staff, and the time to track every possible crime and campaign finance law violation? With this in mind, the idea of shifting responsibility for the election hack from Russia to some other country, or collection of countries, held real appeal. Throughout his life, in business and politics, Trump had answered inquiries and investigations with furious attacks on those who challenged him and on the facts that gave rise to any concern. In this case, he would practice character assassination against Mueller and his team while also discrediting the very basis for the probe, namely that Russia helped Trump win in 2016.

Among the other tried-and-true techniques that could be used against Mueller's findings was a classic of Soviet/Russian propaganda called *whataboutism*. This method required identifying some flaw in a critic's background or behavior and using it to change the subject whenever a legitimate issue is raised. The Soviets used racial strife in the United States in this way, raising it to suggest that Americans could not credibly criticize the ways Moscow systematically deprived all who lived in the USSR of basic freedoms. What about your racism problem? Soviet apologists would ask as they refused to address their government's abuses. One had nothing to do with the other, but the deflection made meaningful dialogue impossible.

Trump had used whataboutism throughout his life and during the 2016 campaign; however, it was not his only propaganda skill. He was also a champion obfuscator, and his ability to promote lies, distortions, and conspiracy theories was legendary. *The Washington Post* would tally this effort on a regular basis, and readers would marvel as the total quickly ran into the thousands and then tens of thousands. He could only do this through a willingness to offer so many competing arguments about what may have occurred in the past or was currently occurring that he overwhelmed the methods people might use to sort things out. Jokes could be offered in a serious tone. Policy proposals might be suggested with a laugh. Experts call the confusion caused by this way of communicating *censorship by noise*. In the internet age, it is a simple thing for armies of media helpers or internet trolls to amplify the noise for power or profit. When conspiracy theories are then suggested to explain what's happening, they might seem like life rafts and, as people climb in, they discover their candidate at the rudder promising, as Trump did, "To Make America Great Again."[9]

The modern practice of political censorship by noise was pioneered by Vladimir Putin, who used it first at home to establish himself as his nation's one true source of reliable information, authority, and leadership. (Before Trump promised to return America to greatness, Putin pledged he would "raise Russia from its knees.") He turned the practice against the outside world when he smirkingly denied the photographic evidence of Russian forces invading Crimea, insisting it just didn't happen. Trump used Twitter in a similar defensive way, to deny events, but also as an offensive weapon that could lob ideas into the political landscape where they exploded like bombs. In March, for example, he claimed, without evidence, that President Obama had wiretapped Trump's offices. This was not something that could be disproved, and so it lingered for the president's loyalists to embrace as fact. Experts call this technique *censorship* by noise because its main effect is to destroy the value of even seeking the truth. The propaganda worked if, like a plausible theory of the case offered by a clever courtroom attorney, it created a doubt that felt reasonable to some minds.

Trump performed a similar trick a month later when he sat for an interview with the Associated Press. In that session, he claimed, falsely, that in 2016, hackers attacked the Republican National Committee but failed because the RNC had superior defenses. The point he hoped to make was that both sides faced equal assaults. It wasn't true that the RNC had superior defenses. In fact, its computer servers were breached and data was stolen. The difference was that the information was not made public, suggesting that the attackers favored the GOP. The president also used the interview to advance a false claim that a Ukrainian-owned consulting firm covered up evidence related to the hacking attack against the Democrats. No part of this narrative was true. The firm, called CrowdStrike, cooperated with FBI investigators, and Trump was wrong about its base of operations and ownership. But as the president offered this tall tale, it became a competing theory to be deployed by his supporters whenever convenient. The name CrowdStrike would be uttered with ominous overtones, and in time, people would even declare as uncontested truth the lie that the Democrats had physically destroyed computer equipment to keep it from the FBI.[10]

•   •   •

When it came to Russia's attack on the 2016 U.S. election, truth seekers confronted the unusual challenge posed by the fact that the leader of the country that had been the victim was deeply invested in confirming the fact that the attack never took place. With one man eager to sell a false narrative and the other eager to buy it, Putin and Trump spoke in private on July 7, 2017, at a G20 summit of world leaders in Hamburg. This was their first in-person meeting—actually, they would have *two* conversations in a single day—and later Trump aides came to suspect this was when Putin first fed Trump the Ukraine line.

Verification of this fact would be difficult, since after the first session, Trump confiscated his translator's notes and no American aide was present for the second talk. However, White House officials did notice that from this day forward, the president would insist to his side that Ukraine and not Russia had attacked the 2016 election. "Everyone knows I won the election,' he would say. 'The greatest election in the world. The Russians didn't do anything. The Ukrainians tried to do something.'" In conversation, the president would say that he knew Ukraine was responsible for the hacking of the 2016 U.S. election because Putin had told him so. In public, he defended his old associate Paul Manafort, who was under legal scrutiny due to the Black Ledger mess, and he complained about Attorney General Sessions's—the man he had chosen for the job—failure to launch a formal investigation into Ukrainian election interference.[11]

After the Hamburg meetings, Trump increased the noise around the facts by sending out social media messages that repeatedly used terms such as *hoax* and *witch hunt* in reference to accurate reports on Russia's effort to support his election campaign. With the aid of the Caps Lock key, he called his bursts of complaint "MODERN DAY PRESIDENTIAL," indicating they were issued with the full authority of his office. And like Putin, who could rely on almost all the Russian press to rebroadcast his propaganda, Trump had media allies who not only rebroadcast his messages but added both their own authority and energy to the spin. So it was that he could quote an article published by the pro-Trump *Washington Times*, which blamed Democrats for "disinformation" as if it were authoritative. He could also appear on one of the rabidly partisan Fox News programs like *Hannity* or *Tucker Carlson Tonight* and pretend that he had actually engaged with the American people. In his capacity as the head of government, he stepped up his attacks on public officials such as Attorney General Sessions and Special Counsel Mueller, who, acting outside the president's exclusive direction, were part of an independent effort to gather actual evidence.[12]

• • •

Just after 6:00 a.m. on the morning of Wednesday, July 26, 2017, three weeks after Trump had chatted with Putin in Hamburg, FBI agents knocked three times on an apartment door in Alexandria, Virginia. They got no answer, so the lead agent, Matthew Mikuska, took out a key and, armed with a search warrant, opened the door. He and his team walked into the luxury 2,700-square-foot condo that Paul Manafort had purchased for $2.7 million in 2015. Manafort was standing at the door by the time the agents entered and did nothing to hinder them.[13]

The agents gathered up boxes full of tax and banking records and other files. The papers included receipts and documents showing the purchase of a Mercedes-Benz and a home purchase for $1.9 million in cash for Manafort's daughter. This cache would help FBI accountants identify suspicious transactions related to a number of assets including: a Brooklyn residence valued at $3 million and a $6.6 million home improvement loan from a bank in Chicago, the Federal Savings Bank. The bank was owned by Steve Calk, a Trump supporter who was trying to get a high-level administration job.

FBI searchers also uncovered information about thirty foreign bank accounts, mostly in Cyprus, that held funds totaling at least $75 million. They also found signs of lavish spending by Manafort which they described in their reports: a "custom $15,000 jacket made from an ostrich," a "$9,500 vest made from ostrich," an "$18,500 jacket made from python skin," and a "waterproof silk blouson." This was the lifestyle of wealth and a profile of fund transfers characteristic of money launderers. The raid, which could only have been carried out after a judge heard evidence that indicated Manafort had committed criminal acts, suggested he was headed, inexorably, toward arrest, indictment, and trial.[14]

The former Trump campaign manager's troubles, which had begun months before the election, were unprecedented in American politics. It would be safe to assume that with any other president's team, Manafort's experience would have signaled an end to the kind of foreign engagements that led to FBI agents pouring through his door at six o'clock in the morning. In President Trump's circle, at least one prominent figure failed to heed the warning. Rudy Giuliani, passed over for his dream job at the State Department, quickly took himself back to the former Soviet state of Ukraine, where he was recognized as an advisor and friend to the president and as a businessman. (As president, Trump had helped create the idea that Giuliani enjoyed a quasi-official status, describing him in public as a cybersecurity advisor who would be "sharing his expertise and insight as a trusted friend.")

With Trump just getting settled in the White House, Giuliani began traveling back and forth to Ukraine, where he found himself giving a lecture on corruption and democracy in one moment and talking business deals with then president Petro Poroshenko in another. He met the American ambassador to Ukraine, Marie Yovanovitch, at an event hosted by oligarch Victor Pinchuk and was greeted at the airport in the northern city of Kharkiv by a group of girls in traditional dress offering ceremonial welcome gifts of salt and bread.

On one of his Ukraine trips, Giuliani invited Yovanovitch to breakfast at the hotel where he was staying in Kiev. Yovanovitch recognized one of the other men at the table as Pavel Fuks, an oligarch who became wealthy in post-Soviet Russia in the gas, finance, and real estate businesses. They discussed two projects: one would involve Giuliani's firm in security work, the other had something to do with municipal finance. Both would supposedly benefit Kharkiv. The Wall Street Journal would eventually report that though Giuliani had made a deal with the Kharkiv government, it was actually Fuks who had paid for the work. Fuks, in turn, would say he expected Giuliani to lobby the Trump administration for Ukraine. "I would call him the lobbyist for Kharkiv and Ukraine—this is stated in the contract. It is very important for me that such a person as Giuliani tells people that we are a good country, that people can do business with us. That's what we would like to bring to America's leaders."[15]

Typical of the shadowy characters Giuliani seemed to attract in his foreign escapades, Fuks was an opportunist who had used political connections to become rich and powerful. Like many oligarchs, he had a rough edge. He bragged about forcing workers who smoked on the job to eat cigarette butts and once said, "When I was young, I beat people up." Fuks had met with Ivanka Trump and Donald Trump Jr. in 2006 and considered licensing the Trump name for one of his Moscow building projects. After the 2016 election, he had paid a GOP fundraiser $200,000 for tickets to exclusive Trump inaugural events. The arrangement was supposed to help Fuks get around legal prohibitions of foreign payments to inaugural organizations, but in the end, he never got the access he believed he had purchased. He watched the inauguration on the TV at a hotel bar.[16]

Although his schemes seemed extraordinarily complex and exotic, Fuks actually fit into a common category of post-Soviet entrepreneurs who used relationships with politicians and (sometimes) crime bosses to buy properties, win government contracts, and dominate competitors. It was common for these actors to use shell companies based in places where scrutiny was scant, to avoid detection, and they played the game on an international scale, moving between cities like Moscow, Kiev, London, New York, and Washington and popping up in resort towns where they might encounter the global rich at play. Big players like Fuks became famous as they made their deals, but for every billionaire, there were countless strivers who imitated them with their own plots, doing all they could to look like they were more successful than they were. In this category, Giuliani would know Igor Fruman and Lev Parnas.

Like Giuliani, Parnas and Fruman were loyal to Trump in a way that someone like James Comey could never be. But they were devoted to themselves as much as to the president. All three had much to gain personally by presenting themselves as his emissaries in Ukraine. For Giuliani, Ukraine offered the chance to gain relevance, wield power, and make money. Cash flow was important for him, as he had seen his market value decline from the early period of his post-mayoral life, when clients were eager to hire the man who had been in charge during the 9/11 attacks. Although his reputation had dimmed, he maintained a lifestyle that included multiple homes and country club memberships. He was also headed toward his third divorce.

Giuliani's new associates, Parnas and Fruman, evidenced no designs on power or political relevance, but like the former mayor, they both needed money. Fruman was facing the prospect of a messy and expensive divorce. He was also burdened by the recent bankruptcy of his Ukrainian food company. When Andrew Roth, a reporter for the London-based *Guardian*, set out to discover Fruman's background, he found a former prosecutor who knew all about him. Roth wrote:

> "He was just a bankrupt guy, a crook I would say, who was looking for some fortune and opportunities," said David Sakvarelidze, a former Ukrainian regional prosecutor who met Fruman after he was assigned to work in Odessa in 2015. "He had big financial troubles and I was told he basically already was living in the United States at that time, in Miami. He was looking for some opportunities to settle his financial problems. Maybe he could use his connections to Giuliani's team to settle his financial troubles, that's my presumption."[17]

Lev Parnas was eager for cash but hindered by a record that would scare off any client or potential partner who performed even a cursory check on his background. The biggest red flag was the $500,000 federal judgment for *Anatomy of an Assassin*, but the movie financing fraud was the culmination of a life devoted to schemes and hustles. In the 1990s, Parnas worked for eight different investment sales firms with names like Euro-Atlantic Securities and Program Trading. Typical of the outfits that earned a Boca Raton business area the nickname "the Maggot Mile," these companies pushed senior citizens to make high-commission risky investments. Euro-Atlantic was shuttered amid charges that it was a front for organized crime. Program Trading was shut down after assuming millions in debt. In 2010, Parnas was assaulted by an angry investor who saw him in a park. Two years later, he was skipping out on the $14,000 per month rent on a mansion he occupied and driving potential clients around Boca in his Bentley. Friendly, energetic, and always eager to have his picture snapped, he had a knack for finding new pathways to people who either didn't look at his past, including links to the Russian mafia, or knew all about it, and saw some advantage in working with him.[18]

5

FORREST GUMPS OF THE GOP

@SeanHannity is having a DEEP STATE SHOW tonight on Fox News at 9:00 PM (E), exposing the tremendous abuse of power that has been uncovered. Tremendous guests, a must see—Enjoy!

—Donald Trump, president of the United States, via Twitter,
May 31, 2019

By all appearances, Lev Parnas and Igor Fruman were men who believed you had to spend money—and get noticed doing it—to make money. Upscale addresses. Fancy cars. First-class travel. Expensive jewelry. (Parnas once offered a Rolex to settle a debt.) In the spring and summer of 2018, they spent large sums that were sure to get them attention, access, and perhaps acceptance in high-roller GOP circles.[1]

April found Parnas and Fruman in the largest hotel suite in Washington, the Townhouse at the Trump International Hotel, where they would join a small group of top political donors for dinner with the president. At some point during this ninety-minute event, Fruman and Parnas had the president's ear and used the moment to complain about America's ambassador to Ukraine, Marie Yovanovitch. Igor Fruman took the liberty of recording the exchange on his phone:

"I think, if you take a look, the biggest problem there, I think where we—where you need to start is, we got to get rid of the ambassador," said Parnas.

"Where? The ambassador where, Ukraine?" Trump asked.

"Yeah, she's basically walking around telling everybody, 'Wait, he's gonna get impeached, just wait.'"

No degree in psychology was required for Parnas to understand that this kind of gossip, especially the suggestion that someone might be disloyal, would provoke a response from the president. The whole world knew he was a suspicious and insecure man obsessed with how others talked about him.

"Really?" Trump asked Parnas.

"Yeah, it's incredible," Parnas answered.

Then as if on cue, the president's son Donald Jr., who was seated nearby, offered an unhelpful, frat-boy kind of joke. "She'll be gone tomorrow!" This, too, was the kind of remark guaranteed to get a rise out of the president.

"What's her name?" the president asked.

Neither Parnas nor Fruman could summon the ambassador's name, which would cause a careful listener to wonder whether the matter was at all serious. Their poor grasp of the facts prompted another person at the table to note the recent appointment of the new secretary of state, Mike Pompeo. This speaker, John DeStefano, who was the head of the Office of Presidential Personnel, seemed to suggest there was an orderly way to review embassy staffing, but by this time, the red flag that had been waved by Parnas and the president's son had had its effect.

"Get rid of her," the president suddenly said. "Get her out tomorrow."

As others at the table chuckled at the thought of hearing the president suddenly decide the fate of an unsuspecting ambassador five thousand miles to the east, DeStefano suggested again that a normal process could be followed to consider Parnas's claim. But now that he was in the middle of a decisive act, and getting an excited response from those listening in, Trump wasn't about to relent. Not waiting for DeStefano to finish, he said, "I don't care. Get her out tomorrow. Take her out. OK?"

Less than a minute had passed from the president's question—"Where? The ambassador where, Ukraine?"—to an order—"Take her out"—that sounded like something a movie mob boss might say. Trump still didn't know the ambassador's name, but he apparently trusted Lev Parnas enough that he would fire an ambassador he didn't know on the basis of Parnas's say-so. To their credit, John DeStefano and Mike Pompeo took no immediate action, which meant that for the time being, U.S. policy was not being directed by a sketchy character who happened to sit next to the president and that the well-respected ambassador could continue in her work unmolested.

A career diplomat with an unblemished record, Yovanovitch had never been involved in political controversy. However, her posting in Ukraine, where anti-corruption policies were a top American priority, had landed her at the epicenter of intrigue. Corruption was such a prominent feature of local political affairs that the Obama administration had conditioned economic aid on efforts to clean up the informal system of bribes and payoffs that hung over the government at every level. In December 2015, Vice President Joe Biden made corruption the focus of a pointed address to the Ukrainian parliament. When American diplomats pushed for the removal of national prosecutor Viktor Shokin, whom they considered corrupt, he was replaced by a politician with no legal background. Yuriy Lutsenko refused to dismiss Shokin's deputies and engaged in a turf war with a new, independent, U.S.-backed National Anti-Corruption Bureau of Ukraine (NABU). By the time Lev Parnas was urging the president to fire Yovanovitch, Lutsenko considered her an enemy and had begun his own campaign for her removal.[2]

As they undertook the same mission at the same time, no evidence proved that Lutsenko and Parnas were working together in the summer of 2018. No cooperation or coordination was necessary, of course, since they would each have ample motivation. Lutsenko blamed Yovanovitch and Biden for undermining him and harbored animosity toward them both. Parnas and his partner Fruman were eager to get involved in the notoriously corrupt Ukrainian energy business. As an anti-corruption crusader, Yovanovitch would be an impediment to the kind of business they hoped to conduct.

After their chat with the president, Parnas and Fruman arranged to send $325,000 to America First Action, a pro-Trump political action committee run by Texas oilman Tommy Hicks Jr. However, this donation was not a simple transaction. The first complicating act came when Parnas and Fruman requested that when the PAC listed its receipts for the Federal Election Commission, as the law required, it declare that the donation came from a company called Global Energy Producers, which they had created two weeks prior to the payment. A third partner in GEP was longtime Republican donor Harry Sargeant III of Boca Raton, whose family and corporate entities had given well over $1 million to Republican causes, including $10,000 to the Trump Victory fund and $14,000 to Rudy Giuliani's ill-fated 2008 presidential run. Sargeant was a shipping magnate who created a start-up company that became the single largest supplier of fuel to U.S. forces in the Iraq War. He won this business despite often being the highest bidder on contracts. A Pentagon audit concluded the government had overpaid him by as much as $204 million.[3]

Although Sargeant had proven he could ramp up a big energy company in very little time, Parnas and Fruman had no comparable experience, and as of May 2018, Global Energy Producers had no internet presence and no record of producing energy anywhere on the globe. It didn't even have offices. Its address was a home in a gated community in Boca Raton occupied by a Soviet-born man named Victor Imber. However, the firm's gossamer status wasn't the only strange thing about the donation. As would later be revealed, the actual payment to America First Action had been made not by GEP but by a limited liability corporation, Aaron Investments I, LLC, which Parnas controlled and which was named for his son.

And where did Aaron Investments get the money? Here, the facts become a swirl of transactions. It appears to have come out of $1.2 million delivered to Aaron by a South Florida–based lawyer on behalf of an unnamed client. In time, it would be revealed that the client may have been Igor Fruman and the money came from a private mortgage taken out against a North Miami condo. The transactions behind the cash were obscured by the use of shell corporations. This was a perfectly legal but also purposely opaque way for people to turn the value held in some piece of property into useful cash.[4]

Aaron Investments got the $1.2 million on May 15, 2018. Two days later, the same LLC wired $325,000 to America First Action, where it was recorded as received from Global Energy Producers. The strange transactions didn't end there. On the day after paying the PAC, Aaron wired Igor Fruman's company, FD Import & Export, $490,000. On the next day, May 18, Aaron paid $11,500 to a private jet service called JetSmarter that had been founded by a man who had recently been indicted on charges of embezzling $11 million in a real estate scheme. In his absence, JetSmarter was being run by the thirty-year-old son of a man who had been linked in published reports to FBI investigations of the Russian mob.[5]

In the same month when they were establishing themselves as money-men for the president, Parnas and Fruman were in the middle of a political donation spree, sending payments to GOP organizations and candidates across the country. Fruman's payments would be difficult to trace, as each one was reported as coming from a man named Furman, not Fruman. However, the most accurate information recorded by the Federal Election Commission showed it was indeed Parnas's partner who gave money to campaigns for the likes of House minority leader Kevin McCarthy and Congressman Pete Sessions of Texas.

On May 1, Lev Parnas visited the White House, where he and Trump had their photo snapped as they stood between two American flags. (Lev flashed a thumbs-up.) Later in the month, Fruman and Parnas visited Representative Sessions on Capitol Hill. The congressman was facing a big challenge in his bid for reelection in November. Parnas and Fruman promised to raise $20,000 for Sessions, and they would make good on the pledge. Sessions promptly sent a letter to Secretary of State Mike Pompeo to complain about Marie Yovanovitch. "I have received notice from close companions that Ambassador Yovanovitch has spoken privately and repeatedly about her disdain for the current administration," wrote Sessions.

(In a little-noted echo of Sessions's complaint, former Republican representative Robert Livingston had also been agitating against Yovanovitch. In phone calls made to Catherine Croft, a Ukraine specialist at the National Security Council, Livingston complained that Yovanovitch was an "Obama holdover" associated with George Soros. Once in line to be Speaker of the House, Livingston had built a powerful lobbying firm based on his access to government officials. Former Ukrainian premier Gas Princess Yulia Tymoshenko, whose vast fortune was acquired in the energy business, was a client. Croft notified her superior Fiona Hill of his complaints and mentioned them to the senior State Department official George Kent and took no other action.[6])

After seeing Sessions in Washington, Parnas and Fruman jetted off to Los Angeles, where they had a private breakfast with Donald Trump Jr. and investor Tommy Hicks Jr. at the swanky Polo Lounge in Beverly Hills. In a photo that Parnas posted online on May 21, 2018, the body language says it all. A relaxed Parnas, seated in the middle of a round banquette, has his right arm draped over Hicks's shoulder and his left across Fruman's back. He smiles broadly. Hicks, who had connections to the oil and gas business and was also cochairman of the Republican National Committee, offers a bland glance at the photographer. Fruman, who has conspicuously opened three buttons on his white shirt to expose the hair on his chest, grins. Opposite Fruman, on the other side of the banquette, Donald Trump Jr. stares warily at the camera, his left arm turned as if to separate himself from the others. His body is coiled, as if he's preparing for a getaway.[7]

If some part of Donald Trump Jr. wanted to escape Parnas and Fruman, he would have to sublimate it as the two newcomers became regulars at high-level events. In June, when Donald Trump Jr. attended an America First Action party for top donors in Washington, Fruman and Parnas were there, alongside former White House press secretary Sean Spicer and Oklahoma oilman Harold Hamm. A few weeks later, when an avid Trump supporter named

Joseph Frager organized a tour of Israel for prominent Americans, Fruman and Parnas were included.[8]

Frager was first vice president of a century-old service organization called the National Council of Young Israel, which, before Trump, had confined its work to helping synagogues. As enthusiastic Trump supporters, Frager and others had turned Young Israel toward partisan politics. This shift helped explain why the summer 2019 Israel tour group included former White House communications director Anthony Scaramucci and former Arkansas governor Mike Huckabee, whose daughter had recently resigned as press secretary. During one stop on the tour, Huckabee, dressed in a black suit, white shirt, and pink tie, joined a band on a rooftop patio to play the Southern political anthem "Sweet Home Alabama." The crowd of right-wing Americans and Israelis included the prime minister's son Yair Netanyahu, who was in the middle of a scandal arising out of a video recording made of him at a strip club in Tel Aviv.

The "Sweet Home Alabama" evening in Jerusalem was followed, a few months later, by a pilgrimage to a cemetery in Queens, New York, where Joseph Frager led Parnas, Fruman, and Giuliani to the grave of Rabbi Menachem Mendel Schneerson, who had been leader of the Chabad-Lubavitch Hasidic movement. Considered by some to be the Messiah, Schneerson was widely credited with performing miracles, and decades after his death, some followers insisted he was still alive. The group joined other politically conservative Jewish leaders for dinner at Frager's home, and soon Parnas and Fruman would be invited to the annual gala of Young Israel, where they would receive a Lovers of Zion award.[9]

Like a couple of political Forrest Gumps, Parnas and Fruman kept popping up in crowds of important GOP figures. When the president's son and Fox News commentator Jeanine Pirro hosted a fancy seaside party in Florida, there they were. The election-night celebration for candidate Ron DeSantis's narrow victory in the race for governor of Florida? By the fall of 2018, Fruman and Parnas had moved from the edges of Trumpworld to the center of it. All of this was made possible by the money they gave to candidates and party organizations across the country and by their newly formalized relationship with the newest member of the legal team helping the president deal with the Mueller investigation, Rudy Giuliani. The former mayor had joined the Trump legal defense group in April when its lead lawyer, John Dowd, resigned over conflicts with his client. Giuliani was soon the face and voice of the team, appearing regularly in the press to criticize the investigation. In August 2018,

Parnas and Fruman had hired Giuliani at a cost of $500,000, ostensibly to help them promote Fraud Guarantee.[10]

On one level, the idea that Giuliani might help promote a company with some vague connection to online security was not far-fetched. His fame was due in part to his law-and-order days as a public official, and he had been a paid endorser for a security service called LifeLock. Fruman and Parnas imagined that Giuliani could perform in TV infomercials for them. However, Fraud Guarantee was still not a real company, and from the start, the relationship among the three men was not businesslike. The $500,000 paid to Giuliani didn't come from a start-up fund or line of credit. It actually came from a Long Island–based personal injury lawyer with a history in Republican politics.

Somewhere, someone may have been keeping track of all the money flowing to and through Parnas, Fruman, Giuliani, Republican politicians, and the various organizations that supported them. Certainly, in the regular business world, these transactions would be expected to produce a return. But this wasn't the regular world. This was a secret world where six-figure payments bought nothing more tangible than proximity to wealth and power. With this proximity came the chance that you might be useful in some way and then be rewarded. But for this to happen, you needed to show you belonged and to inspire confidence.

As Lev Parnas moved into this world, he began collecting photographic evidence to show others and post on social media. Here was a picture of himself aboard a private jet with Rudy Giuliani. There was another photo of Giuliani with the Parnas kids. After they made a $10,000 campaign donation, Parnas and Fruman flashed thumbs-ups with Nevada gubernatorial candidate Adam Laxalt. A photo of the Polo Lounge moment with Donald Trump Jr. and oilman Hicks went online with the caption "Power breakfast." Like the recording Fruman had made of that chat with the president, the one where Trump ordered that an ambassador be fired, the pictures would become proof that Parnas had entered the realm that lies beyond the press conferences, announcements, ceremonies, and other displays of power produced for the press and public.[11]

•   •   •

Just as Parnas seized his chance, another ambitious political operator who had chased his fortune in Ukraine and America and pinned his hopes on Donald Trump offered living proof that this was a high-risk pursuit. In Alexandria, Virginia, Paul Manafort defended himself in a federal courtroom, where he was charged with eighteen different felonies related to tax evasion and the Black Ledger. As he fought the charges and refused to cooperate with prosecutors, President Trump praised him as a "brave man" who "refused to break and make up stories in order to get a deal." Despite the president's support, and his high-priced and highly skilled legal team, Manafort was found guilty on eight charges.

At the conclusion of his trial in Virginia, Manafort was scheduled to appear in a federal court in Washington for a second trial on various fraud charges, for failing to register as a foreign lobbyist, for witness tampering, and for lying to federal investigators. This time, Manafort chose to become a co-operating witness for Robert Mueller's special counsel team and to accept a plea bargain that involved giving up $22 million in real estate and unspecified other assets. When he affirmed this arrangement, Manafort no longer looked like the vigorous man who had deftly fielded interview questions at the 2016 Republican National Convention. After three months in jail, where he ate food from the inmate cafeteria, had limited access to fresh air and sunshine, and couldn't keep up with his cosmetic routines, he looked like a different man. His dyed hair was turning gray, his once-taut skin was sagging, his posture had become stooped, and his gait slowed. In other words, he looked and moved every bit like a man his age and then some. According to federal guidelines, he faced a sentence of up to ten years in prison.[12]

6

MEN ON A (SECRET) MISSION

The Media (Fake News) is pushing Sleepy Joe hard. Funny, I'm only here because of Biden & Obama. They didn't do the job and now you have Trump, who is getting it done–big time!

—Donald Trump, president of the United States, via Twitter,
April 29, 2019

Among the few solemn moments in American political life, state funerals represent an opportunity for setting aside rivalries in favor of respect and amity. As the most disrespectful and abusive president in modern times, Donald Trump's attendance was not welcomed by the family when Senator John McCain's life was celebrated by a Washington National Cathedral gathering of luminaries that included former presidents Barack Obama and George W. Bush, their spouses, and many prominent senators and diplomats. In his remarks on that warm September 1, Bush offered an obvious, if oblique, rebuke of Trump when he noted, "Perhaps above all, John detested the abuse of power." As he spoke, the White House released a photo of Trump, having donned a cap emblazoned with the words *Make America Great Again,* headed to a golf course.

Two months later, in a choice that reflected his own values, George W. Bush permitted President Trump to attend the funeral for his own father at the very same cathedral. Bush delivered a heartfelt eulogy that moved many to tears. It's unlikely that he noticed that somewhere in the enormous cathedral sat Rudy Giuliani, Lev Parnas, and Igor Fruman, but there they were, nonetheless, amid a crowd that could only be described as the elite of American political society.

On the day after Bush's funeral, Giuliani, Parnas, and Fruman attended the White House Hanukkah celebration, where politically conservative Jews from around the world celebrated both their faith and their association with the president. As always, when he visited with Trump, Parnas had his photo taken with the president. In this one, he and Trump were joined by Vice President Mike Pence, Rudy Giuliani, and Igor Fruman. Afterward, Parnas would tell friends that "the big guy," as he called Trump, had brought him into a private room where he assigned him a "secret mission" to help establish that Ukraine, and not Russia, had hacked the 2016 election and to push the Ukrainian government to investigate the family of former vice president Joe Biden, who would be a likely 2020 rival for president.

Though he had been out of politics for years and was renowned for his gaffes, Biden had bested Trump in some recent public opinion polls. The president's inner circle believed Biden could be dragged down by a latent controversy that was conveniently located in Ukraine. The vice president's son Hunter had accepted a lucrative post on the board of a Ukrainian energy company called Burisma. The company obviously wanted the cachet of the Biden name. Hunter obviously wanted the pay. Authorities in Kiev had looked into the issue, and though nothing illegal was uncovered, Biden had left the board. But in politics, nothing is ever really settled, so Hunter Biden became a target for the president and his men. Rudy Giuliani, aided by Parnas and Fruman, would lead an effort that soon became a frenzy of activity. Their hunt was energized by the possibility that they might also help the president get out from under the Russia cloud by proving the Ukraine-did-it conspiracy theory.[1]

· · ·

Soon after his Hanukkah party chat with the president, Lev Parnas went to work as Giuliani's helper. Suddenly, the man paid $500,000 to work for Fraud Guarantee became the boss, and Parnas was eager to please. "Because of my Ukrainian background and my contacts there, I became like Rudy's assistant, his investigator," he would tell Adam Entous of *The New Yorker*. "I don't do anything on my own. I don't lobby people. I go get information. I set up a meeting. I make sure that the call went right. I make sure the translation is done right." What then followed was a game of pseudo investigation and intrigue.[2]

At the end of December, Parnas arranged for Giuliani to speak via Skype with the former Ukrainian prosecutor Viktor Shokin, who claimed that he had been forced out of office because he had begun an inquiry into the matter of Joe Biden's family. In particular, he said, he was looking into the work Hunter Biden had done for Burisma. No evidence was ever offered to suggest anything corrupt in the arrangement, though it was unseemly. Parnas would say that the Skype call marked the first time he had heard about the Bidens and Burisma, and he assumed Shokin was a Ukrainian patriot. Giuliani wanted an in-person meeting with Shokin, but he was denied a visa by embassy officials in Kiev.

Next, Parnas went to work on getting Giuliani a meeting with Viktor Shokin's replacement, Yuriy Lutsenko, the general prosecutor of Ukraine. With the power of the Ukrainian state at his disposal and a conviction that he was being undermined by Ambassador Yovanovitch, Lutsenko had the means and, perhaps, the motivation to cause trouble for her and for Biden. She had been appointed to her post during the Obama-Biden administration and had favored the new National Anti-Corruption Bureau of Ukraine, which had been formed at the insistence of the International Monetary Fund and the U.S. government, over Lutsenko's office, which had a history of corruption.

After Biden had pushed Lutsenko's predecessor, Shokin, out of office, Lutsenko felt he was being bullied by Americans who wanted him to get rid of everyone who had been on Shokin's team. He had resisted and found himself in conflict with Yovanovitch. In 2017, he lost her trust and confidence when he publicly revealed a secret NABU investigation of state officials suspected of selling fraudulent passports. This history meant that Lutsenko needed a way to bypass the normal protocol, which involved the American embassy, to access high-level officials in Washington when he so desired. It was reasonable to think that in exchange for his help with Biden, the president's lawyer, Giuliani, could open such a pathway. In fact, it was Trump who had sent Giuliani on his Ukraine adventure in the first place.[3]

Parnas and Fruman were present in New York when Lutsenko arrived for talks that stretched across three days at the end of January 2019. With no hint of gray in his brown hair and no middle-age paunch, the five-foot-ten Lutsenko looked younger than his fifty-four years. His English was halting but passable, and his wardrobe—suits, shirts with spread collars, fashionable accessories—gave him a look that was more eurozone than post-Soviet. In 2018, his taste for luxury had prompted a scandal when his family spent more than 50,000 euros on a vacation in the Seychelles. Coming two weeks after reports that President Poroshenko's family had spent $500,000 in the Maldives, the publicity about Lutsenko's travel was short-lived.

On one of his mornings in New York, Lutsenko awakened to find the TV news reporting that one of President Trump's advisors had been arrested. Roger Stone had been under investigation for possible federal felonies related to the 2016 campaign and Russia's intervention on Trump's behalf. Captured by a video crew from CNN, the raid was conducted at Stone's luxury rental house in Fort Lauderdale by heavily armed agents who shouted, "FBI! Open the door!" and pounded so hard they could be heard on the street. As Stone was arrested, he was put in handcuffs. It was a shocking event, rare in American political history, but indicated the stakes in the cases being pursued by Robert Mueller and other federal authorities. If Lutsenko, whom an aide would call "a great lover of fairy tales," was inclined to believe that Trump was a legitimate leader facing the kind of intrigue common back home in Ukraine, the Stone raid would have affirmed this notion.

Later on the day Stone was arrested, Lutsenko settled in to talk with Giuliani at his office. According to Giuliani, Lutsenko gave him "information" about Marie Yovanovitch, Hillary Clinton, Joe Biden, and the billionaire investor/philanthropist George Soros. The quality of this material may have varied, but the subjects were of intense interest. Lutsenko resented Yovanovitch and wanted her gone. Clinton had long been the central figure in countless conspiracy theories about political schemes, criminal cover-ups, and even murders. The mere mention of her name would inflame Trump loyalists. Biden was the man most likely to beat Trump in a one-on-one battle for the White House in 2020 and therefore represented a threat to the president's power. Soros was such an object of fear and loathing in the dark recesses of right-wing politics in both Europe and the United States that he often dealt with anti-Semitic rhetoric and credible threats against his life. As much as Clinton was the witch who resided in right-wing nightmares, Soros was the bogeyman.[4]

Lutsenko and Giuliani also talked about Manafort's conspiracy theory that had Ukraine and not Russia at the center of an attack on the 2016 U.S. presidential election. Giuliani would advance this fantasy on behalf of Trump, but it was Biden who was of special personal interest to the former mayor. To put it bluntly, Giuliani had a grudge against Biden going back to 2007, when he was trying to convert his fame as the man who had seen New York through the horror of the terror attacks of September 11, 2001, into the GOP nomination for president. Giuliani was leading the field when Biden said, "There's only three things he mentions in a sentence—a noun, a verb, and 9/11." Three months later, the mayor had not won a single caucus or primary, and he dropped out of the race. Biden became Barack Obama's running mate and was elected vice president. He would serve two terms.[5]

The Burisma issue represented a chance for Giuliani to get even with Biden, and the information Lutsenko shared was tantalizing. Included were records that, according to Lutsenko, showed that Burisma had paid $1 million in order to have Hunter Biden lobby his own father. Lutsenko speculated that taxes had been paid on the $1 million but joked that perhaps "they're as stupid as Manafort" and tried to defraud the government. By the time Lutsenko and Giuliani finished their meetings, they were speculating freely about how they might help each other. Among the items on the table was the possibility of a sit-down between Lutsenko and Trump's new attorney general, William Barr. As Lutsenko left New York, a sweeping set of goals seemed within reach for the prosecutor and his new American friend:[6]

- Rid Ukraine of a meddlesome ambassador.

- Exact revenge on Biden, whose presidential ambitions would be ruined.

- Relieve Trump from the doubt Russia cast on his 2016 election.

- Render moot investigations into Trump and Russia.

- End all efforts to impeach the president.

- Catapult Parnas and Fruman into the Ukrainian gas business.

- Reinforce Trump's relationship with Putin.

In February, after Lutsenko returned to Kiev, Giuliani wrote a proposal for an American legal team to work for the Ukrainian government. True to the spirit of his scheming, he proposed that Ukraine hire him, as well as his allies, the husband-and-wife lawyer team of Joseph E. diGenova and Victoria Toensing. In return, they would try to recover stolen Ukrainian assets. A second plan upped the cost to $300,000 and designated the Ministry of Justice as the client. Giuliani signed it, but no one from the ministry ever did.[7]

While Giuliani devised proposals, Parnas and Fruman followed Lutsenko to Kiev. As emissaries from Donald Trump's lawyer, they managed to get a meeting with Ukraine's president, Petro Poroshenko. Present at the dawn of

Ukraine's independence, Poroshenko had purchased former Soviet-era enterprises like the Karl Marx Bakery (originator of a local delicacy called Kiev Cake) to create the country's largest confectionery company. Although he was known as the "Chocolate King of Ukraine," his wealth, which at one time was estimated to exceed $1 billion, was also derived from investments in car and truck manufacturing and shipbuilding. The two small Ukrainian navy ships captured by Russia when it seized Crimea were built at Poroshenko's shipyard. As a politician, Poroshenko had cultivated an image as a moderate, pro-Western leader, but he could be ruthless. In 2015, he signed a decree banning dozens of journalists from the country and designating them, along with hundreds of others, national security threats.

Poroshenko met with Parnas and Fruman at Lutsenko's office in the Ministry of Justice, which was in a quiet neighborhood far from the bustling downtown and the massive Soviet-era building where the president's office was located. With Lutsenko in attendance, the men discussed the notion that Poroshenko would launch two investigations important to President Trump. One would look into the Bidens and Burisma. The other would explore the possibility that Ukraine had meddled in America's 2016 election. In exchange, Fruman and Parnas said, Poroshenko would be invited to Washington for a state visit.

What would the Ukrainian president have to gain from such a deal? Well, Poroshenko was beginning his own run for reelection and, in a country still dependent on U.S. aid in its fight against Russia, he might benefit politically from a show of solidarity with Washington. Also, if he had anything in common with Parnas, Fruman, Giuliani, and Trump, it may have been an antipathy toward Joe Biden. The two had a falling-out in 2016, when the Americans caught Poroshenko's government moving to return corruption to a part of the Ukrainian energy sector that was just getting cleaned up. At a meeting in Kiev, Biden had refused to accept Poroshenko's claim that he knew nothing about the issue. "This is bullshit," Biden had said. "If you do it again you've lost me."

As the men in Lutsenko's office discussed the proposal made by Parnas and Fruman, the details of a possible arrangement came into sharper focus. *The Wall Street Journal* would eventually report that according to someone involved in the effort, Poroshenko "had wanted to come to Washington and meet with Trump and then after the state dinner he would have an interview with a major news outlet." The interview would provide the opportunity for the investigations to be announced. However, something about the deal—perhaps it was the emissaries or the fact that it would involve Ukraine directly in U.S. politics—didn't sit well with Poroshenko, and he turned it down. By this time, thanks to a chance meeting between Lutsenko and Giuliani, their scheming against Ambassador Yovanovitch would become known in American diplomatic circles.[8]

•   •   •

Although they had failed to help President Trump with Poroshenko, Parnas and Fruman were still having one heck of an adventure. It wasn't so long ago that they were a couple of knock-around guys with sketchy records trying to make deals in South Florida. Now they were on a first-name basis with Republican moneymen and members of Congress. They flew on private jets, puffed expensive cigars, and had shuffled along with the mourning elite at George H. W. Bush's state funeral. They even had managed, against great odds, to make themselves known to presidents on both sides of the Atlantic. This might even qualify them as statesmen. And they still hoped to help themselves to business opportunities in Ukraine.

Parnas and Fruman's main idea involved turning Global Energy Producers into a functioning company that would deliver as many as one hundred shiploads of U.S.-produced liquid natural gas to Ukraine. In order to do this, they sought to make the largest gas producer/distributor there, Naftogaz, into a partner. However, as they pursued this strategy, they kept running into Ukrainians who said that the U.S. government, and in particular Ambassador Marie Yovanovitch, was watching the energy sector and would act to stop a return to the bad old days when executives at state-owned entities like Naftogaz played favorites. This anti-corruption posture was affirmed by Washington in early March as the State Department requested that Yovanovitch stay in her post through 2020. As news of this decision spread around Kiev, her local antagonists grew more eager to find ways to have her removed. Toward this end, state prosecutor Lutsenko agreed to help Giuliani and Parnas go after Biden.

The Biden threat to a second Trump term was reflected in polls that showed Biden doing well in states Trump needed to win in 2020, as well as in the president's own state of mind. On March 5, Trump brought his top political advisors to the White House to discuss how they might run against an opponent who had done a creditable job as Barack Obama's vice president and was more appealing to moderate and independent voters than any of the Democrats seeking the nomination. (This was before Biden formally declared.) Publicly, Trump had said Biden was "weak" and he was "not worried" about running against him. However, at the White House, he said that Biden was "the least crazy" of the Democrats he might face. In fact, Biden's moderate image and blue-collar background were valued by the working-class white voters who had helped Trump prevail in 2016 and whom he needed to retain in his base to be reelected. If Biden won over just a few of them, Trump's path to reelection would be much more difficult.[9]

•   •   •

Trump's concern about Biden was well known to insiders like Giuliani, Parnas, and Fruman, and they kept up their efforts to bring him down. In mid-February Lev Parnas traveled to a Washington TV studio operated by *The Hill*, a media company that offered news and opinion about politics and government. It was a big moment for the Giuliani-Parnas-Fruman team. Parnas had arranged for the Ukrainian prosecutor Lutsenko to sit for a web-based, remote video interview with *Hill* columnist John Solomon. Once a wire service reporter, Solomon had gradually transformed himself into a right-wing political advocate. Along the way, he had become identified with overly hyped articles about Hillary Clinton, Senator John McCain, and others that appeared to reveal scandals but failed to deliver substance and left their targets unscathed. By 2012, the *Columbia Journalism Review* would say Solomon "has a history of bending the truth to his storyline." At *The Hill*, his publisher had expressed concerns about his ethics and his work, and he was eventually moved from the news columns to opinion. Still, Solomon came across as a professional, which gave him an air of credibility, and among partisans, he enjoyed a following.

Parnas and Solomon first met through Texas congressman Pete Sessions, who had been defeated in 2018 despite a $3 million effort by America First Action, a pro-Trump committee that had received more than $300,000 from Fruman and Parnas. (The election had seen Democrats seize control of the House of Representatives, thanks to an anti-Trump voter backlash.) Before they started to work in earnest, Solomon involved his attorneys, Joseph diGenova and Victoria Toensing, who were themselves conservative media stars. Solomon said they gave him "an extra layer of protection" as he worked with Parnas.[10]

When the video link was established, the screens in Washington showed Lutsenko seated at a desk with the blue-and-yellow Ukrainian flag behind him. It was nighttime in Ukraine, and streetlights were visible through a window. Lutsenko looked tired and peered at the camera through thick glasses. He wore a rumpled white shirt and a red tie. Solomon's first question was not subtle. "How do you gauge the relationship between Ukraine," he asked, "and specifically the U.S. ambassador, Miss Yovanovitch?"

Solomon mispronounced the ambassador's name, which was understandable given his limited exposure to Ukrainian-American affairs and her low profile. Before the Trump team arrived in the capital and began monitoring State Department officials for signs that they were Deep State operatives disloyal to their cause, career diplomats almost never became the subject of political conversations in Washington. Indeed, it would seem strange to anyone outside the scheme cooked up by Parnas, Fruman, and Giuliani that she would suddenly be subject number one for an American news site's interview with Ukraine's top prosecutor. But then again, it was strange that Lutsenko and Solomon were doing this interview in the first place.

Lutsenko's reply, in Ukrainian that was translated off camera by Lev Parnas, began with a reminder that as the representative of an important country, Yovanovitch deserved his respect. However, he added, "it is true that I have some difficult personal relationships with Miss Ambassador. Unfortunately, from the first meeting with the U.S. ambassador in Kiev this ambassador gave me a list of people to not prosecute. My response is this is inadmissible." If true, Lutsenko's accusation described an American official interfering with another nation's affairs in a way that no country should tolerate. As Lutsenko told Solomon, the demand came in the context of a discussion about $4 million the United States could provide his office for anti-corruption work, but only if he followed the ambassador's orders.

Imagine how Solomon's report about a poor, embattled little country getting pushed around by a supposed Deep State actor like Yovanovitch would be heard by the most Trumpy people in his audience. They would, of course, be outraged. However, they would find something to cheer as they also learned that Lutsenko was open to the idea that Ukraine had attacked the 2016 U.S. election to help Hillary Clinton. He also said he was going to look into Burisma and the Bidens and that he had more information that he wanted to share in a one-on-one meeting with U.S. attorney general William Barr if that could be arranged.[11]

The Lutsenko interview became the basis for video and print reports that Solomon posted in installments on *The Hill*'s website. The first headline— "Top Ukrainian Justice Official Says US Ambassador Gave Him a Do Not Prosecute List"—established that an authoritative source was making a serious charge, while the body of the article included claims that Yovanovitch had expressed "disdain" for the Trump administration. Here was all anyone needed in order to confirm the Deep State was real and dangerous. Solomon did not explore Lutsenko's motivations or note that Ukraine would soon hold elections that might determine his future. He did, however, write that Yovanovitch had been first appointed to her post by Barack Obama. The ambassador, having never seen this kind of political pressure applied to a diplomat, struggled to respond. Gordon Sondland, U.S. ambassador to the European Union, counseled her to "go big or go home."

A wealthy hotelier who had supported Trump financially, Sondland was a tall, rather gangly fellow with an affable manner that helped explain how he had, as a college dropout, spun a career as a real estate salesman into a majority stake in a chain of thirteen luxury hotels. By telling Yovanovitch to "go big or go home," he meant that she should make a show of pledging personal loyalty to the president or resign. Neither seemed right to her, so she delayed action.

• • •

Solomon's attacks, fueled by Lutsenko, echoed across the internet and hit several targets in Ukraine, where an anti-corruption activist got a hint of what was happening when Solomon telephoned her to discuss a piece he was about to publish. Daria Kaleniuk was cofounder of a nonpartisan pro-democracy organization called the Anti-Corruption Action Center. The center, which received 18 percent of its funding from a Soros foundation, backed conferences, protests, and publications aimed at ending political and economic corruption and as a result often ran afoul of the powerful, who routinely made Soros into a bogeyman as they tried to paint the anti-corruption group itself as corrupt.

Recalling her contact with Solomon, Kaleniuk said, "He asked me, 'When did Soros start funding you? How did the FBI help you to set up your organization? How did you cooperate with them on Dmytro Firtash?' It's absolute nonsense, we have never cooperated with FBI or on Firtash case. They tried to plant this story much earlier, and it didn't work out well until they found Lutsenko."

With Lutsenko supplying cover in the form of his official position, Solomon's articles included a claim, which would be debunked, that Marie Yovanovitch had shut down a legitimate investigation into Kaleniuk's group. In a tour de force of innuendo and inference, Solomon swirled Soros, Hillary Clinton, Barack Obama, and the FBI into a mix sure to inflame conspiracy-minded conservatives who loved President Trump. He also managed to make the fugitive oligarch Dmytro Firtash and the freshly convicted felon Paul Manafort into their victims.

When she read what Solomon wrote, Daria Kaleniuk immediately thought, *Yuriy Lutsenko went nuts.* Then, as she tried to understand how Ukraine's top prosecutor might land in the middle of a wild attack on a U.S. ambassador, she began to worry. "We understood it's very dangerous, because it wasn't an initiative of Lutsenko. Lutsenko was just playing his role either intentionally or unintentionally. It was a very well-planned, designed operation to discredit Ukraine and drag [us] into American internal politics."

In 2013, at age twenty-six, Kaleniuk had jumped into the protest movement that began in Kiev's main square and ended with Viktor Yanukovych's flight from the country. Her main contribution had been a website named YanukovychInfo, where, day by day, leaked and public documents were posted to create a picture of the president's wealth and lifestyle. Here, Ukrainians learned of his palace, his exclusive access to a vast state-owned hunting preserve, his state-purchased aircraft, and real estate deals that saw him become a millionaire many times over thanks to the sale of properties at astoundingly inflated prices. When the protests succeeded in outing Yanukovych, the website became the base for Kaleniuk and others to create the Anti-Corruption Center, which was best known for the T-shirts emblazoned with a simple message: UKRAINE FUCK CORRUPTION. The center became one of many pro-democracy organizations led by young women who confronted the powerful in the press, in political campaigns, and in the streets.

By the time Solomon and Lutsenko went after the Anti-Corruption Center, Kaleniuk had been subjected to so many disinformation campaigns that she immediately recognized what was happening. "I understood that it's very serious when the son of Trump started retweeting that and then it went viral in the conservative media. It was discussed in the Fox News and by various trolls, dubious English-speaking sources. You know we deal a lot with disinformation campaigns, and I can identify when it's happening—coordinated fakes campaign. And it was like that."

Fluent in English, thanks to a Fulbright award that had brought her to study in the United States, Kaleniuk wrote a rebuttal, which *The Hill* published and which refuted Solomon when it came to her group's funding, its contact with U.S. officials, and its supposed abuse of Manafort. Most effective was her take on the notion that Yovanovitch shut down an investigation into her organization. In fact, she pointed out, the probe was closed for lack of evidence months before Yovanovitch arrived in Kiev, and Lutsenko himself had called the case "stupid."

Seen through Kaleniuk's lens, Lutsenko's statements seemed like a desperate attempt to grasp at future power. When she was asked where Lutsenko could have gotten the idea to do this, she concluded, "Probably it was Giuliani." However, this only prompted her to ask more questions. "Who convinced Giuliani? What is his interest to portray Ukraine as the most toxic country in the world? Actually, he was praising the most corrupt people here, who we are fighting against. He was attacking reformers who were trying to change the country and the rules. He praised Shokin, Lutsenko as good prosecutors and says we are Soros charity that interferes into U.S. elections." In all this she saw "Ukraine and U.S. are losers" and Russia gaining as "the truth is being challenged."[12]

• • •

John Solomon repeated his claims a month after they were first published when he appeared on Fox News. This time, President Trump grabbed his phone to tap out a message to his more than sixty million Twitter followers to boost the reports, saying, "John Solomon: As Russia collusion fades, Ukrainian plot to help Clinton emerges." In full cheerleader mode, Rudy Giuliani added his boosting remark: "Maybe now we can find out how it all began. @realDonaldTrump may turn out to once again be correct."[13]

If Giuliani was actually seeking real proof for the Ukraine-did-it conspiracy theory, he wasn't well focused on finding reliable sources of information. In fact, at this stage of his supposed investigation, he wasted precious time reaching out to federal prison inmate Paul Manafort. As Giuliani himself would later relate, he asked Manafort's lawyer to forward questions about the Black Ledger. "I said, 'Was there really a black book? If there wasn't, I really need to know. Please tell him I've got to know.'" The answer that came back—no, there was no Black Ledger—suited Giuliani's purpose in the moment even though it wasn't true.

In this period Giuliani, Solomon, Parnas, and Fruman began meeting regularly, as a team, in a private room at the BLT Prime steak house inside the Trump hotel in Washington. Joe diGenova and Victoria Toensing were sometimes part of this group, as was Capitol Hill staffer Derek Harvey. Long close to Mike Flynn, Harvey was no ordinary congressional aide. He had been a colonel in the army and until recently worked at the National Security Council. In Congress, he worked directly for Representative Devin Nunes, who was the ranking Republican on the House Intelligence Committee.[14]

Few in Congress were more devoted to Donald Trump or more lost in his world of alternative facts. And altogether this gang—they called themselves the BLT Group—constituted more of an amen chorus for Giuliani's strange notions than an investigative team that would come up with real evidence. Much of their effort involved creating the impression that a groundswell of concern about Ukraine was forming. "Keep your eye on Ukraine," warned Giuliani in response to the president's tweet about Russian collusion versus the supposed "Ukrainian plot."

In fact, nothing was emerging from any source other than Trump's circle of helpers, but since the whole idea of this activity was to create the odor of scandal, whether or not one existed, the facts didn't matter. Soon, the president's son Donald Trump Jr. would publicly brand Ambassador Yovanovitch a "joker." This statement, coming from someone who was hardly an expert on diplomacy, could only be understood as part of a publicity campaign. As a longtime foreign service officer, Yovanovitch was professionalism itself. But as a deterrent to partisan manipulators and profiteers, she was an impediment that required removal.[15]

With no actual events or facts to use against the ambassador, who, despite Trump Jr.'s smear, was widely respected, the BLT Group would try to create the illusion of a scandal with the help of right-wing media. John Solomon's interview with Lutsenko was essential to this effort since he was a widely followed pundit and Lutsenko was a high-level official. They had both put whatever credibility they possessed behind conspiracy theories that showed Trump to be the victim of an evil bureaucracy. As links to Solomon's video were shared among the Trump faithful, the media landscape was seeded with lies and distortions that sprouted into more reports in conservative media. Typical was a breathless article on a conservative website called the Daily Wire, which announced:

> Calls to remove former President Barack Obama's U.S. Ambassador to Ukraine, Marie Yovanovitch, have intensified over the last week as a scandal in Ukraine surrounding the 2016 U.S. presidential election has started to gain more attention.

A masterful bit of hype, the article based the claim that calls for the ambassador's removal "have intensified" on a statement made by Joe diGenova—who held no office—and on a reference to Representative Pete Sessions's year-old complaint about Yovanovitch made by a Fox News opinion host. Weak as this evidence was, it seemed substantial when compared with the argument that a scandal involving Ukraine and the 2016 election in America "has started to gain more attention."

No one was paying attention except the press outlets that served as an echo chamber for pro-Trump voices, such as Solomon and Giuliani. However, in that world, Lutsenko's original statements were amplified, interpreted, and reinterpreted to seem more serious with every news cycle. After one of his colleagues said Lutsenko had outlined a case that "has all the markings of bribery and extortion," Fox opinion host Sean Hannity, an informal advisor to the president, discussed the issue with Trump on his broadcast. Trump said it "sounds like big stuff" and wondered aloud if Solomon should be awarded a Pulitzer Prize. Weeks later, as Solomon again promoted his baseless claims, President Trump played his role as the public official who could abuse his office to give weight to accusations by boosting them on social media.[16]

Trump's game of innuendo and inference depended on the fact that he said so many outlandish things at such a rapid pace that it was impossible for them to be fully reviewed by anyone and on the cohesion of the conspirators. Each one, from the president down to Lev Parnas, had something to gain from the effort to take down Biden, destroy Yovanovitch's career, and rewrite the history of the 2016 election. And together, they were obviously disinterested in the truth, unconcerned about Russia's threat to American democracy, and dismissive of the ambassador's expertise. What mattered was what could be gained via the deception, and the plot would hold just as long as the crew stuck together.

The weakest player on the team, the one with the least to gain and who was least vulnerable to pressure, was the Ukrainian prosecutor Lutsenko. Although he may have been motivated by his frustration with Yovanovitch and the possibility of some future gain from renewing corruption in his country's energy business, what he really wanted was to keep his job. In the best-case scenario, his patron, Poroshenko, would be reelected when Ukrainians went to the polls on March 31. However, Lutsenko might also hang on to his position by raising his own profile through high-level contacts with powerful American officials like Attorney General Barr. Hence, his desire to get rid of Yovanovitch, who had disapproved of him, and his effort to signal to the Trumpists that he was on their side. Trouble was, Lutsenko wanted to see results, and none were forthcoming.

In texts he sent to Parnas via the secret messaging service WhatsApp, Lutsenko complained strenuously. "I'm sorry, but this is all simply bullshitt,"

Lutsenko wrote. "I'm fuckingg sick of all this. I haven't received a visit. My [boss] hasn't received jack all. I'm prepared to [thrash] your opponent [Biden]. But you want more and more. We're over."

In other messages, Lutsenko complained that Yovanovitch was still in place. "If you don't make a decision about Madam," he wrote, "you're placing into doubt all of my statements. Including about B." In this case, *Madam* was the ambassador and *B* was either Biden or Burisma. Next, he sent a message saying he was moving forward in his investigation of Burisma chief Mykola Zlochevsky but was still upset about receiving nothing in return. "My Zlochevsky case is moving along successfully. There's evidence about transfers to B," Lutsenko wrote, apparently referring to Zlochevsky and the Bidens. "And yet you can't even get rid of one fool."

"She's not a simple fool, trust me," Parnas replied. "But she's not getting away." Later, Parnas added, "I was asked to personally convey to you that America supports you and will not let you be harmed no matter how it looks now, everything will soon turn around and will be on the right track."[17]

Unfortunately for Lutsenko, Lev Parnas was in no position to say whom "America" might support and protect and whether what his correspondent in Kiev hoped to achieve was even remotely possible. No one in this Keystone Cops outfit held an actual government position, and so Lutsenko, in committing himself to a supposed back-channel route to Washington, wound up nowhere closer than when he set out. For his part, Parnas was discussing the BLT Group's schemes in a rather indiscriminate way. In encrypted texts, he got a message from a Trumpworld acquaintance named Robert F. Hyde. A Connecticut-based landscaper who was running for Congress, Hyde hung around the edges of the same Republican establishment that Parnas had managed to join. Near the end of March 2019, Hyde exclaimed to Parnas, "Wow. Can't believe Trumo [*sic*] hasn't fired this bitch." Soon afterward, he sent messages indicating that associates in Ukraine were surveilling Yovanovitch and were ready to take some action against her if they were given the orders and paid for their effort. "They will let me know when she's on the move," he said. Parnas, who was in Washington meeting with Giuliani and others, didn't respond.[18]

Nothing came of Hyde's offer, but by this time, Parnas was a whirlwind of activity and he may not have had time to determine whether the offer was even serious. His main focus, above aiding Trump politically, remained his drive to revive corruption in the Ukrainian gas and oil business so that he could reap a windfall. As anyone eyeing the Ukrainian energy sector knew, Naftogaz was subject to international scrutiny, as foreign authorities (the International Monetary Fund and the United States) advised the president on appointments to its management team. These watchdogs helped assure that the country was fulfilling promises to reduce corruption. Ambassador Yovanovitch had lent key support to the current Naftogaz chief, Andriy Kobolyev, an anti-corruption crusader who might look askance at an unproven but politically connected company entering the market with a scheme to bring a new supply from across the Atlantic. Kobolyev had earned the ire of the indicted oligarch Dmytro Firtash, whose companies distributed about 70 percent of the fuel shipped by Naftogaz to households and businesses. Under law, Naftogaz had to deliver supplies for home heating to distributors even if they didn't pay for what they took. Firtash often didn't pay. At one point, Naftogaz fought back by ceasing the flow of gas to two Firtash chemical plants for nonpayment. With Firtash in mind as a partner in future shady energy business, Parnas and Igor Fruman wanted Kobolyev replaced by someone less concerned about corruption. The next person in line was an official named Andrew Favorov.

In March, when Favorov visited Houston for an oil and gas industry meeting, Parnas, Fruman, and Harry Sergeant III hosted him at the swanky H Bar in the newly opened Post Oak Hotel, where they sat on a red leather banquette under a huge black-and-white photo of Brigitte Bardot, cigarette dangling from her mouth, playing cards. After a bit of blather about George Soros and some bragging about their relationship with the president of the United States, Fruman and Parnas talked about their plan for shipping gas to Ukraine. They advised Favorov that Marie Yovanovitch would be gone soon, which would make business easier, but they still needed someone like him to help at Naftogaz. Perhaps he would be willing to take over there should Kobolyev be squeezed out.

The scene at H Bar, where managers were about to add a $1,600 gold-garnished burger to the menu, was flabbergasting to Favorov. As far as he could tell, Fruman and Parnas knew nothing about the energy business and too little about him to be asking if he might want to usurp his boss back in Kiev. However, if their political connections were real, then they could be capable of causing trouble. Favorov avoided responding to their suggestion and, after the meeting, promptly informed Kobolyev about what had transpired. Only then did he let Parnas and Fruman know he wouldn't be able to help them. When asked about the incident months later, Favorov would tell *The*

Wall Street Journal, "They don't teach you how to deal with this in business school."[19]

Nothing in Parnas and Fruman's Ukrainian energy play aligned with what Andrew Favorov had studied at Georgetown University's business school. Except for Sargeant, whose real experience lay in energy transport, their company, if it really existed, had no relevant expertise. The fancy hangouts they favored and first-class travel they preferred suggested there was at least some money behind them, but the source was not apparent. For all Favorov knew, the flash was being charged to credit cards belonging to others who were happy to risk $10,000 or even $100,000 on the chance to make oligarch-style profits by reintroducing corruption to the Ukrainian energy trade.

After Houston, the peripatetic Parnas and Fruman turned up in New York, where they were to be honored at Young Israel's annual black-tie gala. On the last Sunday in March, they joined hundreds who streamed past tables offering Trump-themed swag including yarmulkes, sweatshirts, and other items emblazoned with TRUMP 2020. The master of ceremonies for the event was a Fox News personality named Peter Hegseth, and featured speakers were the leader of the House Republicans, Kevin McCarthy, Parnas and Fruman's GOP fundraiser friend Tommy Hicks Jr., and Mike Huckabee. Hicks told the crowd that Trump's reelection in 2020 should be "the most important thing in our life." The chief organizer of the event, Yechezkel Moskowitz, said, "President Trump is the most benevolent leader the Jewish people have ever known in their 2,000 years in the diaspora." Then, in a Trumpian flourish, he added, "Believe me."

The hour was late by the time Parnas and Fruman received the Lovers of Zion award, but at least they weren't the last to be called. After them came *Friend* of Zion Charles Gucciardo, a Long Island–based personal injury lawyer, who received his honor as the festivities ended. This was the same Charles Gucciardo whose $500,000 seemed to have funded Rudy Giuliani's alliance with the Fraud Guarantee fellows. Giuliani was on hand to applaud his friend.[20]

Superficially, Charles Gucciardo's moment in the spotlight showed he was being recognized by a religious organization for some sort of service he had performed for the Zionist cause. In reality, it seemed more like a reward for one Italian American's aid to the wild-eyed scheme of another Italian American seeking political and financial gain. The little ego boost that came with the award was delivered at no real cost to Young Israel and could help Giuliani maintain some order in his network of support. In a similar way, Lev

Parnas and Igor Fruman were fortified by their first-class travel to make contact with the rich and powerful in exotic settings. Maintaining Yuriy Lutsenko's loyalty posed a bigger challenge, because he wanted a more substantial payoff—namely Yovanovitch's dismissal—and he wanted it to be delivered by Ukraine's election day, March 31.

Giuliani appeared to put some effort into making Lutsenko happy. He discussed Yovanovitch with his client, the president of the United States, who, according to Giuliani, told him to work on the issue with Secretary of State Mike Pompeo. (Giuliani would tell *The New York Times* President Trump said "either 'discuss it with Mike' or 'turn it over to Mike.'")

On March 28, Giuliani gave Pompeo a file of news reports and other documents that suggested Ambassador Yovanovitch was not a faithful representative of U.S. interests and should be replaced. (Giuliani would offer competing accounts of how the material was transmitted. In one, he handed Pompeo the material directly. In another, it was passed along to Pompeo by intermediaries.) The papers were contained in a manila envelope that bore the words *Secretary Pompeo* in over-the-top, wedding-invitation-style calligraphy and a hand-lettered return address of THE WHITE HOUSE. It was as if a talented child artist had been playing at "government" and created a mock official letter.

The papers included notes from Giuliani's meetings with Shokin and Lutsenko as well as the news clippings and crude memos making wild claims that even a cursory investigation would have knocked down. Among the more ridiculous was the suggestion that somehow Yovanovitch had set up Ukraine's independent anti-corruption agency in order to protect the Biden family from investigations into Hunter's involvement with Burisma. The packet also called attention to a conspiratorial breakfast meeting between Hunter Biden and a top State Department official that occurred on May 26, 2015, and noted that because he supposedly arranged for Yovanovitch's posting, George Soros "has as much, or more, power over Yovanovitch as the President and Secretary of State."

The mere mention of a deep, dark Soros connection meant that whoever filled the envelope was, at the very least, susceptible to ridiculous conspiracy theories. (At worst, the Soros bit showed an inclination to pander to anti-Semitism.) The claims about Yovanovitch ignored the fact that she had been appointed to her post in Kiev two years after the anti-corruption bureau was formed. And that conspiratorial breakfast Hunter Biden supposedly attended on May 26, 2015, happened to coincide with a moment when he was at the hospital bedside of his brother, Beau, who would die of brain cancer four days later.

Rudy Giuliani clearly expected that the mishmash he sent to Pompeo would be taken seriously. With the White House serving as intermediary, he had a brief phone call with the secretary early the next morning. As he later told *The New Yorker,* he thought that "State's going to look at that, and they're going to see that what they're saying about Yovanovitch is true. And then they're going to see, holy shit, there's a whole big bribery or money-laundering case here. We'll give it to the Justice Department, so now I'm home free."

In fact, nothing happened in response to Giuliani's file, because inside the State Department, high-level officials had already begun assessing the public claims he, Lutsenko, and Solomon had made and were debunking them one by one. In a memo to Secretary Pompeo's top legal advisor, Assistant Secretary of State George P. Kent described the claims about Yovanovitch as a "false narrative" and said the supposed do-not-prosecute list was a sham. "This list appears to be an effort by Lutsenko to inoculate himself for why he did not pursue corrupt Poroshenko associates and political allies—to claim that the US told him not to," wrote Kent. "Complete poppycock." He noted that names on the list were misspelled and suggested the United States borrow a page from the American embassy in Moscow's playbook to respond. "I know Embassy Moscow has in the past derided fake letters by circling in red all of the misspellings and grammar mistakes and reposting it," wrote Kent. "If we wanted to push back hard(er), we could consider a similar approach."[21]

A career foreign service officer first appointed by President George H. W. Bush in 1992, Kent had served under presidents of both parties. Well seasoned in the affairs of Eastern and Central Europe, he spoke Ukrainian and Russian. Prior to his appointment to the position of deputy assistant under secretary for European and Eurasian affairs, he worked in the embassy in Kiev and had been a leader in America's anti-corruption and rule-of-law advocacy work around the world. Few American officials knew more about political affairs in Ukraine or how Yovanovitch would be smeared by those who longed for the more corrupt past.

Kent wasn't alone in rising to defend Yovanovitch. At the time when he wrote his memo, others at the State Department were calling attention to her difficulties and to the larger problem of political interference with the diplomatic corps. A political appointee who had previously worked as a lobbyist and wine blogger (she called herself Vino Vixen) was searching out diplomats she deemed insufficiently loyal and singling them out for bullying and berating. An inspector general report would find Vixen had mistreated employees. Her behavior was viewed by many career officials as context for the difficulties Marie Yovanovitch was experiencing in Ukraine. Two key members of Congress, majority leader Steny Hoyer and the chairman of the House Committee on Foreign Affairs, Eliot Engel, were so concerned about what was happening to her that they wrote to Pompeo to say they thought she deserved his full support. They asked Pompeo to make clear, in public statements, that diplomats "will not be subjected to any politically motivated attacks."[22]

Engel and Hoyer did not receive an immediate reply from the secretary of state, and Pompeo did not make any public statements defending his team. However, Yovanovitch stayed in her post as Lutsenko's March 31 election-day deadline passed. Ukraine's voters narrowed the field of presidential contenders to just two, the incumbent, Poroshenko, and a remarkable new political figure named Volodymyr Zelensky. A comedian and actor, Zelensky had become a household name playing a high school history teacher who, thanks to an anticorruption rant that went viral on the internet, becomes president of Ukraine. On the hit show, which was called *Servant of the People*, the "president" named his friends to ministerial positions, lived with his parents, and rode a bike to work.[23]

In the real world, the election results showed that Zelensky, running under the aegis of his new Servant of the People Party, was about to make life imitate art. In a field of thirty-eight, he was unable to win the absolute majority required to win in the first round. However, his 5.7 million vote total, the most of all the candidates, was almost double the second-place Poroshenko's tally, and public support for his campaign was growing. A growing number of people seemed to believe that Zelensky could apply the ideals of a TV character to the presidency.

After the election, Yuriy Lutsenko remained in regular contact with Lev Parnas, who was also frequently consulting with GOP representative Devin Nunes, who, prior to the 2018 election, had been chairman of the House Permanent Select Committee on Intelligence. But while the Americans devoted to Trump's cause and to driving Yovanovitch out of her job kept up the pressure, Lutsenko was losing heart. With his sponsor, Poroshenko, almost certain to lose his bid for reelection, he finally made his move. He told the press in Kiev that Yovanovitch had never given him a do-not-prosecute list. In fact, it was he who, in a meeting with the ambassador, wrote a list of names on a piece of paper and suggested they be considered out of bounds for prosecutors. This came in an exchange that was marked by confusion and a bit of emotion. The list was not something she sought, and she did not approve of the one Lutsenko wrote.

Lutsenko's retraction did not occasion any corrections by John Solomon or gain attention in the pro-Trump mediasphere, where his original lies had been deployed to smear Marie Yovanovitch. His reversal signaled both his departure from the Giuliani team and the content of his character. He had been willing to lead a platoon of liars in an attack on Yovanovitch in order to exact a little revenge and perhaps save his job. When he didn't get the result he wanted fast enough, he recanted. In a few months' time, he would also reverse himself on the Bidens and Burisma, saying, "From the perspective of Ukrainian legislation, he [Hunter Biden] did not violate anything."

Of course, in hyper-partisan America, where formerly mainstream journalists like John Solomon were partnering with characters like Lev Parnas and a once-respected figure like Giuliani was devoted to conspiracy theories, nothing could repair the damage Lutsenko had done. He had served their purpose, and they would carry on their campaign. There was an election coming. There was money to be made. And their Ukraine scheme was about to enter a new phase.[24]

7

AMBASSADORS, OLIGARCHS, AND
MENTAL MIDGETS

*Welcome to the race Sleepy Joe. I only hope you have the intelligence, long
in doubt, to wage a successful primary campaign. It will be nasty–you will
be dealing with people who truly have some very sick & demented ideas.
But if you make it, I will see you at the Starting Gate!*

—Donald Trump, president of the United States, via Twitter,

April 25, 2019

Ukraine's two-man runoff for the presidency pitted the media-savvy forty-
one-year-old Volodymyr Zelensky, whose social media outreach and advertising were first rate, against a stolid, fifty-four-year-old Petro Poroshenko,
whose perfectly blow-dried gray hair made him look like a man from an era
long gone. He had made things worse by adopting the slogan "Army! Language! Faith!" which needed all those exclamation marks, because otherwise
very few people would realize they were supposed to be excited by these
words. In contrast, Zelensky declined most of the staples of politics, choosing to substitute comedy club gigs for stump speeches and posting videos on
Instagram.

At the debate that concluded the campaign, which took place in front of
twenty-two thousand at Kiev's National Sports Complex, rock music blared
from loudspeakers, and police took pains to separate the two camps. Poroshenko described Zelensky's candidacy as "a bright candy wrapper. There
are Russians inside and fugitive oligarchs." Zelensky answered Poroshenko's
warnings about his inexperience with jabs about the failures of veteran politicians. "I am the result of your mistakes," he said.

On election day the result was so lopsided—73 percent to 25 percent—that exit polls persuaded the incumbent to concede early in the evening. Dressed in a business suit, white shirt, and striped tie, Poroshenko offered his congratulations to the victor via a television appearance, where his silent and grim-faced wife stood behind him and off to his right. At Zelensky's victory party the results were posted, confetti flew, and the five-foot-seven president-elect hopped up and down like a birthday boy getting the first glimpse of his new bike. He spoke briefly in English and then in Ukrainian, saying, "Though I'm still not president, I can say as a Ukrainian citizen to all the countries of the former Soviet Union: Look at us. Everything is possible."[1]

Zelensky's 2019 win was even more unlikely than Donald Trump's capture of the White House in 2016. An extremely wealthy man who had spent forty years seeking publicity, Trump had dabbled in politics since the 1980s and previously feinted at presidential runs. His drive for the GOP nomination actually began in 2011, when he made himself a leader of the so-called birther movement, which played on racial and partisan feelings to insist, against the evidence, that Barack Obama had not been born in the United States and was therefore not a legitimate president. Zelensky had barely begun his run as a TV president when Trump first grabbed the lead in the polls that ranked Republican contenders.

If their individual achievements were unlikely, the phone call that Trump placed to congratulate Zelensky after his win was almost impossible to imagine. Nevertheless, after Zelensky was declared the winner, Trump called him from Air Force One to praise his "incredible election" and then stepped into the spotlight himself by adding, "I guess, in a way, I did something similar." In fact, compared with the way Trump had gained his office with a losing tally, Zelensky's win was the kind of landslide the American president knew only in his fantasies. Popular with virtually every demographic group and almost every region of the country, Zelensky had a true mandate. What he didn't have was full confidence in the West's continued support for Ukraine's war against Russian-backed rebels. With this need in mind, he invited Trump to his inauguration, which would take place on May 20. Trump did not give him a definitive response but said that Vice President Mike Pence would attend if he could not.

As he and Zelensky spoke, Trump was well aware of his lawyer Giuliani's campaign against Yovanovitch and the conspiracy theories holding Ukraine responsible for interference in the 2016 U.S. election. With Joe Biden announcing his drive for the presidency on April 25, and most polls showing him doing well against Trump, Ukraine remained a tantalizing locale for mischief. The president got into this game himself by calling in to the Fox News program hosted by his friend and informal advisor Sean Hannity.

An unabashed Trump booster, Hannity let Trump talk about the "big" and "incredible" revelations he thought were coming about Biden and Ukraine. He thought that Attorney General William Barr should look into it and said, "I would certainly defer to the attorney general." For a president to tell a TV audience that the attorney general should look into a matter that had yet to become a legal issue was unusual, if not unprecedented. Add the fact that prosecutor general Yuriy Lutsenko had reversed himself on Biden and the president's comments seemed nonsensical. However, Fox News had not reported Lutsenko's change of heart, and neither Trump nor Hannity seemed to have much reason to inform viewers of a development that contradicted the narrative they had been pushing. For them, words that might evoke partisan energy—Biden! Burisma! Ukraine!—merited repeating as often as possible whether they corresponded with anything real or not.[2]

Although the president could use his stature to keep Fox News focused on almost any subject, moving the story out of the right-wing-media ghetto would require more than mere rhetoric. If new evidence couldn't be discovered, then an official action that signaled a possible development might work. Eager to cultivate the incoming Zelensky for this purpose, Giuliani first tried an indirect route. He dispatched Lev Parnas and Igor Fruman to Israel to see if they could win over the oligarch who owned the TV company that made *Servant of the People* a hit and who was one of the president-elect's most important backers.

A pudgy bespectacled man whose bushy gray hair and beard gave him a cuddly look, fifty-six-year-old Ihor Kolomoisky was a study in contrasts. He was a bare-knuckles kind of competitor who had risen out of the sometimes-violent struggle of the immediate post-Soviet era to be one of the two or three richest people in Ukraine. He was also a thoughtful social observer who saw himself as a product of the turmoil that was a natural first stage of Ukraine's progress toward democracy and rule of law. He expected his ilk to disappear as the country matured. In the meantime, he and his fellow oligarchs would play outsize roles in Ukraine's affairs, pursuing both personal and social goals simultaneously. When Ukraine received foreign aid, he inevitably benefited. When Russia invaded Ukraine and armed local militants, he paid to outfit defenders and paid $10,000 bounties for any armed pro-Russian fighters cap-tured in battle. At one point, he was spending an estimated $10 million per month on militias known as Kolomoisky's Army.

By the time Zelensky was challenging Poroshenko for the presidency, Kolomoisky was living mainly in Israel as he fought to regain control of a bank called PrivatBank, which Poroshenko had nationalized. With Zelensky's vic-tory, he might be expected to have some influence over the president-elect, but he pushed back against any suggestion that he was some sort of puppet master. As Parnas and Fruman arrived at his office in Israel, they assumed Kolomoisky really did control Zelensky but were cautious enough to first approach him as businessmen entering Ukraine's natural gas business. Soon, the conversation turned to Rudy Giuliani's desire for a meeting with Zelensky. Would it be pos-sible, they asked, for him to put the two men together? When he later described this moment to *The New York Times,* he said it went something like this:

> "Did you see a sign on the door that says, 'Meetings with Zelensky
>   arranged here'?"
> "No."
> "Well then, you've ended up in the wrong place."

After Parnas and Fruman struck out in Tel Aviv, Rudy Giuliani decided that Kolomoisky was no longer worthy of the respect he showed when he had dispatched his emissaries. He made this clear in an interview with a Ukrainian journalist, whom he told that Volodymyr Zelensky "must cleanse himself from hangers-on from his past and from criminal oligarchs—Kolomoisky and oth-ers." Kolomoisky responded with his own warning. "A big scandal may break out," he said, "and not only in Ukraine, but in the United States. That is, it may turn out to be a clear conspiracy against Biden."

With the former vice president looming large as his client's political op-ponent, Giuliani and his helpers maintained their effort to turn Hunter Biden's work for Burisma into a scandal and, as part of this campaign, to remove Am-bassador Yovanovitch. (If this also cleared the way for whatever business op-portunities they sought in Ukraine, so much the better.) On April 23, Giuliani texted Lev Parnas to say, "He fired her again." This appeared to mean the pres-ident had fired the ambassador. On the very next day, Yovanovitch received a late-night call from the State Department advising her to leave Kiev on the next available flight.

The call, from the director general of the U.S. Foreign Service, Carol Perez, had sounded urgent, if not ominous. Yovanovitch correctly sensed that Perez meant to indicate that her professional status, and not her life, was in jeopardy. For months, she had heard about the campaign being waged against her. Her boss, the secretary of state, had done nothing in response to this threat other than to ask Fox News host Sean Hannity, who was part of the effort, what was going on. This had prepared her to depart Kiev without knowing whether she would ever go back.[3]

In Washington, Yovanovitch met with Deputy Secretary of State John Sullivan, who told her that the White House no longer wanted her in the Kiev post. Her sudden recall had been ordered so that she could be spared the embarrassment of a nasty presidential tweet or public outburst. Yovanovitch accepted the decision without making a stir that would attract the attention of members of Congress who conducted oversight of the State Department. A few weeks later, a State Department official would write to House Foreign Affairs Committee Chairman Eliot Engel, noting Yovanovitch had left her post because the three-year term set for her time in Kiev had run out. Considering that Yovanovitch had been asked to extend her time in Kiev beyond this three-year term and had accepted the offer, this letter was a lie.[4]

In Marie Yovanovitch's absence, Americans who sought access to the incoming Zelensky team, and Ukrainians who might like to revive the bad old days of flagrant corruption, enjoyed more wide-open access to Kiev. With his operatives Parnas and Fruman already in Ukraine, Rudy Giuliani told *The New York Times* he would soon go to Kiev, where he would urge officials to investigate Biden, Burisma, and the 2016 election. He said intermediaries were working to set up a meeting with Zelensky. He intended to tell Zelensky "what I know about the people that are surrounding him, and how important it is to do a full, complete and fair investigation."

Giuliani finally approached Zelensky directly two days *after* he told *The New York Times* what he was up to. In the letter, he described himself as President Trump's "private counsel" and offered his congratulations on the election result. Then he said, "In my capacity as personal counsel to President Trump, and with his knowledge and consent, I request a meeting with you on this upcoming Monday, May 13 or Tuesday May 14th."

Though his statement was drenched in legalese that might deflect critics who said he was trading on the president's power, the words didn't hide the reality. In fact Giuliani was trading on the president's power. He left no doubt about it when he didn't just ask for a meeting but suggested specific days when, presumably, it would be convenient for *him* to visit with a man who faced the daunting task of becoming the leader of a nation of forty-two million. This was a high-handed move. However, it didn't work. Zelensky didn't arrange for a meeting, and Giuliani, who had previously announced that he was heading to Kiev to investigate Joe Biden, suddenly told the press the whole thing was off. Sounding a bit like a mobster afraid of a setup, he said he had discovered he would have "been walking into a group of people that are enemies of the president, and in some cases, enemies of the United States."[5]

Giuliani's talk of "enemies of the president" and "enemies of the United States" was more unhinged than his usual rants and likely reflected a fear that he was failing his client in Ukraine. In Kiev, Lutsenko spent several hours with Zelensky, who was trying to understand the running conflict between the prosecutor's office and the National Anti-Corruption Bureau. As Lutsenko left the meeting, he still held his job. However, in the small world that was Ukrainian national politics, gossip was spreading about how he had worked with Giuliani against Yovanovitch and the Bidens. George Kent, who arrived in Kiev at about this time, heard about it from several high-level sources, including four current ministers and one former prime minister. Within days, Lutsenko would move to contradict at least some of the talk by telling the U.S.-based *Bloomberg* news service that the Bidens were not under investigation and that as far as he knew, the younger Biden had not violated any laws in Ukraine.[6]

Lutsenko had spoken to *Bloomberg* as Lev Parnas had been furiously attempting to set up a call with Giuliani. Parnas had already warned the Zelensky team that if they didn't make sure the Bidens were investigated, the vice president would cancel his plan to attend the inauguration. With Parnas getting nowhere, Giuliani put Igor Fruman on the case, and at last, Lutsenko accepted a call from Giuliani. They connected in the middle of the night in Ukraine, just days before the inauguration. Giuliani was livid. As he would recall it for *New Yorker* writer Adam Entous, the president's personal lawyer said: "Have you ever read your goddam bribery statute? Let me read it to you. This takes a mental midget to do one plus two equals crime. You don't need to be a lawyer, Yuriy, you just need to be an honest man."[7]

Lutsenko would add that Giuliani loudly repeated the word *bribery*. The bribery Giuliani referenced involved then vice president Biden's threat to withhold American assistance if Ukraine didn't act to reduce corruption by, among other things, replacing chief prosecutor Shokin. At the same moment, the International Monetary Fund was also pressuring Ukraine to dismiss Shokin or it, too, would withdraw assistance. Lutsenko saw Biden's threat, which worked, as a matter of one country pressuring another to achieve a policy goal. It happens all the time, he told Giuliani. And it's not bribery. Giuliani's reply was, "I'm a lawyer, you're not."[8]

A lawyer reduced to declaring "I'm a lawyer" has ceased to function as one. In this case, it was immediately clear that the client would take matters into his own hands. Always inclined to stake out a position he felt favored him and then labor to find an argument to support it, Trump was certain that Ukraine was a terribly corrupt place and that this corruption was somehow hurting him in particular. He would find support for this view from his favorite Eastern European autocrats, Putin and Viktor Orbán of Hungary. On May 3, Trump had spent ninety minutes on the phone with Putin and discussed, among other things, Ukraine—Putin denigrated the leadership in Kiev—and what Trump termed the "hoax" of Russia's 2016 election interferences.

It was a measure of Trump's attitude toward Putin that the call was their thirteenth conversation, and Trump initiated the call. Ten days later, Orbán had nasty things to say about Ukraine in general and President-Elect Zelensky in particular. Orbán even indulged in some trash talk about Ihor Kolomoisky, the oligarch Giuliani had been attacking on the internet. This was no mean feat on Orbán's part, since anyone with access to the internet would know that the president's lawyer hated Kolomoisky and that Trump was the kind of man who liked to have his preconceived notions confirmed. Taken together, the comments undermined the promise that seemed evident in Trump's April phone call with Zelensky and worked against the State Department's interest in supporting the Ukrainians.[9]

President Trump relieved Giuliani of responsibility for the Ukraine propaganda machine and assumed that duty himself. In a Fox News appearance, the president advanced the lie that Joe Biden had committed bribery in Ukraine on behalf of his son. "He calls them and says 'Don't you dare prosecute, if you don't fire this prosecutor'—The prosecutor was after his son. Then he said, 'If you fire the prosecutor, you'll be OK. And if you don't fire the prosecutor, we're not giving you $2 billion in loan guarantees,' or whatever he was supposed to give."

Untrue in all respects, Trump's statement would not be explored by the Fox interviewer Steve Hilton, who, despite appearing on a network that claimed to offer "news," had no training in journalism and was, in fact, a pro-Trump political consultant. As an exercise in reality bending, the TV appearance showed Trump exercising the kind of power he lacked as a private citizen. Back then, he would have needed the aid of some official entity—a court, an agency, a bureau—to make his deceptions worthy of attention. As president, everything he said came with a weight of authority that he often wielded for purely political purposes and without concern for truth or fairness. In this way, he orchestrated the destruction of any sense that Americans occupied a shared factual universe. As numerous studies had shown, political prejudices increasingly predicted what people thought to be true. Depending on the interpretations offered by leading figures on their side, the more they saw their champions challenged, the more attached they became to their preconceptions. Thus, when the president said Biden had abused Ukraine, roughly half the nation would accept it.

The power that allowed the president to affect what millions thought presented him with seemingly endless opportunities to practice self-serving manipulations. In this pursuit, his long career as a promoter and reality TV star meant that he was more experienced than any of those who tried to assist him. He also was so persistent in his efforts and so resistant to facts that he would never yield to, for example, all the evidence of Russia's effort to help him win in 2016. He would instead insist on his alternative narrative and thereby deprive the country of the chance to close the books on the matter and move on. For this reason, he would in both public and secret ways maintain his effort to make America's ally Ukraine, a struggling democracy vulnerable to ongoing Russian aggression, a coconspirator in his partisan schemes.[10]

8

THE THREE AMIGOS

If it weren't for Donald Trump, we would never know how corrupt these
Democrats are, we would never know for sure that there was a Deep State.
Now we know it. @JudgeJeanine

—Donald Trump, president of the United States, via Twitter,
July 28, 2019

With the Ukrainians refusing to cooperate with Rudy Giuliani, there was no
way that President Trump was going to send Vice President Mike Pence to the
Zelensky inauguration. After canceling the plan for Pence to fly to Kiev, he
picked Secretary of Energy Rick Perry to lead the U.S. delegation. Although no
formal pecking order exists, the world recognizes that the cabinet posts come
with differing levels of status. After the vice president follow, in order, the secretaries of state, defense, treasury, and commerce. Because the Department of
Energy is sometimes engaged with global issues and nuclear weapons treaties,
the Ukrainians could take some solace in the fact that Perry had a substantial
international portfolio. And at least he wasn't, say, the secretary of education.[1]

Perry put together a delegation that would include the American ambassador to the European Union, Gordon Sondland, a special envoy to Ukraine
named Kurt Volker, and National Security Council Ukraine expert Alexander Vindman. (A U.S. Army lieutenant colonel and combat veteran, Vindman
was born in Ukraine and brought to America in 1979, at age three, after his
mother's death. His twin brother, Yevgeny, also worked for the NSC as an
ethics expert.) With this group, Perry would not be prepared for high-level diplomacy, but he would have enough expertise on hand to steer clear of foreign
policy trouble.

While Perry took the point position for the federal government, Giuliani used social media to remind anyone who paid attention that he still had his eye on Kiev. In a post on Twitter, he wrote: "Billionaire Ukrainian Oligarch Ihor Kolomoisky under investigation by FBI He has now returned to Ukraine from exile in Israel and the first thing he did is threaten American citizens. This is real test for President. Will he be arrested?"[2]

Giuliani's May 18 message would be passing strange to most of the former mayor's social media followers. However, anyone who knew Ukrainian politics, including President Zelensky, would understand that at the very least, Donald Trump's lawyer had a beef with Kolomoisky and was sending a message to Zelensky. Equally strange, to the uninformed, would be the photos Lev Parnas posted days later. The images, snapped at fire-ravaged Notre Dame Cathedral and in a private cigar bar at Le Royal Monceau, made it seem as if he was touring the City of Light with his friends Giuliani and Igor Fruman. In the cigar bar picture, they were joined by a fourth man. Younger, slimmer, and better dressed than the others, Dmitry Torner was employed by the energy oligarch Dmytro Firtash. He was considering a run for the Ukrainian parliament under the banner of a pro-Russia party and, according to one source, had escaped from prison in his native Moldova and assumed the name Torner as he began a new life in Ukraine. Soon after he met with Giuliani, Torner was disqualified from running for election when authorities discovered he held multiple passports under different names.

In former Soviet states, well-made fake passports were sold for as little as one hundred dollars. Other false documents, obtained from corrupt officials, made it easy for criminals to avoid detection and difficult for honest people to feel confident in any of their dealings with strangers. Since this fog also served those who wanted to claim they were shocked—shocked!—to learn they had been associating with shadowy figures, Rudy Giuliani could plausibly claim he didn't recall meeting Torner or what was discussed at the posh cigar bar. This line became less believable when Giuliani extended it, a month later, to a similar meeting with Firtash representatives in London. As Giuliani was dealing with Firtash's folks in London, Parnas and Fruman, apparently vouched for by Torner, went to Vienna for an audience with the man himself.

More than a little irony attended the effort to draw Firtash into the Giuliani-Parnas-Fruman endeavor. Just months before the president's personal lawyer had drawn the news media's attention to Firtash's associations with "[Semion] Mogilevich, who is the head of Russian organized crime, who is

Putin's best friend." He also said that Firtash himself was "considered to be one of the high-level Russian organized crime members or associates."

Giuliani's slaps at Firtash were offered in an interview on which his main target was the attorney Lanny Davis, who was representing the president's previous personal lawyer, Michael Cohen. As often happened in Trump's world, Cohen had gone from trusted confidant and advocate—he called himself Trump's "fixer"—to antagonist and enemy. This transformation had begun when federal prosecutors raided his home and offices in search of evidence of campaign finance law violations related to payments made to women—a *Playboy* model and an adult film star—who said they had sexual affairs with then candidate Trump. By the time Giuliani spoke about Davis, Cohen was helping the congressional committees investigating the president and his campaign, and he had testified publicly for ten hours.[3]

Firtash had been arrested in Austria in 2013, where he devoted substantial time and money to fighting extradition to the United States. He had been charged with bribing officials in India in order to pull off a deal he had arranged to supply titanium to the American aerospace company Boeing. The titanium was never mined, but Firtash was caught paying millions in bribes. When the Austrians arrested him on a U.S. warrant, another Putin-linked oligarch helped him with a $174 million bond. He remained in Vienna, conducting business and fighting to stay out of U.S. courts. In this cause, he could be helped by forming relationships with those who held sway with Donald Trump, who had made no secret of the fact that he did not respect the norms that generally separated the White House from the Justice Department.[4]

As Parnas saw it, he went to Vienna to make a deal: legal help in the United States for Firtash's assistance in getting dirt on the Bidens and advancing Trump's fringe theories about Ukraine and the 2016 election. With his vast wealth, numerous businesses, links with Yanukovych-era politicians, and connections to Putin and his crowd, Firtash could be a useful supplier of anything from verifiable information to harebrained notions supported by fake evidence. Indeed, under the right circumstances, his connections in Moscow might provide weapons-grade propaganda useful to both Trump's political cause and to Parnas's and Fruman's business ambitions. On his side of the arrangement, Firtash could seek either direct access to the U.S. government, via the president's personal lawyer and his helpers, or he could seek a referral to American lawyers who might bring the right competence and connections to a fight he saw in both legal and political terms.

Notes Parnas scribbled on Ritz-Carlton Vienna stationery indicated that he planned to suggest to Firtash that he dismiss Lanny Davis and replace him with Giuliani's friends Victoria Toensing and Joe diGenova. (DiGenova had known Attorney General Barr for thirty years.) Parnas, who would say he scratched the notes while talking to Giuliani, wrote, "Get rid of Lenny Davis (nicely!)" and "Victoria/Joe retained" and "$100,000-month." On another sheet of the same stationery, he wrote, "Get Zelensky to Announce that the Biden case will be Investigated."

Firtash didn't change lawyers right away; things went well enough between them that he and Parnas would keep talking. Parnas dashed off to London, where he and Giuliani watched the Boston Red Sox and New York Yankees play two games. (The Yankees won both.) Like much of his adventure, the games in London were a first-class experience for Parnas. With Giuliani a kind of mascot for the Yankees, both men were welcomed onto the field to chat with players as they warmed up. When the game started, they watched from some of the best seats in the house. During their time together, they also attended a speech Giuliani gave to a charity luncheon for Jewish residents of a Ukrainian community called Anatevka.

Like so much in the saga of Giuliani, Parnas, and Fruman, the Anatevka episode was an odd occurrence full of strange little twists, beginning with the name. If it sounds to you like something from *Fiddler on the Roof,* you are right. Anatevka was, until 2014, a purely fictional place. Only then did a Hasidic rabbi named Moshe Azman begin to build a gated community called Anatevka intended to house Jewish refugees from the war in the east. He raised money for the project from wealthy Jews in former Soviet states, where his kind of ultra-Orthodox Judaism was favored by Putin. He also got help from Friends of Anatevka organizations in various Jewish communities in the West. He made his son Yoel administrator for the community. As of spring 2019, the $6–$7 million spent on Anatevka had funded housing for about 150 people.

Although he was well known in Kiev, Azman was a bit of a self-promoter, and his political connections were a subject of some debate. When Parnas and Fruman introduced him to Giuliani, it wasn't clear who could help the other more. Azman named Giuliani honorary mayor of Anatevka and gave him a two-foot-long ceremonial key to the village. Giuliani called the rabbi "Moshe baby" and posted a photo of himself and Azman puffing on cigars. Fruman founded a New York branch of Friends of Anatevka in 2018. His main efforts involved sending the village a shipment of used school buses, written off on donors' taxes, which turned out to be too decrepit to be driven.[5]

Ultimately, the Giuliani team's Anatevka engagement was just a moment in a long-tortured effort to help the president and profit by restoring corruption to the Ukrainian gas business. However, it does illustrate one of their main methods, which was seeking relationships with those who might help them directly or, through their reputations and contacts, introduce them to powerful associates. On social media, Giuliani hyped Azman as Ukraine's most important rabbi, which he was not. In fact, if Giuliani had wanted access to the incoming Zelensky government, he would have been better off reaching out to Rabbi Shmuel Kamenetsky of Dnipro, who had been the only rabbi in attendance at Zelensky's inauguration.

Days after the group was together in London, Parnas learned that Firtash was willing to see him again. When he dashed off a text message informing Giuliani, the former mayor replied, "Wow!" Soon, he was with the oligarch in Vienna. In a few weeks' time, Firtash would end his arrangement with Lanny Davis and embark on a four-month arrangement with Toensing and diGenova, for which he said he paid $1.2 million. He hoped the new lawyers would do something to make Attorney General William Barr, if not the president himself, more receptive to his effort to get out from under the charges he faced in the United States. Firtash also made a first payment to Parnas of $200,000. Parnas would joke that the money, ostensibly for translation services, made him "the best paid interpreter in the world." He was hiring private jets and moving around with an entourage that included bodyguards. On the ground, the Parnas team traveled in a pair of big black sport utility vehicles like the ones favored by the Secret Service.[6]

• • •

The most remarkable thing about the BLT Group's long campaign to help the president, and also help themselves, was how little was gained from all the effort. Try as they did, they couldn't get the news media beyond John Solomon's *The Hill* and the partisans of the right-wing press to buy what they were selling about the Bidens and how Ukraine had been the real culprit in the 2016 election. Similarly, Parnas and Fruman were not much closer to the big money they had hoped to make in the gas business. Indeed, the only way one could consider this crowd a success was in the way they had been able to serve themselves in smaller ways.

Rudy Giuliani had, through his advocacy for Trump, made himself relevant in national affairs, if only as a person whom journalists turned to for snappy quotes and pot stirring. And after being denied the job of secretary of state, he had nevertheless become a transatlantic figure who played at foreign policy. For a seventy-five-year-old politician whose last campaign had ended in abject failure a decade earlier, these developments may have been reward enough.

Like Giuliani, Fruman and Parnas had also gained a kind of relevance they could not have imagined prior to their arrival in Trumpworld. Parnas and Fruman had spent their lives on the scuffling fringe of America's deal-seeking subculture. Fruman had been moderately successful back in Ukraine (except for the bankrupt milk company and associations with crime figures). However, in the United States, his limited English had made it hard for him to make progress and led to dependence on partners like Parnas. More comfortably American, Parnas had spent decades in frenetic efforts to achieve a gilded version of the American dream through imagination and persuasion. If one ignored Donald Trump's vast inheritance and many bankruptcies and focused on his TV show image as a glamorous deal maker, he had a godlike ability to achieve ever-expanding success. Look at the houses! Look at the jets! It was no wonder that Parnas tried so hard to get close to the man, and when he did, he memorialized each occasion with photos and recordings. As he created what he called a "shrine" to Trump in his home, he could display the evidence that he actually knew his patron saint. He was like a pilgrim who came home from Lourdes with a photo of himself flashing a thumbs-up with the Virgin Mary.[7]

Flip through the record of Parnas and Fruman's political adventure and you will see them displaying upturned thumbs or flashing big grins with all sorts of powerful people and in a wide variety of exclusive settings. The president and members of his family—daughter Ivanka; son-in-law, Jared Kushner; Donald Trump Jr.; even the president's grandchildren—would appear all over an album of these pictures. Other pages would show them with the vice president, the governor of Florida, Nevada's attorney general, a former White House chief of staff, and Attorney General Jeff Sessions. The settings ranged from the White House, to hotel ballrooms, to members-only cigar bars. For two years, Parnas and Fruman had been in with the in crowd of wealthy GOP players, and even if it were to end at that moment, they would always have the rooftop at 666 Fifth Avenue and the H Bar at the Post Oak Hotel.

•   •   •

If Parnas and Fruman were scrappy prospects getting a few swings at what ballplayers call *the Show*, Rick Perry was a bona fide big-leaguer who strode into Zelensky's inauguration ready to play. The former governor of Texas was a Lone Star cosmopolitan who wore expensive suits accessorized with fancy cowboy boots and designer eyeglasses. (The late Molly Ivins called Perry "the Coiffure" and "Governor Goodhair.") In Austin, Perry had wielded his power and state money to reward donors. More than one thousand were appointed to state positions, and they in turn poured $17 million into his campaign coffers. This naked favoritism led *The Atlantic* to compare him with the caudillos of Latin America. A failed 2016 presidential campaign didn't disqualify Perry from Trump's cabinet, where, as energy secretary, his main role seemed to be salesman for American fuels and technologies. In Ukraine, he, like Parnas and Fruman, had his eye on the gas business and the operation of Naftogaz. But where Parnas and Fruman tried to corrupt the state-owned company's executive team, Perry aimed a little higher.[8]

When Perry met with Zelensky, he was accompanied by EU ambassador Gordon Sondland, who had qualified for his post by donating $1 million to Trump's inaugural fund, and by Kurt Volker, who had been appointed to an unpaid, quasi-official role as U.S. representative in Ukraine's nascent peace talks with Russia. Volker had a foreign policy background but also brought with him to Kiev some remarkable conflicts of interest. Although he had an official-sounding title, he was not a federal employee. His diplomatic activity was a side gig he performed while remaining an executive with a Washington lobbying firm called BGR, which counted the Ukrainian government as a client. BGR also represented Raytheon, which made the Javelin antitank missiles that the Trump administration had sent to Ukraine for its defense against Russia. More Javelins, as well as sniper rifles, night vision goggles, and launchers for rocket-propelled grenades, were to be included in another U.S. military aid package Ukraine would receive on the condition that it make progress in its anti-corruption efforts. At the time of Zelensky's inauguration, the Pentagon determined that indeed Kiev had satisfied this condition, which was a U.S. taxpayer–funded win-win-win for Ukraine, Raytheon, and Volker's firm. Defense Department officials would soon send notice of Ukraine's compliance to the corners of the federal bureaucracy where the aid would be authorized and implemented.[9]

At the sit-down with Zelensky, Rick Perry targeted the international board of advisors for Naftogaz and suggested the new president replace the American member Amos Hochstein. A veteran foreign policy expert, Hochstein's experience ranged from fact-finding in the hermit kingdom of North Korea to disrupting oil revenues going to terrorist organizations in the Middle East. In Ukraine, he had helped officials cope with the loss of Russian energy supplies after the start of the war in the east. However, he was a Democrat, and this alone would make some in the president's camp unhappy. Perry gave Zelensky a list of those who might replace Hochstein. It included a Ukrainian American named Michael Bleyzer, who happened to be in Kiev and also a longtime donor to Perry's various political campaigns.

In the colorful world of the Texas oil and gas industries, Bleyzer was a noteworthy figure. Although he spoke with a Slavic accent, his English was flawless and rapid fire. He wore his hair, which was completely white, so long that it cascaded down his shoulders. His fifteen-thousand-square-foot house, which was featured on the American Institute of Architects national home tour, featured a meditation room equipped with a life-size statue of the Buddha and a wall of TV screens that Bleyzer used to watch nine channels at a time. His initial fortune had been acquired through the purchase of more than eighty state-owned companies that went private at rock-bottom prices as Communism crumbled in Ukraine. In time, his purchases would include a shipyard, an ice cream factory, a cable TV provider, and a bakery that made Happiness to You brand cookies. Along the way, he became a significant political player in his home country, where he even paid for one president's inaugural ball.[10]

Bleyzer promoted himself as an anti-corruption, free-market capitalist, but in Rick Perry's Texas, he operated in an environment where political donors were rewarded with plum jobs and favorable treatment. Donors received a big share of the $439 million grant doled out by the governor's Texas Enterprise Fund. After Bleyzer himself was appointed to an advisory board for another Perry-controlled fund that awarded grants to those who promised to start new companies in the state, he donated $30,000 to one of Perry's political campaigns. The sums were small compared with Ukraine, where oligarchs poured millions into political parties, but the dynamic was the same.[11]

Although he was new to public office, Zelensky had lived his entire adult life in the corrupt post-Soviet chaos of modern Ukraine. He had been trained as a lawyer, which meant he knew how things were supposed to work, and with his star turn on *Servant of the People,* he had demonstrated a full understanding of the slippery ways of the rich and powerful in real life. In his encounter with Perry, Zelensky followed the only logical path: delay. He made no commitment to move against anyone on the Naftogaz board, but he did have a request of his own.

Like Poroshenko before him, Zelensky wanted a good relationship with the president, if only to demonstrate to the Russians that Ukraine remained under U.S. protection, and was hoping to meet him at the White House. This desire meant that Zelensky was vulnerable and his government might be looking for ways to make U.S. officials happy. An immediate move against a watchdog appointed to check corruption wasn't going to happen, but there might be other ways for the Ukrainians to make the Americans happy. One favored by Perry's patron Michael Bleyzer would involve getting more Americans into the Ukrainian energy business. This wasn't exactly a sign that Perry was some sort of cronyism savant. Everyone from Parnas and Fruman to Dmytro Firtash knew that was where the money was. However, out of all the possible candidates, Bleyzer had the best chance. He was an experienced oil and gas investor, and in Rick Perry, he had an apex-level political operator who, unlike Giuliani, possessed actual political power. (Perry and Bleyzer had appeared together in Kiev at a recent meeting of the U.S.-Ukraine Business Council, which, not surprisingly, was funded mainly by the nonprofit Bleyzer Foundation and was run by a Bleyzer employee. In this way, an organization that appeared to be devoted to the greater good related to Ukraine was, in fact, a vehicle that aided Bleyzer's interests.) Bleyzer also had a deep-pocketed partner who also came from Rick Perry's crowd. A week after Zelensky's inaugural, this partner, Alex Cranberg, bid for the rights to drill on a large government tract where geologists suspected they would find significant gas reserves.

Cranberg was a longtime Republican moneyman whom Perry had rewarded with one of his choicest plums: a seat on the University of Texas system's board of regents. The appointment came just two weeks after he moved to the state from Colorado, and Cranberg dove headlong into controversy as critics accused him of attacking scientific research and organizing a drive to oust the university's president. Perry's 2012 reelection campaign leased Cranberg's private jets to whisk him to events and visits with donors. The campaign initially paid below-market fees for aircraft but in an amended finance report it noted additional payments to bring the numbers in line with commercial prices. Cranberg would later hire Perry's presidential campaign manager, Jeff Miller, as a lobbyist. Miller would serve as vice chairman of Donald Trump's inaugural committee and sat behind Perry during his Senate confirmation hearing. He visited Perry's Department of Energy a dozen times prior to the secretary's trip to see Zelensky in Kiev.[12]

If Perry didn't make a direct pitch for the Bleyzer-Cranberg drilling proposal, he had made his feelings clear by pushing Zelensky to put his friend on the Naftogaz advisory board. The field they wanted to exploit was called Varvynska, in the Dnieper-Donets Basin, where scientists estimated reserves of 1.6 million barrels of oil and 59 trillion cubic meters of gas. Bids for the drilling rights were due on May 28, and on that day, Bleyzer appeared at the energy ministry in Kiev to hand in the proposal personally. Bleyzer's hair made him impossible to overlook, but he made certain that he got noticed by wearing a Western-style shirt fashioned out of stars-and-stripes fabric.

Contracts for exploiting resources on state-controlled land in Ukraine were awarded by a process that gave a significant role to the president's cabinet. The cabinet considered just two bids for the Varvynska parcel. The Cranberg-Bleyzer proposal was countered by one from Naftogaz, which offered a higher price for the drilling rights but somehow lost the competition. (When contacted by *Time*, the Naftogaz CEO, whom Parnas and associates had sought to oust a year earlier, said simply, "We know our offer was better.") Perry's guys, and presumably their successors, would be free to exploit the 1,340-square-mile territory for the next fifty years. Just how much they might gain would depend on prices, competing energy sources, and the cost associated with getting the oil and gas out of the earth.[13]

•   •   •

With his wealthy Texas friends poised to get even wealthier in Ukraine, Rick Perry turned to the main concerns affecting U.S.-Ukraine relations, namely President Trump's drive to use Kiev to take down Joe Biden and rewrite the history of the 2016 election. Just as Rudy Giuliani had Lev Parnas and Igor Fruman to round out his team, Perry could count on Gordon Sondland and Kurt Volker. For the president, this new team was an overall upgrade. Yes, superficially, Giuliani, Parnas, and Fruman were extremely loyal to him, but this devotion was also a matter of intense self-interest. The new trio was, as a group, fawning. But they also were less in need of money, attention, or access to circles of power. However, they weren't so experienced and mature that they could resist borrowing from a mostly dumb 1980s film comedy—*The Three Amigos*—to give their little band a name.

Upon their return to Washington, the Amigos went to the White House to see the president and attend a meeting arranged by acting chief of staff Mick Mulvaney. Among themselves, the Amigos agreed that Ukraine deserved U.S. support but found, in President Trump, a man who seemed all but hypnotized by the misinformation he had been fed by his lawyer and conservative talk shows on Fox News. As Volker would recall, Trump complained that "they [Ukraine] tried to take me down." Sondland, perhaps naïvely, pointed to the way Russia had abused Ukraine as a reason for America to favor Kiev, but Trump wasn't moved. Instead, he kept talking about what he had heard from Giuliani.

"It was apparent to all of us that the key to changing the President's mind on Ukraine was Mr. Giuliani," Sondland would eventually recall. "I did not understand until much later that Mr. Giuliani's agenda might have also included an effort to prompt the Ukrainians to investigate Vice President Biden or his son." As the Oval Office meeting ended, the president told the Amigos they should consult with Giuliani in order to truly understand Ukraine. Sondland even thought that Giuliani might help him, Volker, and Perry by influencing the president to regard Ukraine with less suspicion and treat Zelensky more generously.

If Sondland and his Amigos actually expected Giuliani to help them, they had not paid close attention to what the president's lawyer had been saying and doing. For more than a year, Giuliani had been acting as if he was both a private attorney and a representative of the White House. The confusion caused by his boundary crossing was something the president tolerated and may have even preferred, but it was anathema to government professionals. It caused the veteran diplomat William Taylor to pause when George Kent approached him about replacing Marie Yovanovitch in the ambassador's post in Ukraine, where he had previously served. He would consult with his wife—who recommended against it—and with friends who offered varied responses. His text exchanges with Kurt Volker indicated he had a good sense of the challenges he would meet: "Can anyone hope to succeed with the Giuliani-Biden issue swirling for the next 18 months? Can [Secretary of State Pompeo] offer any reassurance on this issue?" wrote Taylor.

"I don't know if there is much to do about the Giuliani thing, but I do think the key thing is to do what we can right now since the future of the country is in play right now," replied Volker.

In a subsequent exchange, the two men discussed how the White House staff had circumvented established channels for communicating with President Zelensky. At one point, Volker seemed to agree with a criticism Taylor offered, noting that "in a normal world," things would be handled differently.

"Do I want to enter this non-normal world?" wrote Taylor.

"Despite everything," answered Volker, "I feel like we have moved the ball substantially forward over the last 2 years. I think it is worth it to continue to keep pushing."[14]

Taylor would accept the assignment, even though he would step into a situation that he would later describe as "a weird combination of encouraging, confusing and ultimately alarming circumstances." In fact, he would say, "I found a confusing and unusual arrangement for making U.S. policy towards Ukraine. There appeared to be two channels of U.S. policy-making and implementation, one regular and one highly irregular." Giuliani's involvement was quite irregular and so, too, was the plan hatched at the White House after the Three Amigos saw the president. In a meeting called by Mulvaney, it was decided that Ukraine policy would be taken out of the hands of career experts at the State Department and given to the Amigos plus Giuliani. State's deputy assistant secretary for Ukraine, George Kent, was informed that he should, in his words, "lie low" for a while. Like Sondland, Volker, and Perry, Kent harbored hopes for Zelensky, and what happened next was encouraging. On May 29, President Trump sent Zelensky a letter noting America's "unwavering" support for Ukrainian sovereignty and inviting him to the White House "as soon as we can find a mutually convenient time."

In Kiev, Trump's letter was considered a breakthrough, and its arrival was noted in the press. However, a careful reading would reveal something odd. Although Trump framed the message as an invitation, the fact that no date had been worked out in advance by aides made it conditional. Indeed, a White House visit was so important to Zelensky that there would have been very few dates when he wouldn't make himself available to shake Trump's hand and have his photo taken in front of the Resolute desk. By not setting a date, Trump followed his lifelong habit of keeping his options open and dangling opportunities as inducements. The letter was not so much an invitation as a suggestion that the president was thinking about Zelensky's situation—he was an untested neophyte whose country was outmatched against Russia—but withholding the truer sign of support he needed.[15]

One certainty in the U.S.-Ukraine relationship was the American demand for Kiev to attack corruption, and Zelensky took a step in that direction by informing parliament that he wanted to replace prosecutor Yuriy Lutsenko, whose campaign to drive Marie Yovanovitch out of the U.S. embassy was an embarrassment for the new government. This move was also a way for Zelensky to signal that he would continue to do what the United States required if

Ukraine were to qualify for the Javelin missiles and other aid promised so he could resist the Russian-backed fighters in the east.

For the new president, whose previous political experience was confined to playing a comic version of a president on TV, the responsibilities of office were, no doubt, heavy. The political landscape in Ukraine was, at best, a hall of mirrors where motivations were opaque, alliances were ever shifting, and corruption lurked in every encounter. At worst, it was a blood sport that had seen many participants killed and imprisoned. Add the perils posed by Russia and the challenge of relating with an American president who was unpredictable to the point of psychopathy, and Zelensky must have wondered, at times, why he ever wanted the job in the first place.

Zelensky would be helped the most by quick action on the two big asks he had been raising in his contacts with U.S. officials: a meeting at the White House, and approval and shipment of the war-fighting aid Washington had promised. Unfortunately for him, it was going to fall to the Three Amigos to deliver.

9

THE DRUG DEAL

*So much Fake News about what is going on in the White House. Very
calm and calculated with a big focus on open and fair trade with China,
the coming North Korea meeting and, of course, the vicious gas attack in
Syria. Feels great to have Bolton & Larry K on board.*

—Donald Trump, president of the United States, via Twitter,
April 11, 2018

Of all the Amigos, Kurt Volker was the most experienced in foreign affairs,
and so President Volodymyr Zelensky was fortunate to find him leading the
U.S. delegation at the Third Annual Ukraine Reform Conference, which was
held in Toronto from July 2 to July 4. Always alert, and immaculate in his
Euro-style spread-collar shirts, the soft-spoken Volker was the very model of a
modern Western diplomat. He was generally well informed, attentive, and able
to understand how other states might regard America's power. But Volker had
never operated in a world where that power was wielded in a context as chaotic
as the Trump presidency, where, in the case of Ukraine, the usual process was
being warped by partisan politics.

The conference gave Western countries a chance to assess Ukraine's progress toward true democracy and rule of law. Attended by representatives of
Ukraine's trading partners, lenders, and financial regulators, the conference
took place at the Depression-era Fairmont Royal York hotel, which, when it
was built, was the tallest building in the British Empire. Among the hundred
who attended, many praised Zelensky for ridding the government of Yuriy
Lutsenko, and the end-of-session communiqué noted Ukraine's ongoing efforts
at integration with Europe. However, the matters addressed in the official

cochairs statement represented just the public product of a meeting where more immediate problems were considered in quiet conversations in the Fairmont's smaller meeting rooms. Normally, these contacts would be opportunities for the exchange of more honest and reliable truths, and in Toronto, Volker used one of his side sessions to explain what he would come to call "the Giuliani factor" to Zelensky, his foreign policy advisor, Andriy Yermak (a former film and TV producer), and his chief of staff, Andriy Budhan.[1]

A lawyer and economist, Budhan was barely a year older than Zelensky but vastly more experienced in politics, thanks to his training as a lawyer and economist and a career spent moving in and out of government and private business. Like everyone in Kiev's circles of power, Budhan's record was an easy target for skeptics. Prior to joining Zelensky's campaign, he had been an attorney for Ihor Kolomoisky. A new law that barred the appointment of those who had worked in government during the Yanukovych regime prompted a lawsuit challenging his appointment by Zelensky, but while the suit was unresolved, he remained a trusted aide.

In Toronto, Budhan, Yermak, and Zelensky listened as Volker explained the ways in which Giuliani influenced Trump to accept a negative view of Ukraine that played into his fascination with schemes and conspiracy theories. A supremely gifted manipulator, Trump relished opportunities to determine the outcome of events before they occurred or rewrite the results after everyone else believed things had been settled. As president, he practiced this gamesmanship at the highest level but was constrained by two factors: objective reality and the integrity of individuals within the government. Trump could overwhelm reality with rhetoric sufficient to throw it into doubt. But overcoming the integrity of dedicated officials was more difficult. For this, he needed to use rogue agents—a role that gave meaning to Giuliani's life—and techniques that forced those with a moral compass to make a choice.

Volker confessed to Zelensky, Yermak, and Budhan that the president's private lawyer was having a negative effect on Ukraine-American relations. He accomplished this mischief through his conversations with the president and other officials and in his interactions with the press, where he talked about Ukraine and certain Ukrainian figures as if they posed a continual threat to the United States. Like many others, Giuliani understood that the president paid close attention to television news and opinion programs—Trump called them "the shows"—where many players in American politics believed they were speaking directly to him during their appearances. The shows, most especially the ones on the Fox cable news network, constituted a feedback loop where propaganda was offered and either accepted and recycled by others, including the president himself, or passed over for one reason or another.

When the president's lawyer wasn't sharing his agitprop on television or in interviews with print reporters, he was doing it on social media, where he could leverage whatever credibility and celebrity he had earned as mayor of New York City to offer lies and innuendo without fear of fact-checking. Just a month after Zelensky took office, Giuliani turned to Twitter to complain in a message that was garbled but obvious in its intention, which was to use lies and innuendo to pressure Zelensky and suggest he was somehow stonewalling a legitimate concern.

> New Pres of Ukraine still silent on investigation of Ukrainian interference in 2016 election and alleged Biden bribery of Pres Poroshenko. Time for leadership and investigate both if you want to purge how Ukraine was abused by Hillary and Obama people.

The Giuliani factor was not the only strange element Zelensky had to accommodate. As Volker told him, the Three Amigos were in charge of the U.S. government's relationship with Ukraine, which meant that the embassy and State Department were not the places to go to work on sensitive issues, like, say, the president's desire for Ukraine to help him by going after the Bidens and supporting his false narrative about 2016. Volker said it might be a good idea to work on those agenda items and for Zelensky to signal to the president, in some way, that Ukraine might give him and Giuliani what they wanted.

Standing feet away from this conversation, and informed about it by Volker, Deputy Assistant Secretary of State George Kent had doubts about Volker's approach, because asking Ukraine to help Trump politically ran contrary to America's worldwide effort to discourage countries from interfering in each other's domestic political affairs. For Ukraine to do so and for Trump to accept such help might even be a violation of U.S. law. Of course, the president had recently told ABC TV's George Stephanopoulos that he would accept foreign assistance for a political campaign, so perhaps Volker was just following his lead. Kent opted to believe that Volker was trying to smooth things over in ways that would ultimately help Zelensky improve Ukraine's security.

"He was trying to get through what seemed to be a hiccup in the communications," Kent would say later on. "And [he] wanted to get President Trump and President Zelensky together, counting on Zelensky's personal interactive skills to build rapport and carry the relationship forward."

As Kent was watching Zelensky and Volker wrap up their sidebar discussion in Toronto, he noticed there might be a hiccup there, too. Volker, perhaps not recalling that Trump had sent a letter inviting the president of Ukraine to the White House, told him that the Three Amigos were working to connect the two leaders on the phone. This was something akin to the *Peanuts* character Lucy van Pelt yanking away the football just as Charlie Brown approached to kick it. As Kent would recall, Zelensky cut Volker off to say:

"Just a phone call? How about the visit?"

"First a phone call," replied Volker. "We'll aim for that perhaps next week and hopefully that will lead to a meeting by the end of the month. July 29–30."

• • •

As Zelensky returned to Kiev more aware that the Americans were unreliable and potentially corrupt, President Trump's White House team was preparing to squeeze him harder. Like high-pressure salesmen, they were going to build so much suspense around Zelensky's next contact with Trump that they might as well have used all capital letters whenever they communicated about it. More than a prelude to a more substantial event, THE CALL was framed as momentous in and of itself, as if the sound of Donald Trump's voice, ringing in Zelensky's ears, would stop the bullets from flying and the bombs from falling.

Two weeks earlier, President Trump signaled his interest in Ukraine during an on-air interview, via telephone, with Fox TV commentator Sean Hannity. In addition to bragging about his campaign rally crowds and recalling how many people tell him, "Thank you, sir, for saving our country," Trump brought up Ukraine and the discredited notion that somehow Hillary Clinton campaign chairman John Podesta prevented the FBI from gathering information on online election interference. "And Ukraine, take a look at Ukraine," said the president. "How come the FBI didn't take the server? Podesta told him to get out. He said, 'get out.'"[2]

Trump may have had Ukraine on his mind because earlier on the same day, he had been shown an article from the conservative *Washington Examiner* website titled "Pentagon to Send $250M in Weapons to Ukraine." (In fact, with a separate portion funded by the State Department included, the total aid scheduled for Ukraine was $391 million.) The president apparently made his concerns known because Robert Blair, top aide to acting chief of staff Mick

Mulvaney, immediately called Russell Vought, the deputy director of the Office of Management and Budget, to say, "We need to hold it up." Vought, a political appointee drawn from the ranks of one of the president's most ardent support groups—right-wing Christians—would join a small group of half a dozen White House and OMB officials who began working, out of public view, to slow the aid.

The effort was clearly directed by Mulvaney, who, consistent with the president's strange management practices, had retained his previous title of director of OMB, though Vought carried out many of the director's duties. Mulvaney considered the Ukraine matter such a high priority that as he flew with the president to an economic summit in Japan, he used some of his time aboard Air Force One to check in with Blair. "I'm just trying to tie up some loose ends," wrote Mulvaney in an email. "Did we ever find out about the money for Ukraine and whether we can hold it back?"

Blair, who had previously worked on Capitol Hill and in the State Department, had determined that what the president wanted could be done, but not without some risk. "Expect Congress to become unhinged," he wrote. He also warned that holding up the arms intended to help Ukraine withstand Russian-backed fighters might feed into the argument of critics who said Trump was pro-Moscow.[3]

Whatever the risk, the president had a point of leverage, and he was going to use it to get for himself what Giuliani and the BLT Group, with all their wanderings and propaganda, couldn't obtain. For him, the appeal in this course of action was likely twofold. First, it was based on his reflexive tendency to use threats to achieve his goals. (He once told writer Bob Woodward, "Real power is, I don't even want to use the word, 'Fear.'") The tactic also allowed the president to show that he could succeed where others had failed, establishing that he had the ability to close a deal that those acting in his name couldn't.[4]

As the president's men swung into action, they could find inspiration in his prior record of simplistic foreign policy ideas. Especially helpful were Trump's oft-stated complaints about how the United States paid too much on the North Atlantic Treaty Organization and his claim that European allies "owe massive amounts of money from past years." In fact, the member countries were meeting their obligations to fund NATO's operations. Trump was mixing up this NATO cost sharing with separate, voluntary goals for overall national military spending, which many countries did not meet. This deceit enabled an attack on NATO that surely pleased Vladimir Putin and resonated with xenophobic voters drawn to his "America first" posture. Trump was also concerned about the revenues U.S. arms makers could reap from military aid programs and agreements for weapons sales. Increasing these revenues was official administration policy, and U.S. diplomats the world over had been instructed to aid the effort. The president had boasted of his own salesmanship in this regard, inflating by 400 percent the value of an arms sale to Saudi Arabia, which was signed in Riyadh on his first visit to a foreign nation as president.[5]

With the president's rhetoric and priorities well established, Trump's political appointees began peppering the career officials who were actually managing the aid to Ukraine with questions about NATO members' spending to support Ukraine and whether the money bought arms from American companies.

In response, Deputy Under Secretary of Defense Elaine McCusker, the Pentagon comptroller, told her superiors that other NATO countries—most notably Canada, the United Kingdom, and Lithuania—were supplying substantial aid to Ukraine. (In fact, together the Europeans contributed much more than the United States.) Also, nearly all the money in the American aid package would be spent on U.S.-made matériel, and thus find it's way back to America.

The questions McCusker was asked to answer were irrelevant to the work she did on this type of aid disbursement, which should have been routine. What did matter to her was that if the White House held it up, it would risk violating a federal law, the Impoundment Control Act. Moved by Richard Nixon's abuses, Congress had approved the act in 1974 to prevent the executive branch from simply refusing to spend money appropriated to implement policies it opposed. Of course, in this case, the interference wasn't necessarily related to some policy disagreement but rather to the president's personal political agenda. He wanted Ukraine to dirty up Joe Biden and change the record of the 2016 election, and he seemed ready to hold up the defense aid until Kiev complied.

•   •   •

Elaine McCusker and other frontline officials, many wondering about President Trump's intentions, met on July 10 with a delegation representing Zelensky at the White House to prepare for the two leaders to speak on the phone and then meet in person in the Oval Office. The Ukrainian group, including Andriy Yermak and Ukraine defense minister Oleksandr Danylyuk, was operating on the assumption that Trump had been sincere when he invited Zelensky to come to the White House. Danylyuk was the senior member of the group and comparatively well traveled. Fluent in five languages, he had studied in the United States and worked in London and Moscow for the consulting giant

McKinsey. On the American side, they met the Three Amigos—Perry, Sondland, and Volker—plus national security advisor John Bolton and a few members of Bolton's NSC team, including Alexander Vindman and White House
Russia advisor Fiona Hill. A hard-liner where Russia was concerned, Bolton
had advocated strong U.S. support for Ukraine. When the group posed in front
of the White House for a photo, he positioned himself next to Danylyuk and
far from Sondland and Volker.

Danylyuk considered Bolton the most reliable friend Ukraine had in the
administration, and the two men had been responsible for setting up the meeting to discuss a plan Zelensky had approved for his government's relationship
with Washington under Trump. However, as Danylyuk laid out the plan in
Bolton's office, Sondland repeatedly interrupted him to ask about Trump's demands for investigations into the Bidens and Ukraine's supposed interference
in the 2016 election. Investigations that had been dropped, he said, "needed
to be started up again." (In an email he wrote at this time, Sondland said that
the only "purpose" of any phone call between Zelensky and Trump should be
"for Zelensky to give [Trump] assurances of 'new sheriff' in town," including
a promise that "any hampered investigations will be allowed to move forward
transparently." With such assurances made, added Sondland, the "goal is for
Potus to invite him to Oval.")[6]

At the call-planning session, Danylyuk was taken aback by Sondland's
interruptions but quickly recognized that the ambassador was trying to draw
Ukraine into American political affairs and that could be, as he said later,
"really bad" for his country. He noted the peril this posed for a young and
inexperienced Zelensky and that what was being proposed might actually violate U.S. law. The meeting ended abruptly with an annoyed Bolton, who had
suspected some sort of shadow policy was being pursued on Ukraine, asking
the group to leave his office.

Banished from Bolton's office, Sondland asked the group to continue the
conversation in the Ward Room, which is near the Navy Mess and the highly
secure Situation Room in the White House basement. The space could be accessed via a stairway close to Bolton's office, and in a moment, the group was
gone. Hill stayed behind to speak with Bolton.

Downstairs, Sondland resumed talking about the investigations. This
time, it was Vindman's turn to feel perturbed. He interjected, telling Sondland
his requests were inappropriate and that the National Security Council was
not going to support them in any way. When Vindman spoke up, Sondland

suddenly asked the Ukrainians to leave so that the American side could deal with what had become an internal disagreement. When the Ukrainians were out of earshot, Sondland made it clear that the investigations the president wanted would be required before Zelensky received a formal invitation to the White House. He also said that Mulvaney had instructed him on this point. Vindman said that unlike Mulvaney and Sondland, he was not a political appointee, but as a national security specialist, he viewed the request as inappropriate.

Outside the Ward Room door, the Ukrainians found themselves standing just feet away from the Situation Room, a facility the Central Intelligence Agency calls "a national nerve center." Behind a locked door, in a suite of cramped rooms, staff received and collated reports from around the world, alert to national security messages that would be routed to officials in various White House offices. Few people ever get as close to the Sit Room as the Ukrainians were that day. That was one reason why Fiona Hill was a bit startled when she descended the stairs to discover them standing there.

Inside the Ward Room, Hill got an instant update on the discussion from Vindman. In short, the kind of talk that Bolton had found problematic—you give us investigations, we give you a White House meeting—had simply been shifted to a new location. The same demands were being made, and the same pushback was being offered by the national security experts. Hill supported Vindman, and in a matter of minutes, the whole episode ended. Vindman opened the door and let the Ukrainians inside just so they could say goodbye to the Americans. He would walk the visitors back up the stairs and accompany them outside, to the gate, and watch them depart.[7]

After the Ward Room meeting, Hill returned to Bolton's office to report what she had seen and heard. His reaction was characteristically blunt. He described Rudy Giuliani as "a live hand grenade" and said, "I am not part of whatever drug deal Sondland and Mulvaney are cooking up." He then told Hill she should inform the NSC's lead attorney, John Eisenberg. Vindman would make a similar report, and the NSC would not be part of future meetings intended to draw Ukraine into the president's political scheme. However, this did not mean that anyone else in the White House was deterred. In fact, two days later, administration officials were discussing, via email, the fact that the president had actually decided to put a formal hold on Ukraine's aid. Robert Blair, top aide to Mick Mulvaney, told Michael Duffey at OMB that the president had decided to freeze the aid. This news was not widely shared within the administration or with those who needed the money, but as the person in charge of OMB's oversight of national security programs, Duffey was the one who could make sure the president's order was followed.

In relying on Mulvaney, Blair, and Duffey, President Trump bypassed officials like Bolton, who understood U.S. policy toward Ukraine and the geopolitical implications of the delay in military aid. Among them was William Taylor, the U.S. ambassador in Kiev, who learned about the decision when he logged in to a video conference on July 18. More than a dozen high-ranking officials listened as a young staffer from OMB chimed in. As Taylor would eventually recall, she "said that she was from OMB and that her boss had instructed her not to approve any additional spending of security assistance for Ukraine until further notice." The woman added that "the directive had come from the President to the Chief of Staff to OMB."

After the video conference, Taylor and his colleagues spoke among themselves and reached what he would describe as a "unanimous" conclusion that the aid should not be delayed. They then went to work on the secretaries of state and defense and on the directors of the CIA and NSC. According to Taylor, all four agreed to take the matter up with Trump, but weeks would pass as they tried to get time in his schedule. Officials at the Ukrainian embassy in Washington, who had many friends in the government, learned about the hold and cabled word to the foreign ministry and president's office in Kiev. Defense minister Danylyuk was soon on the phone with Taylor to explain that President Zelensky did not want to be used as a pawn in Trump's election scheme. Taylor relayed this concern to Sondland and Volker, who, it seemed, were the ones who knew the president's mind and were driving U.S. policy.

That the ambassador to Ukraine, one of the most seasoned and respected diplomats in the State Department, would find himself working through Sondland and Volker was, of course, both insulting and reckless. Sondland was not just out of his depth in his first-ever government job, he was operating outside his remit as ambassador to the European Union, which didn't include Ukraine. Volker's actual position, which was unpaid and gave him no real authority, involved watching and advising from the sidelines whenever Ukraine might talk. But while their limitations cast doubt on the wisdom of relying on Volker and Sondland, Taylor had no real choice.

Sondland, who had Trump's private phone number and wasn't shy about using it, derived his power from his personal relationship with him. Though he was a loyalist, he wasn't abject in his commitment. He wanted Ukraine to receive American aid but judged it necessary for Zelensky to play along with Trump's game. When Taylor told him the Ukrainian president was "sensitive about Ukraine being taken seriously, not merely as an instrument in Washington domestic, reelection politics," Sondland agreed but added, "We need to get the conversation started and the relationship built, irrespective of the pretext. I am worried about the alternative."[8]

Acting a bit like Sondland's wingman, Volker sent Taylor a text reminding him, "Most impt is for Zelensky to say that he will help investigation." He also met with Rudy Giuliani and immediately introduced the former mayor to Zelensky's advisor Andriy Yermak. When they spoke by phone on July 22, Giuliani pushed Yermak on the investigations that Trump wanted Ukraine to conduct. Yermak, the former TV producer, wasn't certain whether Giuliani was representing the president as his private attorney or acting as some sort of quasi-official emissary. What he and other top Ukrainian officials knew for certain was that the U.S. aid they needed, and the moral support it represented, was of vital importance. Ukrainians were continuing to die in a war that had already killed more than thirteen thousand. With his decision, Trump put a new and unnecessary burden on an ally the United States had promised to help. With every day that then passed, the pressure felt by Zelensky's team would increase.[9]

• • • •

Though Donald Trump often talked about his "total" and "absolute" authority to command the machinery of the federal government, the idea that he could get whatever he wanted accomplished by merely issuing orders was a fantasy. Presidents are bound by acts of Congress, constrained by the checks and balances created by the Constitution, and limited by the decisions of the judiciary. Within the government, which Trump believed he commanded, were systems created to keep him inside the legal limits. These systems were operated by people who understood that the United States was not an autocracy and knew how to respond when this standard was threatened.

Next door to the White House, in the colossal Eisenhower Executive Office Building, a career OMB official named Mark Sandy came back from vacation on July 18 to learn of the president's decision. Trained in economics and public policy, Sandy had spent more than twenty years in government service. He was so well regarded that in the first weeks of his administration, President Trump had asked him to serve as interim chief of OMB. Once Mick Mulvaney was installed in that job, Sandy became Michael Duffey's second in command at the National Security Division (NSD), which meant he handled the everyday work of overseeing budgeting and spending for defense, nuclear security, intelligence, and veterans affairs. Duffey spoke to Sandy in a hallway of the Eisenhower Building, telling him about Trump's decision and asking him to devise an apportionment to implement it.

Apportionments are legal documents that tell federal agencies just how funds appropriated by Congress are to be spent. Often, they generally affirm a process that is well understood throughout the government. In this case, Duffey wanted to deviate from the pro forma practice without offering a specific justification. This was, for Sandy, a red flag. In a follow-up phone call, Sandy told his boss that his request raised a number of questions that required him to consult with OMB's legal counsel.

Sandy's inquiry at the office of the legal counsel touched off a struggle that would lead one lawyer to resign after submitting to higher-ups an argument against the apportionment document Duffey wanted approved. As others inside the agency inevitably became involved, they began discussing the Impoundment Control Act. When Sandy spoke to Elaine McCusker at the Department of Defense, she said she thought a brief hold could be accomplished in a way that would not violate the law. Sandy heard again from Duffey, who forwarded him an email from *his boss*, which directed that the hold be enacted but that the whole matter would be revisited with Trump later.

In the meantime, the men Trump had trusted to get him results in Kiev tried to prepare the Ukrainians so that when Trump called Zelensky, the heads of state could perform like actors in a scripted scene who understood in advance all that was to be said. One problem was that no one seemed certain about the schedule. Believing it would happen on July 20, Gordon Sondland spoke with President Zelensky the day before. Afterward, he sent a text to Volker.

> Looks like Potus call tomorrow. I spike [*sic*] directly to Zelensky and gave him a full briefing. He's got it.

Minutes later, Volker replied, referencing his own efforts with Giuliani.

> Good. Had breakfast with Rudy this morning-teeing up call w Yermak Monday. Must have helped. Most impt is for Zelensky to say that he will help investigation-and address any specific personnel issues-if there are any.

When THE CALL didn't happen on July 20, Volker and Sondland maintained their effort to make sure the Ukrainians would please President Trump, if only to ensure they received the aid they were due. By this time, Rudy Giuliani was back in the picture. He was, by no means, a fourth Amigo, but he was working alongside them, which meant the president's trusted friend, outspoken propagandist, and private attorney would be aware of their work and positioned to influence it. In turn, as a July 22 text exchange between Sondland and Volker showed, they were trying to both manipulate and exploit him. As of this point in the effort, Fiona Hill, John Bolton's top Russia expert on the National Security Council, had announced her resignation.

> **VOLKER:** Orchestrated a great phone call w Rudy and Yermak. They are going to get together when Rudy is in Madrid. In the meantime Rudy is now advocating for phone call. I have call into Fiona's replacement and will call Bolton if needed. But I can tell Bolton and you can tell Mick that Rudy agrees on a call if that helps.

> **SONDLAND:** I talked to Tim Morrison, Fiona's replacement. He is pushing, but feel free as well.

Thanks to Sondland, Volker, Giuliani, and others, when word came that THE CALL would take place on July 25 at 9:00 a.m. Washington time, President Zelensky surely knew what was expected of him. Trump wanted Ukraine to give credibility to his ideas about the Bidens and the 2016 election so that the Russia controversy would be lessened and his likely rival in 2020 would be diminished. Trump might not talk about the quid pro quo he was proposing—the aid would be unfrozen should Zelensky acquiesce—but it couldn't be clearer. Though he was in a difficult spot, Zelensky wasn't completely without options. Trump may have been determined, but Ukraine had friends elsewhere in the United States—in the State and Defense Departments, in the U.S. Senate, and in the press—and its military needs were not so desperate that its dignity would have to be sacrificed. At least not yet.[10]

•   •   •

On the morning of August 25, 2019, President Trump awakened in the White House residence and turned to one of his main sources of comfort, the *Fox & Friends* morning TV show. There, he got some bad news from the network's newest poll. A slight improvement in his approval rating in the previous survey, which had been done in February, had disappeared. Now just 46 percent of surveyed voters said he was doing well in his job. Worse was the continued strength of Joe Biden's numbers. Fox's pollsters asked about the huge field of Democrats running; Biden held a commanding lead over them all. When respondents were then asked about a Trump-versus-Biden election in 2020, the former vice president beat Trump by ten points. This result, in a poll conducted after Trump and his helpers worked hard to tar Biden with Ukraine pseudoscandals, was two points *more* than the lead Biden had enjoyed in March.

Ever the president's silver-lining finders, the show's producers plucked a positive item from a subcategory of the survey for a headline that read, "Poll Shows Most Approve of Trump on Economy." In fact, 52 percent did approve of Trump's handling of the economy, but this number was lower than his score on the same question the previous year. Nevertheless, one of the hosts loudly proclaimed, "There is a lot of credit being given to President Trump." Others seated on the studio sofa murmured agreement and then expressed fears about what could happen with the election of a Democrat who might champion an increase in the minimum wage. No one mentioned that with inflation factored in, the federal minimum wage of $7.25 was a third lower than it was in 1968.

Fox, which was broadcast on channel five in Washington, featured the poll numbers during a segment that began at 6:41 a.m. and ended at 6:45. (The president often watched the show with the help of a video recorder, which meant that there might have been a lag between when the segment was presented and when he actually saw it.) Sometime in the 7:00 hour, the president took a call from Gordon Sondland, who was in Europe. The two talked briefly. Later, Sondland would say only that the president had given him a message to relay to the Ukrainian government. At roughly the same moment, Sondland's Amigo Kurt Volker was having lunch in Kiev with Andriy Yermak. Afterward, he dashed off a thank-you text to his companion. It included some optimistic words about THE CALL, which was imminent, and then referenced the next carrot to be dangled, which he could have called THE VISIT:

> Good lunch—thanks, Heard from White House—assuming President [Zelensky] convinces trump he will investigate / "get to the bottom of what happened" in 2016, we will nail down date for visit to Washington.

At the White House, the president took a few minutes to compose and send to his millions of Twitter followers a message about his favorite part of the Fox poll. Composed using the strange third-person voice he often adopted when boasting, perhaps to suggest he was merely reporting facts, the president's message said:

> President Trump's Approval Rating on Economy is at 52%, a 4 point jump. Fox Poll @foxandfriends Shouldn't this be at 100%? Best stock market, economy and unemployment numbers ever! Most people working within U.S. ever! Low interest rates, very low inflation! Country doing great!

The president bragged to the world at 8:07 a.m. Apparently still tuned to *Fox & Friends,* he followed this message with one recommending that his seventy million Twitter fans tune in to watch the "great guy" Mark Levin, a national radio host who was about to appear as a guest. A study published in 2016 by Oxford University Press judged Levin to be the most extreme of America's top right-wing radio ideologues. Devoted to Trump, he often said the Deep State was conducting a silent coup against the president. This kind of talk earned Levin a spot in the synergistic dynamic that found the president of the United States continuously promoting those who promoted him. Everyone in this circle—Trump, Fox, Levin—would gain in power, and perhaps money, from whatever extra attention grew out of their mutual promotion.

Maintaining this cycle was second nature for Trump, who reflexively praised those who supported him and could do it even as he was anticipating getting on the phone with Zelensky.

Trump was a master of phone calls, too. In his decades as a businessman and then as a candidate, he spent countless hours in gossipy conversations and negotiations. While others relied on emails and text messaging to a degree that made many uncomfortable on the telephone, Trump eschewed both these forms of communication and maintained his telephone talent. He wouldn't need much time, or for that matter much intellectual focus, to prepare for a conversation that others had been busily arranging for weeks. He knew what he wanted, and he surely expected to get it.

10

THE CALL

The call to the Ukrainian President was PERFECT. Read the Transcript! There was NOTHING said that was in any way wrong. Republicans, don't be led into the fools trap of saying it was not perfect, but is not impeachable. No, it is much stronger than that. NOTHING WAS DONE WRONG!

—Donald Trump, president of the United States, via Twitter,
November 10, 2019

The technical aspects of THE CALL had been orchestrated in advance with Ukrainian authorities. According to the plan, secure telephone connections would be made by the staff of the White House Situation Room, which is not actually a room but rather a suite of facilities, including a communications hub that looks like a miniature version of NASA's Mission Control Center. In this space, operators sit at stations, staring at multiple computer screens, and work with keyboards and sophisticated communications equipment. Wall-mounted displays stream data and video. Digital clocks mounted near the ceiling mark local time, Greenwich mean time, and the time at key locales. One labeled *President* indicates the time wherever the commander in chief might be.

Although the Situation Room staff could record calls to heads of state, the scandal caused by Richard Nixon's secretly recording his Oval Office conversations led to a strict no-record policy. Instead, duty officers join any number of officials authorized to listen in, and type everything they hear. An extra officer, listening in a separate room, repeats what the speakers say for a speech-to-text transcription program. This effort produces a Memcom (memorandum of conversation) that is not a transcript but nevertheless quite accurate.

It is sometimes corrected by one of the many officials—from the White House, intelligence agencies, and State Department among them—who listen in at the president's request or when a call relates to their areas of expertise or duties.[1]

On July 25, at least seven officials, including Secretary of State Mike Pompeo, the NSC's Ukraine specialist Alexander Vindman, and Robert Blair, aide to the chief of staff, Mick Mulvaney, were poised to listen to Trump and Volodymyr Zelensky talk. Blair had been in on the president's plan to leverage Ukraine's aid from the very start. After the *Washington Examiner* reported that the aid had been approved by the Pentagon, he was the one who had contacted OMB to say, "We need to hold it up." He had also used the word *unhinged* to warn Mulvaney of how Congress might react.[2]

By 9:00 a.m., Blair, Vindman, and the rest were in position, and a line was opened to Kiev, where it was 4 p.m. At 9:03, Zelensky was ready, and in the First Family residence, Donald Trump was connected to the call. Though not precisely scripted, the conversation would proceed along a preordained path. This wouldn't be difficult for two men who, in their previous lives, had been TV performers. Indeed, it would be hard to imagine an instance when two first-time officeholders were better prepared to speak as heads of state. One had played the role of president through four seasons. The other had spent his entire adult life, including a fifteen-year run on television, pretending to be someone he was not.

Trump started the call with a gush of praise that was based, at least in part, on a misreading of Zelensky's recent success in parliamentary elections, which had been expected by Ukrainian pollsters and political experts.

> **TRUMP:** Congratulations on a great victory. We all watched from the United States and you did a terrific job. The way you came from behind, somebody who wasn't given much of a chance, and you ended up winning easily. It's a fantastic achievement. Congratulations.

Zelensky replied in a way that showed he understood how to deal with a naked emperor. He bypassed the president's inaccuracies to quickly engage in the kind of flattery that those who succeeded with Trump practiced as an art form.

> **ZELENSKY:** You are absolutely right Mr. President. We did win big and we worked hard for this. We worked a lot but I would like to confess to you that I had an opportunity to learn from you. We used quite a few of your skills and knowledge and were able to use it as

an example to our elections and yes it is true that these were unique elections. We were in a unique situation that we were able to achieve a unique success. I'm able to tell you the following; the first time, you called me to congratulate me when I won my presidential election, and the second time you are now calling me when my party won the parliamentary election. I think I should run more often so you can call me more often and we can talk over the phone more often.

Another American president, one with more refined skills, would have next acknowledged Ukraine's vulnerability or offered Zelensky some kind words of advice to begin a mentoring relationship. Trump did neither. Instead, he talked about how "we do a lot for Ukraine," which is "much more than the European countries are doing." (He took pains to single out Germany and its chancellor, Angela Merkel, specifically on this count.) This claim wasn't true. European military aid to Ukraine far exceeded America's, and its economic assistance of $15 billion was also much higher. However, Trump's statement supported his predetermined path of complaint, which would take him to a place where he could say that Ukraine wasn't holding up its side of its relationship with the United States.[3]

> **TRUMP:** I wouldn't say that it's reciprocal necessarily, because things are happening that are not good but the United States has been very very good to Ukraine.

Zelensky knew where Trump was headed. He said that he agreed with him that the United States was a better friend to Ukraine than Europe was. He even joined Trump in a negative exchange about Merkel. He then found a way to step lightly into the matter of defense aid.

> **ZELENSKY:** I would also like to thank you for your great support in the area of defense. We are ready to continue to cooperate for the next steps. Specifically, we are almost ready to buy more Javelins from the United States for defense purposes.

Although he named them specifically, the Javelin antitank missiles were not something Zelensky needed right away. In fact, a previous shipment of Javelins remained stored far from the front because his forces were not fighting against tanks but against squads of raiders who used small arms. What they needed were the sniper rifles, night vision goggles, grenade launchers, and other items that could keep the Russian proxies contained. So why all the talk of Javelins? Two likely factors would explain the focus on the Javelin. One was that they fit the way Trump imagined all wars. Trump often spoke admiringly of General George Patton, whom he knew only from the film *Patton,* which is full of World War II tank battles. The fact was that the Javelins were the big-ticket items that mattered most to Trump politically. They would be manufactured by the U.S. arms maker Raytheon with American workers. High-paying jobs secured by taxpayer funds poured into a big corporation, which kept a portion for its profits; this was a Trumpian dream come true. By mentioning the missiles, Zelensky focused Trump on them and prompted him to lurch into his scheme.

The president's decision to condition military aid on political favors was sordid, and the way he spoke suggested he knew it. In this part of the conversation, he leaned more heavily on half-truths, distortions, and conspiracy theories, and his way of speaking became even more disjointed. His sentence fragments and suggestive phrases required Zelensky to fill in much of the true meaning for himself. This is the way that mobsters talk when they want to communicate a threat while maintaining deniability:

> **TRUMP:** I would like you to do us a favor though because our country has been through a lot and Ukraine knows a lot about it. I would like you to find out what happened with this whole situation with Ukraine. They say Crowdstrike. I guess you have one of your wealthy people. The server, they say Ukraine has it. There are a lot of things that went on with the whole situation. I think you are surrounding yourself with some of the same people. I would like to have the Attorney General call you or your people and I would like you to get to the bottom of it.
>
> As you saw yesterday, that whole nonsense ended with a very poor performance by a man named Robert Mueller, an incompetent performance, but they say a lot of it started with Ukraine. Whatever you can do, it's very important that you do it if that's possible.

Zelensky had undoubtedly been briefed well enough to understand Trump's meaning. Besides, the key had been offered in Trump's first phrase—10 little words—which was the only clear part of a statement that was actually 155 words long. "I would like you to do us a favor though" is the kind of thing said as a condition is placed on a promise. What follows is never good for the listener.

Here, Zelensky had to know that the military aid Ukraine needed was being conditioned on a favor and what followed let him know he was required to give credence to the crazy idea that his country had messed with the U.S. to help Hillary Clinton. Although Zelensky shouldn't have required a glossary to understand the coherent parts of the president's side of the conversation, one would be helpful for those unfamiliar with Trump's peculiar way of talking and the conspiracy theories of the conservative fringe.

- Robert Mueller, of course, was not a performer but the special prose-cutor who had been appointed to examine Russia's interference in the 2016 election on Trump's behalf. He had testified before Congress on the previous day, and President Trump had concluded that he did not do well and therefore the matter was settled.

- "They," as in "They say," represented unnamed sources of information that the president credits for one reason or another. "They" could be top-level national security experts or random folks sending messages on social media, or no one at all. What mattered was not the quality of the source but whether the information was helpful. In this case, "they" were likely the right-wing media outlets that continuously provided him with suggestions for conspiracy theories.

- CrowdStrike is the California cybersecurity firm hired by Democrats to respond to Russia's hacking of campaign emails, which traced the attacks to two Russian espionage groups.

- "You have one of your wealthy people" suggested that someone in Ukraine controlled CrowdStrike. It was in fact founded by a tech and business entrepreneur from New Jersey and a Moscow-born cybersecurity expert who immigrated to Chattanooga with his par-ents at age fourteen.

- "The server, they say Ukraine has it" references a conspiracy theory about Democratic Party computer equipment hidden in Ukraine by CrowdStrike. In fact, the firm worked on digital versions of the servers' contents. All this material was given to U.S. authorities, per widely accepted security practice.

Ukraine's president didn't fall into the trap of trying to unpack, in the moment, what the president of the United States said or to seek any clarifications. Instead, he did what any astute person would do while being threatened by someone with more power and a well-established malevolent streak. He immediately offered his agreement and quickly followed it with acquiescence and flattery.

ZELENSKY: Yes, it is very important for me and everything that you just mentioned earlier. For me as a President, it is very important and we are open for any future cooperation. We are ready to open a new page on cooperation in relations between the United States and Ukraine. For that purpose, I just recalled our ambassador from United States and he will be replaced by a very competent and very experienced ambassador who will work hard on making sure that our two nations are getting closer. I would also like and hope to see him having your trust and your confidence and have personal relations with you so we can cooperate even more so.

I will personally tell you that one of my assistants spoke with Mr. Giuliani just recently and we are hoping very much that Mr. Giuliani will be able to travel to Ukraine and we will meet once he comes to Ukraine.

I just wanted to assure you once again that you have nobody but friends around us. I will make sure that I surround myself with the best and most experienced people. I also wanted to tell you that we are friends. We are great friends and you Mr. President have friends in our country so we can continue our strategic partnership. I also plan to surround myself with great people and in addition to that investigation, I guarantee as the President of Ukraine that all the investigations will be done openly and candidly. That I can assure you.

In all, the two presidents would speak for twenty-nine minutes. Trump would reference the recently fired prosecutor Yuriy Lutsenko—"I heard you had a prosecutor who was very good"—and note that "a lot of people are talking about that, the way they shut your very good prosecutor down." He also mentioned that he was going to ask Rudy Giuliani to contact Zelensky, because "Rudy very much knows what's happening and he is a very capable guy." Trump also made sure that he communicated his disdain for Ambassador Yovanovitch and Vice President Biden.

> TRUMP: The former ambassador from the United States, the woman, was bad news and the people she was dealing with in the Ukraine were bad news so I just want to let you know that.
>
> The other thing, There's a lot of talk about Biden's son, that Biden stopped the prosecution and a lot of people want to find out about that so whatever you can do with the Attorney General would be great. Biden went around bragging that he stopped the prosecution so if you can look into it. It sounds horrible to me.

Zelensky did not signal that Yuriy Lutsenko, whom many Ukrainians associated with corruption, would be coming back. Instead, he protected his prerogative, saying only that "the next prosecutor general will be one hundred percent my person." Zelensky made vague pledges to appoint a prosecutor who "will look into the situation, specifically to the company that you mentioned in this issue. The issue of the investigation of the case is actually the issue of making sure to resolve with honesty so we will take care of that and will work on the investigation of the case. On top of that, I would kindly ask you if you have any additional information that you can provide to us it would be very helpful for the investigation to make sure that we administer justice in our country."

On the other end of the call, President Trump was free to hear either a pledge to go after Biden and Burisma or a hedging response that promised nothing more than "honesty." Indeed, Zelensky had been so imprecise that he seemed, for the moment, a master of the kind of doublespeak that Trump had practiced for decades. The Ukrainian president was far more direct when it came to Marie Yovanovitch, joining with Trump to say:

> ZELENSKY: With regard to the Ambassador to the United States from Ukraine as far as I recall her name was Yovanovicli. It was great that you were the first one who told me that she was a bad

ambassador because I agree with you one hundred percent. Her attitude towards me was far from the best as she admired the previous
president and she was on his side. She would not accept me as a new
president well enough.

No public record indicated that Zelensky and Yovanovitch had ever been
at odds, and she had never exhibited any special coziness with Poroshenko.
(Diplomats in Kiev concurred with that assessment.) However, Yovanovitch
was no longer in Ukraine, and in this private man-to-man talk, Zelensky could
assume there was no risk, for him, in trashing her. Apparently encouraged by
the gossip, Trump stayed with the topic but assumed a more menacing tone,
saying, "Well, she's going to go through some things. I will have Mr. Giuliani
give you a call and I am also going to have Attorney General Barr call and we
will get to the bottom of it."

In movies and television programs, mobsters use phrases like *she's going to
go through some things* to foreshadow a move against an enemy. Can't you hear
Tony Soprano saying it? As president of the United States, Donald Trump
could back up his comment with more power than anyone, and in this case,
his gadfly personal lawyer, Rudy Giuliani, and Attorney General William
Barr came immediately to his mind. Given that Yovanovitch's supposed sin
involved being insufficiently loyal to Trump, an ethical attorney general would
resent being joined with Giuliani in the mission the president imagined. However, William Barr had already shown he was willing to act as an agent of the
president's ego who indulged his conspiracy theories, so he could be expected
to join Giuliani in a Ukrainian misadventure.

Twenty-five minutes into the conversation, Trump and Zelensky had
completed their agenda and were ready to close the circle they opened with
mutual admiration. Zelensky offered some glowing commentary about his visits to the United States and, in particular, a stay at a Trump-branded hotel.
He reminded Trump of the open-ended offer of a White House visit, made
months before, promised again to look into Biden and Burisma, and dangled
the possibility that Ukraine could buy lots of American oil. The president then
ended the call.

TRUMP: Good. Well thank you very much and I appreciate that. I will
tell Rudy and Attorney General Barr to call. Thank you. Whenever you

would like to come to the White House feel free to call. Give us a
date and we'll work that out. I look forward to seeing you.[4]

•   •   •

Having said all he needed to say and heard the reassurance he needed to hear,
President Trump felt the call had gone well. This didn't mean he would act to
ease the pressure on Zelensky. In fact, hours after Trump and Zelensky spoke,
Michael Duffey of OMB notified officials at the Pentagon that they were to
"hold off" sending assistance to Ukraine. Duffey noted "the sensitive nature"
of what he was doing and asked it be hidden from everyone other than "those
who need to know to execute the direction." What he meant by "direction" was,
in fact, an order coming from the White House and delivered to him. At this
time, Blair declined to explain the exact rationale for the hold even to Mark
Sandy, director of national security at OMB. As a career official, Sandy had
never heard of a case in which this kind of hold had been imposed by a political
appointee without explanation, but he chose to trust Duffey and immediately
added a footnote to a budget document that formalized it.[5]

With officials moving to enact his squeeze play, the president spent the
remainder of the day in performance mode. He threatened to place tariffs on
French wine, making the absurd observation that "I've always liked American
wines better than French wines. Even though I don't drink wine. I just like
the way they look." He used the social media platform Twitter to demand
that the World Trade Organization act against countries "CHEATING the
system at the expense of the USA!" And he welcomed officials from Guate-
mala to the Oval Office, where they promised, under the threat of U.S. sanctions, that their country would house asylum seekers from around the world
who were being turned away by American authorities. In other words, for the
president, it had been just another day.

For those who had listened to Trump and Zelensky talk, it was not just another day. Alexander Vindman, the Ukraine-born army officer on the National
Security Council staff, had been shocked by Trump's attempt to leverage promised military aid for domestic political favors. Instead of offering inducements
to encourage positive change, the president was pressuring Ukraine to double
down on corruption and, in the process, affirming the worst a foreign leader
might imagine about the United States. The country that had, for generations,
lectured others on democracy and the rule of law was, Trump demonstrated,
not just hypocritical but also willing to endanger an ally in order to achieve a
transient leader's short-term goal.

For Vindman, a twenty-year army veteran with an immigrant's passion for his adopted homeland, the call was doubly disturbing because he had also become optimistic about Ukraine's future under America's protection. No one in the U.S. government was better versed in Ukraine-U.S. affairs, and no one cared more deeply about the relationship. Vindman had to know that if Zelensky kept his promise and backed an investigation into the Bidens, Ukraine could expect ongoing support from the White House. However, no objective review would find justification for such an investigation, just as no evidence would support the president's criticism of Ambassador Yovanovitch or the conspiracy theories about CrowdStrike, an internet server, and Ukraine trying to help Clinton in the 2016 U.S. election.

Vindman wasn't the only listener who recognized something strange and concerning in the call. Jennifer Williams, advisor to Vice President Mike Pence, had never heard a president make direct political requests in the way Trump had done with Zelensky. And as far as she knew, her boss, Pence, had never talked about the political investigations with any of the Ukrainians he ever dealt with. She included the readout produced by the two Situation Room recorders in her daily briefing packet for the vice president and, on the day after the call, joined in a review with officials from all the agencies that would deal with the aid. Many in this group agreed that the hold should be lifted immediately.

As he reflected on the call, Vindman turned to the National Security Council computer system, where he expected to find a copy of the notetaker's report of the conversation. This system was where records of the president's high-level conversations would be stored for revision by others who listened in. In this case, Vindman discovered that the text had been quickly sequestered in a different way that was generally used for highly classified material, which only those with the most advanced clearances could access. Vindman was able to get a printout of the document, and as he sat and reviewed it, he noted problems and began jotting down corrections in a classified notebook.

In several spots, the record showed changes that obscured what Vindman recalled had been said. In one passage, where Trump talked about Biden supposedly stopping a Ukrainian investigation into his son, an ellipsis marked some missing words. Vindman recalled that what Trump had said was "there are recordings." This referred to recordings of Biden. In another spot, where the record quotes Zelensky promising that "the company you mentioned in this issue" would be investigated, Vindman saw a wordy effort to obscure the

fact that Zelensky had, instead, mentioned Burisma by name. In a third location, where Trump references CrowdStrike and a server, the words *they say you
have it* were apparently excised.

It seemed beyond coincidence that all the changes Vindman identified
would make the conversation seem inflammatory to someone looking for evidence of a president seeking to have his conspiracy theories affirmed and his
political opponent harmed. Vindman let the team know what he had discovered and recommended corrections to make the document more accurate. He
did this so that the record would be more useful if national security officials
needed to consult it and so that history would be better informed.

Vindman also understood that many Ukrainian and American officials were
aware of the game Trump was playing. He had even heard about it from diplomats in the Ukrainian embassy. This foreknowledge would have given Zelensky
reason to make his own recording of the call, which could be used to turn the
table on Trump. Add the general trouble the administration had with leaks to
the press and, as the hours passed, the chance that the call would become THE
CALL and a scandal would rise. If this occurred, the White House would be
best served by an accurate record and not one with which many witnesses might
disagree.

To be clear, Vindman did not know whether a federal statute had been
violated or whether he had observed what might turn out to be a cover-up.
However, he was certain that something strange—he would use the word
inappropriate—had gone on, and it was not likely to stay contained. Later in
the day, the office of the president of Ukraine issued its own report on the
phone call, which included the following: "Donald Trump expressed his conviction that the new Ukrainian government will be able to quickly improve
Ukraine's image and complete the investigation of corruption cases that have
held back cooperation between Ukraine and the United States." This was an
invitation for alert journalists on both sides of the Atlantic to start asking
questions.[6]

11

SHO?

Our Country is the envy of the World. Thank you, Mr. President!

—Donald Trump, president of the United States, via Twitter,
July 6, 2019

On the day after THE CALL, Gordon Sondland and Kurt Volker made William Taylor and David Holmes temporary Amigos for a visit with Volodymyr Zelensky at the Ukrainian president's office. (Taylor had replaced Ambassador Marie Yovanovitch, and Holmes was his top counselor for Ukraine affairs.) Zelensky greeted the group in a ceremonial room decorated in muted tones of cream, blue, and gold. True to his identity as a TV president turned real president, he wore a white shirt with the collar unbuttoned and no necktie.

When they sat down to talk, Zelensky told the Americans that President Trump had "three times raised some very sensitive issues" and made it clear that they would have to be addressed by Ukraine before any White House visit. (Local embassy staff were in the dark about the Zelensky-Trump chat because, in a departure from standard practice, no memo on the call had been sent to them.) Sondland offered Zelensky advice on how to deal with Trump. When this meeting ended, Sondland then spent thirty minutes alone with Zelensky's foreign policy advisor, Andriy Yermak. Although Holmes had been assigned to take notes during this outing, Sondland decided this would be a one-on-one session with no notetakers. The president had done something similar when he met with Vladimir Putin in 2017.[1]

After he finished his private chat, Sondland invited Holmes and two others to lunch at one of Kiev's few high-end restaurants. Sho, which means "What" in Ukrainian, offered a gourmet take on traditional dishes, which made it special in a city where "fancy" was generally associated with classical French or even Asian cuisines. Locals with the money to afford the place appreciated the creativity applied to rabbit served with cabbage, borscht, and of course, chicken Kiev. Sondland inspected the wine list and ordered a bottle for the table to share. This would have been a treat for mid-level foreign service officers whose expense accounts weren't geared toward such high-end entertaining.

At Sho, the Americans were seated in an outdoor section of the restaurant. Sondland interrupted a sociable conversation to use his unsecured cell phone to place a call to the president. (Although most American embassy officials took extra precautions with calls in Kiev, where they assumed Russia could intercept almost any cell signal, Sondland was known to be cavalier in his cell phone habits.) Sondland waited to be connected and, at more than one point told someone on the other end of the call, "Gordon Sondland waiting for the president."

When Trump finally came on the line, he spoke so loudly that Sondland winced and held the phone away from his ear. Holmes was able to hear every word that was said. He heard Sondland explain to Trump that he was calling from Ukraine. He said he had spoken with Zelensky and told the president, "He loves your ass." Trump asked, "So he's going to do the investigation?" Sondland answered, "He's going to do it," and Zelensky would do "anything you ask him to do."

Trump and Sondland chatted like a couple of buddies who happened to be in charge of the world. After dealing with Ukraine, they turned their attention to Sweden and the problems of an American rap performer whose stage name was A$AP Rocky. Mr. Rocky had been arrested after a brawl, held, promptly tried, and convicted of assault. Prompted by the Kardashian family of reality TV fame, Trump had sent the special presidential envoy for hostage affairs to watch the trial. Since under Swedish law A$AP Rocky was unlikely to receive a prison sentence, Sondland suggested Trump take no action. Actually, what he said was that the president should wait for Rocky to be sentenced, and then he, Trump, could "play the racism card" against Swedish authorities. Upon his return, said Sondland, Trump could arrange for him to be honored with "a ticker tape parade." In the meantime, "You can tell the Kardashians you tried."[2]

If Sondland was interested only in moving the president to free the aid for Ukraine, this was the kind of talk that might do it. However, his take on the president's attitude wasn't encouraging. After the call ended, he turned to his lunch companions and said the president had been in a bad mood. He blamed this in part on the hour. It was about 6:00 a.m. and, though Trump was famously an early riser, this didn't mean he was even-tempered at such an hour.

When Holmes then asked about Trump's views on Ukraine, he slipped into the vernacular Sondland had demonstrated, asking whether he knew if the president actually gave "a shit" about Ukraine. Sondland said, "No," because Trump was focused only on "big stuff." Holmes said something about how the war Ukraine was fighting in the east and Russia's occupation of its territory in Crimea amounted to "big stuff." Sondland replied that for the president, the big stuff was anything that might relate to his political future, including the "Biden investigation."[3]

For professionals like Holmes, who had joined the foreign service in 2002, the idea that an American president would seek domestic political help from a war-ravaged ally was more than dismaying. That he might hold U.S. war aid to apply pressure to that ally was almost unimaginable. However, Holmes had been at Marie Yovanovitch's side when Rudy Giuliani and the BLT Group began making mischief, so he wasn't surprised.

●　　●　　●

In the week after THE CALL, Rudy Giuliani arrived in Madrid, where he and Lev Parnas met with Zelensky's man Yermak. Among them, only Yermak could claim official foreign affairs experience, and he had only been at it for a couple of months. But there they were, seeking to determine the fate of nations. Nothing much had changed when it came to Giuliani's agenda. He told Yermak that President Trump was still keen on Ukraine opening the investigations that would put an official sheen on conspiracy theories about the Bidens and the 2016 election.

A bit of progress was suggested when the two men discussed how officials in Kiev could make a public statement that assured President Trump his request was being fulfilled. The president would be satisfied if the statement addressed the Burisma-Biden theory specifically, as well as the 2016 election, and Yermak said it might be helpful for the U.S. government to issue an official request for an investigation. This would, of course, provide nonpolitical cover for Ukraine while forcing the Americans to act openly on a demand that, up to this point, had been voiced only in secret.[4]

While they were in Spain, Giuliani and Parnas visited a bullring where Giuliani posed between two young matadors who wore their ornate skintight costumes. In the photo, a grinning, slightly hunched Giuliani squints into the sunlight while grasping two fuchsia-colored bullfighting capes. The mayor and Parnas's destination was a vast hunting estate owned by a jet-setting Venezuelan businessman named Alejandro Betancourt López. The host had hired Giuliani to help his associates with some legal problems with the U.S. government. (They were suspected of money laundering. López was not.)

The estate was fifty miles southwest of Madrid by car and accessed via a narrow paved highway that ended at a steel gate opening upon a long and winding gravel road. At the end of this dusty path, they entered a complex of paved courtyards, green gardens, fountains, and stone buildings. A pool, a tennis court, and a soccer field lay behind the main house.

Once the site of a Moorish fortress called the Castillo de Alamín, the riverside hilltop had been occupied by royals for more than a thousand years. Betancourt and partners had acquired the place as courts cleaned up a financial mess reminiscent of Donald Trump's own bankruptcy in the early 1990s. Like Trump, the former owner of Alamín had operated an airline, hotels, and other enterprises. He went to prison for his financial crimes.

At Alamín, Betancourt introduced Giuliani to another guest—the father of Venezuelan opposition leader Juan Guaidó. As leader of the movement against Venezuela's leftist government, Guaidó was a favorite of the Trump administration. Betancourt wanted the Trump administration to know that he was funding Guaidó. Giuliani taped an interview with Betancourt so he would have testimony to present to the Justice Department. Thus, the lawyer who represented the president would intercede with the president's administration on behalf of another client, who just happened to be a foreign national tangentially involved in an international criminal case. While staying with Betancourt, the former mayor of New York also tapped out a Twitter post about Joe Biden and his son Hunter. This one cited a new baseless conspiracy theory connecting the Bidens and China and ended with the declaration, "It stinks!!"[5]

The China fantasy had been devised inside a pro-Trump political shop blandly called the Government Accountability Institute that functioned as a political version of Dr. Frankenstein's laboratory. Founded by Steve Bannon before he became Trump's campaign manager, GAI employed lawyers, researchers, and writers to develop articles and reports that smeared Trump's opponents. The team was led by a writer named Peter Schweizer, who pasted together this material to produce books that became huge bestsellers thanks to heavy promotion in conservative media. By inflating some facts and leaving out others, Schweizer cleverly affirmed the worst about people his readers had already been taught to hate. So doing, he also supplied inflammatory ideas for the likes of Giuliani and Trump who could talk about how they had heard, or read, something startling that deserves more attention.[6]

• • •

With Rudy and Lev globe-trotting again, ordinary diplomats and national security experts had no reason to hope that Ukraine would be freed from the president's squeeze any time soon. In fact, as the talks in Madrid were finished, OMB political appointee Michael Duffey signed a letter notifying officials at the State Department of a "reapportionment" of the nearly $400 million slated to go to Ukraine. This seemingly innocuous term indicated that not only was the hold still in effect but that the administration was considering other options for the money. This move confirmed that Duffey had taken control of the process away from the government workers charged with managing the machinery at the Departments of State and Defense. At the Pentagon, Elaine McCusker warned that the further delay meant the administration could no longer be sure the aid could be sent in a "timely" way, which Duffey still claimed. Later in the month, McCusker would ask about the reason for the hold. This echoed her concern, early in the tussle over the aid, about whether Duffey's moves could be justified within the law on impoundment.[7]

The continued hold also indicated that despite THE CALL, the pressure was still on Zelensky. Yermak understood this was true, and when he returned to Kiev, he spoke with Kurt Volker about how to satisfy Trump. Volker circled back to Giuliani, who was, it seemed, once again the main interpreter of the president's demands. In a cheery August 8 text that was also sent to Sondland, he wrote:

> **VOLKER:** Hi Mr Mayor! Had a good chat with Yermak last night. He was pleased with your phone call. Mentioned Z making a statement. Can we all get on the phone to make sure I advise Z correctly as to what he should be saying? Want to make sure we get this done right. Thanks!

> **SONDLAND:** Good idea Kurt. I am on Pacific time.

> **GIULIANI:** Yes can you call now going to Fundraiser at 12:30.

The fundraiser was one of several that would be attended by wealthy Trump loyalists in the tony Long Island resort towns known, collectively, as the Hamptons. The Trump 2020 campaign expected to raise $10 million at two events where attendees who paid $100,000 got a photo with the president and those who paid $250,000 got to sit with him. Others would be kept at a distance. Rudy attended the bigger bash, where five hundred people listened to Trump speak in his version of a Japanese accent as he explained how he asked Prime Minister Shinzo Abe about the motivations of World War II kamikaze pilots. Abe replied that they acted out of love for their country.

In addition to offering the Abe anecdote and inside jokes about recent corporate controversies, Trump commiserated with real estate tycoons who disliked New York rent control laws and complained about the press—"Fake News!" He also scanned the crowd for familiar faces and, like the master of ceremonies at a banquet, called out greetings to those he recognized. Having visited the sites of two mass shootings two days earlier, guns were on the president's mind. When he noticed his son Donald Jr. in the crowd, he quipped, "Don Jr. is my gun expert. He knows more about guns than anyone I know." He hastily added, "We need meaningful [gun purchase] background checks. It is time."[8]

In a crowd that was heavy on New York real estate developers and investment bankers, Rudy Giuliani fit in well. It wasn't just that he had become immensely wealthy himself, although that helped. No, he benefited more from the fact that these people remembered his rallying performance as mayor of New York City during 9/11 and that he was very close to the president. Giuliani mattered in a way that he hadn't in nearly twenty years. And though they couldn't be aware of what Giuliani was quietly doing to help the president as he flitted between Washington, New York, Kiev, Paris, London, and Madrid, the story might be told one day, and it was possible that then Rudy Giuliani would be a hero and a leader once again.

That Giuliani, the private lawyer, was in charge of the federal diplomats working on the Ukraine problem was evident in text messages that eventually became public. With the U.S. government's fiscal year, and the chance for sending authorized aid, ending on October 1, Andriy Yermak began pressing Kurt Volker about setting a date for Zelensky's White House visit. Yermak wanted the assurance of a firm date for the visit before Zelensky made a public statement on what Sondland called the "deliverables" Trump wanted. The president's team wanted Zelensky to go first.

On Saturday, August 10, Yermak worked into the night in Kiev while the dinner hour approached where Volker was in the United States. Finally, the two men struck what seemed to be a diplomatic solution to the puzzle of who was to take the first step. They agreed to work together on Zelensky's statement, which would be sent to the White House for review. With this draft indicating the process had begun, Washington could then specify when the Ukrainian president could come visit. It was after midnight in Kiev when they agreed on this approach. In the coming week, Sondland would acknowledge when Volker wrote to him that in Zelensky's statement:

> Special attention should be paid to the problem of interference in the political processes of the United States especially with the alleged involvement of some Ukrainian politicians. I want to declare that this is unacceptable. We intend to initiate and complete a transparent and unbiased investigation of all available facts and episodes, including those involving Burisma and the 2016 U.S. elections, which in turn will prevent the recurrence of this problem in the future.[9]

As numerous fact-checking organizations would confirm, the two notions Volker mentioned—that Ukraine had interfered with the 2016 U.S. election and that the Burisma issue was a serious concern—were not supported by real evidence and not accepted by well-informed people outside the president's circle of political and media supporters. Biden's son did take a high-paying position on Burisma's board, but the vice president had done nothing to help him or the firm. More troubling for the Ukrainians was the convoluted tale the president's side told about Ukraine boosting Hillary Clinton in 2016.

The story of Ukraine helping Clinton was told to suggest that both candidates had benefited from outside help in 2016 and therefore Trump had not been especially advantaged. Of course, this wasn't true. National intelligence officials had briefed the president himself on a government investigation that found no evidence that hackers who attacked the Democrats were Ukrainians. A second branch of the conspiracy theory, which suggested the Ukrainian government itself helped Clinton, was based on reports that some officials in Kiev hoped she would win. In fact, while the Kremlin conducted a massive criminal assault on the American election, there had been no Ukrainian government–backed interference of any kind. However, U.S. experts did discover a years-long Russian propaganda effort to smear Ukraine with this suggestion.

All the important facts would have been available to Sondland and Volker from inside the State Department and were available in news reports. But they did not serve the president's purpose, which he chose to advance himself by again dangling the carrot Kiev desired. This move came when Trump paused to speak with reporters as he left the White House for a flight aboard the presidential helicopter, Marine One. Journalists had come to refer to these moments as "Chopper Talks" because they were accompanied by the sound of the helicopter's engines and rotors, which added to the stagecraft—it made things seem more urgent—and allowed him to pretend to not hear certain questions. In this particular Chopper Talk, Trump seemed to send signals to both Zelensky and Putin:[10]

REPORTER: Mr. President, do you plan to invite your Ukrainian counterpart, Volodymyr Zelensky, to the White House? And what would be your advice for him—

TRUMP: Who are you talking about?

REPORTER: The President of Ukraine, Volodymyr Zelensky.

TRUMP: Yeah.

REPORTER: Do you plan to invite him to the White House? And what would be your advice for him on how to communicate with Vladimir Putin to stop the conflict in Eastern Ukraine?

TRUMP: I think he's going to make a deal with President Putin, and he will be invited to the White House. And we look forward to seeing him. He's already been invited to the White House, and he wants to come. And I think he will. He's a very reasonable guy. He wants to see peace in Ukraine. And I think he will be coming very soon, actually.[11]

As the president spoke and the blades of Marine One noisily whirred, *The Washington Post* noted on its website that he had crossed the twelve thousand mark in its tally of his false and misleading statements. *The Post* and others had begun to count and report this number as a way to cope with the sheer volume of Trump's distortions, which ranged from outright lies to deceptive wordplay. No public figure had ever presented the news media of the American people with the challenge Trump posed as he reflexively mutilated the truth. In the past, presidents so rarely offered the kind of distortions Trump spouted that, when they occurred, the press would pore over them for days, or even weeks, until the facts were firmly established. In Trump's case, they came at a rate of more than a dozen per day, which made this kind of examination impossible. With so much poison pouring into the political environment, the press was reduced to pointing out the phenomenon rather than each element of it.[12]

• • •

Following the president's other forms of subterfuge required more than mere counting and observation. At the Department of Defense, Elaine McCusker kept a close watch on Michael Duffey's manipulation of Ukraine's military aid. On August 9, she sent him a reminder that a long hold on the funds could make it impossible for them to be sent on time. "As we discussed," she wrote, "as of 12 AUG I don't think we can agree that the pause 'will not preclude timely execution.' We hope it won't and will do all we can to execute once the policy decision is made, but can no longer make that declarative statement."

When August 12 rolled around, she wrote again, and copied Mark Sandy of OMB. This time she wanted confirmation that OMB understood "that exe cution risk increases with continued delays." As a career civil servant, McCusker wrote in the legalese that was required in her profession, but the words conveyed something plainly serious. In this exchange, McCusker and Duffey discussed a meeting the president would soon convene at his golf club in Bedminster, New Jersey, where the heads of national security agencies were expected to be in attendance. Since Bolton was to participate, it was possible, if not likely, that the Ukraine situation would be discussed. However, the lawyer who worked with McCusker would not wait for this group to get together. They began studying what the White House was doing to determine whether the policy of holding the aid hostage until Zelensky performed a political favor could, in any way, be legal.[13]

As the official whom Michael Duffey was required to notify so that the president's wishes would be heeded, McCusker was a serious, by-the-book type with a deep commitment to the mission of the Defense Department. Her position as comptroller made her the chief financial officer of an entity that churned through more than $700 billion per year. If the Pentagon were a country, its budget would make it the twentieth largest in the world, by gross domestic product. The office McCusker led was so important that it occupied a large section in the Pentagon's coveted E Ring, which offered the building's only views of the exterior world.

Born and raised in the small city of Pekin, Illinois, where Everett Dirksen was a favorite son, McCusker had excelled in every prior position, developing expertise in both finance and military technology. She had led an effort to design a safe combat transport for troops in Iraq and visited the war zone to evaluate its performance. Though a Republican, she had won awards from both Republican and Democratic presidents, and she had climbed steadily in the Pentagon bureaucracy. She had been named to her current job by President Trump and came to it from a top position managing the flow of resources for the U.S. Central Command at MacDill Air Force Base in Florida.

Her path through adult life, in which she moved from one highly responsible but low-visibility position to another, had brought her to one of the highest positions in the vast Pentagon management scheme, where she reported directly to the deputy secretary of defense. No one could reach her position without mastering a vast system of checks and balances that required adherence to laws and regulations. In contrast, Duffey had devoted his adult life to the practice of politics and public relations, where he manipulated perceptions and found ways to carry out the dictates of his superiors despite the obstacles.[14]

If Duffey didn't know that in McCusker he had encountered a formidable bureaucrat, he should have. When the Bedminster meeting happened and he informed her that "Ukraine was not discussed," she was in the middle of devising a way for the aid to be expedited the moment the hold was lifted. Inside the Department of Defense, she alerted her colleagues that members of Congress who were headed to Ukraine had asked for information about the funding. At the end of August, when Duffey again extended the freeze on the aid, McCusker asked him, "What is the status of the impoundment paperwork?"

"I am not tracking that. Is that something you are expecting from OMB?" replied Duffey.

"Yes, it is now necessary—legal teams were discussing last week."

McCusker's eleven-word message indicated that she was not alone in her concerns about the mission Duffey had been conducting and signaled that problems lay ahead. Later on the very same day, she vented frustration, telling Duffey that the top lawyer at OMB, Mark Paoletta, "appears to continue to consistently misunderstand the process and the timelines we have provided for funds execution. Are you working with him and can you help?" She also informed Duffey that members of the Senate Armed Services Committee and the House Appropriations Committee were "asking questions." This not-so-veiled warning suggested that the scheme to exploit Ukraine's vulnerability would not remain secret for very long. Indeed, within a day, an executive for a U.S. contractor awaiting funds to cover equipment it was producing for Ukraine went straight to the secretary of defense with their questions about the money they were supposed to receive. The question quickly found its way to McCusker, who responded with restrained exasperation: "Recognizing the importance of decision space, but this situation is really unworkable [and] made particularly difficult because OMB lawyers continue to consistently mis-characterize the process—and the information we have provided. They keep repeating that this pause will not impact DOD's ability to execute on time."

Within the Department of Defense, concerns for Ukraine's military vulnerability and the Pentagon's responsibilities were rising. Federal law did not seem to permit the delay that Michael Duffey was orchestrating. One level up from McCusker, the deputy secretary of defense was drafting a letter to OMB chief Russell Vought that would spell out the legal ramifications of the hold. It would suggest that the administration would soon be obligated to go to Congress and formally propose eliminating or delaying the aid into the next fiscal year.[15]

· · ·

As Elaine McCusker had watched the clock tick in Washington, the new U.S. ambassador to Ukraine, William Taylor, had been trying to keep track of the aid funding from his post in Kiev. On August 22, he called Tim Morrison at the National Security Council, who told him that the president "doesn't want to provide any assistance at all." Months before, as he had accepted the assignment to replace Marie Yovanovitch, Taylor had warned the secretary of state that he would resign if America failed to support Ukraine in its standoff with Russia. When he heard Morrison's assessment of the president's intentions, he began to think that he might have to follow through on his condition.

Finally, someone, somewhere, took the path followed by countless disgruntled Washington players and told the press that Ukraine's aid package had been held up. On the last Wednesday of August, the website *Politico* published an article by writers Caitlin Emma and Connor O'Brien titled "Trump Holds Up Ukraine Military Aid Meant to Confront Russia." Although the report understated the value of the aid, it properly focused attention on all the key concerns. It noted that the money was an important symbol of America's attitude toward Russia and that "scaling back that assistance could expose Trump to allegations that his policies are favoring Moscow."

Other than a vague statement that American interests were at stake, *Politico* was unable to obtain a clear explanation for the hold from the White House. The Defense Department was more direct, as a source there explained that a Pentagon review had approved the spending. Touching all the bases, the reporters went to Congress and got an earful from both Republicans and Democrats. The most pungent comment came from Senator Bob Menendez, a Democrat from New Jersey, who was the lead member of the minority on the Foreign Relations Committee. Menendez had been aware of the struggle over the money and had run out of patience. "Enough is enough," he said. "President Trump should stop worrying about disappointing Vladimir Putin and stand up for U.S. national security priorities."

Published just before Labor Day, which is the quietest period on Washington's calendar, the *Politico* article was all but ignored by the rest of the press. What did capture attention was Hurricane Dorian, which was bearing down on Florida. President Trump made certain the storm would dominate the news when he used a Sharpie to alter a National Weather Service map in order to score a political point. As he was caught in the act, his ridiculous behavior served to distract from serious issues like the struggle over the aid to Ukraine. Such distractions were essential to Trump's political method.[16]

Inside the government, Elaine McCusker was not going to let the Pentagon fall into a controversy born of the president's political selfishness. When the OMB lawyer Paoletta suggested that everyone could say that "no action has been taken by OMB that would preclude the obligation of these funds before the end of the fiscal year," McCusker pushed back, writing in terms that showed she could break the bureaucrat mold any time she chose: "I don't agree to the revised TPs [talking points]—the last one is just not accurate from a financial execution standpoint, something we have been consistently conveying for a few weeks."

Among her Department of Defense colleagues, McCusker warned that "OMB continues to ignore our repeated explanation regarding how the process works." On August 29, the chief of staff to Secretary of Defense Mark Esper told her that his boss and Secretary of State Mike Pompeo would discuss the Ukraine aid with the president "tomorrow." When tomorrow came, it was Duffey who told McCusker, "Clear direction from POTUS to hold" the funds.

As far as anyone at the Pentagon or the Office of Management and Budget knew, the next steps would involve Vice President Mike Pence and Volodymyr Zelensky, who were to meet at ceremonies marking the eightieth anniversary of the start of World War II. At this point, just thirty days remained before the fiscal year would end, and the administration could find itself in violation of the impoundment act. For McCusker, this was such a concern that she dashed off another note to Esper's chief of staff, asking, "Do you believe DOD is adequately protected from what may happen as a result of the Ukraine obligation pause? I realize we need to continue to give the WH has [*sic*] much decision space as possible, but am concerned we have not officially documented the fact that we cannot promise full execution at this point in the [fiscal year]."[17]

At the White House, the president, whose very identity had been built on breaking the rules others followed, proceeded with business as usual. He took to Twitter to feud with the actress Debra Messing, who had criticized him, and to rail at former FBI director James Comey. In one two-day span, he played weatherman as he issued more than one hundred social media updates about the hurricane. The president also gave a symbolic middle-finger salute to conservationists by reversing a bipartisan policy that called for energy-efficient lightbulbs, and he ordered funds shifted from defense to the construction of a wall on America's southern border, which he had promised to build with funds from Mexico.[18]

12

THE WHISTLEBLOWER

In addition, I want to meet not only my accuser, who presented SECOND & THIRD HAND INFORMATION, but also the person who illegally gave this information, which was largely incorrect, to the "Whistleblower." Was this person SPYING on the U.S. President? Big Consequences!

—Donald Trump, president of the United States, via Twitter,
September 29, 2019

A man who functioned much like a shark, moving ever forward and never looking back, Donald Trump was not the type to suffer over his phone call with Volodymyr Zelensky. Having seen that his trusted men—Giuliani, Parnas, Sondland, and Volker—had almost overcome the Deep State to win Ukraine's political cooperation, the president had assumed the role of the supersalesman, or "closer," who would seal the deal. And given the way Zelensky sounded—friendly, cooperative, eager—it seemed like he had played things just right.

But standing on the sideline, close enough to hear THE CALL and access the record of it before it was buried in a secure electronic repository, were national security experts who couldn't stop looking back at it. One of them was Lieutenant Colonel Alexander Vindman, who had submitted corrections for the call record and shared his concerns with his twin brother, Yevgeny, who held the proper clearances and also worked for the National Security Council. Another insider considered the call, and other actions taken by the president and his helpers, and began drafting a letter to the chairmen of the Intelligence Committees of the House and Senate. The first sentence of the letter was direct and concise: "I am reporting an 'urgent concern' in accordance with the procedures outlined in 50 U.S.C. §3033(k)(5)(A). This letter is UNCLASSI-FIED when separated from the attachment."[1]

The statute cited by the writer lays out the process that must be followed when someone inside the United States Intelligence Community wants to report potential wrongdoing to Congress. Known by the shorthand IC, this community is composed of powerful organizations with acronyms that can send shivers up the spine. The CIA (Central Intelligence Agency), DIA (Defense Intelligence Agency), and NSA (National Security Agency) are among the big ones, but the membership includes more than a dozen others. In this community, the landscape is shadowed by secrecy, and inhabitants assume that double agents walk among them. Arrests and assassinations occur with a frequency that makes vigilance part of everyone's job description. The stakes are so high that everyone is expected to be on the look-out for double agents, and paranoia is an occupational hazard.

Theoretically, 50 U.S.C. §3033(k)(5)(A) created a way for insiders—you might call them *whistleblowers*—to report "a serious or flagrant problem, abuse, or violation of law" to the congressional committees that oversee the IC without revealing secrets or running afoul of their superiors. It allows a whistleblower to act anonymously and, given the explosive nature of the complaint and the high probability that Trump would seek retribution, this one requested this protection.[2]

As used in the letter, the term *urgent concern* was intended to draw the attention of Intelligence Community inspector general Michael Atkinson, whose office would be the first stop for any complaint directed at the committees. Appointed in 2018 by President Trump, Atkinson had worked for fifteen years in the Department of Justice. As inspector general, he operated apart from the IC but with access to its resources. It was his job to separate personal quarrels and trivial matters from credible alerts that deserved attention at the highest level. In this case, the whistleblower pointed to a problem that would have been unimaginable during any other administration. He (the person was almost certainly male) said he had received information that: "The President of the United States is using the power of his office to solicit interference of a country in the 2020 U.S. election. This interference includes, among other things, pressuring a foreign country to investigate one of the President's main domestic political rivals. The President's personal lawyer, Mr. Rudolph Giuliani, is a central figure in this effort. Attorney General Barr appears to be involved as well."

By framing the complaint in the present tense, the whistleblower emphasized that his concern was as urgent as a crime being reported in progress. By referencing the president and attorney general, along with the president's private lawyer, he surely captured Atkinson's attention for the information that was to follow in seven single-spaced, footnoted pages that contained no classified material. Though not laden with intelligence secrets, it was shocking in what it revealed about a monthslong campaign, witnessed by more than half a dozen high-level officials, to use Ukraine's military aid as bait to get President Zelensky to work for Donald Trump's political cause.

First in the whistleblower's accounting of the evidence was "the 25 July Presidential phone call," which was described in detail. The writer said that officials who had listened in—he had only seen the readout—were concerned that they were witnesses to the president committing a possible "abuse of his office for personal gain." After the call came an attempted cover-up as White House personnel sought to "lock down" all records of the call, "especially the official word-for-word transcript." According to the complaint, a senior White House lawyer moved the transcript to a computer system outside the one usually used for records of a president's contacts with foreign leaders.

"One White House official described this act as an abuse of this electronic system," wrote the whistleblower, "because the call did not contain anything remotely sensitive from a national security perspective." With this in mind, the whistleblower suggested that "White House officials understood the gravity of what had transpired in the call."

The rest of the letter reviewed the whistleblower's insider knowledge about the BLT Group's effort to remove Ambassador Yovanovitch and the scheme to get Ukraine to both smear the Bidens and rewrite the history of the 2016 election. Though rife with deceit, these plots were not especially complex when compared with the byzantine norms of spy craft. However, they were exceptional because they had been directed by the president of the United States, who involved himself as the schemes' ultimate agent. He was the one who at the key moment picked up the phone and said, "I would like you to do us a favor though." This phrase announced that the president was attaching a new condition to aid that had already been promised to Ukraine. What he wanted was a series of personal political favors, and he was using authorized federal aid, nearly $400 million, to get them.

To Atkinson's eye, the complaint met the urgent concern standard, and following procedure, he sent it to the director of national intelligence, who, as a member of the president's cabinet, oversaw the entire intelligence community.

The DNI position had been created after the terrorist attacks of September 11, 2001, exposed communication breakdowns among the many agencies responsible for various aspects of national security. On August 26, when Atkinson forwarded the whistleblower's complaint and observed that it was "urgent and credible," the DNI, Joseph Maguire, had been on the job for all of two full days. His title came with the qualifier *acting* because, like so many administration officials, he had not been confirmed by the United States Senate.[3]

Maguire, who had just turned sixty-eight, had been a commander of a Navy SEAL team and served in the wars in Iraq and Afghanistan. He retired from military service in 2010 with the rank of vice admiral. In the period since, he had worked as a consultant for the international firm Booz Allen Hamilton. His appointment was made after the president's initial choice, an intensely argumentative and partisan Republican congressman named John Ratcliffe, was found to have inflated his personal résumé. Having been suddenly drafted back into government service, Maguire was still using a satellite navigation device to find his way to work every morning. The whistleblower's letter was the political equivalent of a massive improvised explosive device discovered in the middle of a roadway back in Afghanistan. He would need a bit of time to get his bearings and figure out how to deal with it.

In the meantime, the whistleblower, anxious to see his concern taken seriously but worried for himself, contacted one of the few Washington attorneys known for representing whistleblowers in the intelligence community. Andrew Bakaj had been a senior investigator in the Pentagon's inspector general office and had also worked at the CIA. When he entered private legal practice, he cofounded a group dedicated to IC whistleblowers. It was called Compass Rose, after the compass emblem on the CIA seal, which refers to the agency's worldwide mission to gather accurate intelligence. Whistleblowers sometimes do occupy points on that compass and can supply vital, if occasionally disruptive, information.

Bakaj and his partner, Mark Zaid, had always understood that bureaucracies tend to treat whistleblowers with skepticism, resistance, and worse, but they believed that with his many public complaints about leaks to the press and demands for personal loyalty, President Trump had created an atmosphere of unprecedented hostility toward those who felt a duty to report suspected wrongdoing. Bakaj was known in the intelligence community because he had led the development of the system devised to make whistleblowing possible. However, he had misgivings about the way different agencies would treat whistleblowers and was especially concerned about how the CIA, where this one worked, would respond.

Worried about the intrigue and crosscurrents of the intelligence and political worlds, the whistleblower contacted Bakaj even as the complaint letter was still under official consideration. In their first conversations, Bakaj tested the caller for telltale signs of trouble. Effective whistleblowers are devoted to their jobs but also have well-rounded lives. They have supportive friends and family. They have outside interests. They aren't inclined toward obsessive and paranoid thinking. (In the world of spies, a little paranoia can be helpful. More than a little is crippling.) Good whistleblowers understand that whatever concerns they're raising, it's about the national interest and not themselves. This whistleblower seemed the kind of person who was acting for all the right reasons and could withstand what might come.

Given the whistleblower's need to be discreet, which meant he couldn't be overheard, Bakaj sometimes conducted calls while in his car. A favorite route, because traffic was typically light and slow moving, would take him around and around the White House. He would follow the route ten or more times before a conversation ended. It wasn't lost on him that he was listening to someone who could cause a big problem for the president while literally circling 1600 Pennsylvania Avenue.

At home, Bakaj's wife and daughter noticed he was a little more preoccupied than usual and putting in somewhat longer hours. One evening as he came home late and poked around in the refrigerator, his wife asked how his work was going. "Well, I've got this new case. I can't talk about it, but it's pretty significant, I think, and either you'll know about it or you won't. But it's pretty big and it involves some pretty senior people."

Bakaj didn't act until Joseph Maguire missed the deadline for sending a notice about the complaint. "I got a status update that it was being prohibited from going to the Hill," recalled Bakaj months later. "That had never happened before." In fact, in the normal process the inspector general would send a complaint to the director of national intelligence, in this case Maguire, who would tell the IG to notify Capitol Hill and conduct a full investigation. Sometimes the DNI might add a comment to the notice but otherwise let the IG carry out the work. When this didn't happen, Bakaj had what he would call an "oh shit moment." He thought, *Who can conduct oversight of the president? Congress.* In fact, if Maguire did what he was supposed to do, Democrats and Republicans in Congress "would battle it out. But that's not our battle. We're just transmitting information." When he asked why his client's complaint wasn't being forwarded, Bakaj was told that DNI Maguire had concluded that it was "outside the scope" of the whistleblower law.

On September 9, 2019, after the deadline for sending notice to Congress passed, Bakaj left home in the morning after telling his wife, rather cryptically, "Just so you know, I'm going to go up to the Hill today and something's about to go down, because there's some crazy shit happening." Her response was, "Okay."

He then went to Capitol Hill carrying letters for Senator Richard Burr and Representative Adam Schiff, who chaired the Intelligence Committees of Congress. He intended to hand deliver them to aides he knew at both committees. To do this, he had to pass through security stations, deposit electronic devices in a holding area, and be cleared by guards to enter spy-proof rooms. In the Senate, committee staff did not want to see Bakaj, but they accepted his letter and recorded its delivery. When they read it, they learned only that Bakaj was representing an anonymous whistleblower whose complaint had been submitted but was stuck in the DNI's office. Bakaj wrote nothing about the content of the complaint and didn't request that anything be done.

In the House, Intelligence Committee staff were willing to see Bakaj, and they asked him to sit with them in their windowless hushed office while they opened and read the letter. As they finished a brief conversation in which Bakaj still wouldn't disclose the subject of his client's complaint, one of the three lawyers left and quickly returned with a document. The three staffers asked him to wait while they huddled.

"They all just go pale," explained Bakaj later. "They're like, 'We just received an email from the ICIG. We can't show you just yet.' They put the letter now underneath the one that I sent. 'And everything that the ICIG just transmitted matches up exactly with what you're providing us.' It's freaking them out. They said, 'It's a mirror image. Let's just say we view it as very credible. And I said, 'Well, thank you.'"

ICIG Atkinson's email discussed, at length, the problem with the whistleblower complaint. He reviewed the course of action prescribed by the law and noted that everything had proceeded normally until acting DNI Maguire determined that he was "not required to transmit my determination of a credible and urgent concern, or any of the Complainant's information." Atkinson was careful to note that he believed Maguire was acting "in good faith" but added that the DNI's decision "does not appear to be consistent with past practice."

Atkinson also said he would continue to work with Maguire to resolve the apparent stalemate and keep the committee informed of his progress.[4]

Atkinson's letter, which like the one from Bakaj was unclassified, put down a marker. He believed something strange was going on, and he wasn't going to leave it unresolved. The copy he sent to Maguire meant that the DNI and, presumably the White House, would be very aware of the brewing conflict. If this wasn't clear, it would have become clear on September 13 when Schiff, the only Democrat with the power to act, sent a subpoena to Maguire requesting not only the complaint but also any correspondence he had related to it.

Schiff's letter noted that the deadline for Maguire to forward the notice of complaint had been September 2: "More than ten days later, the Committee has not received the disclosure, in violation of the law." Blunt as this note was, Schiff made the impending crisis plain with a paragraph he chose to make bold in the typescript:

> **The Committee can only conclude . . . that the serious misconduct at issue involves the President of the United States and/or other senior White House or Administration officials. This raises grave concerns that your office, together with the Department of Justice and possibly the White House, are engaged in an unlawful effort to protect the President and conceal from the Committee information related to his possible serious or flagrant misconduct abuse of power, or violation of law.**

As Schiff wrote, Maguire had worked in concert with the Justice Department's Office of Legal Counsel, which, despite its rather innocuous name, wields enormous power as it advises the executive branch on legal and constitutional matters. Often treated as an authority equal to a federal court, the OLC's opinions are used by the attorney general to support key decisions and positions. For example, it was the OLC that determined that the Constitution protects the president from many legal actions until he or she leaves office. Short of a Supreme Court decision overturning it, the opinion is regarded as the law of the land. The OLC also produced the infamous memos that justified the use of torture in the post-9/11 war on terror and in the Trump era had been responsible for a slew of opinions supporting controversial policies. Some OLC opinions are rendered in secret, which makes it hard for anyone to challenge them. When Barr headed the office during the George H. W. Bush administration, it produced a secret memo to support kidnappings, in foreign countries, by U.S. agents.[5]

Barr's opinion justifying kidnappings was revealed as a result of congressional and public pressure. The same factors started to work in the case of the whistleblower. On September 18, *The Washington Post* reported on a building conflict between the House and the administration over a whistleblower complaint related to the president's contacts with an unnamed foreign leader. After Atkinson met the next day with Schiff's committee, the press reported that the country at issue was Ukraine. A cascade of public statements by the president and Rudy Giuliani made it clear that Trump had repeatedly urged Ukraine to investigate the Bidens and that this was one of the whistleblower's concerns.

Then on September 20, with the prime minister of Australia on hand in the Oval Office, Trump responded to reporters' questions about the complaint. He said that, at the White House, "everybody has read it and they laugh at it. And it's another—it's another media disaster. The media has lost so much credibility in this country. Our media has become the laughingstock of the world."[6]

Within days, Trump would confess that he had withheld Ukraine's military aid but claimed he did so because he was concerned about corruption in Kiev and about whether the European Union shouldered its share of the burden of helping an ally. This was when he began describing the call with Zelensky as "perfect." To be precise, he called it "absolutely perfect." Two days later, having advertised it as flawless, he tried to get ahead of the controversy by releasing the rough transcript of the call, as made by officials who had listened in.[7]

So few Americans would read the document that the president's claim would suffice to persuade his supporters that it was indeed perfect. In the months ahead, he would repeat the claim over and over again, and at his rallies, his loyalists would wave signs that read "Read the Transcript," as if it proved he did nothing wrong. In fact, the transcript revealed that Trump had tried to force Zelensky to serve him politically and used taxpayer funds to do it. It was such an egregious abuse of an ally and of presidential power that it could only be described as perfect by someone who was looking for an example of how a president might put the lives of allied soldiers at risk to satisfy a partisan whim.

The release of the call record freed Maguire to talk about the whistleblower's complaint in public at a hearing of the House Intelligence Committee. Maguire defended his decision to seek an OLC opinion on the complaint but also said he believed it was made in "good faith" and that he supported the whistleblower's decision to file it. In its report, *The Washington Post* noted that it may have been a "dry run" of future impeachment hearings.

Eight weeks prior to this moment, Special Counsel Robert Mueller's halting testimony before Congress about his report on the president and Russia's attack on the U.S. election had seemed to foreclose the possibility of impeaching the president. That the president had, on the very next day, made the "absolutely perfect call" that revived the possibility of his removal was head spinning. However, what Mueller had revealed was, for those who cared to read his report, a picture of a president who took extraordinary risks and did things that would shock the conscience in order to advance his own interests. Mueller and the whistleblower had observed the same heedless, reckless, and unfit man, and it was the totality of the record that would demand that Congress act.

PART II

MUELLER AND HIS REPORT

13

WAITING FOR MUELLER

The Phony Witch Hunt continues, but Mueller and his gang of Angry Dems are only looking at one side, not the other. Wait until it comes out how horribly & viciously they are treating people, ruining lives for them refusing to lie. Mueller is a conflicted prosecutor gone rogue.

—Donald Trump, president of the United States, via Twitter,
November 27, 2018

Democrats almost swept the boards in the 2018 midterm election, a result born of smart campaigning on their part and the two years of chaos and scandal produced by Donald Trump and his White House team. Thanks to victories in more than forty Republican-held districts, the Democrats gained a majority in the House of Representatives. Big wins in various statehouses, where they picked up more than three hundred seats, threatened the redistricting schemes Republicans had used to whittle safe congressional districts out of regions that would, without gerrymandering, go to their opponents.

However, as big as the so-called Blue Wave of 2018 was, it could not wash the GOP out of its controlling position in the United States Senate. Here, the outcome was determined by the fact that only nine Republican senators needed to defend their seats compared with twenty-six Democrats. This imbalance allowed them to actually add to their Senate majority, which grew from fifty-one seats to fifty-three. This result made majority leader Mitch McConnell of Kentucky an even more powerful ally for the president.

Once a party elder who abhorred Trump's bad manners, McConnell had become his chief protector and enabler. By controlling Senate confirmation votes, he guaranteed the lifetime appointments of nearly two hundred right-wing judges, including many deemed unqualified by the American Bar Association. One example: Justin Walker, age thirty-seven, joined the powerful U.S. Court of Appeals in the District of Columbia. He had never tried a case in any court, and it wasn't clear that he had spent much time at all practicing law. However, he was ideologically pure, and McConnell had mentored him since he had been a high schooler. In addition to helping Trump's nominees, the majority leader also shepherded his one big legislative initiative—a massive tax cut that overwhelmingly favored the rich—through Congress, and he denied Democrats the chance to have their proposals ever considered.[1]

McConnell had become devoted to Trump after polls had shown that in his own state, he was far less popular than the president. Trump had won Kentucky by thirty points in 2016. By 2018, McConnell's approval rating was drifting toward 33 percent. His political security depended on demonstrating he was as loyal to the president as any dog would be to his master. Thus, after the election, McConnell's most important duty would be to protect Trump from whatever accountability—including impeachment—might be suggested by the results of Special Counsel Robert Mueller's investigations into Russia's attack on the 2016 election and Team Trump's response to it.

Ever since Rod Rosenstein had named Mueller special counsel, in an effort to put the Russia probe beyond the president's reach, the probe had cast a shadow over the political landscape. As Trump grew ever more angry and critical of Mueller, many Democrats anticipated a report from him that would support Trump's removal. Mitch McConnell, carefully managing his relationship with Trump, reminded Democrats that even if the House managed to impeach Trump, the effort might backfire since his GOP-controlled Senate was certain to find him not guilty. "I think it'll help the president get re-elected," he said of impeachment. "This business of presidential harassment may or may not quite be the winner they think it is."[2]

Unimaginable in most political eras, impeachment had become a viable option when a Republican-controlled House impeached Bill Clinton for lying about a sexual affair. Prior to his trial, the only presidential impeachment proceeding ever brought in the Senate had been against Andrew Johnson in 1868. He was found not guilty and, more than a century later, Clinton was found not guilty too. Afterward, talk of impeachment arose during the presidencies of both George W. Bush and Barack Obama. However, neither Bush nor Obama had crossed lines in the way that Trump had. As the 2018 election gave Democrats the power to initiate the process, it was possible to suggest that the voters had, with their ballots, indicated impeachment should be considered.

If impeachment was in the air, then the person selected to be Speaker of the House would occupy the second most pressurized job in Washington. Nancy Pelosi, who had held the post the last time the Democrats controlled the House, from 2007 to 2011, had broad support to return to it. A seventy-eight-year-old with more than three decades in the House, a professed lover of chocolate and the *New York Times* crossword puzzle, Pelosi faced opposition from her left, where some emboldened young liberals were not willing to wait for the evolution of national political affairs. They preferred a revolution, and in the heady period that followed Election Day 2018, they dreamed it was at hand.

Although newcomers like Alexandria Ocasio-Cortez of New York had used modern methods and boldly liberal ideas to become overnight political sensations, decades in the House had taught Pelosi how to maintain both her individual claim to power and her party's majority in the House. When sixty-six members decided to withhold their support for her bid to return to the Speaker's post, she called in some markers and made some promises, including a pledge to make way for a younger generation's leader in 2022. (By then, Trump would either be out of office or approaching lame duck status.) When House members finally chose their leaders, Pelosi got all but fifteen Democrats to select her.[3]

Those constituents—or rather, voters—occupied Pelosi's mind as she contemplated the ways that the House, under her party's control, could conduct oversight over Trump. The lack of such oversight, owing to the fact that the president's party had held both the House and Senate in the past two years, had made it relatively easy for him to escape examination and ignore all those Americans who had voted for his opponent in 2016 and opposed his agenda. With political polls showing a majority of Americans uncertain about impeachment but concerned about a reckless president, Pelosi planned to move cautiously. What was important to her was that the House retain the power to check the president, and this would only happen if the Democrats held it for as long as possible.

Fortunately for Pelosi, she had an advantage over McConnell, who faced real political peril in his home state, where voters were rabidly pro-Trump. In the last two elections, she won with between 72 and 87 percent of the vote and enjoyed her constituents' trust to such a degree that she could resist those who called for Trump's immediate impeachment and thereby protect vulnerable Democrats in closely contested districts. In these so-called frontline districts moderate voters, who might choose a Republican in one election and a Democrat in the next, held sway. To assure them that her party was also moderate, Pelosi could cool the impeachment fever. This was the choice she made, and the front lines would become some of her most loyal troops.

"We believe that we have a responsibility to seek common ground where we can," said Pelosi. "Where we cannot we must stand our ground, but we must try." Impeachment hearings may come, she said, but she preferred that the Democrats not go it alone. "When we go down any of these paths, we'll know what we're doing, and we'll do it right," while trying to "unify the country."[4]

•   •   •

No one could take Trump seriously when he mentioned bipartisanship in the wake of the election. Consensus had never been his way. Nevertheless, he talked about it. "It really could be a beautiful bipartisan type of situation," said Trump on the morning after the election. "There are a lot of great things we can do together."[5]

Unity would be difficult with America so divided and a president so strident. Trump's popularity depended on a style nasty enough to thrill supporters who spat on journalists and screamed "Fuck the media!" at his rallies and agreed with him when he said that Democrats committed treason when they failed to applaud sufficiently for his State of the Union address. Trump also indulged in applying demeaning nicknames to his critics and political opponents. These labels were profane, bigoted, misogynistic, and puerile, but they resonated with his core supporters. They had been drawn into his camp by Trump's message of rage and grievance against the political establishment and stayed because they were entertained by his pro-wrestling style of politics.[6]

For Pelosi, Trump's abuse brought a new kind of challenge. Many Democrats had become weary of their side playing by the old rules of decorum while the president fought dirty. They wanted someone to fight back more vigorously, and with the Democrats finally seizing one part of the government, Pelosi became her party's most powerful figure and the obvious choice for this duty. However, taking on Trump was no simple matter. He had always traveled the low road so, for him, the nastiness was authentic. Others had to find a way to respond to Trump without abandoning their own values. Pelosi apparently did her homework, and determined which tone would work for her before she needed to strike back.

Pelosi's opportunity came on Tuesday, December 11, 2018, a month after the midterms. The president had scheduled one of his cameras-rolling live encounters, as if he were still the fake impresario holding sway on his TV show *The Apprentice*. The difference was that he sat in the White House and not a TV studio. And the subject was not some made-up task for contestants to complete but his demand for funds to build his controversial wall at the border with Mexico, the one he had promised that Mexico would pay for. Also, in the Oval Office, he faced not reality show contestants but seasoned political pros. Pelosi was perhaps the most gifted lawmaker on Capitol Hill. Next to her sat Chuck Schumer, the Democratic minority leader in the Senate and Trump's fellow New Yorker. Also present was Vice President Mike Pence, who sat stolid and silent during the entire encounter.

With Pence glancing from side to side, like a spectator at a tennis match, Trump tried to engage Pelosi in a game of power signaling. He called her "Nancy." She called him "Mr. President." When he tried to say she was politically weak because some in her caucus opposed her selection as Speaker, she responded firmly, "Mr. President, please don't characterize the strength that I bring to this meeting." Indeed, as Pelosi held the high ground and batted away Trump's insults, she demonstrated to wavering House Democrats that she had the fortitude to stand against him.

Trump tried to goad her into an argument about the border wall funding. He threatened to shut down the government over it. She noted that Republicans would control the House until January 1. If Trump had a grievance, he should take it up with them.

"We are here to have a conversation in a careful way," she said. "I don't think we should have a debate in front of the press." Then she turned the tables on the president, saying, "You should not have a Trump shutdown."

"Did you say Trump?" said the president.

"A Trump shutdown," replied Pelosi.

"I was going to call it a Pelosi shutdown."

Pelosi was daring Trump to shut down the government and was not intimidated. Now Schumer forcefully took up the argument. "Elections have consequences," he said. Democrats held new power but were willing to negotiate. However, he added, "you just said 'my way or we'll shut down the government.'"[7]

To the horror of many Republicans, Trump confirmed that "if we don't have border security, we'll shut down the government." Schumer half smiled and shook his head knowingly. Now, if there were a government shutdown, it would be blamed on Trump—it would be the Trump shutdown.

When the fifteen-minute verbal brawl was over, Pelosi and Schumer marched out of the White House to stand before the press. In the short walk from the Oval Office to the White House door, Pelosi had donned a stylish burnt-orange, high-neck coat. As she strode toward the microphones, she donned a pair of sunglasses and walked in a way that exuded strength. The reporters asked her to discuss not the content of the Oval Office conversation but the subtext.

The wall is "like a manhood thing for him," Pelosi said. "I was trying to be the mom. I can't explain it to you. It was so wild. It goes to show you: you get into a tinkle contest with a skunk, you get tinkle all over you."

The word *tinkle,* chosen as a substitute for the cruder *piss,* was indeed a mom word. It signaled that Pelosi had been the adult in the room while Trump had played the toddler.

Her performance erased all doubt about her leadership. Her coat became an instant sensation, with American women turning to the internet to identify the maker and try to purchase it. It was a product of the Italian company Max Mara and was no longer available. In an article published the next day, the chief fashion critic of *The New York Times* wrote, "Along with her dark glasses, sharp heels and smile of post-combat exhilaration, the coat whispered 'burn' with a wink and a swish." It also helped to transform her from a seemingly tired symbol of the establishment to one of well-dressed revolt.[8]

If Pelosi were to lead a revolt against President Trump, it was going to be a careful one. While the most agitated members of her caucus wanted to impeach Trump immediately, she was keenly aware of opinion polls that showed the American people were evenly divided. Roughly 49 percent of Americans wanted him removed and about 46 percent did not. Among independents, support for impeachment was much lower. Democrats would need these independents if they were going to get rid of the president in the 2020 election. This was, in her mind, the surest path to sparing the country two full terms of the chaos and division that were Trump's hallmarks.

The political path appealed to many who, like Pelosi, had been present for the Clinton impeachment and hoped to spare the country a similar political trauma. With McConnell in control of the Senate, it was all but certain that even if the House did impeach Trump, the Senate would find him not guilty and he would remain in office. Nevertheless, dozens of House Democrats believed

Trump was trampling the Constitution and felt that they were required to hold him accountable. With them in mind, Pelosi would allow House committees to do the normal work of oversight, gathering information and examining controversies. Trump, who to date had shown no ability to change his methods, was certain to dig his own impeachment hole as time passed.[9]

In the meantime, Democrats outside of Pelosi's sphere maintained the impeachment drumbeat. Tom Steyer, a liberal hedge fund billionaire, formed an organization called Need to Impeach and flooded cable news programs with ads that demanded action. "Congress and his own administration know," said Steyer in one of the ads. "This president is a clear and present danger who's mentally unstable and armed with nuclear weapons. And they do nothing."[10]

Steyer's advertising blitz meant that many House Democrats heard the points he made every time they met with constituents back in their districts. As the anger at Trump grew, so did the pressure on House Democrats. Pelosi found refuge in the methodical work of Special Counsel Robert Mueller, who was expected to issue a public report on his findings. "We have to wait and see what happens with the Mueller report," Pelosi said. "We shouldn't be impeaching for a political reason, and we shouldn't avoid impeachment for a political reason. So, we'll just have to see how it comes."[11]

•   •   •

On January 3, 2019, the first day of the 116th Congress, the Trump Shutdown, which he declared in a fit of pique when he didn't get his wall-building money, was already two weeks old. Christmas had been spoiled for many federal workers and contractors, and Americans were growing restive over service cutbacks and shuttered facilities. Garbage piled up at national parks. Airport security lines slowed to a crawl. Businesses that catered to federal workers lost millions of dollars. Weeks would pass as the shutdown became the longest in history and, in the end, Trump wouldn't get what he wanted.

In the meantime, impeachment and the pending Mueller report loomed over Pelosi as she appeared on the House floor. Ever conscious of the message she could send with symbols, she wore a cheerful, bright fuchsia dress as she took the oath of office, surrounded by her grandchildren and children, who were admitted to the chamber for this special day. Trump may have cast a temporary shadow, but Pelosi was determined to emphasize the hope inherent in American democracy. She was inspired especially by the arrival of a congressional class that had record numbers of female, Native American, and Latino/Hispanic members. Nearly all the diversity came from the Democratic side of the aisle, and it represented the demographic future of the nation. "When our new Members take the oath, our Congress will be refreshed, and our Democracy will be strengthened by the optimism, idealism and patriotism of this transformative Freshman Class," she said. "Working together, we will redeem the promise of the American Dream for every family, advancing progress for every community."

True to her political core, Pelosi had encouraged her party to promote an agenda called A Better Deal that emphasized improved access to health care, tax cuts for the poor and middle class, and jobs through public works projects. These policies brought the party voters who, when joined with anti-Trump Democrats, made for a solid national majority. Although the president and Senate Republicans would block everything the House might approve in pursuit of this agenda, the point was to establish a record and require them to do so. In this way, Pelosi would show that Democrats were not so affected by what their critics called Trump Derangement Syndrome that they couldn't do the work they had promised to take up.

Unfortunately for the Speaker, a caucus was not an army, and members of Congress were elected by their own constituencies who were their real commanders. Among the freshmen Democrats were several who, like Ocasio-Cortez, represented voters who felt most outraged by Trump's anti-immigrant and anti-Muslim rhetoric and yearned for someone to stand against him. The president had offended them, made them feel unsafe, and made them feel angry. On the evening after she took her oath of office, their outrage burned in the heart of freshman Representative Rashida Tlaib, whose Detroit-area district was among the poorest in the country. Tlaib would represent many black, Hispanic/Latino, and Muslim voters, and they wanted a hero. Within hours of being sworn in, Tlaib stood up at a party where friends and family celebrated her achievement and recalled an election-night exchange she had with her son. As she explained, he had said, "'Mama, look, you won. Bullies don't win,' and I said, 'Baby, they don't'—because we're going to go in there and we're going to impeach the motherfucker."

As fate and technology would have it, someone's recording of Tlaib, *motherfucker* and all, made its way to the internet and then to every journalist, political operative, commentator, and citizen who cared to view it. As reporters sought reactions, a few Republicans feigned pearl-clutching concern, but for the most part, Tlaib's comment was regarded as a lapse in judgment brought about by overexuberance.[12]

The next evening, January 4, Pelosi sat before a live audience in a town hall setting with Joy Reid of MSNBC, who asked for her reaction to Tlaib. "I probably have a generational reaction to it. But in any event, I'm not in the censorship business. I don't like that language, I wouldn't use that language. I don't . . . establish any language standards for my colleagues, but I don't think it's anything worse than what the president has said. Generationally, that would not be language I would use. But nonetheless, I don't think we should make a big deal of it." Tlaib soon apologized for her choice of words but not her sentiment.[13]

While Tlaib captured headlines, other Democrats began to do the work to determine whether Trump had committed offenses that met the Constitution's standard of "high crimes and misdemeanors." As chair of the House Financial Services Committee, Maxine Waters turned her attention to the president's borrowing practices, especially his relationship with the scandal-plagued Deutsche Bank of Frankfurt, Germany. The bank, which had been under investigation for links to money-laundering schemes, had lent Trump hundreds of millions of dollars when others considered him a bad risk. When asked if she thought the work would lead to impeachment, she said, "I have not called for the impeachment yet. He's doing it himself."[14]

Waters's committee would not, under normal circumstances, lead Congress down the road to impeachment. This role would more likely fall to the House Committee on the Judiciary. It was this committee that did most of the work when Richard Nixon was nearly impeached during the Watergate scandal. Judiciary also developed the articles that were approved when Clinton was impeached in December 1998. In the 116th Congress, the House Judiciary Committee came under the control of Jerrold Nadler of New York.

Nadler had watched Trump for decades as he proposed and canceled big development projects and floated from bankruptcy to bankruptcy. From the very start of Trump's presidency, Nadler had suspected him of violating the emoluments clause of the Constitution, which bars the president from accepting payments from any foreign or domestic sources. This happened daily at various Trump hotels and resorts scattered across America and the world. In fact, foreigners conducting business with the federal government had been so intent on buying rooms and conference services at the Trump hotel in Washington that they were squeezing out other guests.

Long before Democrats seized the House, Nadler had called for an inquiry into Trump and the emoluments clause and for a House investigation into Russia's interference in the 2016 election on Trump's behalf. Now that he controlled the House Judiciary Committee, he had the power to proceed on both fronts. However, he had accepted Pelosi's go-slow strategy. So, too, had the leaders of other relevant committees—government oversight, foreign relations, intelligence—and all would wait for Mueller.

•   •   •

While the Democrats waited, the president and his boosters denigrated Mueller publicly while preparing to blunt him administratively. The denigration had begun soon after Mueller's appointment and was led by the president himself, who said that:

- Mueller had it out for him because of a long-ago dispute over a charge at a Trump golf course.

- Mueller's team was stocked with lawyers who had been registered Democrats and were therefore untrustworthy.

- Mueller relied on the federal agents whose anti-Trump views made their work invalid.

- Mueller was wasting time and federal dollars on a politically inspired "Witch Hunt."

Repeated ad nauseam—especially the phrase *witch hunt*—the personal attacks on Mueller did not dent his reputation. His service alone as a decorated and injured Vietnam War veteran—he received a Bronze Star for rescuing a wounded fellow marine under enemy fire—stood in withering contrast to the president who sought to diminish him. And by now, Mueller had served three decades in the Justice Department, including twelve years as a highly praised director of the FBI.

With Mueller's credibility still intact, Trump moved to use the federal bureaucracy against him. Though legally independent, the special counsel relied on the resources of the Department of Justice and would eventually report to the attorney general. This gave the person in this post certain leverage, but only if he or she were inclined to use it on the president's behalf. Given the broad expectation that American justice is "blind," attorneys general had typically sought to avoid the appearance of political bias. The attorney general is not the president's lawyer, and, in fact, when previous top prosecutors appeared to play this role, they ran into trouble. (Nixon's attorney general, John Mitchell, went to prison for this.) However, President Trump wanted an attorney general who would act as his advocate and protector, and when his first AG refused to play this role, he was fired.

With Jeff Sessions gone and Trump asking, "Where is my Roy Cohn?" the president passed over Deputy Attorney General Rod Rosenstein and Solicitor General Noel Francisco, and for a brief time, he relied on a modestly experienced lawyer named Matthew Whitaker to serve as acting attorney general. Whitaker had been Sessions's chief of staff and was a board member for a patent company that was subject to a class-action lawsuit from inventors who alleged they had been scammed. One of the failed inventions it hawked was a "masculine toilet" for the well endowed. It was clear that Whitaker would never be more than an "acting" attorney general, and for this reason, Trump was frequently questioned about the leadership gap at the top of the Department of Justice.[15]

On the day after the 2018 election, Trump had appeared in the White House East Room, under the watch of Gilbert Stuart's larger-than-life portrait of George Washington, to offer his assessment of the outcome. In essence, he said that others were to blame for the GOP's losses, and he felt the result was not a referendum on his presidency. Then a reporter tried to change the subject.

"Can you give us clarity, sir, on your thinking, currently, now after the midterms, about your Attorney General and your Deputy Attorney General?"

"I'd rather answer that at a little bit different time," said Trump. "We're looking at a lot of different things."[16]

On December 7, one month later, Trump announced the permanent appointment of William Barr as attorney general, predictably a conservative Republican, and a Justice Department veteran who had served as attorney general once before, from 1991 to 1993, during the administration of George H. W. Bush. In the moment, Justice Department employees were reportedly pleased because they considered Barr supportive of their mission. "Worthy of consideration," was how Democratic senator Amy Klobuchar put it. Others noted how William Barr and his wife, Christine, were "good friends" with Robert Mueller and his wife, Ann, and suggested this relationship would shield Mueller. Missing from this analysis was something insiders knew: Barr has long regarded Mueller as an intellectual inferior, a good investigator with a less-than-brilliant legal mind.[17]

Those who were present when Barr was last attorney general were less sanguine.

Barr's nomination was "deeply concerning," said Pelosi, who added that Barr "has spent the past two years auditioning for this job by stoking partisan attacks on our nation's law enforcement community, and encouraging the President to use the Justice Department as a political weapon to pursue his rivals and undermine investigations into Trump and his family's scandals." Schumer said Barr "will have a steep hill to climb in order to be confirmed by the Senate." He also suggested the conflict ahead as he said that Mueller's work should "proceed unimpeded" and his ultimate report should be made available, in toto, to Congress and the public.[18]

January 1, 2019 — Number of House members in favor of impeaching the president: 1

14

ENTER WILLIAM BARR

Why should Radical Left Democrats in Congress have a right to retry and examine the $35,000,000 (two years in the making) No Collusion Mueller Report, when the crime committed was by Crooked Hillary, the DNC and Dirty Cops? Attorney General Barr will make the decision!

—Donald Trump, president of the United States, via Twitter,
April 13, 2019

At a little after 9:00 a.m. on the morning of Tuesday, January 15, 2019, William Pelham Barr entered the hearing room of the Senate Committee on the Judiciary in the Dirksen Building on Capitol Hill. An austere space with a high ceiling and dark wood paneling, the room was almost devoid of decoration, which only served to focus attention more keenly on the man of the moment. As photographers jostled nearby, he moved serenely, as if he understood the choreography and knew all the steps.

Nearly seventy years old, Barr looked prosperous in a soft and jowly way that recalled the days before senior citizens began to turn to gyms and plastic surgeons to make themselves into status symbols. He wore a blue suit, white starched shirt with neat cuffs showing, and a blue-and-white-print tie. The round frames of his glasses gave him an owlish look that he sometimes aided by pursing his lips and puffing out his cheeks. His one concession to fashion was the stylish cut of his salt-and-pepper hair. As he seated himself at the witness table, the family members seated behind him completed the civic tableau of the elder summoned from the mountaintop to once again serve.

After almost thirty years away from public office, Barr was seeking the Senate's approval to return as the chief law enforcement officer of the United

States. As he addressed the senators, he spoke in a monotone that threatened to become a mumble. This lent him an air of confidence augmented by a whiff of boredom. "I did not pursue this position," he said. "When my name was first raised, I was reluctant to be considered. I am sixty-eight years old, partially retired, and nearing the end of a long legal career," said Barr. "But ultimately, I agreed to serve because I believe strongly in public service, I revere the law, and I love the Department of Justice and the dedicated professionals who serve there. I believe I can do a good job leading the department in these times."

There was good—and very public—reason to reject what Barr was selling. Six months earlier, he had sent an unsolicited memo titled "Mueller's 'Obstruction' Theory" to Deputy Attorney General Rod Rosenstein that was so scathing in its criticism of what Barr assumed Mueller was doing that it amounted to a defense manifesto for President Trump. At nineteen single-spaced pages, replete with citations, it was the kind of document that a client might pay $20,000 or more for a top lawyer to produce. It began with Barr's confession that he was "in the dark about many facts" and assumed that Mueller was guided by a "theory" he had never propounded. Nevertheless, he would attack Mueller's work for what he assumed was sweeping overreach and mis-application of legal standards.[1]

Made public prior to the confirmation hearing, the memo contended that the Mueller investigation was unfair and unconstitutional. Barr argued that "Mueller should not be permitted to demand that the President submit to inter-rogation about alleged obstruction," because his "obstruction theory is fatally misconceived." If accepted, he continued, Mueller's view "would do lasting damage to the presidency and to the administration of law within the exec-utive branch."[2]

Barr wrote as a man who had long believed that he understood what America's Founders had intended when they declared independence, and it was not what the overwhelming majority of scholars had assumed. He insisted that Franklin, Jefferson, and the rest had intended to give the executive branch more power than others appreciated and that the president had been improp-erly constrained, especially after the Watergate scandal. In this moment, he saw more improper encroachment. Although Trump would admit he had fired James Comey to protect himself legally, Barr would argue that his right to do so shouldn't be challenged. "Mueller is proposing an unprecedented expansion of obstruction laws so as to reach facially-lawful actions taken by the President in exercising the discretion vested in him by the Constitution."

Having all but pledged to be President Trump's Roy Cohn, Barr could sometimes display some of the charm and humor that Cohn had been known for during his long and corrupt career. (This was what had made him, for some, a lovable scoundrel.)

However, no charm was required for Barr to please the Republican majority on the committee. The chairman, Lindsey Graham of South Carolina, set the tone: "I just can't think of a better person to pick than Mr. Barr," said Graham. "I don't know who is going to do better than him in terms of experience, judgment, and temperament. If this guy doesn't cut it, I'm at a loss of who we can pick."[3]

The memo informed many of the questions posed by Democrats on the Judiciary Committee. As the ranking member of the minority, Senator Dianne Feinstein got to ask about it first. At age eighty-five, Feinstein had been a senator for twenty-seven years and, though not a lawyer, had deep experience with judicial issues. As a member of the Intelligence Committee, she had been instrumental in making public a Senate report on America's use of torture in the so-called war on terror. When it came to Barr's memo, she was not shy about saying, "It does raise questions about your willingness to reach conclusions before knowing the facts and whether you prejudge the Mueller investigation and I hope you'll make that clear today."

No one in the hearing room was surprised by the question, and Barr was more than ready.

"I believe it is vitally important that the Special Counsel be allowed to complete his investigation," he said. "I have known Bob Mueller personally and professionally for 30 years. We worked closely together throughout my previous tenure at the Department of Justice under President Bush. We've been friends since. I have the utmost respect for Bob and his distinguished record of public service. When he was named special counsel, I said that his selection was 'good news' and that, knowing him, I had confidence he would handle the matter properly. I still have that confidence today."

Later in the hearing, as he was pressed again on the matter, Barr repeated that Mueller was his friend and that he didn't believe he would engage in the kind of investigation the president had repeatedly called a "witch hunt." He promised to publish Mueller's final report. Then he added a subtle caveat. The report would be made public in a way "consistent with regulations and the law."[4]

Other comments offered by the nominee were less reassuring. When asked about when Trump could act on matters that would impact his businesses, which he still owned, Barr said, "There is no legal prohibition against the President's acting on a matter in which he has a personal stake." Questioned about the president's authority over judicial concerns, he skated close to Richard Nixon's infamous claim that "when the president does it, that means that it is not illegal." In Barr's version, "when the President exercises these discretionary powers, it is presumed he does so lawfully, and his decisions are generally nonreviewable."[5]

Returning to the memo, Feinstein said, "You repeatedly referred to Mueller's 'sweeping and all-encompassing interpretation of section 1512,' which is a statute on obstruction. How do you know what Mueller's interpretation of 1512 is?"

Pausing as the question hung in the air, Barr reached up to his glasses and adjusted them, and then glanced briefly away. A grimace pulled his lips upward into a tight semicircle, then his face went slack as he began to speak.

"Well, as I said, I was speculating . . . I was writing in the dark. We are all in the dark." Then he waved his hands outward in a gesture to the world. "Every lawyer, every talking head, everyone who thinks about or talks about it doesn't have the facts."

On the raised dais where senators sat and looked down upon the witness, Feinstein stared straight ahead, serious, tight-faced herself. Then a twinkle appeared in her eye. "I spent my Saturday reading that memorandum," she noted. "So you are saying this is all your speculation? It's a big memo."

Now Barr put his hands up, as if he were defending himself from a punch. "Well, it was informed to the extent that I thought that that was one of the theories being considered. I don't know how seriously. . . . but as a shorthand way in the memo of referring to what I was speculating might be the theory I referred to it as Mueller's theory."

Feinstein moved on, but the point was clear. Barr had been quite specific in his memo. He wrote as if he knew and understood Mueller's theory and plan for investigating Trump, and he rejected it outright. "Mueller's overly aggressive use of the obstruction laws should not be embraced by the Department," he had said, "and cannot support interrogation of the President to evaluate his subjective state of mind."[6]

Since no Republican on the committee or in the Senate would defect from the president's side, questions about Barr's memo—or for that matter, his view of the presidency—were, in the end, almost academic. All that mattered for the Democrats was that they put on record their concerns about Mueller's independence. Aside from this, they were left to pray that Barr would serve a purpose higher than to function as the president's guard dog. "While I opposed Bill Barr's nomination," said Feinstein after he was confirmed, "it's my hope that he'll remember he is the people's lawyer, not the president's lawyer."[7]

•   •   •

Senator Feinstein could hope that William Barr might be guided by some higher loyalty, but his life's record suggested he would not. He was born in 1950 into a deeply conservative Catholic family. Like so many of his generation, he was shaped by the tumult of the '60s and, as a keenly intelligent youngster, seemed to choose a side quite early. While many of his peers challenged authority, he was eager to join the so-called establishment and fight for its right to power. His earliest political views, which he shared freely at the exclusive Horace Mann School in New York, favored the president's power to wage an unpopular and undeclared war in Vietnam, where eventually more than fifty thousand of Barr's generation perished. (Thanks to many years of higher education, Barr was among the millions of middle-class and wealthy young men who were not drafted and did not serve in the military.)[8]

As writer Marie Brenner would discover when she researched Barr's background, his cast of mind was inherited from his iconoclastic father, Donald. "My father once said to me that we have been used to being different and it doesn't bother us at all," Barr said. "I have always been in situations where I had no problem being politically different. I don't govern my life by polls or by what other people think about what I do." In fact, according to someone who knew Barr well in high a school and college, in the 1960s he was a bully who physically attacked protesters.

Barr's father, Donald, was headmaster of the Dalton School, which, like Horace Mann, was a prestigious feeder to top universities. A traditionalist at a time when tradition was under assault, Barr seemed to view himself as a bulwark against change. "Everyone knows that I am somewhat anachronistic in my views of the educational leadership of a school," he said after a conflict with the Dalton board. "I am not comfortable with the definition of board-head relations that I see becoming current in schools everywhere." Not unlike Donald Trump, the elder Barr basked in press attention and stretched the truth. He asked that he be called "Dr." Barr, though he never completed his Ph.D. He was also capable of Trumpian cruelty. When writer Betty Friedan's son Jonathan was president of his class and applying to top-rated colleges, he got turned down by every one. Eventually, he learned that Barr had sabotaged his chances, with a letter describing him as a troublemaker and a homosexual. When other students at Dalton sought to change the dress code, Barr couldn't restrain himself. "Your desire to wear slacks is masturbatory ego gratification," he declared. Blue jeans were not just masturbatory, they were unacceptable because "we are elites." Soon he was no longer headmaster.[9]

As Donald Barr faded from public view, his son William became prominent in conservative legal circles. Brilliant and assertive, William Barr was a leader among those who hoped to not just undo the post-Nixon constraints on the presidency but to expand the executive's power to act unilaterally. He argued for expanding the executive's ability to keep its work secret, and serving in the Justice Department's office of legal counsel in 1989 under President George H. W. Bush, Barr wrote a memo that justified, for the first time, America's conduct of a preemptive war. Bush relied on it to justify the invasion of Panama and arrest of strongman General Manuel Antonio Noriega for prosecution on drug trafficking charges. Barr was soon made attorney general.[10]

Controversial as his war memo was, Barr's tenure in the Bush administration was better known for his influence in criminal cases that arose from the Iran-Contra scandal of the Reagan administration. (U.S. officials had evaded congressional prohibitions in order to aid rightist Contras in a civil war against a socialist regime in Nicaragua.) First, he opposed appointment of a special prosecutor to investigate Iran-Contra. Then, on the eve of former defense secretary Caspar Weinberger's trial for obstruction and lying to Congress, President Bush pardoned Weinberger and five other officials implicated in the affair. Independent Counsel Lawrence Walsh bitterly declared, "The Iran-contra cover-up, which has continued for more than six years, has now been completed." Barr said, "People in the Iran-Contra affair have been treated very unfairly." In contrast, in a memo titled "The Case for More Incarceration," he would argue for vastly more spending on prisons so that more of those convicted of ordinary crimes could be locked away for longer periods of time.[11]

After Bush's defeat in the 1992 election, Barr practiced law, served on corporate boards, and involved himself with a number of right-wing religious groups, notably the Catholic Information Center, where he served on the board of directors and occasionally railed against secularism in American society. He became a fixture in a community of right-wing lawyers who booster their own as candidates for judicial appointments and, when someone they preferred held the office, campaigned for an expansive view of presidential power. Barr also grew so wealthy that, by 2016, he could contribute $55,000 to Jeb Bush's failed presidential primary campaign. (Bush, smeared by Trump as "low energy Jeb." was one of the first to be knocked out of the race by the eventual winner.)[12]

• • •

In 2019, as the Senate considered his return to the post of attorney general, Barr's record became fodder for critics such as Katherine Stewart and Caroline Fredrickson, who saw him as a Christian nationalist. "When religious nationalists invoke 'religious freedom,' it is typically code for religious privilege. The freedom they have in mind is the freedom of people of certain conservative and authoritarian varieties of religion to discriminate against those of whom they disapprove or over whom they wish to exert power."[13]

The problem for Stewart, a writer, and Fredrickson, a legal scholar, was that no argument or recitation of Barr's record would affect his nomination. He was the president's man, chosen precisely because of his commitment to the president's authority, and the senators in the president's party could confirm him on their own. Ultimately, three Democrats from states where they were vulnerable to GOP opponents seized the chance to appear bipartisan and voted for him. The *Los Angeles Times* editorial board captured the divided opinion about Barr, noting he was perhaps the best Americans could hope for under the circumstances, though "a leap of faith is required."[14]

Hours after he was confirmed by the Senate confirmation, Barr stood in the Oval Office, placed his hand on a Bible held by his wife, Christine, and took the oath of office administered to him by Chief Justice John Roberts. The ceremony was witnessed by Senator Lindsey Graham, chairman of the Senate Judiciary Committee, and the president himself. Such formalities were not always conducted at the White House in the presence of the president, but it was understandable in this case. After two years of frustration with the surprisingly independent Jeff Sessions and the marginally qualified Matthew Whitaker, Trump had every reason to believe that he finally had gotten an attorney general who would safeguard his prerogatives and advance his agenda. From a policy point of view, this meant that Barr would defend what Trump would call his "absolute right" to direct the department once revered for its political neutrality. This meant the Justice Department would crack down on undocumented immigrants, permit state efforts that made voting more difficult, and protect Trump from any fallout related to Russia's interference in the 2016 election.

Barr, who described himself as a humble servant compelled by a sense of duty, was now ready to defend presidential authority and pursue his own personal crusade, which would include raising suspicions about what Trump enjoyed calling the Deep State. In an address at the University of Notre Dame, which had become a hub for academic holy warriors, he would describe his opponents as "secularists . . . responsible for the steady erosion of our traditional Judeo-Christian moral system."[15]

Barr's moralism would reassure Christian conservatives who voted for Trump and stood in contrast to the president's reputation, which included his numerous marriages, his penchant for profanity, his unethical conduct in business, and personal conduct that led to dozens of allegations of sexual harassment and worse. Two weeks after Barr put his hand on the Bible in the Oval Office to swear his oath, Trump's former private attorney Michael Cohen appeared on national television to call his former boss a con man, a cheat, and a racist. During a decade in Trump's employ, Cohen had used Trump's money to buy the silence of women who alleged affairs with his boss and labored to intimidate others who might speak against him. In sworn testimony before Congress, Cohen contradicted the president's claims that he knew nothing of efforts to build a Trump project in Moscow and said his former boss knew, in advance, about elements of Russia's attack on the 2016 election.

Cohen spoke after being sentenced to prison for crimes he committed while trying to protect himself and Trump from investigations into the 2016 election, but the most chilling thing he said related to the election that lay ahead. "I fear that if he loses the election in 2020, that there will never be a peaceful transition of power," he told Congress. "And this is why I agreed to appear before you today."

These words had chilled Democrats in Congress, who worried that Trump represented a threat to the basic norms that had governed civic life back to the founding of the republic. They considered Trump's resistance to congressional oversight and efforts to intimidate judges and journalists to be attacks on the independent institutions that assured that power wasn't concentrated in the hands of one man. Speaker Pelosi, who often considered the sweep of history, wasn't persuaded that the crisis was so dire or that the American people were sufficiently alarmed.

"I'm not for impeachment," said Pelosi in a question-and-answer session with *Washington Post* writer Joe Heim soon after Cohen's testimony. "Impeachment is so divisive to the country that unless there's something so compelling and overwhelming and bipartisan, I don't think we should go down that path, because it divides the country. And he's just not worth it."

The line about how Trump wasn't worth it reverberated around the mediasphere, but it was not the most important thing that Heim and *The Post* reported about Pelosi's thinking. Before the Q&A section of the article, Heim described Pelosi gazing out the window of her office, which overlooks the Mall, and then picking up a small plaque she had received from Representative Cheri Bustos of Illinois, who, as head of the Democratic Congressional Campaign Committee, was responsible for helping Pelosi maintain her majority. The Speaker had lost it once, and the experience had driven home the age-old wisdom that teaches that elections have consequences.

The plaque was inscribed with a Lincoln quote, which Pelosi read aloud. "Public sentiment is everything. With public sentiment, nothing can fail. Without it, nothing can succeed." She was not going to make the mistake of rushing toward impeachment without knowing that public sentiment was substantially behind her.[16]

February 1, 2019 — Number of House members in favor of impeaching the president: 1

15

ROBERT MUELLER REPORTING

50% of Americans AGREE that Robert Mueller's investigation is a Witch Hunt.

—Donald Trump, president of the United States, via Twitter,
March 15, 2019

At 4:00 p.m. on Friday, March 22, a thunderstorm rumbled through Washington, D.C., rattling windows in older houses on Capitol Hill. Friday evenings bring the witching hour when it comes to news in the nation's capital. With Congress typically adjourned, its members racing for home, it's a moment political creatures favor when they seek some advantage as they make something public. And sometimes a late Friday release means that workers used up every last minute before the arrival of a deadline.[1]

In the case of Special Counsel Robert Mueller's report, Washington journalists had spent several Fridays wondering when it would be safe to leave their posts. Few, if any, knew that William Barr had actually received Mueller's findings and given President Trump's private attorneys two days of exclusive access to the report. They had read it, taken notes, and reported to their client. Since at least two of the participants in this process, Rudy Giuliani and Donald Trump, were famously loose-lipped, Barr couldn't expect the secret to stay secret.

Mueller had been conducting his Russia probe for twenty-two months. In that time, President Trump had consistently denigrated him and demanded a quick conclusion to his work. Trump and his boosters repeatedly said there had been "no collusion" between the Trump campaign and the Russians who attacked the U.S. election on his behalf. Since "collusion" is not a federal crime and Mueller was not looking for it, he was never going to find it. But this wouldn't preclude anyone from declaring victory when it was absent from the prosecutor's findings.

The "no collusion" game was just one of the many publicity techniques Team Trump used to deal with Mueller. They also complained mightily about both the expense of the investigation and what they deemed a paltry work product. These criticisms ignored the tens of millions of dollars Mueller would recover for taxpayers in the Manafort prosecutions and all the charges brought on the basis of his work by U.S. attorneys in New York, Washington, and Virginia. (In fact, Mueller's work would lead to the indictment of thirty-four people, including six who had worked directly for the Trump campaign.)

A similar dishonesty lay at the heart of Trump's repeated claims that those who worked for the prosecutor were incapable of acting honestly because they may have donated to Democratic candidates or voted for his rival in the 2016 election. His constant talk of their supposed unfairness presumed that professionals who had devoted much of their lives to public service could not act ethically. It was a slur, but it would appeal to Trump supporters who believed all of the government was corrupt and their man never got a fair shake.

The final element of the Trump team's effort to deter the prosecutor involved the deft parrying of his many requests for an interview with the president. Here, Trump's lawyers used a legal version of boxer Muhammad Ali's rope-a-dope strategy. As Mueller pressed to depose the president, his lawyers repeatedly hinted that he would do it, but demanded more information about the questions Mueller would ask. In this way, they determined the breadth of his interests while delaying a resolution of the requests. With the president declaring he was eager to meet with Mueller because he had nothing to hide, his lawyers ultimately ruled against it. Trump would only entertain written questions, which his many attorneys would help him answer.

Mueller could have asked the courts to compel the president to testify. However, this would have caused an enormous political conflict; taken weeks, even months of ligitation; and in the end he couldn't be sure of the results. But in settling for the written questions and answers, the special counsel gave up on the chance that he might obtain anything more than the self-serving responses of a politician well served by some of the best lawyers in the country.[2]

The special prosecutor's original charge had included a mandate to probe all issues related to Russia's attack on the election, any activities that indicated the Trump team conspired with the attack, and evidence of crimes discovered along the way, including obstruction of justice. This last part, common when special prosecutors set to work, ensured that witnesses or subjects who tried to impede or obstruct justice could be held to account. In this case, Mueller was concerned with signs that campaign aides and even the candidate himself had known of the attacks and, rather than report the impending crimes, sought advantage in them. An infamous June 9, 2016, meeting at Trump Tower, attended by a lawyer with Kremlin connections and Donald Trump Jr., was of great interest. So, too, were the circumstances of James Comey's firing and the activities of the candidate's longtime friend Roger Stone, who had appeared to have inside knowledge of the timing of the public release of emails hacked by Russian agents.

When Mueller submitted his questions to Trump and his lawyers, the replies to twenty-nine of them included some version of "I do not remember." In fact, the president, who had recently said he had "one of the greatest memories of all time" couldn't even remember whether he had been at Trump Tower on June 9, 2016, or when he heard that hackers had obtained records from the Clinton campaign and the Democratic Party. He had himself expressed the hope that Russia would release emails stolen from Clinton, then told Mueller, "I do not recall being told during the campaign of any efforts by Russia to infiltrate or hack the computer systems and I have no recollection of any particular conversation in that regard."[3]

•   •   •

In the nearly two years that he spent investigating the political crime of the century and all its effects, Robert Mueller did not once speak to the press about his work. His communications chief Peter Carr's duties involved refusing to comment, hundreds of times, even when critics lied about the special prosecutor's work, intentions, and motivations. (This included the time President Trump announced that the Russia controversy was "all made up by this den of thieves and lowlifes.") With Carr deflecting the press, Mueller's reticence became the subject of speculation, punditry, and jokes. After the prosecutor was photographed one weekend at an Apple Store's Genius Bar, *Late Show* host Stephen Colbert described Mueller asking a computer technician, "Let's just say, hypothetically, someone lost a very, very important file. It's called ivanka-confession.pdf."[4]

Journalists assigned to monitor Mueller took to photographing his comings and goings at his home and office and describing the color of the frosting on the cupcakes he sometimes brought to his colleagues. With Mueller's office located in a building where the parking garage had three entrances, photographers were hard-pressed to keep track of his gray Subaru, which he drove himself. What little credible information dribbled out to the press came from Justice Department sources who had occasional contact with Mueller's group. They suggested that Mueller would deliver his final product in February or March, after Barr assumed his duties.

On Wednesday, March 20, Rudy Giuliani arrived in Washington to await the news, telling reporters he wanted to be close to the White House "just in case."

On Thursday, March 21, Mueller was spotted arriving at work at 7:00 a.m., which was especially early for him.

On the morning of Friday, March 22, President Trump stopped in front of reporters for a bit of Chopper Talk as he began a trip to his Florida home. He said he had "no idea" about Mueller's schedule but was certain the prosecutor's investigation had been bad for the country.

Finally, at 4:40 p.m., Mueller sent a security officer to the Department of Justice to deliver a letter notifying Barr that the report was finished and would be given to him. Within twenty minutes, the leaders of key Congressional committees received letters from Barr notifying them that the report had been submitted.

Cable news outlets issued "Breaking News" alerts informing viewers that Mueller had spoken but could offer nothing of what he had actually said. In his letter to Congress, Barr said he would review the report immediately and "I may be in a position to advise you of the Special Counsel's principal conclusions as soon as this weekend."[5]

•   •   •

William Barr spent his weekend with a few colleagues, poring over the 448-plus pages Mueller had produced. He was aided, most closely, by Deputy Attorney General Rod Rosenstein, who had been responsible for Mueller's appointment and had been directly involved in supporting the special counsel's effort. It was Rosenstein who watched over Mueller's budget, and assigned FBI agents as needed. As he and Barr reviewed the report, Democrats on Capitol Hill called for the release of the full text and any underlying documents, including interview transcripts, FBI notes, and depositions.

In the absence of real information, analysts and TV pundits recalled the moment when another independent investigator, Kenneth Starr, issued his report on President Clinton. In that case, Congress received the entire report and thirty-six boxes filled with evidence, which were delivered rather showily for the press to observe. Within hours, the public could also view the full report, which in certain sections read like a salacious novel, on the internet. Twenty years later, Nancy Pelosi and Chuck Schumer issued a joint statement calling for a similar approach, adding, "The American people have the right to the truth. The watchword is transparency."[6]

What Schumer and Pelosi sought was, on the surface, equal treatment for two presidents who had been subject to intense investigation. But however similar the circumstances were, the differences were greater. In the case of Clinton, yearslong reviews of a failed real estate development called Whitewater did not produce meaningful evidence but had led to further investigation of sexual affairs. Finally, interrogation of the president, in which he appeared to lie about his relationship with a White House intern, led to impeachment. The conduct in question, while reprehensible, had not involved official duties, and his deception, while possibly illegal, was hardly momentous. In the case of Donald Trump, the reprehensible sexual behavior was widely known but beside the point. His scandal revolved around the conduct of an election and obvious indications of attempts to hinder the special counsel's work.

The Trump case involved nothing but official concerns and implicated not only national but international political affairs. Far more serious than Clinton's transgressions, the Russian election attack and Trump's response would seem to merit more sunlight, not less. However, in the Clinton case, Starr was not tightly supervised by the president's attorney general and was free to report to a Congress that was eager to humiliate Bill Clinton even if that meant putting the country through only the second impeachment trial in the history of the republic. In contrast, Mueller worked under an attorney general who was devoted to protecting the president and who would control what the world would see of his report.

Having signaled his attitude in his nineteen-page memo / job application, in which he declared that Mueller's nonexistent obstruction theory was "fatally misconceived," Barr worked against competing pressures. First, Congress, the president, and the public were eagerly waiting for news of the report's contents. (Rudy Giuliani told reporters he was ready to light a celebratory cigar.) Second, Barr labored under the shadow of his own expansive view of presidential power and the importance of maintaining it. Finally, having assumed the power to review Mueller's work, he seemed obligated to at least appear to be conducting a thorough examination.

Although Americans generally believed that all *should* be subject to equal justice under the law, this was an ideal that was belied by a system in which money routinely prevailed through the purchase of expert lawyering. Less routine, but just as real, was the effect of the special status afforded to government officials, which culminated in the extraordinary exceptions carved out for the president. As the nation's one and only chief executive, presidents are either exempted from, or can temporarily evade, many legal procedures. A widely recognized executive privilege permitted presidents to keep secret some national security matters and some elements of their administrations' inner workings. However, this right was not well defined, and many in the law, politics, and academia would restrain it out of concern for abuse. Advocates of executive power, like William Barr, saw this privilege as exceedingly broad and would say it extended to many who worked for the president. They were, in his view, part of a "unitary executive."[7]

As a high-ranking member of the (still theoretical) unitary executive, Barr did not even pretend to carefully examine Mueller's work or reflect on his duty. Instead, in less than forty-eight hours, during which he presumably enjoyed two nights' sleep, he read and analyzed Mueller's work and wrote his own review of its findings. It was this review, and only this review, that he would make public, and it was accomplished in just four pages. In fact, if one removed the salutations, footnotes, and description of the process, Barr offered less than two pages' worth of information, which was, of course, filtered through his lens. These two pages led to two very elemental observations:

> The investigation did not establish that members of the Trump Campaign conspired or coordinated with the Russian government in its election interference activities.

And:

> [Deputy Attorney General] Rosenstein and I have concluded that the evidence developed during the Special Counsel's investigation is not sufficient to establish that the President committed an obstruction-of-justice offense.[8]

Since Barr alone had access to Mueller's work, no one else was informed in a way that made it possible to fully challenge his distillation. However, the context raised immediate concerns. In the twenty-two-month investigation overseen by Robert Mueller, 19 lawyers aided by 40 staff members had used 2,800 subpoenas, 500 search warrants, 230 domestic record requests, 13 requests of information from foreign governments, and the testimony of 500 witnesses. Although Mueller and his team had not granted interviews or published commentaries on their effort, documents filed with the courts had revealed meaningful connections between the Trump campaign and the Russian attack. Indeed, just weeks prior to Barr's letter, Mueller had presented evidence that showed Trump's friend Roger Stone had been in contact with the two main actors in the theft and publication of thousands of emails from the Clinton campaign and the Democratic Party. Stone and those working with him had communicated with an online front for Russian hackers called Guccifer 2.0 and with WikiLeaks, which served as the clearinghouse for the hacked documents.

Those who had followed Mueller closely and understood what he had accomplished would recognize the disservice and deception in Barr's letter. However, as a document issued by the highest legal official in the federal government, it arrived with the power to influence what Americans would think and say about the 2016 election and the president's conduct.

The Department of Justice was, by tradition, respected as an institution above partisan politics. (Among the few who publicly disparaged the institution was President Trump, who frequently branded its officials as venal and corrupt.) Barr, who had called himself a traditionalist who revered the Justice Department, inherited the credibility that accompanied that respect. In his letter, he had risked both his own and his department's credibility and taken the chance that his friend Robert Mueller would maintain the silence that he had embraced as his duty.[9]

•   •   •

In his letter to Congress, William Barr did not go so far as to introduce the irrelevant topic of collusion. Nor did he declare the president had been deemed, by Mueller, to be somehow innocent. Indeed, as Barr tried to signal good news for Trump, he had written in a remarkably passive way. In Barr's telling, Mueller "did not establish" that Trump and team conspired with the Russians and the evidence was "not sufficient" to establish that Trump committed a crime. And, while Barr observed that Mueller had noted ten episodes in which the president could be seen to have obstructed justice, the evidence did not establish an offense.

Trump converted Barr's cautious, lawyerly words into his own much more categorically pleasing headline for the day. (He had done this before, when he coaxed the *New York Post* into declaring that his mistress said sex with him was THE BEST SEX I EVER HAD. This time, he didn't need the *Post,* since he had a Twitter account and tens of millions of followers.) "No Collusion, No Obstruction," announced the president of the United States hours after Barr's letter was made public. "Complete and Total EXONERATION. KEEP AMERICA GREAT!"[10]

Trump's gleeful legal take, decorated with his reelection campaign slogan, took advantage of the pre-report effort he and his advocates in the media and politics had made to guide public perceptions. The president had first denied "collusion" with Russia in March of 2017, months before Robert Mueller was even appointed. In the eighteen months that followed, his side made this claim so often and so adamantly that some in the press had adopted it as a standard. Guaranteed that the special counsel wouldn't find it, the president was ready to declare victory on that point and did so soon after Barr's letter was released. Similarly, although neither Barr nor Mueller had used the term *exoneration,* the president did, and he added "complete and total" just to amplify the distortion.[11]

Once the president had spoken, his allies added their voices. Kellyanne Conway, his combative counselor, declared that Trump had won the 2016 election "all over again" and "got a gift for the 2020 election. They'll never get you because they'll never 'get' you."

At Fox News, Sean Hannity, the president's loyal booster, announced that his TV show would be a "NO COLLUSION EDITION!" He also declared "mainstream media have lied to the American [people] for 2 plus years. Now they will be held accountable." At the Republican National Committee, a spokesman said, "For years, Democrats & many in the media promised us there was collusion between the Trump campaign and Russia. They guaranteed us that Special Counsel Mueller would find the proof of it. They were wrong."

Fully committed to a celebration based on a deliberate miscasting of events, Trump and his team kept crowing for days. At a Tuesday luncheon with Republican senators, the president gushed, "I love the A.G. He works fast. I love this guy. You told me I would." House Republicans gleefully, if prematurely, announced the end to the president's troubles. "There was no collusion," said Representative Doug Collins of Georgia. "There is no constitutional crisis."

At a rally in Michigan where he kicked off his 2020 reelection campaign, the president whipped the crowd into a frenzy of "Lock them up!" chants directed at reporters and his political opponents and declared "the Russia hoax is finally dead" and "the collusion delusion is over." He said that "Robert Mueller was a god to the Democrats . . . until he said no collusion," and now "they will need to decide whether they will continue defrauding the public with ridiculous bullshit, partisan investigations." With a few conspiracy theory flourishes about the Deep State, he completed what was a greatest-hits version of his pitch for public support and made sure his supporters knew he would win again in 2020.[12]

As the victory cries continued, Robert Mueller's equanimity thinned. He and his team wrote their own letter, which they sent to Attorney General Barr on March 27. Made public six weeks later, this document was, for a man like Mueller, remarkable in the way that it challenged those who were above him in the chain of command.

> The summary letter the Department sent to Congress and released to the public late in the afternoon of March 24 did not fully capture the context, nature, and substance of this Office's work and conclusions. There is now public confusion about critical aspects of the results of our investigation. This threatens to undermine a central purpose for which the Department appointed the Special Counsel: to assure full public confidence in the outcome of the investigations.

Although Mueller did not invoke Barr's name, the letter was as close to a personal rebuke as one could expect in the circumstances. It noted that in person and in writing, Mueller had informed the attorney general that "introductions and executive summaries" supplied with the two-volume report were accurate summaries of their contents. No redacted information was included in these pages, and Mueller encouraged Barr to make them public immediately. Mueller sent along fresh copies of these parts of his report, just in case.[13]

Barr did not act directly on Mueller's letter, but its mere existence guaranteed that others would learn of it; he couldn't ignore the issues it raised. At the same time, as Democrats reflected on the attorney general's four pages, they began to question his parsing of the report. For example, where Barr quoted Mueller on the issue of conspiring or coordinating with Russia, he began with a pair of brackets that indicated that the snippet he used was preceded by something not included. It would be reasonable for anyone to wonder what Barr had left out. Also, Barr had been so critical of Mueller's efforts before he became attorney general that he did not get the leeway a less partisan figure would have enjoyed. "Maybe Barr's interpretation is right. Maybe it's not," said Senator Chris Murphy of Connecticut. "But why the heck would we be okay with an ally of the president, appointed because of his hostility to the Mueller investigation, tell us what the report says?"

Having inflamed interest in what Mueller had actually found, Barr quickly issued another statement explaining that his description of the special counsel's "principal conclusions" had not been intended as even a "summary" of the report. He said a summary or "serial or piecemeal" release of the report would be a disservice, and so he planned, upon completing his review, to make it public all at once. Fortunately, this effort was proceeding well, he said, and it would likely be finished by mid-April.

The attorney general made this promise when he went to Capitol Hill to testify before House and Senate committees that had previously scheduled sessions to discuss the Department of Justice budget. In the Senate, where fellow Republicans were in control of the proceedings, he took the opportunity to signal his continued loyalty to President Trump by joining him on the lunatic fringe, where a conspiracy theory saw something nefarious in the federal government's investigation of Russia's cyberattacks on the 2016 election. After several reviews had confirmed the attacks and that they were done to benefit Trump, the federal authorities who had labored to avoid disrupting the election themselves had come under attack by the president and his allies. Inside the Justice Department, Barr had commenced an investigation of the investigators. Senator Jeanne Shaheen of New Hampshire, a Democrat, asked, "Can you share with us why you feel the need to do that?"

> BARR: Well, for the same reason, we're worried about foreign influence in elections, we want to make sure that during—I think spying on a political campaign is a big deal. It's a big deal. The generation I grew up in, which is the Vietnam War period, people were all concerned about spying on anti-war people and so forth by the government and there were a lot of rules put in place to make sure that there's an adequate basis before our law enforcement agencies get involved in political surveillance. I'm not suggesting that those rules were violated but I think it's important to look at that. And I'm not—I'm not talking about the FBI necessarily but intelligence agencies more broadly.

SHAHEEN: You're not suggesting, though, that spying occurred?

BARR: I don't—well, I guess you could—I think that spying did occur. Yes, I think spying did occur.[14]

Barr's observation echoed Donald Trump's unsubstantiated, two-year-old complaint that somehow President Obama had ordered that his phones be tapped. "Terrible!" was how Trump put it. "Just found out that Obama had my 'wires tapped' in Trump Tower just before the victory. Nothing found. This is McCarthyism!" Trump would never say how he "just found out," and no evidence ever emerged to support this harebrained idea, but it became rooted in the places where Trump's most rabid supporters imagined vast conspiracies arrayed against their champion. There, it became one of several conspiracy theories that prominent allies of the president, like Barr, would pluck up when they needed to say something extreme in order to show they were good soldiers.[15]

When done well, the rhetorical game played by the president and his helpers became an improvisational performance in which he always got to deliver the best lines. The complaint about spying had been a kind of running gag for at least a year. In fact, in May of 2018, Rudy Giuliani had admitted that the complaint was a public relations gambit aimed at shaping opinion about whether Trump deserved impeachment. "It is for public opinion," said Giuliani. "Because eventually the decision here is going to be impeach or not impeach. Members of Congress, Democrats and Republicans, are going to be informed a lot by their constituents. And so, our jury—and it should be—is the American people."[16]

One year later, when Barr talked of spying, Trump one-upped him by telling the White House press corps that Mueller had actually attempted to overthrow his government. "It was an illegal investigation. It was started illegally. Everything about it was crooked," said Trump as he stood outside the White House. "This was an attempted coup," he added. "This was an attempted takedown of a president, and we beat them."

Having declared victory, the president cavalierly announced, "I don't care about the Mueller Report." If this were true, then he may have been the only person in American politics to hold this view. All the others were so eager to read it that not even the attorney general's talk of spies would move their focus from the pledge he made to release the Mueller report within a week. No one could predict which parts Barr might redact—black out—to accommodate national security or executive privilege, and the attorney general had, with his spying remark, stoked fears that he would use his redaction pen for political purposes. Still, after nearly two years of waiting, there was a thrill in the air as the country anticipated reading the report.

The anticipation would end a bit early for Rudy Giuliani, Jay Sekulow, and others on the president's legal term as William Barr quietly permitted them to visit the Justice Department and pore over the Mueller report in advance of anyone else seeing it. On Tuesday, April 16, they sat down to read at 4:00 p.m. and stayed until 9:00 p.m. They returned the following day and worked from 10:30 a.m. to 3:30 p.m. Although they weren't permitted to make copies of any pages, they scratched away on legal pads so that when they were finished, they could write an outline of the report's contents. The sneak peek—or rather, the full access—allowed for the president's lawyers to be better prepared than others when the report was finally distributed.

March 31, 2019 — Number of House members in favor of impeaching the president: 1

16

"[NOT] FULL EXONERATION"

Why should I be defending a fraudulent Russian Witch Hunt. It's about time the perpetrators of this fraud on me and the American People start defending their dishonest and treasonous acts. How and why did this terrible event begin? Never Forget!

—Donald Trump, president of the United States, via Twitter,
April 2, 2019

With his provocative talk of spying, William Barr had shown he could play Donald Trump's game of distortion and deflection. Eight days later, with his coy handling of the release of the Mueller report, he would prove he was an expert.

Barr chose to release the report on a date—Thursday, April 18—when Congress would be out of town and much of America was about to begin days of solemn religious observance. On Friday, Christians would begin the long Easter weekend. Saturday would commence the Jewish week of Passover.

Having selected a date when few would be watching, Barr did his best to manipulate those who did pay attention. Instead of merely sending the document to Congress and releasing it publicly, he opted for a reality TV show—style event where the press was summoned to be seated like movie extras, and he walked onto a small lighted stage decorated with flags. As Barr stood at a lectern adorned with the eagle-and-shield seal of the Department of Justice, Rod Rosenstein and his main deputy, Ed O'Callaghan, positioned themselves behind him. They stood silently, grim-faced, like the steadfast G-men of James Cagney movies. Neither man would crack a smile in the ensuing half hour.

The reporters were not going to actually receive the report. That moment was still ninety minutes away. Instead, they were to listen as the attorney general offered pre-show remarks that might influence what everyone—public officials, journalists, legal experts, citizens—might think about it when they finally read it.

Barr spoke first of the special counsel's charge, which did not summon him to search for "collusion" but which the attorney general quickly described as an effort that led to "no evidence of Trump campaign collusion with the Russian government's hacking." In the printed version of this speech, the collusion was written with quotation marks to indicate a vernacular term. Since TV cameras don't capture quote marks, the live broadcast and later replays of this key statement gave the president the political display he needed. The attorney general said it. No collusion.

But wait, there was more. After providing the president a sound bite worthy of a reelection campaign ad, Barr offered an empathetic review of how the president was affected, emotionally, by the investigation. "And as the Special Counsel's report acknowledges," said Barr, "there is substantial evidence to show that the President was frustrated and angered by a sincere belief that the investigation was undermining his presidency, propelled by his political opponents, and fueled by illegal leaks." Barr made no mention of Trump's refusal to be deposed, but praised him for not asserting executive privilege when "he would have been well within his rights to do so."[1]

With the president sufficiently served, Barr said he would answer reporters' questions, which, since they had not received the report, revolved around the very strange exercise they had been asked to indulge. First, he denied that he had just offered an analysis of the report, insisting that instead he was "really focused on the process of releasing the report," as if this activity, which had entered a phase that would be handled by couriers, required his devotion. When one reporter asked him to respond to those who said he was "overly generous" to Trump, Barr acted as if he couldn't fathom the question. Finally, when someone asked, "Is it an impropriety for you to come out and sort of spin the report before people are able to read it?" Barr said, simply, "No," picked up the folder he had brought to the stage, turned, and exited stage right.

The advantage Barr enjoyed as he performed at his press conference was aided by his timing. Congress was on a long-scheduled holiday, and few members were in Washington, where they might be interviewed by the press.

Instead, they would access the report via the internet (Pelosi would do so while on business in Ireland) and monitor news outlets, where journalists raced to read, absorb, and then report on what Mueller had written. In larger newsrooms, teams divided up Mueller's two volumes and began sharing bits of what they learned. This process began when the report was posted online at 11:00 a.m. ABC News was quick to offer a first take, reporting at 11:16. The probe, it said:

> Uncovered numerous links—i.e. contacts—between Trump campaign officials and individuals having or claiming to have ties to the Russian government.

> Among the people: Carter Page, an unpaid adviser to Trump's campaign, George Papadopoulos, one-time campaign foreign policy adviser, Jared Kushner, the president's son-in-law, JD Gordon, a campaign adviser, Paul Manafort, former Trump campaign chairman, Erik Prince, Trump ally and Blackwater founder, and Jeff Sessions, a former senator and attorney general.

Nine minutes later, ABC News updated its report to explain that, in fact, Robert Mueller had not cleared Trump of obstruction of justice. Instead, he had offered detailed evidence of ten instances where Trump may have committed obstruction but left open the ultimate conclusion about the evidence. ABC then reported that Mueller's team considered Trump's written replies to its questions "inadequate" but chose not to subpoena him for an interview because such a demand would lead to long and difficult litigation. As more time passed, more news was offered so that by the end of the day, a long list of troublesome facts had been revealed. Among them were:

- Michael Cohen, Trump's former personal lawyer, had been coached to provide inaccurate testimony to Congress.

- Trump had tried to influence White House counsel Don McGahn to lie about how he had ordered the firing of Special Counsel Mueller.

- Candidate Trump had repeatedly ordered campaign staffers to obtain Hillary Clinton's emails.

- Trump may have been aware that Russian agents possessed a compromising videotape of him that could have been damaging to his campaign for the White House.

- Mueller found "multiple links between Trump campaign officials and individuals tied to the Russian government." This included a Russian source who told campaign official George Papadopoulos that Moscow possessed thousands of Clinton emails. He then bragged about it to others and emailed many updates on plans to make the emails public.

- "The President's efforts to influence the investigation were mostly unsuccessful, but that is largely because the persons who surrounded the President declined to carry out orders or accede to his requests."

- Mueller found ample but not conclusive evidence of the president's obstruction of justice, and "if we had confidence after a thorough investigation of the facts that the President clearly did not commit obstruction of justice, we would so state."

Mueller seemed to suggest the next step was up to Congress with its impeachment and removal powers, writing, "Congress has the authority to prohibit a president's corrupt use of his authority in order to protect the integrity of the administration of justice," according to the report.[2]

The most trenchant news reports on Mueller's findings came from the few major newspapers with sufficient staff to carry out deeper analyses. At *The New York Times*, Charlie Savage revealed that prior to the release of the full report, Attorney General Barr had quoted snippets of Mueller's work in deceptive ways and remained silent on other key passages. For example, Mueller had presented extensive evidence that Trump may have obstructed justice but did not recommend immediate prosecution due to the immunity granted the office. He actually left the door open for prosecution of Trump once he no longer enjoyed special protection from being charged. Mueller explained that with this in mind, he had produced a thorough factual investigation "in order to preserve the evidence when memories were fresh and documentary materials were available."[3]

At *The Wall Street Journal*, Aruna Viswanatha and Sadie Gurman also drew attention to the way Barr had skipped over the fact that Mueller had stopped short of recommending charges against Trump because of presidential immunity even though he presented ample evidence that the president had tried to obstruct justice. As Mueller reported, when the special counsel was named, Trump said, "Oh my God. This is terrible. This is the end of my Presidency. I'm fucked." He then embarked on a campaign of "public attacks on the investigation, nonpublic efforts to control it, and efforts in both public and private to encourage witnesses not to cooperate."[4]

The breadth of the president's effort to undermine and influence the investigation and thereby obstruct justice was clear to see in the Mueller report, but recognizing it required a thorough reading. More obvious, because he stated it in the bluntest way possible, was the fact that Mueller did not exonerate Trump. The report noted this explicitly, saying, "The evidence we obtained about the President's actions and intent presents difficult issues that prevent us from conclusively determining that no criminal conduct occurred. Accordingly, while this report does not conclude that the President committed a crime, it also does not exonerate him."

In another country, where tradition and practice led newly elected governments to prosecute their predecessors, the Mueller report would have been a road map for future indictments. In the United States, where political stability is highly valued, the prosecution of an ex-president is essentially unthinkable. This meant that impeachment by Congress and a Senate trial ending in Trump's removal represented the only means for holding the president legally accountable. Barring this unlikely outcome, individuals in Congress, alone and through their committees, could use the report as a starting point for further investigations and public hearings. The White House would refuse to cooperate, of course, and Republicans in Congress would oppose this kind of oversight and describe it as a meritless, partisan enterprise.

The political peril represented by unified GOP opposition and the president's continued support among a sizable minority of the electorate meant that even House Democrats were divided over which steps they should take. To be precise, they agreed on the president's transgressions. He was, in their minds, a dangerous rogue actor. However, worthy debates raged over how to best check Trump. The continuum of Democratic opinion began, on one side, with those who had already drafted articles of impeachment to those who believed it was best to pursue a regular legislative agenda and let the voters decide the president's fate in 2020. In between these poles the majority of

House Democrats seemed to want to proceed with oversight while leaving the impeachment option available.

In the immediate term, the House Judiciary Committee would bear most of the responsibility for responding to the Mueller report. Mueller's silence, motivated by his powerful sense of ethics, had allowed Barr to play politics in ways that effectively neutered his report.

The committee had seen a full month pass while the president's declarations of "No Collusion" and "Full Exoneration" reverberated in the echo chamber of Fox News and its ilk. If members were to respond in an effective way, they would have to determine what Mueller had actually discovered and communicate it in a way that could compete with pithy slogans that, despite or perhaps because they were lies, had shaped public opinion. The work of analysis and response would begin with a close reading of Mueller's 448 pages informed by all that had transpired around the Russian election attack. This would be no easy task.

• • •

Like every other alert American, Representative Pramila Jayapal, a member of Congress whose district included Seattle and nearby communities, had spent months waiting for Mueller to issue his findings. She had spent much longer—fifteen years to be exact—waiting for the honeymoon she and her husband, Steven, had postponed when they were married. When the legislative calendar offered an opening in April 2019, they planned a trip to Italy and decided that barring an emergency, they would take the trip.

They flew to Rome, where on landing they heard the news that the report would be released. As dusk cast shadows on the ancient piazzas, Jayapal went online and downloaded the report to her iPad. She read the first pages, which are dense with legalese, and then set it aside for the evening. She would dip in and out of the report as she and her husband toured Rome and Venice. (Her first reaction involved a football metaphor—"We were hurt when Barr obviously intercepted the ball.") Finally, in Tuscany, where they planned to spend several quiet days at a farmhouse/hotel, Jayapal would have time for deeper study.

A second-term member of the House, Jayapal was one of two nonlawyers on the Judiciary Committee, but she was a quick study, and her perspective often helped her see issues with greater clarity than those who were distracted by finer points of the law. She valued the accountability inherent in an American system that established three branches of government and a free press. As a

young person born and raised in India, she had been drawn to the ideals represented by this system, and she remained idealistic about a country that had
welcomed her to become a citizen in 2000 and a member of Congress sixteen
years later. If the Trump presidency struck her as a deviation from the best of
American tradition, the fact that she would be part of the effort to check his
excesses affirmed it.

In Tuscany, the pages Jayapal read seemed, to her, more like a novel
than a legal filing. Trump was the bully whose behavior created powerful
adversaries like James Comey and converted toadies like Michael Cohen into
dangerous truth-tellers. Mueller and his team appeared as dogged and ethical
lawmen who maintained their principles. Legions of White House officials
tried to save Trump from his worst impulses, while hangers-on like Corey
Lewandowski tried to figure out how to please the boss without risking too
much.

In addition to the characters, the story told by Mueller was full of intrigue
and set in iconic locales that reeked of drama. For Jayapal, even the redactions,
which often seemed to obscure juicy details, were of dramatic interest. Like puz-
zles set inside the story, they invited her to try to figure out what was missing.

Having absorbed the arc of the story in her first read, Jayapal returned to
the document two more times, hoping to identify the constitutional concerns
she would want to address in her work on the Judiciary Committee. In general,
she recognized that Trump had systematically abused his power in a way that
required thorough examination. More specifically, she whittled Mueller's ten instances of possible obstruction to five that were most serious and, based on the
evidence, all but impossible to explain away. Before she left Italy, she completed
three full readings, jotted hundreds of notes, and concluded that Trump had
created a constitutional crisis that seemed to require impeachment proceedings.[5]

Meanwhile, back in the States, Jayapal's colleagues on the Judiciary Committee pored over the pages of the report knowing that they would soon question both the special counsel and Attorney General Barr at hearings devoted
to the report. With the exception of Chairman Jerrold Nadler, who could rely
on a small staff of lawyers, committee members could count on perhaps one
or two experienced aides to help them. Some were on their own completely.
Most but not all held law degrees, but this training did not confer much of an
advantage to those who hadn't practiced in many years.

As a former defense lawyer who had extensive experience representing mob
figures in Rhode Island, Representative David Cicilline recognized something

familiar in the quotes Mueller used and the schemes he described. Cicilline, who isolated himself at his home in Providence so that he could read uninterrupted, needed five hours to complete this task. "It was like reading transcripts of mobsters I had represented," said Cicilline months later. "I mean the language he uses; this is not only not presidential language; this is the language of an experienced criminal." When he read that Trump had told FBI director Comey, "I need loyalty, I expect loyalty," Cicilline heard a gangster making things clear to a member of his crew. Michael Cohen's decision to tell the truth to investigators made him, in Trump's words, a "rat." During one of several attempts to fire Mueller, Trump ordered his White House counsel Don McGahn to do his dirty work "and call me back when you do it."

Besides Trump's language, Cicilline found familiar criminal patterns in the president's behavior. He didn't want the lawyers who served him in the White House to take notes, presumably because notes would create a potentially troublesome paper trail. As revealed by Mueller, Trump wanted those who might testify against him to stay silent and trust they would be taken care of later. When he felt that a member of his team needed encouragement, he sent a third party to remind him that the president "really like[s] him."[6]

Like others, Cicilline saw in the report evidence of ten instances of obstruction of justice that, but for the president's protected status, would have led to criminal charges. The facts indicated the opposite of what William Barr had suggested, and this conflict had led Chairman Nadler to demand that the House be provided the documents underpinning the report and be given access, perhaps in a secure facility, to an unredacted version of it. This handling would bring the Mueller report in line with the Starr report, which was used to impeach Bill Clinton.

Finally, Cicilline saw that, contrary to claims that the administration cooperated with Mueller, many who were asked for testimony and evidence responded like gangsters with something to hide. As Mueller's team wrote, they had been hampered by witnesses who "invoked their Fifth Amendment right against compelled self-incrimination." In some cases, "even when individuals testified or agreed to be interviewed, they sometimes provided information that was false or incomplete." Some of the interviewees, "including some associated with the Trump campaign—deleted relevant communications or communicated during the relevant period using applications [such as Signal and WhatsApp] that feature encryption or that do not provide for long-term retention of data or communications records."

By the day after its release, Cicilline was ready to discuss the report on national television, where he referenced a passage in which Mueller explained that "charging the President with a crime was therefore not an option we could consider" but "the Constitution requires a process other than the criminal-justice system to formally accuse a sitting President of wrongdoing." The other process would be impeachment, and when asked about it on television, Cicilline said, "There's no question that impeachment must be on the table," but he was just not ready to take it up.

Others in the Democratic Party, including Massachusetts senator Elizabeth Warren, who was running for president, had already announced they believed Trump deserved to be impeached. She likely had in mind the polls that showed registered Democrats were lining up in favor of impeachment. According to the survey company Morning Consult, these voters had crossed the 50 percent pro-impeachment threshold in mid-January and remained there. (The number of independents who considered impeachment a "top priority" approached one-third.) The polls meant that a candidate for the party's presidential nomination—like, say, Elizabeth Warren—might find votes by getting out in front of the impeachment parade.

Cicilline voiced his respect for her but noted that she was not on the House Judiciary Committee, which would have to "do the work" to determine what should happen next. He seemed to frustrate the interviewer who questioned him on live television. In one breath, Cicilline stressed that Trump had committed impeachable offenses "by firing people, by encouraging people to lie and by lying himself." However, he also repeatedly passed on opportunities to call for immediate action on impeachment, saying instead that the House needed to conduct "our own fact gathering, our own evidence gathering." In this careful performance, Cicilline communicated the tension inside the House Democratic Caucus, where Nancy Pelosi and her leadership team were trying to restrain members who were furious about William Barr's deceptions and certain that Trump should be impeached.

On the eve of the report's release, Pelosi had spoken at length about staying focused on the "kitchen table" issues that concerned voters, including jobs and health care costs. In Dublin, she reminded a reporter that most Americans would have trouble paying an unexpected car repair bill or health care expense over a few hundred dollars. Their concerns were on her mind, and so, she said, "I have not been one of those focused on impeachment."

When she returned to the United States, Pelosi was blunter with the two-hundred-plus Democrats who dialed into a massive telephone conference call. "I hate to disappoint some of you," she said about restraining the impeachment impulse, "but I'm not struggling with this decision." However, she said she shared the belief, expressed by others on the call, that many in the administration had "decided they're not going to honor their oath of office."[7] Those more committed to impeachment were from secure and very liberal districts or members of the Judiciary Committee who, because of the committee's responsibilities, had been most immersed in the growing record created by Mueller and other investigators. News accounts of the caucus call noted that committee members Madeleine Dean of Pennsylvania and Val Demings of Florida said any careful review of the evidence in Mueller's report led inevitably to the conclusion that some sort of move toward impeachment would be the logical next step. Their views carried little extra weight since they were from swing districts that could easily go Republican. Though not quite front liners, they would assume some political risk by leading the drive toward impeachment yet were willing to do it.[8]

For months, members of the Judiciary Committee had been working in small groups to analyze the president's behavior and determine whether it met the standard for impeachment set by Article II of the Constitution. The key passage declares that a president could be impeached for "treason, bribery, or other high crimes and misdemeanors." Although many Americans assumed the phrase *high crimes and misdemeanors* referred to actual crimes, like the obstruction of justice Mueller outlined, it did not. At the time of its enactment, there were no federal statutes that defined such crimes. Constitutional scholars generally agree that the language in Article II, which had been borrowed from British law, related to abuses of presidential power as Congress would define them on a case-by-case basis. The choice to leave things vague was intentional, because the authors of the Constitution recognized that future presidents could find ingenious new ways to exceed their powers while evading any specific, detailed list of offenses. In addition to comparing Trump's abuses with Article II, members of the committee would consider the Constitution's ban on presidents' receiving emoluments—gifts or payments of anything of value—from foreign or domestic sources. Committee Chairman Nadler would ask Representative Jamie Raskin of Maryland, a Harvard-educated former professor of constitutional law, to lead the group study on emoluments.[9]

Given his committee's purview and the president's record, Nadler had ample reason to prepare for impeachment. He also understood, as well as anyone in Congress could, who Donald Trump was. Born a year less a day after Trump and raised in the same city of New York, Nadler's life was vastly different from Trump's. Nadler's father had been a New Jersey chicken farmer who moved to the city when the farm went bust during the Great Depression. Trump's father had begun assembling a real estate empire by purchasing foreclosed properties and became one of the richest men in America. He had groomed Donald to be his successor and financed his success. Nadler's father gave him liberal political values. As Nadler worked his way through college and law school and entered politics, he had witnessed Trump's very rise from self-anointed real estate wunderkind to tabloid headline-grabber. The two men came into direct conflict in the 1980s, when Trump proposed a massive development, to be called Television City, for the Upper West Side of Manhattan district Nadler represented on the city council. The centerpiece would be a 150-story tower that would overshadow a residential neighborhood where few buildings exceeded six stories.

The battle over Television City was a classic case of a developer determined to single-handedly reshape a large, established community versus a populace defended by a scrappy local politician. In this time, Nadler concluded that Trump was a greedy, heedless, and insatiable man with no regard for the damage he might do. Trump decided that Nadler was an annoying impediment to his greatness. Trump took to calling him "dumb" and "fat Jerry." A Nadler aide quipped that his boss "never went bankrupt and had to spend his father's fortune to keep his family's business afloat." Television City was never built, and the bad feeling between the two men never went away.[10]

Nadler, who said Trump had been elected "legally but not legitimately" due to Russia's election attack, understood what mischief his old nemesis might get up to. He had boycotted Trump's inauguration and, while in the minority, bided his time. "There's so much to look into, but we can't call a hearing," he said before the 2018 election. After the election assured he would chair the Judiciary Committee, Nadler had considered how Michael Cohen had violated election laws to help Trump's campaign and "was at the center of a massive fraud, several massive frauds against the American people."[11]

Nadler's experience with Trump and his position as chairman of a relevant committee made him the logical choice to lead House efforts to hold Trump accountable. He had also shown a keen appetite to do so. However, his path was not entirely clear. The history that informed his perspective on Trump could also be cited by those who would discredit him. It was easy to imagine Trump and his allies complaining that Nadler had it out for him and couldn't be fair.

Among House Democrats, Nadler was respected, beloved, and the source of some anxiety. Decades spent representing one of the most liberal districts in the country had rendered him a bit tone deaf to the sensibilities of middle America. He also had a way of talking that made him seem like a big-city pol from a bygone era. Finally, he was not a true insider on the Pelosi leadership team. The Speaker had her favorites. Among them were several rising stars from California, a handful of close personal friends, and others who had achieved, on their own, reputations for integrity and good judgment.

No one in Congress was more respected by Pelosi than Elijah Cummings, chairman of the House Committee on Oversight and Reform. When the first opportunity arose for a high-profile hearing on a Trump scandal, Cummings got the nod, even though the issue at hand—the crimes Michael Cohen committed on Trump's behalf—could be seen as falling under Nadler's purview. A giant of the civil rights movement who represented Pelosi's native Baltimore, Cummings enjoyed a special rapport with House Republicans and had a gift for addressing political issues in moral terms.

Although it wasn't well appreciated in the moment, the fact that Cummings had this first public opportunity indicated, in the jockeying for leading positions in what was sure to be a long-running drama, that Jerrold Nadler stood at a disadvantage. His status was also evident in the fact that prior to the televised hearing conducted by Cummings, Cohen met behind closed doors with the House Permanent Select Committee on Intelligence, chaired by Representative Adam Schiff of California. Well before most knew there was even a competition under way, Schiff's personal style and his politics made him the front-runner in the competition to determine who would be the leading voice of any effort to impeach the president.[12]

April 30, 2019 — Number of House members in favor of impeaching the president: 10

17

"YOU LIED, AND NOW WE KNOW"

*Mueller, and the A.G. based on Mueller findings (and great intelligence),
have already ruled No Collusion, No Obstruction. These were crimes
committed by Crooked Hillary, the DNC, Dirty Cops and others!
INVESTIGATE THE INVESTIGATORS!*

—Donald Trump, president of the United States, via Twitter,
April 15, 2019

As a former mayor of Providence who loved retail politics, Representative David Cicilline couldn't go to the grocery store or a coffee shop without being stopped by a constituent, or two, or ten. Cicilline relied on these contacts to keep him up on public sentiment and, after Robert Mueller reported, these conversations suggested that, Democratic partisans aside, Rhode Islanders were not as concerned about the special counsel's findings as he'd expected them to be.

Mueller had described in detail many times when the president met the legal criteria for the crime of obstruction of justice. He made it clear that he had not brought charges due to the Justice Department guidelines prohibiting the indictment of a sitting president, and he had practically invited Congress to begin down the path to impeachment. However, when Mueller submitted his report, Attorney General William Barr had announced that the wait was over and that the special counsel had cleared the president. Add Donald Trump's victory declarations and the celebrations on Fox News, and one might assume that the cycle had been completed and it was time to focus on something else.[1]

For most of a month, the president had the story to himself, and he repeated his version over and over again in a brief and pithy way. No collusion.

No obstruction. Full exoneration. There was no way others could compete with an opposition message that said something like: *We should all wait to read the 448-page report ourselves and, besides, "collusion" wasn't even on the table in the first place.* That narrative favored Trump, yet cautious Democrats went with it, often with the addendum: let's-wait-and-see. It had been unrealistic for anyone to believe that a typical voter would have the time to make reading the Mueller report a priority.

Cicilline, like other Democrats, discovered that many of his constituents had no idea what was actually in the report and had no sense of what Trump had done to obstruct Mueller. This gave him a growing sense of doubt about how his party was responding to the report. As he explained it months later, he began to think, *What if we made a mistake? Maybe we should have announced the filing of articles of impeachment the day after we got the report. The Mueller report warranted it. And if we had done that, I think the American people would have reacted the way they should have reacted as, "Oh my God, this is deadly serious."*

One person who seemed to agree that the details of the Mueller report were quite serious and were being obscured was its author. On Tuesday, April 30, *The New York Times* revealed that back in March, Mueller had written to his good old friend William Barr to express his frustration over his public description of the report, which had given President Trump room for his victory dance. With the attorney general set to testify before the Senate Judiciary Committee the very next day, the Department of Justice chose to make it public. Brief as it was, the letter's tone and the specific complaint that Barr had created "public confusion about critical aspects of the results of our investigation" made it obvious that the most important person in the debate over the Mueller report disagreed with the attorney general's take.

In the House, Jerrold Nadler was among the first to react to the news of Mueller's complaint. He issued a statement saying, "The Special Counsel's concerns reflect our own. The Attorney General should not have taken it upon himself to describe the Special Counsel's findings in a light more favorable to the President. It was only a matter of time before the facts caught up to him." The next morning, before Barr appeared in the Senate, Adam Schiff went on national television to say that Barr should resign. "I think his statement is deliberately false and misleading, and yes, most people would consider that to be a lie," said Schiff. Later in the interview, he added, "After two years of work and investigation implicating the president of the United States, for the attorney general to mislead the public for an entire month before releasing that report is inexcusable."

The news that Mueller had complained breathed new life into the controversy over Russia's election interference, the Trump campaign, and the president's apparent obstruction of justice. Barr's bizarre but carefully conducted rollout of the report had been interrupted by Mueller's letter and his appearance before the committee promised even greater drama. TV networks cleared their schedules to broadcast the entire session live, and many news outlets set up teams of journalists who provided running commentary on the internet. On the website of *The New York Times*, the live coverage was moderated by veteran White House correspondent Maggie Haberman, who, in the run-up to Barr's swearing in, struck a tone that might have been perfect for a broadcast of a ball game.

"Katie, what are you watching for as we begin?" she asked her colleague Katie Benner, who covered the Department of Justice. After Benner said she'd watch to see if Barr would "obscure the fuller truth of his relationship with the special counsel's office," Haberman turned to congressional correspondent Nick Fandos to say, "Nick, how do you anticipate the senators are going to handle Barr? I assume there will be a difference between the Democrats and the Republicans."[2]

There was indeed a difference as the Republicans and the Democrats waged the equivalent of political warfare in a hearing room. Committee Chairman Lindsey Graham, who had transformed himself from a fierce Trump antagonist to a loyalist beyond compare, opened the proceedings with a tirade about Hillary Clinton and a declaration that the real scandal of the Russia-Trump affair was the conduct of the investigators who first dug into the attack on the U.S. election. These two themes reeked of the president's Deep State conspiracy theories, and by sounding them, Graham signaled to the president and voters in his home state of South Carolina that he was fully committed to the cause.

"No collusion, no coordination, no conspiracy between the Trump campaign and the Russian government regarding the 2016 election," said Senator Graham. "As to obstruction of justice, Mr. Mueller left it to Mr. Barr to decide after two years and all this time. He said 'Mr. Barr, you decide.' Mr. Barr did." At the end of his remarks, Graham held up the Mueller report as a prop for photographers and declared, "I have read most of the report. For me, it is over."

Setting aside the humor in a senator's confession that, weeks after it was published, he had still not finished reading the report he waved in his hand, Graham's speech was a purposeful attempt to distract from the real controversy of the moment. Mueller's letter had raised serious concerns about Barr's honesty and integrity. The report itself showed that Barr had deliberately mischaracterized it to favor the president. But Graham wanted to talk about Clinton's email issue, which had been settled for nearly three years, and FBI intelligence expert Peter Strzok, who had expressed private disdain for Trump. This was the rhetorical equivalent of setting a backfire to create a line of ashes so that a larger, raging forest fire would die for lack of fuel. The technique works for smoke jumpers in the mountainous West, but it didn't work for Graham. Instead of redirecting the proceedings, his diatribe inflamed Democrats who went after Barr in a way that showed they had each assumed responsibility for a specific area of interest so that they could cover as much ground as possible in the time available. As the day proceeded, it became clear that in addition to the facts of the Mueller report, they wanted to raise concerns about the independence of the Barr Justice Department. To be specific, they wanted to know if the post-Nixon reforms, which had been intended to protect the department from a president's politics, had been set aside. The Nixon reforms had been developed in response to revelations that the thirty-seventh president had used the Justice Department to harass his political critics.

Senator Kamala Harris of California suspected that Barr was taking orders from the White House, and so, when she got her chance to question Barr, she went straight at him with this question: "Mr. Barr, has the president or anyone at the White House ever asked or suggested that you open an investigation of anyone?"

It was a clearly worded question, and Harris offered it in a tone that was so matter-of-fact that a listener might need a moment to absorb it. As she paused, tilted her head slightly to her left and rested her chin on her hand, she punctuated the drama and demonstrated the skills she had employed in her previous job as attorney general of California.

Barr, unable to look Harris in the face, gazed up and to his right, as if looking to heaven for inspiration.

"Uhhhh. I wouldn't, I wouldn't, uhh."

Barr paused here, cotton-mouthed, his tongue flickering to his lips. He began to twist and turn a pen with his fingers, making it look like he was manipulating some worry beads or perhaps a rosary.

"Yes or no?" said Harris, now adding pressure to the moment.

"Uh, can you repeat the question?" Now Barr was a spelling bee kid or a game show contestant, playing for time.

"I will repeat it," said Harris chirpily. Now her elbows were on the dais, and she was staring straight at Barr. "Has the president or anyone at the White House ever asked or suggested that you open an investigation of anyone? Yes or no, please, sir."

Barr, still playing for time, began with another, "Uhhhh," and then tilted his head to indicate thoughtfulness and said, as if to himself, "The president or anybody else."

"It seems you would remember something like that and be able to tell us."

"Yeah, but I'm trying to grapple with the word *suggest*." By this point, more than thirty seconds had passed. "I mean, there have been discussions of matters out there"—here, he lifted his right hand into the air—"that they've not asked me to open an investigation."

"Perhaps they suggested."

"I don't know, I wouldn't say suggest."

"Hinted?"

"I don't know."

"Inferred?"

Here Barr simply stopped responding. He gazed to his right and fell silent, his mouth twitched, but he didn't make a sound.

"You don't know." This wasn't a question. It was a statement. Harris then said, mercifully, "Okay," and moved on to the matter of Barr's March 24 four-page interpretation of the Mueller report. As she spoke, Barr suddenly thought of a reply to her previous query.

"But I will say that no investigation . . . ," he said, interrupting.

"Sir, I am asking a question," said Harris, cutting him off. Harris then noted the vast body of testimony, records, and FBI reports Mueller had accrued as the evidence Barr referenced to decide, two days after receiving the report, that no obstruction had occurred. "In reaching your conclusion, did you personally review all of the underlying evidence?" asked Harris.

"Uh, no," said Barr. As he tried to explain, Harris intervened.

"Did Mr. Rosenstein?"

"No." He then explained that no one in his office had considered any of the evidence Mueller had presented on the ten possible acts of obstruction.

"Yet you represented to the American public that the evidence was not quote 'sufficient' to support an obstruction of justice offense," said Harris. Indeed, in a case involving the president of the United States, and a report that offered a strong argument that he had committed multiple crimes, Barr had decided no charges would be made without anyone in his office looking at a single bit of underlying proof.

Harris was not the only senator who brought a prosecutor's experience to the hearing. Senator Sheldon Whitehouse had been U.S. attorney in Rhode Island for six years and attorney general of his state for four. He was concerned with the complaint letter Barr had received from Mueller, and, like a prosecutor, he was eager to establish a timeline. Whitehouse determined that Barr read the letter and spoke with Mueller about it on March 28. On April 4, Barr attended an Appropriations Committee hearing, where Congressman Charlie Crist of Florida asked him if he knew if members of the Mueller office felt "frustration" over his four-page description of the report. At that time, Barr had said, "No, I don't."

As Whitehouse explored this issue, it became clear he believed that Barr had misled Crist and delayed telling the truth until he had been trapped by news reports about the Mueller complaint. "Would you concede you had an opportunity to make this letter public on April 4 when Representative Crist asked you a very related question?"

"I don't know what you mean by 'related question.' It seems to me it would be a different question."

By this point, an exasperated Whitehouse said, "I can't follow that down the road. That's masterful hairsplitting. I mean, boy."

Whitehouse chased the attorney general down a different road when he returned to the controversy Barr had sparked by using the politically charged term *spying* to denigrate the federal investigation of the Russian election attack. This word was consistent with the long-running effort Trump and others had made to rewrite history so that those who learned of Russia's theft of campaign documents and commenced an investigation would be painted as evildoers. "In your entire career, have you ever referred to authorized department investigative activities, officially or publicly, as spying? I'm not asking for private conversations."

"I'm not going to abjure the use of the word *spying*," said Barr as he then recalled that he had worked at the Central Intelligence Agency and considered the term a "common" word with no "pejorative" meaning. He also said he considered it a "big deal" that spying had taken place. Barr did not, however, recall any previous instance when he had used it in public. And the former U.S. attorney Whitehouse, again impatient, observed, "It is not commonly used by the department."

As the Democrats exposed Barr on various aspects of his deceptions, they also displayed different emotional tones. Whitehouse was incredulous. Harris was coolly commanding. It would fall to Senator Mazie Hirono of Hawaii to express the anger that many of her colleagues and many Americans felt as Barr had hijacked the Mueller report and used the Department of Justice to support the president's political agenda.

Hirono, who wore a red jacket for the occasion, offered the kind of heated criticism, and judgment, rarely heard in the United States Senate. Under the rules, she had just minutes to speak, and since she had much to say, she barely took a breath:

Mr. Barr: Now that the American people know you are no different from Rudy Giuliani or [White House counselor] Kellyanne Conway, or any of the other people who sacrificed their once decent reputations for the grifter liar who sits in the Oval Office. You once turned down a job offer from Donald Trump to represent him as his private attorney. At your confirmation hearing you told Senator Feinstein that "the job of attorney general is not the same as representing the president" so you know the difference but you've chosen to be the president's lawyer and side with him over the interest of the American people.

To start with, you should never have been involved in supervising the Robert Mueller investigation. You wrote a 19-page unsolicited memo, which you admit was not based on any fact, attacking the premise of half of the investigation. And you also should have insisted that Deputy Attorney General Rod Rosenstein recuse himself. He was not just a witness to some of the president's obstructive behavior, we now know he was in frequent personal contact of the president, a subject of the investigation.

As Hirono continued with a withering review of Barr's handling of the Mueller report, the attorney general took sips of water and Republican senators began to squirm in their seats. Where Senator Whitehouse had stopped short of saying it, Hirono went ahead and declared that Barr had "lied to

Congress" when he told Representative Crist he wasn't aware that Mueller's team had objected to his handling of the report. "You lied," she said, "and now we know." A moment later, she spoke of the public trust held by the attorney general and said, "You have betrayed that trust. America deserves better. You should resign."

When she finally reached a point where she asked questions, Hirono set aside the matter of crimes, which she believed the president had committed, and simply asked whether Barr, as attorney general, thought certain acts had been "okay." Had it been "okay" for the president to fire James Comey because he had been investigating links between the Trump campaign and Russia? (Trump had said this was his motivation.) Barr said, "I do think it's okay for the president to do what he did." Next came a question about Trump's request that White House counsel Don McGahn to lie about efforts to fire Mueller. Was that "okay"? Here, Barr paused and said, "Well, I'm going to talk about what's criminal."

"No," said Hirono, waving her hand. "We've already acknowledged that you think it was not a crime. I'm just asking whether you think it's okay. Even if it's not a crime, do you think it's okay for the president to ask his White House counsel to lie?"

As Barr stammered, Hirono took his nonanswer to indicate he thought the president had acted properly. Then, noticing she had little time left, she raced ahead. "Do you think it is okay for a president to offer pardons to people who don't testify against him? To threaten the family of someone who does? Is that okay?"

Barr sputtered some protests, suggesting these things had not occurred when, in fact, one of the president's lawyers had talked about pardons for Michael Flynn and Paul Manafort and the president himself had tweeted ominously about Michael Cohen's family.

"Please, please, Mr. Attorney General. You know, give us some credit for knowing what the hell is going on around here with you."

Suddenly, from the center of the Senate panel came a voice that interrupted Hirono.

"Not really," said Senator Graham, the committee chairman. "Listen, you've slandered this man."

Now, emboldened by Graham's interruption, Barr decided that he would pose questions to the room.

"What I sort of want to know, how did we get to this point?"

Graham said, "You've slandered this man from top to bottom. If you want more of this, you're not going to get it."[3]

•   •   •

Before he finished testifying on May 1, William Barr would dismiss Robert Mueller's complaint about his effort to spin the findings in his report as "a little bit snitty" and blame the press for making his friend upset. In this, he followed the Donald Trump playbook, which calls for endless attacks on the news media in order to shape public opinion. Barr would use Rod Rosenstein as a shield, saying the deputy attorney general had supported his handling of the report. And he would denigrate those in his own department who had dug into the Russia issue. Barr said Mueller's prosecutors were "not necessarily" the best and the brightest, and some FBI officials had acted improperly because they believed "they know better than the American people."

Five hours passed between the start of the dramatic hearing and its end. Over at the website of *The New York Times,* the running commentary, which had included more than one baseball metaphor, ended its blow-by-blow reporting with correspondent Charlie Savage's announcement that "there's your final" (a common phrase sports announcers use to note the end of a game and the final score).

Barr left behind an astonishing record of an attorney general repeatedly declaring "no collusion" as he played the role of the president's defender. Instead of putting to rest concerns about his handling of the report, he inspired calls for Mueller himself to testify and moved others to join in with Senator Hirono's demand that he resign. Although the attorney general had labored to seem unruffled and at times even bored by the hearing, his behavior in the hours after the hearing indicated he had, in fact, been unsettled, as he abruptly refused to appear at a House Committee on the Judiciary hearing, which he had planned to attend.

Barr blamed his sudden change of heart on the committee's plan to let its staff lawyer join the questioning, but in fact, he was acting in line with an overall administration strategy to stonewall Congress's attempts to oversee the executive branch in any way that caused it discomfort. Although Democrats had only held the House for four months, President Trump and his administration had refused requests for information and documents related to eight different controversies and were resisting many more. The blatant partisanship in this practice was obvious in the administration's ready cooperation with the Senate, where fellow Republicans were in charge and would lead to court battles as Congress sought to use its oversight power.

In the moment, though, the stonewall strategy gave William Barr, who would turn sixty-nine in three weeks, a chance to catch his breath. It was unusual, but not unprecedented as the administration claimed, for committee attorneys to interview a witness. When the Trump administration rejected allowing Barr to submit to such questioning, Jerrold Nadler lashed back.

"He is terrified of having to face a skilled attorney," Nadler said, referring to lawyers for committee Democrats. "That's the most effective way at getting at the facts and getting at the truth . . . I can understand why he's afraid of facing more effective examination." The next step, announced Nadler, would be for the committee to consider holding Barr in contempt of Congress.[4]

May 1, 2019 — Number of House members in favor of impeaching the president: 10

18

CONFLICT ESCALATION

Why are the Democrats not looking into all of the crimes committed by Crooked Hillary and the phony Russia Investigation? They would get back their credibility. Jerry Nadler, Schiff, would have a whole new future open to them. Perhaps they could even run for President!

—Donald Trump, president of the United States, via Twitter,
May 20, 2019

William Barr's retreat fulfilled a declaration Donald Trump had made days before. The occasion had been one of the president's Chopper Talk performances outside the White House. "We're fighting all the subpoenas," he shouted hoarsely at the gathered reporters. "These aren't, like, impartial people. The Democrats are trying to win 2020."

The subpoena that concerned Trump most had been sent to Don McGahn. The former White House counsel had told Robert Mueller's team that the president had pressured him to create a false document. It would have been used to cover up the fact that Trump had tried to fire the special counsel. The House wanted to get to the bottom of this episode and others. The fact that McGahn had already discussed this event with Mueller, thus letting the horse out of the barn, made it unlikely the president would ultimately win in a court battle over the subpoena, but with a trial and appeals, he could delay resolution of the issue, perhaps even past Election Day 2020.

When Trump announced his sweeping refusal to comply with House subpoenas, experts noted that no president in memory—and perhaps history—had ever said he would defy every writ issued by the House. In this case, it seemed inevitable that when committees filed suit to enforce demands for witnesses and documents, they would win some cases. However, this process could take many months or even years, which meant that the president's announcement, and Barr's decision to break his commitment to testify in the House, brought the country closer to the grave condition known as a *constitutional crisis*.

Scholars defined this phenomenon in different ways but generally agreed that it amounted to a state of war between branches of the government. Such wars arise when one branch breaks faith with the power-balancing rules created by the Constitution. Andrew Jackson, who presided over the murder of Native Americans and whom Trump much admired, did this when he refused to enforce a Supreme Court decision granting a tribe nation status. Another of Trump's favorites, Richard Nixon, created a constitutional crisis during Watergate when he refused to hand over tape recordings and documents subpoenaed by Congress. Nixon lost a court battle over the issue, and his refusal moved the House to proceed toward impeachment. The crisis ended when Nixon resigned to spare the country the trauma of seeing a president impeached and possibly convicted. Trump believed Nixon had made a mistake and should have dared Congress to follow through.[1]

• • •

Conflict escalation was Donald Trump's lifelong habit, and his rule was to push beyond the point where propriety suggested he stop. In business, he proudly rejected the common belief that parties to a negotiation should leave something *on the table* as a gesture of goodwill that might encourage a future deal. Trump adhered to a take-it-all-now strategy even when it guaranteed him an enemy. As a public personality and politician, he reliably answered criticism with personal attacks and crossed lines that others respected. So it was that he insulted others' appearance, questioned their intelligence, and even demeaned their loved ones. As president, he routinely relied on powers that others used lightly. To avoid the Senate's confirmation authority, he filled the upper echelons of his administration with "acting" officials. He used his tariff powers to score political points and abused his pardon privilege to short-circuit the criminal justice system.

During the House investigation of his conduct, Trump would systematically refuse to provide documents requested by committees conducting oversight. As the House tried to look into emoluments, he would deny them access to financial records, including tax returns, which, unlike every president back to Nixon, he had refused to make public. He withheld records of hush-money payments Michael Cohen had made to an adult film star and a nude model, ignored a subpoena for evidence on the transfer of nuclear technology to Saudi Arabia, and denied a request for information on the separation of infants and children from asylum-seeking parents. These varied examples represented the breadth of the issues Trump refused to discuss but hardly the volume, which, as time passed, grew ever larger and clogged the courts with legal proceedings.[2]

With each provocative step, the president caused actors in other branches of government to consider how to defend against him. In November 2018, John Roberts, chief justice of the Supreme Court, actually rebuked Trump for complaining about judges whom other presidents had named to various courts. "We do not have Obama judges or Trump judges, Bush judges or Clinton judges," Roberts said. "What we have is an extraordinary group of dedicated judges doing their level best to do equal right to those appearing before them. The independent judiciary is something we should all be thankful for." Unable to feel chastened, Trump replied on Twitter. "Sorry Chief Justice Roberts, but you do indeed have 'Obama judges,' and they have a much different point of view than the people who are charged with the safety of our country." Trump went on to deny that the Ninth Circuit represented "an 'independent judiciary.'"[3]

Mild as it was, Roberts's statement was noteworthy because legal experts could not recall when any modern chief justice had said a similar thing in response to a president. It was also noteworthy that, despite holding an office that was, by definition, overtly political, Speaker of the House Nancy Pelosi had chosen to refrain from actually saying the country had reached the point of crisis that would make impeachment thinkable. An astute observer of the president's behavior, she had refused to be goaded into overreacting. However, many in Pelosi's caucus believed that only tough action could stop Trump from doing damage to essential elements of American democracy.

Away from law schools and universities where such things are studied and discussed, the elements of democracy are not regularly considered as people go about their lives, as we rightly rely on the clockwork to function and depend on those in charge to keep it in good repair. Even inside the government, it is rare to find someone with a true sense of mission when it comes to defending the system. Sure, most members of Congress can give a patriotic speech about the American Revolution or the Constitutional Convention, but in the hurly-burly of Washington, it is natural for different branches of government, especially the legislative and executive, to compete for dominance.

Some members of Congress were cut out for the political slugfest. Representative Steve Cohen of Tennessee showed how this was done at a hearing where he mocked William Barr as "chicken," produced a bucket of golden-fried legs and thighs, and began chowing down. It wasn't all that unusual for members of Congress to add a dash of vaudeville to their public appearances, but Cohen's level of theatricality was rare. Similarly rare was the member of Congress with the inclination and the expertise to blend politics and constitutional law in a way that could inspire. One of those few was Democrat Jamie Raskin, who had just begun his second term representing a Maryland district that borders Washington, D.C. When he decided to speak out, it became obvious that he had been preparing for this moment for his entire life.

• • •

Jamie Raskin had been born into what might be called the liberal activist elite. His father, Marcus Raskin, had set aside a promising classical music career to become a lawyer and aide to prominent congressional Democrats, including FDR's eldest son. In the 1960s, he rose to prominence as a writer and organizer. At age six, Jamie found himself working in coloring books in a federal courtroom, where his father was on trial on charges of aiding and abetting men trying to evade the draft for the Vietnam War. One of a group of defendants called the Boston Five, Marcus Raskin was acquitted, but his four codefendants, including Dr. Benjamin Spock and Rev. William Sloane Coffin, were found guilty. (Their convictions were overturned on appeal.)

Three years later, Marcus Raskin helped *The New York Times* obtain the Pentagon Papers from defense analyst Daniel Ellsberg, who had chosen to release the official history of the war effort after learning of Richard Nixon's plan to use tactical nuclear weapons to end the conflict. The papers revealed how four presidents had misled the public on the conduct of the war. In response to their publication, a furious Nixon ordered the use of burglaries and blackmail schemes to limit the damage to his government. After Nixon declared, "We've got to get this son of a bitch," the White House authorized a break-in at a psychiatrist's office to obtain Ellsberg's file. (Nixon's men also planned to attack Ellsberg physically, with the intent to incapacitate him, but did not follow through.) These abuses, joined with other revelations about how Nixon had tried to use the FBI and other agencies against his critics, became the basis for the post-Watergate reforms intended to separate the Justice Department from direct presidential control.[4]

With William Barr mouthing the president's political slogan—"No collusion"—and participating in the White House practice of stonewalling the House, Jamie Raskin could sense history repeating itself. He also recognized the threat Trump posed to a system devised by the Founders that depended upon every generation of citizens—and most especially presidents—to respect it. He had been keeping track of Donald Trump's record in this regard.

As the Judiciary Committee's point man on the issue of emoluments, Raskin had watched with amazement as the president's businesses profited and his Republican colleagues, many of whom claimed to revere the Constitution, said nothing. "They said they were going to drain the swamp," said Raskin, citing a Trump campaign promise. "They moved into the swamp. They built a hotel on it and they started renting out rooms to foreign princes and kings and despots and dictators and tyrants. They've converted the government into an instrument of money making. It's a for profit enterprise."

When it came to the Constitution, Raskin was so adept that he was able to quote the *Federalist Papers* from memory and liked to entertain his colleagues by singing about his favorite text. In his study of emoluments he had been reminded that many of the Founders, but especially George Mason of Virginia, believed that accepting emoluments would be an impeachable offense. He also noted that presidents were not just prohibited from accepting things of value from foreigners. Much overlooked was the fact that domestic emoluments violated the Constitution as well, and the only way a president could get around the ban involved obtaining Congress's permission to accept a payment or gift.

In early 2019 Raskin helped form a group that communicated via the secure messaging service called Signal, which allowed them to exchange information and opinions without concern for them being compromised by hackers. This practice didn't grow out of paranoia, although the Nixon example showed that crossing a president could be dangerous. Instead, they wanted to prevent even the possibility of leaks that could affect House leaders trying to manage a caucus that was already divided over what to do about the president. Raskin also reread *The Federalist Papers,* to remind himself of how the Founders thought as they drafted the Constitution.

The more he studied, the more Raskin came to believe that Trump's actions had provoked a constitutional duty for the House to respond via the impeachment mechanism. Colleagues who remained reluctant noted that even if the House did approve articles charging Trump, Senate majority leader Mitch McConnell had already declared "case closed" and would, with his lock on his caucus, guarantee Trump a victory in any trial on charges referred by the House.

In May of 2019, Raskin's group certainly understood this reality but also wondered about the possibility that a handful of GOP senators who had previously criticized Donald Trump might be persuaded and thereby make Trump's conviction and removal possible. Among the list they considered at the time were:

- Senator Ted Cruz of Texas, because Trump had insulted his wife and suggested his father was involved in President Kennedy's assassination

- Senator Marco Rubio of Florida, because Trump had called him "Little Marco" and many of his state's voters opposed Trump

- Senator Mitt Romney of Utah, because he had been highly critical of Trump and was a very traditional Republican

No one on this list could be deemed a likely vote against Trump in an impeachment trial, but in their private discussions, they encouraged the idea that the conventional wisdom about the GOP senators walking in lockstep behind McConnell might be wrong. An old joke holds that every morning, one hundred senators wake up in Washington and see a future president in the mirror. This chestnut depended on the idea that senators did imagine themselves to be national figures, and their six-year terms permitted them to take breaks from partisan politics and cast votes that showed their independence.[5]

While some members of the House Judiciary war-gamed a future Senate trial of Donald Trump, the committee as a whole moved behind Jerrold Nadler's continued effort to hold the administration accountable. Days after William Barr refused to keep his commitment to testify about the Mueller report, Nadler called on the committee to consider holding the attorney general in contempt. Congress so rarely held officials in contempt that this move represented a serious escalation of the conflict between the House and the administration. Congress had ceased to arrest and detain those held in contempt, which meant the proceedings were mainly symbolic. However, some shame could still be attached to those whom the House deemed worthy of such powerful condemnation.

Coming so soon after Barr's confrontation with Senate Democrats, Nadler's hearing on the contempt charge brought TV news networks back for hours of live coverage. Every member, Republicans as well as Democrats, tried to match the senators who had gained national attention the week before. Little known outside his district prior, Jamie Raskin became a national political figure with a speech that he began with a quiet reference, drawn from memory, and offered in a professorial tone.

> Thomas Paine said in the monarchies, the king is law, but in the democracies, the law is king. That is the principle at stake in America today. The president of the United States and all of us who seek and attain public office are nothing but the servants of the people and the servants of the law, and the moment that we forget that and we begin to act like the masters of the people and the masters of the law, then we put our jobs at risk.

Raskin was bothered that William Barr had blacked out sections of the Mueller report without explaining in any detail why and by the opposition from those in Congress who wanted to retain the redactions. Anticipating the argument that Barr's cuts only obscured 8 percent of the report, he said, "You could redact eight percent of the Constitution of the United States and get rid of freedom of the speech, freedom of the press, religious freedom, equal protection, and due process."

After a bit more about the Constitution, including a lesson about how the president was expected to enforce the laws established by Congress, Raskin shifted into a more powerful rhetorical gear, raising his voice and accelerating his cadence, to recite the ways that President Trump had degraded his office and American political life. Every item in his long and varied litany noted a specific, documented instance of the president's behavior. He began with things that normal adults know not to do but that Trump had done.

> You don't mock people with disabilities. Men don't mock women's bodies on television. You don't ridicule people and give them obnoxious nicknames, at least after you graduate from the third grade. You don't falsely accuse other political leaders of treason. You don't accuse other political leaders' parents of assassinating President Kennedy. You don't use disgusting, profane language to disparage

other countries, and you don't call neo-Nazis and Klansmen very fine people. You don't give aid and comfort to the dictators of the world like Kim Jong-un and Vladimir Putin by flattering them and being their sycophant.

In this speech, Raskin seemed to channel his father, who had frequently laced his legal arguments with appeals to morality and patriotic ideals. He condemned Trump's repeated attacks on the news media, House committees, the Department of Justice, and the Mueller team and then pivoted to his academic specialty, the Constitution, and how Trump violated constraints designed to protect the presidency from those seeking influence.

You turn the government of the United States into a money-making operation for your family, for your business, and yourself . . . You collect millions of dollars from foreign princes and kings and governments in violation of Article I, Section IX, Clause VII of the Constitution.

And now the president, aided and abetted by the attorney general, tears at the very fabric of our Constitution. He orders that a curtain be pulled down over the executive branch. He says there will be no cooperation with the lawful demands of Congress for information . . . The president declares himself above and beyond the law.

James Madison said knowledge will forever govern ignorance. And those who mean to be their own governors must arm themselves with the power that knowledge gives. The people through the Constitution gave us that power, we must exercise it. If you act with contempt for the people and Congress, we will find you in contempt of the people and of Congress.[6]

•   •   •

At the end of the five-hour hearing, the committee voted along party lines to find William Barr in contempt. Republicans said this vote was little more than an expression of frustration over the limited impact of the Mueller report. They also saw an effort to unfairly vilify William Barr. "Why this rush?" asked Representative Doug Collins of Georgia, the senior Republican on the committee. In answering his own question, he added, "We can only assume Democrats, led by the chairman, have resolved to sully Bill Barr's good name and reputation."

By the end of the day, Adam Schiff, chairman of the House Intelligence Committee, would issue his own subpoena seeking copies of the full Mueller report, unredacted. Schiff's action revealed a growing appetite for confrontation among House members and signs of competition over just who would lead House Democrats into battle. Schiff's committee had jurisdiction over foreign intelligence issues, and Russia's attack on the 2016 election fell into this area of concern. However, the true controversy in the Mueller report grew out of the president's response to being investigated and the vast evidence that he had attempted to obstruct justice. Add that Mueller had worked under the supervision of the Justice Department and that Attorney General Barr controlled his work product, and Jerrold Nadler would seem to have the greater claim to oversight authority.

Nadler's move on contempt would, in two months, be ratified by the entire House. As it occurred, Speaker of the House Pelosi crossed a boundary as she said she agreed with him that the country had entered a constitutional crisis. Her decision to use this language affirmed that the Judiciary Committee had acted with her assent. The Speaker made this point at one of her weekly news conferences where, like the president, she could use the trappings of office, including flags that served as a backdrop, and be certain of getting attention. Unlike him, she never raised her voice, and she spoke in full sentences and even paragraphs. And yet, in her matter-of-fact way, she outlined a future that was threatening to the president. "What we want to do is get the facts. We want to do it in a way that is least divisive to our country and the most productive. . . . We are sailing, in the Constitutional way, for the administration to comply. We still have more opportunities. We'll see if Mueller will testify and that will make a big difference in terms of where we go from here."

When asked whether she was foreshadowing a historic confrontation between Congress and the executive branch, she answered in a quiet way that should have chilled the president. "This is not about Congress or any committee of Congress. It's about the American people and their right to know, and their election that is at stake and that a foreign government intervened in our election and the president thinks this is a laughing matter . . . to look to history, and the Nixon experience, of non-impeachment, or whatever you want to call that, was months of hearings and investigation before they got to a place where they had a compelling argument." Then, she said, Republicans had to "go to the president" and tell him he had to resign.[7]

•　　•　　•

Investigation. Months of hearings. Nixon. Resignation. It was all very ominous. So, of course, Donald Trump would respond as if nothing serious was happening.

As a former television performer and executive, President Trump understood the age-old strategy called *counterprogramming*. It involves presenting a noisy alternative show at the moment when a competitor offers a marquee program. If they broadcast a top-rated drama with gifted actors, you present the finale of a reality show titled, say, *Naked and Afraid* (this is a real program). Done well, counterprogramming will draw most of the viewers who just want entertainment and may even resent all the hubbub about the tony TV show everyone says you should watch. In entertainment and then politics, Trump had long preferred the tight bond that could be formed as he offered adrenaline-pumping fare to folks who were happy to join him in mocking those who sought to elevate and educate. A big audience could be had by a performer who shed all pretense—or at least pretended to—in order to deliver the unvarnished truth.

As president, whenever Donald Trump was besieged by opponents, he used big public rallies to showcase his well-practiced distortions and to reassure himself that he was still a leader with lots of devoted followers. For this reason, he never paused for very long between campaign-style appearances where he delivered stream-of-consciousness monologues that reminded the faithful of why they loved him. They, in turn, provided the cheers and chants that buoyed the president's spirits. With interludes of call-and-response and shouts for favorite tunes—"Lock her up!"—Trump rallies were like rock concerts, religious revivals, and pro-wrestling matches rolled into one. Admission was free, and everyone, but most especially the president, received a jolt of emotional reinforcement.

On the day when the House Judiciary Committee voted to hold William Barr in contempt and Jamie Raskin recited his compendium of Trump's sins and failings, the president of the United States flew to the part of northern Florida known as the Panhandle, where, in 2016, a huge advantage among the voters in rural counties gave him enough support to capture the state's electoral college votes. More like neighboring Alabama than the parts of Florida south of Tallahassee, the Panhandle depended on the federal dollars that flowed to local military installations. The president had promised to rebuild one of them, Tyndall Air Force Base, which had been devastated by a hurricane. Air Force One delivered him to the base as the sun was beginning to set over the Gulf of Mexico. The armored presidential limousine known as the Beast whisked him to the Aaron Bessant Park Amphitheater in Panama City Beach. At a venue where the biggest draw of the summer would be an '80s rock tribute band called Sound Arcade, Trump easily filled the place to overflowing.

The president gave 'em what they came for, including the now-traditional retelling of the Trump-era origin story: his overwhelming election triumph came despite a deficit in the popular vote of more than 2.8 million, which of course had to be the result of voter fraud. Trump had spent years whittling this fluke into a miracle akin to Moses delivering the Israelites from bondage. But like any effective leader, he rewarded his followers with the credit. They were the heroes.

"You came from all over," said the president. "You voted. They didn't know you; they didn't know you folks existed in many cases, the invisible people. And you know what you are? You're the smartest, you're the hardest working, you're paying your taxes. You do all of this stuff, great jobs, great talents, you're the best-looking people, that's for sure.

"They call themselves the elite. They're not elite, you're elite. I always take heat. I say you have better houses, so do I. You have better boats. You have better everything. You have better everything, you're smarter, you know, I say, 'No, we're the elite.' So, let's let them be the elite, but we're the super elite, there's not even a contest."

When he talked about them, the people in the crowd were attentive and engaged. They laughed eagerly and applauded. When he then referred to himself and Congress, their enthusiasm flagged. "Now the Democrats are saying, 'We want more.' You know it was gonna be like, 'We want the Mueller report.' Now they say, 'Mueller report? No. We want to start all over again.' It is a disgrace." The president almost lost them with his detour into Mueller and the way Congress had begun to use it as a guide for its own investigations. This was a recent development in the Trump saga and was, as of May 8, 2019, not something that everyone followed closely.

Fortunately for the president, he had already captured the sound bite that guaranteed the rally would make headlines and divert attention from his trouble in Washington, thanks to a prompt from someone in the audience. As the president reviewed his anti-asylum policies at the border with Mexico, which included mass incarceration and family separation, he mused that soldiers he had posted were not supposed to shoot those who arrived at the border. "Other countries do," he said. "We can't. I would never do that. But how do you stop these people?"

"Shoot them!" shouted a woman in the crowd.

The president paused, chuckled, and gestured at the woman. Milking the moment, he grinned and shook his head as he said, "That's only in the Panhandle that you can get away with that, folks." Met by cheers and laughter, he paused again before repeating, "Only in the Panhandle!"

Reassured and reinvigorated by the cheers, the president roared back to Washington aboard Air Force One, ready to counterattack. He would say that Mueller and the House Democrats were not just investigating him, they were attacking the United States of America and it was time for it all to stop. "So there's no crime. There never was a crime. It was a hoax. It was a witch hunt. So this comes back, and it comes back totally exonerating Donald Trump and a lot of other people. This was a terrible thing that happened to our country."[8]

May 20, 2019 — Number of House members in favor of impeaching the president: 15

19

SELF-IMPEACHMENT

"If they try to Impeach President Trump, who has done nothing wrong (No Collusion), they will end up getting him re-elected" @LindseyGrahamSC Impeachment is for High Crimes and Misdemeanors. There were no High Crimes and Misdemeanors, except for those committed by the other side!

—Donald Trump, president of the United States, via Twitter,
May 24, 2019

On the evening of May 20, when leaders of the Democratic Caucus met in the Speaker's office at the Capitol, three who were members of the Judiciary Committee pressed her on impeachment. David Cicilline of Rhode Island, Jamie Raskin of Maryland, and Joe Neguse of Colorado said that on every visit to their districts, in every log of phone calls and emails, in every delivery of regular mail, they had been overwhelmed by their constituents' concerns about the president.

Bluntly put, the people they represented expected a stronger response from Congress. Most of the Democrats on the Judiciary Committee favored beginning an "impeachment inquiry," which would bring the House right up to the starting line for a formal proceeding without crossing it. Under this strategy, they could investigate indefinitely and use what the president would soon call "a dirty, filthy, disgusting word," without binding the House to any future action.

Clever as the idea was, Speaker Pelosi said that voters were more interested in seeing Congress work on problems that affected them directly. National polls indicated this was true, even if individual members of the House felt their own constituents considered impeachment a first priority.

For months, public appearances had brought Pelosi face-to-face with questions about impeachment, and as time had passed, she had expressed changing views. Firm resistance to the idea of removing Trump gave way to the observation that some things the president did indicated he was almost determined to be charged with high crimes and misdemeanors. She called these actions "self-impeachable."

Having followed her closely, Jamie Raskin couldn't resist using *her* words to make *his* argument. "Madame Speaker, you just made a great argument for an impeachment inquiry," he told her in the leadership meeting. "It could be delegated to the Judiciary Committee, which could then go forward with it."

As others urged the same course, they argued that by opening an impeachment inquiry, Chairman Nadler might strengthen Congress's case if the courts were asked to settle disputes over the president's refusal to comply with subpoenas. This was not a fanciful idea. Impeachment, a power granted only to the House, put Congress on firmer ground when it demanded cooperation from the executive. Why not invoke the term now, so that the courts would have reason to grant House demands for documents and testimony?

With the pressure on Pelosi growing, higher-ranking members of the team came to her side. Hakeem Jeffries of New York was especially firm in pushing back against the three younger members. (In the caucus at large, Pelosi would also depend on fellow Californians Zoe Lofgren and Ro Khanna, and Gerry Connolly of Virginia.) The session ended with the Speaker irritated, rather than moved, and holding to her position. If at all possible, she wanted the process toward impeachment to be bipartisan. With no sign of a Republican defecting from Trump's side, she would wait. However, as Steve Cohen's fried chicken moment had shown, she could not control everything House Democrats did. Shortly after the meeting where Pelosi quashed the impeachment inquiry notion, Chairman Nadler observed, "The president's lawless conduct is making it harder and harder to rule out impeachment."[1]

•   •   •

Tension increased day by day between Pelosi's hope for bipartisanship and the restiveness of members who thought Trump had to be impeached, whether or not any Republicans participated.

Some outside observers believed there was a Brer Rabbit aspect to Pelosi's stance, with her publicly resisting but secretly encouraging the calls for action. This was not true. Pelosi was not persuaded that the best course for the country would be a plunge into an impeachment process. On May 20,

Representative Joaquin Castro, a member of the Intelligence Committee from Texas, said simply, "It's time to start." On May 21, two members from Pennsylvania, Mary Gay Scanlon and Madeleine Dean, said they supported an impeachment inquiry too.

Few members of the House were more outspoken than Raskin, who submitted to a long interview with Greg Sargent of *The Washington Post*, whose Plum Line column was known as a place where political players spoke to each other in public. Raskin noted that members of the Judiciary Committee had more day-to-day involvement with impeachment issues and were "operating with detailed knowledge of the evidence of high crimes and misdemeanors spelled out in the Mueller report." A day later, at an early-morning, closed-door caucus meeting, the Speaker held her ground as more Democrats lined up behind the inquiry idea. Afterward, Raskin pushed her just a little bit harder and borrowed from Malcolm X to say, "Lots of members want to put an impeachment inquiry on the table. We want to use whatever means are necessary in order to defend the Constitution and the rule of law."[2]

• • •

If Nancy Pelosi couldn't control members of her party with any full confidence, she had virtually no influence over House Republicans. In another time, not so long ago, presidents could not expect members of their party to follow them over an impeachment cliff. When Richard Nixon resigned under threat of impeachment in 1974, he did so after Republicans in the House expressed their outrage over Watergate and Barry Goldwater told him he had no choice. Twenty-four years later, five Democrats joined their GOP colleagues to support one or more of the articles of impeachment approved against Bill Clinton.

As Pelosi knew, much had changed since the Clinton impeachment, especially in the Republican Party, which had moved to the right and become far less tolerant of dissent. With hyper-partisans dominating primaries, moderate Republicans in Congress had become a dying breed. Then came Donald Trump, who combined hard-right political positions with a cult leader's personal appeal to make the party over in his own image. In the 2018 election that gave Democrats control of the House, many of the seats they picked up had been abandoned by these so-called moderates. Ironically, many of *them* had arrived in Washington as conservative insurgents, only to watch the trend that brought them to office continue until it produced a president so intolerant of dissent that he attacked officeholders who openly disagreed with him and was so skilled at rallying voters that many resigned rather than seek reelection against the Trump tide. When the new Congress arrived in January 2019, 40 percent of the Republicans who had been present for Trump's inauguration just two years before were gone.[3]

With no one to talk to on the other side of the aisle, Nancy Pelosi had no reason to believe that a single Republican would dare to cross the president. Indeed, where many of them were concerned, the surest way for them to oppose any idea was for the Speaker to say she was for it. So it was that Representative Justin Amash of Michigan, a young Republican who had ridden the wave of anti-Obama sentiment into the House in 2010, surprised her on May 18 when he suddenly announced that after reading the Mueller report he had concluded that the president "has engaged in impeachable conduct."

Amash chose to break from the GOP on the president's favorite social media site, Twitter, where he wrote a series of public messages related to his reading and analysis of the Mueller report. The first began with the statement "Here are my principal conclusions" and then offered a list:

1. Attorney General Barr has deliberately misrepresented Mueller's report.
2. President Trump has engaged in impeachable conduct.
3. Partisanship has eroded our system of checks and balances.
4. Few members of Congress have read the report.

In a flurry of a dozen more tweets, Amash presented an essay for the social media age, explaining that he believed William Barr "intended to mislead the public about Special Counsel Robert Mueller's analysis and findings" and these "misrepresentations are significant but often subtle, frequently taking the form of sleight-of-hand qualifications or logical fallacies, which he hopes people will not notice." Amash saw obstruction of justice in Mueller's report on the president's conduct, and he reminded his colleagues that "America's institutions depend on officials to uphold both the rules and spirit of our constitutional system even when to do so is personally inconvenient or yields a politically unfavorable outcome."

Inevitably, the outcome for Amash included lacerating comments from the president, who said, "Never a fan, never liked him," and declared Amash to be "a total lightweight who opposes me and some of our great Republican ideas and policies just for the sake of getting his name out there through

controversy." He added, "Justin is a loser who sadly plays right into our opponents' hands!"[4]

On the day after Amash spoke out, pro-Trump Republicans back home
were, as if on cue, clamoring to challenge him in a 2020 congressional primary.
One state representative announced, "I am a Pro-Trump, Pro-Life, Pro-Jobs,
Pro-2nd Amendment, Pro-Family Values Republican. Justin Amash's tweets
yesterday calling for President Trump's impeachment show how out of touch
he is with the truth and how out of touch he is with people he represents."[5]

When Amash returned to his district for the long Memorial Day weekend, he found dozens of reporters and camera crews from national news
networks at a long-scheduled town hall–style meeting with his constituents. The setting was his alma mater, Grand Rapids Christian High School,
where the cross and the American eagle (varsity team mascot) were reminders of the distinctly political brand of faith underpinning the educational
program. The meeting was held in an auditorium built with a grant from
the local DeVos family, which included Betsy DeVos, President Trump's
secretary of education.

Amash faced hundreds, including some with placards that read RECALL
AMASH, not from the elevated stage but from the floor in front of it, which
meant that his constituents occupied the high ground. He wore wire-rimmed
glasses, a blue polo shirt, and navy-blue slacks. Among those who spoke to
him were many who were old enough to be his mother or father. Quite a
few expressed views that indicated that they hadn't read the Mueller report
and that what they knew of it came from Fox News or the president's own
remarks.

"We voted for you as a Republican," said a woman wearing a red Make
America Great Again Trump campaign hat. When others jeered at her complaint, Amash asked them to be quiet and let her speak. She continued, "If
you want to go along with violating the public trust, how far does it go? How
can you become a Democrat when we voted for you as a Republican? You just
drank the same Kool-Aid as the Democrats."

For his part, Amash tried to remain down to earth while stressing that he
had studied the report with care before reaching a conclusion.

> So, my birthday was on April 18, and I got a birthday present. Not a
> good one. The Mueller report came out on my birthday. But I took my
> time to read it. I took my time to read it, I was very careful about it.

Volume 1 has more Russians than there are characters in the *Game of Thrones*. I focused most of my tweets on volume 2. Volume 2 deals with obstruction of justice. In volume 2, Robert Mueller very clearly identifies several instances of obstruction of justice.[6]

Gradually, Amash seemed to turn the crowd in his favor. Many in the audience applauded and cheered him on. One man asked jokingly if the Constitution could be amended to allow for presidential recall votes. Another asked about what could be done to provide support for thousands of immigrants—especially children—who were being detained under crowded conditions on the U.S.-Mexican border. And yet another identified himself as a combat veteran and praised Amash's courage to another volley of cheers.

But even as it became clear that Amash enjoyed the support of most in the crowd, it was also evident that his constituents wanted to air their feelings about him, the president, and the turmoil in national political life. These were troubling times, and the folks in Grand Rapids wanted to be heard.

"I was there for you from the very beginning. I would like to say since that time, I have changed my position on you," said thirty-year-old Anna Timmer, pointing at him angrily. "You have spent the last two years failing to do your job, which is to directly represent the popular will of your constituents."

"My job is to uphold the Constitution," said Amash.

Timmer said she thought Amash was grandstanding to gain national attention and said, "You know you have no future in this district as a Republican."[7]

Anna Timmer was correct on both counts. Amash had become instantly known across the country, and he would soon abandon the GOP, declaring himself a member of the Libertarian Party. Since the party had never elected anyone to any federal office, he was immediately its most successful figure.

• • •

If Justin Amash surprised official Washington by giving Democrats one Republican vote in favor of impeachment proceedings, then Robert Mueller shocked them when, on the day after Amash's Grand Rapids town hall, he suddenly announced that he would speak to reporters at the Department of Justice. House Democrats had been calling for him to testify on Capitol Hill, but the special counsel had resisted all suggestions that he discuss his report in public.

Interest in Mueller's work, and in the man himself, was extreme. For two years, Americans had plumbed the limited public record to imagine Mueller as they either dreamed or feared he would be. His prep school upbringing, his military service, his traditional Republicanism, and his churchgoing were the subject of reflections and meditations. Mueller was a do-good lawman, a threatening demon of the Deep State, a Gary Cooper hero of the taciturn old school.

The Gary Cooper fantasy was embraced by the writers at *Saturday Night Live,* the comedy program that, for decades, had skewered presidents and criminals and presidents who seemed to be criminals. *SNL* had long mocked Trump, but his rise to the presidency and apparent abuses of his office had led the show to treat him more acidly. First, the actor Alec Baldwin was enlisted to play him as a relentless buffoon. Then, when Mueller came on the scene, Robert De Niro portrayed the special counsel as an implacable investigator.

In his first turn as this character, De Niro's Mueller appeared with the actor Ben Stiller, who played a nervous Michael Cohen.

"Have you ever used a lie detector before?" the fake Mueller asked. "If you're innocent, you have nothing to worry about."

"I feel like I have," said Stiller's Cohen.

"And you're a lawyer?"

". . . ish."

"Did you make a payment of $130,000 to Stormy Daniels?" asked De Niro, referencing hush money paid to the adult-film star.

"Yes."

"And did President Trump know about it?"

"No."

The lie detector needle began to scribble noisily off the chart.

"I think you're lying."

"Yeah, it was supposed to be a surprise for Stormy, like a gift."

"A gift?"

"Yeah, a gift like a rock that you throw through a window with a note tied to it that says, 'Stop talking.'"[8]

De Niro would impersonate Mueller half a dozen times on *SNL*. President Trump, a television and pop culture addict, was watching. "Nothing funny about tired Saturday Night Live on Fake News NBC!" Trump tweeted after one show. "Question is, how do the Networks get away with these total Republican hit jobs without retribution? Likewise, for many other shows? Very unfair and should be looked into. This is the real Collusion!"[9]

Trump was no doubt watching, too, as news networks broadcast Mueller walking into the same Justice Department auditorium where, in the previous month, William Barr had appeared and offered his interpretation of the special counsel's report. On that occasion, Barr's two silent wingmen—Rod Rosenstein and Ed O'Callaghan—had helped the attorney general establish a commanding stage presence. Mueller appeared alone, a bit dwarfed by the podium where he stood. Grayer and more slightly built than he seemed in photographs from days gone by, he spoke with a voice that was soft and a bit reedy.

Mueller explained that he was shutting down his office and returning to private life and for these reasons felt it was appropriate to say something. True to the values of a bygone age, before a TV showman became president and an attorney general chose to function as his sidekick, Mueller said that once he finished talking, "it is important that the office's written work speak for itself."

Beginning with his report's findings on Russia, Mueller reminded the reporters that Russia had interfered with the election of 2016 with the intention of harming Hillary Clinton. Elements of the Russian military "launched a concerted attack on our political system." Documents were stolen and made public. National security and the cause of justice required that these crimes be investigated. "That is also a reason we investigated efforts to obstruct the investigation."

When it came to the obstruction issue, Mueller said, "If we had had confidence that the president clearly did not commit a crime, we would have said so."

Though Mueller's words were delivered in a slow voice unmarked by emotion, a careful listener could hear his rebuke for all those, including the president, who had spoken of exoneration. He explained that no charges were made against the president because "under longstanding department policy, a president cannot be charged with a federal crime while he is in office. That is unconstitutional." However, the same authority that forbade charges "explicitly permits the investigation of a sitting president, because it is important to preserve evidence while memories are fresh and documents available." Among other things, that evidence could be used if there were coconspirators who could be charged now.[10]

Those who consulted Mueller's report—he very much wanted people to do this—would discover that he had noted many contacts between Russians and Trump officials. By one journalist's count, the report cataloged 272 contacts between Russian operatives and Trump. Thirty-eight of these contacts were in-person meetings. None were reported to U.S. law enforcement, which is general practice for when presidential campaigns are approached by foreign agents. The report also said that "several individuals affiliated with the Trump Campaign" lied to the special counsel's office and "materially impaired the investigation of Russian election interference."[11]

Mueller's evidence indicated that key emails had been destroyed and that the president had attempted many acts of obstruction. Thus, any claim suggesting Trump had been given a clean bill of legal health would be nonsense.

During his ten minutes onstage, Mueller had described, in terms anyone could understand, the charge he had been given, the special status that shielded the president, and the outline of his discoveries. For more, Americans would have to actually read his report. Although the report was available for free online, no one could reasonably expect many to rush to read it. In fact, no evidence suggested that President Trump, notoriously impatient with the written word, had read it. When *The Washington Post* canvassed nearly one hundred representatives and senators, 30 percent declined to reply. In weeks to come, many confessed that they did not read the report. Senator Lisa Murkowski of Alaska said it was "tedious." Senator Tim Scott of South Carolina asked, "What's the point?" The point should have been obvious, and while parts of the report were tedious, much of it was actually quite compelling. Literary critic Laura Miller found some parts read like a thriller with footnotes while others revealed palace intrigue staged in an asylum. In this place, aides are "forced to humor and manipulate their demented old king, who has a schoolchild's conception of his own job." Michiko Kakutani, one of the most respected reviewers in America, found in the report "the visceral drama of a detective novel, spy thriller, or legal procedural."

As its principal author, Robert Mueller understood that he had produced a work that would reward anyone who made the commitment to reading it. A senator traveling from, say, Washington, D.C., to her home state of Alaska could consume its pages before touching down in Anchorage. Understanding the content of the report and respecting those who should feel an obligation to read it, Mueller clearly wanted to believe his task was finished. "The report is my testimony," he said. "So, beyond what I've said here today and what is contained in our written work, I do not believe it is appropriate for me to speak further about the investigation or to comment on the actions of the Justice Department or Congress."[12]

In Robert Mueller's view, his work was finished. In Robert De Niro's view, it wasn't. In a turn of events that would have been strange before the

Trump era, the man who played Mueller on TV addressed him in an article he wrote and published in *The New York Times* almost immediately after the special counsel spoke. He wrote:

> It probably hasn't escaped your attention (in my mind, *nothing* escapes your attention) that I play a version of you on "Saturday Night Live." As "Robert Mueller," my character is intimidating because he is so honest and upright. I do it for comic effect—that's the intention anyway—but there's also a lot of truth to it. To put it another way—it's good-natured fun, but not entirely good-natured.

De Niro offered forthright advice to Mueller.

> The country needs to hear your voice. Your actual voice. And not just because you don't want them to think that your actual voice sounds like Robert De Niro reading from cue cards, but because this is the report your country asked you to do, and now you must give it authority and clarity without, if I may use the term, obstruction.

Like many, De Niro believed that Mueller's work had been obstructed, trumpeted in bizarre terms by the president's absurd personal lawyer, and distorted by the attorney general.

> And if, in fact, you have nothing further to say about the investigation, for your public testimony, you could just read from the report in response to questions from members of Congress. Your life has been a shining example of bravely and selflessly doing things for the good of our country. I urge you to leave your comfort zone and do that again. You are the voice of the Mueller report. Let the country hear that voice.[13]

In an age of celebrity that had produced President Trump, De Niro's call for Mueller to speak was no more remarkable than reality TV star Kim Kardashian's visit to the Oval Office, where she successfully sought a pardon for an imprisoned drug trafficker. The merit of a pardon request, or for that matter a special counsel's report, mattered little if people didn't pay attention, and there was no surer way to capture attention than to connect a cause with a prominent person.

All politicians understand that they can redirect national sentiment with a measured dose of celebrity. On the last day of May, Speaker Pelosi appeared as a guest of talk show host Jimmy Kimmel, who, like every one of his late-night colleagues, had made Trump a regular focus of his commentary. With banter a form of currency in Kimmel's world, Pelosi talked about sports and let him tease her. When, as expected, he pressed her about impeachment, she reminded him that the Democrats had only held the House for five months and that for the first month, the government had been shut down. She quoted the Founders, who remarked, "The times have found us."

In most circumstances, a public official who uses phrases like *E Pluribus Unum* and raises her hand as she says, "We understand our oath of office to support and defend the Constitution of the United States," would not elicit shouts and applause. At Kimmel's taping, people were so attuned to the historical moment that they could not contain themselves. Pelosi could practice restraint. She wouldn't be goaded into saying Trump didn't respect the Constitution. Instead, she said, "He doesn't honor the oath." However, Pelosi understood what was expected of her on the program and so revealed a bit of her own thinking.

"The president wants us to impeach him," she theorized. "He knows it's not a good thing to be impeached, but the silver lining for him is that then he believes that he would be exonerated by the United States Senate." This would happen, she said, because the Senate was "completely in the pocket of Donald Trump."

Kimmel, clearly eager to see Trump impeached, seemed a bit impatient as Pelosi said the House needed to be "as ready as you can possibly be" before it took action. "Will we be ready before 2020?" he said plaintively.

"Yeah, we will," said Pelosi, almost under her breath.[14]

May 31, 2019 — Number of House members in favor of impeaching the president: 45

20

BARR'S PREDICATE

Democrats can't impeach a Republican President for crimes committed by Democrats. The facts are "pouring" in. The Greatest Witch Hunt in American History! Congress, go back to work and help us at the Border, with Drug Prices and on Infrastructure.

—Donald Trump, president of the United States, via Twitter, June 2, 2019

Legal battles are like three-dimensional chess matches, and William Barr was a grand master. As the Mueller report's actual findings started to gain more currency and the truth overcame Barr's attempts at interpretation, the attorney general decided to move backward in time. He wanted to change the foundation—the predicate—on which Mueller's work was built.

Considered as Barr would, the term *predicate* referred to the basis for Mueller's appointment as special counsel. All criminal and civil investigations are predicated on some event, or set of circumstances, that set the justice system in motion. A bullet-riddled body, for example, becomes the predicate for a murder investigation. In less obvious cases, a police officer's suspicions, and perhaps her sense of smell, could be the predicate for searching someone for drugs.

Generally speaking, prosecutors fight back when defense attorneys challenge the predicates that lead to arrests, especially for street crimes. (Defense lawyers often use the term *fruit of the poisonous tree* as they ask for cases to be dismissed because they grew out of improper police actions.) This made it a bit ironic when William Barr hinted, with his use of the word *spying* to describe the FBI's investigation of the Trump campaign, that he would attack the predicate for the special counsel's appointment. He was foreshadowing a campaign to discredit all that was known about Russia, Trump, and even obstruction of justice.

The predicates for the special counsel's appointment included Russia's attack on the 2016 U.S. election, Mike Flynn's deceptions, and the president's firing of James Comey, which he had said, out loud, was prompted by his irritation over the FBI's Russia probe. Functioning as Trump's defense attorney, Barr was able to use the resources of the Justice Department to, in effect, attack its own work. Within weeks of taking office and while the Mueller report was still secret, he created a team of shadow investigators to dig into the way the federal government responded to signs that Russia was attempting to aid Donald Trump.

"I am reviewing the conduct of the investigation and trying to get my arms around all the aspects of the counterintelligence investigation that was conducted during the summer of 2016," he said. Thus began a long and complex effort to, as the president said, "investigate the investigators," as if something nefarious had caused American law enforcement officials to look into Russia's attack on the 2016 election.

In fact, U.S. officials have, for decades, tracked Russian (and Soviet) attempts to use information warfare and other means to influence elections. In July of 2016, American security experts were quite interested, if not alarmed, to hear from an Australian diplomat that a Trump foreign policy advisor had been bragging about his contacts with Russians. The diplomat was Alexander Downer. The advisor was a twenty-nine-year-old named George Papadopoulos, who just a year before had been an unpaid intern at a U.S. think tank.

In May 2016, Papadopoulos had late-night drinks with Downer at a high-end London bar and restaurant called the Kensington Wine Rooms. At some point, Papadopoulos blabbed about how he knew that the Russians had thousands of emails stolen from Hillary Clinton. At the time, hackers *were in the process* of taking the documents from the Clinton campaign and the Democratic National Committee, but this was not publicly known. Downer didn't immediately act on what he had heard, perhaps because Papadopoulos was a neophyte with no credentials in Russian affairs to lend his bragging credibility. (During the campaign, Trump described Papadopoulos as one of his top foreign policy advisors; now, suddenly, he was a "young, low level volunteer." Then the Russian hacks hit the press. The Australians' tip, added to information coming from British and Dutch officials, prompted the FBI to swing into action.

As predicates go, the warnings from three allies combined with public disclosures about the email hacks were more than enough to justify a federal investigation, which was done very quietly to minimize the effect on the election. In September, the investigators received portions of a dossier of raw intelligence on Trump that had been gathered by a former British spy named Christopher Steele. Funded first by a conservative political activist and then by Democrats, Steele's work product indicated, accurately, that Vladimir Putin was trying to aid Trump's campaign and several Trump allies had been dealing with Russian operatives.

More salacious elements of the dossier, including a report that Russians possessed a compromising video of Donald Trump, were never verified, but much of it was confirmed. Likewise, all credible evidence indicated that the dossier was not the predicate for the American investigation of the election hacking. However, by the summer of 2018, President Trump had taken up a conspiracy theory that blamed the dossier and Steele's Washington contacts for the FBI probe. It was nothing unusual for Donald Trump to promote a conspiracy theory. Over the years, he had lent credence to dozens of them, including the idea that the science about the dangers of asbestos was a "con" and that windmills caused cancer. (Asbestos and windmills had actually caused him trouble as a real estate developer.) As he continued to indulge in this kind of talk after he was elected, Trump used conspiracy theories to create public doubt about inconvenient facts and, in the case of Robert Mueller's appointment, establish a false basis for challenging the predicate of his investigation.[1]

With no personal history of promoting conspiracy theories, William Barr's embrace of the notion that the Justice Department may have lacked a predicate to delve into the Russian election hack seemed to reflect not an absence of critical thinking skills but a need to either appease the president or deflect attention from his own abuse of the Mueller report. The president had said it was time to "investigate the investigators," and his ally Senator Lindsey Graham talked of appointing a special counsel to investigate the special counsel. Barr did not go quite as far as Graham suggested, but the steps he did take caused some dismay in the ranks at the department he led, which could not function if the American people came to believe it was untrustworthy.

Weeks after Barr announced his shadow team, FBI director Christopher Wray told a Senate committee that he had seen no evidence of inappropriate surveillance against either candidate Trump or people who worked for his campaign. Like Barr, Wray had been appointed by Donald Trump to replace someone who had made the president angry. When asked directly if the government had spied on the Trump campaign, he said, "That's not the term I would use." He added, "There are lots of people who have different collo-quial phrases. To me, the key question is making sure it's done by the book, consistent with our lawful authorities." Wray said he had not seen evidence to support the idea that lawful authorities had been violated.[2]

Lack of evidence did not inhibit the attorney general who, in mid-May, expanded his effort to attack Mueller's predicate when he did indeed appoint a special counsel to, essentially, go after Special Counsel Mueller. His choice of John Durham, the U.S. attorney in Hartford, Connecticut, would have meant little to a casual consumer of news about federal law enforcement, but insiders saw proof of Barr's determination to serve the president.

In 2011, Durham had appeared in an article titled "Washington's Most Powerful, Least Famous People," where it was noted that he had investigated FBI misconduct in the case of world-famous mobster Whitey Bulger and led a probe into the Central Intelligence Agency's torture of prisoners captured in the wars in Iraq and Afghanistan. In the mob case, which focused on individ-uals, a top FBI agent was convicted of aiding murder. When Durham finished the CIA case, all but 2 of 101 incidents of potential torture were closed without action. Many years later, the end result would include zero convictions. Gina Haspel, who had been in charge at a secret torture facility in Thailand, was named by Donald Trump to be director of the CIA.[3]

Durham's record indicated he was thorough and professional and a team player. With the Bulger investigation, he helped bring down a rogue agent when the FBI ran out of reasons to protect him. The torture probe threatened American prestige and a host of powerful people who had either participated in or approved the abuse of prisoners, and in the end, no one was held ac-countable. In general, Durham was respected by his peers. Richard Gregorie, a former assistant U.S. attorney who had worked with him, said that Durham would "be hard-nosed and report what he finds." On the other hand, Grego-rie and hundreds of other former Justice Department attorneys had signed a letter of protest about the handling of the Mueller report. Many of them saw in Durham's appointment an attorney general aiding a president's effort to dis-credit every institution that had not bent to his will.

•   •   •

If William Barr was going to cap his career with a flourish of norm-busting moves on behalf of an erratic and impulsive president, there was no reason he couldn't also enjoy a bit of adventure and good food. So it was that after appointing Durham, the attorney general found himself on the Via Veneto in Rome, perhaps glancing for reminders of Fellini's *La Dolce Vita*. If he had wanted to, Barr could have walked to one of the places where, during the 2016 election, George Papadopoulos had met with Joseph Mifsud, a Maltese professor and proxy for Russian intelligence. It was Mifsud who had told Papadopoulos that Russia had dirt on Hillary Clinton.

Though generally unrecognized by Romans, Barr could not have gone unnoticed given the retinue of aides and security officers accompanying him everywhere. On a hot summer Tuesday, his motorcade wound through the city streets, past the central train station, to the new headquarters of Italy's intelligence services on Piazza Dante. Known as Italy's Langley (in homage to the CIA's main facility in Virginia), the spy center occupied a massive former post office building. The 1911 façade had been preserved, but the interior featured a modern central open gallery surrounded by vaulted rooms.

Inside, Barr was welcomed by Gennaro Vecchione, the head of Italian intelligence. In Rome, the cognoscenti understood that "Talk to Vecchione" was the answer that Prime Minister Giuseppe Conte gave to anyone who sought sensitive information related to security and international affairs. Barr, acting like Donald Trump's defense lawyer, was looking for information about the predicate to the U.S. investigation of the Trump-Russia connection.[4]

The Italians didn't give Barr much help, even when he came back a second time and saw Conte himself. When asked, the prime minister said, "Our intelligence is completely unrelated to the so-called Russiagate and that has been made clear."

With a long history of intelligence cooperation, especially in the areas of terrorism and organized crime, the Italians would have been inclined to help Barr if they could. This would have been doubly true considering that President Trump had been making personal calls to world leaders to open doors for Barr as he did his personal investigating. Australian prime minister Scott Morrison told Trump his country would cooperate. The Aussies got a chance when Barr attended a conference of the so-called Five Eyes security allies in London.

Formed after World War II by an agreement between the United States and members of the British Commonwealth, the group included the U.S., the United Kingdom, Canada, Australia, and New Zealand. Twenty different agencies shared resources. In London, and also in Washington, the Australians were willing to help Barr but had little to offer. (Alexander Downer would tell a reporter that he believed Trump had embarked on a campaign to show that various powerful entities had engaged "in a conspiracy to bring down the Trump administration, that this is treason, that I should be in Guantanamo Bay . . . it's a little bit sad that people take that kind of thought seriously.")[5]

Barr also struck out with the British, even though he had the ear of Home Secretary Priti Patel. The British mattered because Papadopoulos had operated from London during the 2016 campaign, and Christopher Steele had spent twenty-two years working for MI6. Few British agents had spent more time in Moscow or enjoyed the level of respect accorded to Steele. In the end, the British would give Barr nothing significant to use against Mueller's investigation or to discredit the American response to the Russian election hack. Barr would soon leave the investigative trail to Durham, who labored on without giving a hint to when he would issue his own conclusions.[6]

June 30, 2019 — Number of House members in favor of impeaching the president: 60

21

A PARTISAN THING

The Dems fight us at every turn–in the meantime they are accomplishing
nothing for the people! They have gone absolutely 'Loco,' or Unhinged, as
they like to say!

—Donald Trump, president of the United States, via Twitter,
June 13, 2019

With his attorney general scouring the world for evidence to discredit the
Mueller report, Donald Trump was free to dwell on his political problems,
which he generally reduced to personal terms. Supporters were good and great
and beautiful. Critics and opponents were evildoers with no purpose other
than to destroy him. (He would say that some, notably past president Obama,
Hillary Clinton, and Joe Biden should be imprisoned.) The press, except for the
few outposts that reliably praised him, was devoted to lying about him.

In the president's construct, no room was given to the possibility that
some of the scandals of his administration were genuine. In Trump's political
Wonderland, he was cleaning up "the swamp" in Washington while others
sought to evade his effort. In fact, between his administration's record pace of
high-level firings and resignations and rampant signs of corruption in both his
government and personal affairs, the tally of scandals outside the realm of the
Mueller report was breathtaking. A partial list would include:

- Corruption in a Trump charitable foundation that was forced to close.

- Concealment of the Trump family's negotiation, during the election
  campaign and after it, to build a development in Moscow.

- Irregularities in presidential inaugural committee spending, including $1.5 million paid to a Trump hotel.

- Foreign government purchases from Trump businesses in apparent violation of the Constitution's emoluments clause.

- Commerce Secretary Wilbur Ross's alleged false statements to Congress on the addition of a citizenship question to the census.

- Former Health and Human Services secretary Tom Price's abuse of taxpayer funds for private travel.

- Multiple allegations of corruption against former Environmental Protection Agency head Scott Pruitt.

- Allegations of self-dealing by former Interior secretary Ryan Zinke.

- Irregularities in the handling of a security clearance awarded to the president's son-in-law, Jared Kushner.

- Deaths of children held in federal custody after being separated from their asylum-seeking parents at the U.S. border with Mexico.

- Bungled hurricane relief efforts in Puerto Rico, where thousands of Americans died.

- Increased arms sales to Saudi Arabia *after* Saudi operatives killed and dismembered *Washington Post* journalist Jamal Khashoggi in its embassy in Turkey.

- The Kushner family's pursuit of foreign investors for its businesses.

- Cabinet officials' use of government planes for pleasure junkets.[1]

As the watchdog group Citizens for Responsibility and Ethics in Washington tracked thousands of alleged conflicts of interest involving the president himself, new disclosures were greeted as routine, and the circle of corruption widened. At the end of May 2019, news reports revealed that Secretary of Transportation Elaine Chao had not kept her promise to divest herself of stock in the country's largest highway materials supply company. Highway construction was, of course, one of her department's main activities. Chao oversaw a road building and repair budget of roughly $47 billion per year.[2]

Chao had been caught trying to use her position to benefit her family's shipping company in China, and it was revealed she had created a back channel for her husband, Senator Mitch McConnell, to get special access to $78 million in federal funds to be spent in his home state of Kentucky. As Senate majority leader, McConnell was positioned to save Donald Trump from conviction in the event that he was impeached, then placed on trial in the Senate. This made McConnell the administration's most important friend, and to no one's surprise, Elaine Chao was permitted to retain her position. House Democrats and the press corps, fully absorbed by the Mueller report's aftershocks, let the Chao scandal fade away.

Mueller's public statement had not satisfied those who seemed to think he had, within him, a dramatic persona more like the character played by Robert De Niro. In their imaginations, he could stride into a congressional hearing room and, by simply reading parts of the report aloud, make the country understand. Newspaper readers shared hopes of this sort in letters to the editor. One man asked him to come forward "and speak plainly—not in redacted form or legalese." Another wrote, "Mr. Mueller, speak as a full person, with feeling and conviction, values and principles. The country's moment is your moment. Do not shrink from it."[3]

In Congress, calls for Mueller to testify grew louder, and Democrats continued to struggle among themselves over the best way to deal with what had been revealed in the report. Jamie Raskin, who had challenged Speaker Pelosi in the leadership meeting and in his interview with Greg Sargent of *The Washington Post,* worried that he had pushed too hard. He may have been frustrated with the Speaker's restraint, but he didn't want to be on her bad side. He was relieved when, at the end of May, she had asked him to preside over the House as it met. This he took as a sign that there were no hard feelings.

As Raskin tapped the brake on his drive toward impeachment, others on the Judiciary Committee privately complained about the Speaker's reticence. One member told us, "If she's never going to allow articles of impeachment to come to the floor, if that's really her position, she should say it to Jerry [Nadler] . . . stop creating this impression that you just have to see more evidence. And now the problem for her is that people will quickly realize that it's not actually up to Nancy Pelosi, because any member of the committee can call articles of impeachment which are considered a privileged resolution and they will get a vote."

In the space between Pelosi and the more impatient House Democrats, David Cicilline began to warn that his party risked being thwarted by a disciplined GOP minority. "When some people say, 'Well, we don't want impeachment to be a partisan thing, let's count up those heads and see what we've got,' I don't think that's the way you determine whether or not the impeachment is partisan. You determine it based on what the character of the impeachment articles are. Do they successfully assert the existence of high crimes and misdemeanors? By which we mean, treason, bribery, obstruction of justice, and other crimes against the character of our democracy. What about emoluments? What about the other issues?"[4]

Cicilline and Raskin both hoped that testimony from Mueller would convince reluctant members of the caucus and their constituents that Trump had committed high crimes and misdemeanors and therefore had to be impeached. A month after he believed he had left his duties behind, the special counsel agreed to come to Capitol Hill on July 17.[5]

• • •

For Raskin, Cicilline, and others on the Judiciary Committee, impeachment represented both an immediate political reality and a constitutional power, a responsibility that Trump had forced them to consider. The political matter involved staying responsive to their constituents, who implored them to act. The constitutional concerns were rooted in what they knew of the Founders' intentions as they structured the American form of government. In their time, fresh from a rebellion against a king, they had intentionally constrained the office of the president and, in locating impeachment in the House, gave it to the elected officials who were expected to be most responsive to the American people.

Raskin was able to evoke the meaning of the Constitution and the context of its history in every conversation with colleagues and constituents, and at times, he did see himself as a descendant of the Founders. For this reason, he resented a long-running attempt by the GOP to seize all the symbols of patriotism and deny them to Democrats. He loved the flag and the Fourth of July; when it rolled around in 2019, he spent the day traveling around his district to walk in parades, visit picnics, and cheer for the Scouts and others who marched.

July 4, 2019, dawned in Takoma Park, Maryland, with a sense of excitement that was shared by thousands of communities around the United States. At first light, people were hauling out folding tables and tablecloths and plates with cookies and jugs of lemonade. It was a scene that might surprise those who knew it to be a liberal city in one of the most liberal states in the union and assumed folks there didn't wave the flag. One could see the fervor and joy for this most American of holidays among the drum majors and majorettes and school bands and veterans and firefighters who paraded down Ethan Allen Avenue past the fire station.

The day had started with a chill in the air that soon dissipated as the sun bathed the streets. Raskin marched off with campaign volunteers who carried banners with his name on them, although that was not really necessary. He was already known around town, and televised hearings had made him somewhat famous beyond Takoma Park. From the sidewalks, he heard shouts of "Keep up the good work!" and "We love you, Jamie!" as he raced jauntily from one side of the street to the other, grasping hands and shouting out greetings. A few who knew him well marveled at his stamina. A few years before, when he served in the state legislature, he had been diagnosed with colorectal cancer, and his survival had been in doubt.

After the Takoma Park parade, Raskin attended a few block parties and then hopped into a car for a short ride to Cabin John, a hamlet close to the Potomac River. Legend had it that Cabin John was named after a hermit who lived in the woods around the time they were building the Chesapeake and Ohio Canal alongside the river, decades before the Civil War. In the few minutes of quiet, his mind went to the Mueller testimony that was two weeks away. Committee aides were warning against high expectations. They said that Mueller, at seventy-four, was not the prosecutor some remembered. As Raskin put it, they said Mueller appeared "to have lost a step or two."

"Attorney General Barr set us back several months by holding on to the report, then redacting it into oblivion and lying about its contents to the public," said Raskin. "So, we have the chance for a do-over, against the chaos." Of course, it was likely that House Republicans would bring the chaos into the hearing room and "go after him in mad dog fashion. It will not be pretty, but it will at least show people how extreme and reckless the GOP is. There's a chance of a nationwide backlash against their harassment and their paranoid conspiracy theories and the so-called deep state. They re-created themselves as a cult of personality around Trump and here they are."

As Raskin jumped out of the car in Cabin John, his colleague David Cicilline was walking behind a marching band that had left the mustering point at Mt. Hope High School in the harbor town of Bristol, Rhode Island. He was joined by Representative James Langevin and the state's U.S. senators, Jack Reed and Sheldon Whitehouse.

To say the Fourth was a big deal in Bristol was an understatement. The city's first celebration of Independence Day had occurred in 1777, when the crew of a rebel frigate fired thirteen cannon shots. A British officer stationed nearby reported, "As the evening was very still and fine, the echo of the guns down the bay had a very grand effect, the report of each being repeated three or four times."[6]

The history in a place like Bristol, where the streets and many of the homes dated to colonial times, made it easy for locals and visitors to feel some connection to the nation's founding. Jewish and Italian by heritage, Cicilline had long believed that an unwritten pact of mutual respect kept a diverse America together. In the Trump era, when a president spoke of journalists as "enemies of the people" and Democrats as "traitors," he had begun to wonder if the pact still worked. Retirement and primary defeats had driven from office the Republicans he once counted as friends in the House. He could no longer find anyone on the other side of the aisle willing to talk.

At the end of the two-mile march, Cicilline wondered if he could find common ground with any of his Republican colleagues. "You know, even if we don't agree on one issue, environmental policy is different, immigration policy is different, I've always thought, they're representing their communities," he said. "They believe in different things and they do what they think is right for their country. I always treated them like happy warriors—we just had different ideas. But I've watched for the last two and a half years, as they refuse to stand up in any way for our country, totally enabling the destruction of our democracy and the shredding of our institutions. In many ways our democracy is broken. And they do nothing."

That America had entered a new era was evident near the end of the day in Washington, D.C., where President Trump presided over a militarized Fourth of July celebration on the National Mall he had been promoting excitedly for months. Trump had spent two years pressuring the Pentagon to make a big display of military hardware at the annual parade. In general, the Defense

Department resisted this kind of show in order to limit the ways a political figure might co-opt the symbols of the military for his or her purpose. After insisting that a parade of tanks would tear up city streets, the department had reached a compromise with the president, which allowed for the display for some parked armored vehicles at the Lincoln Memorial and flyovers by various types of aircraft. On February 24, Trump hyped the resulting compromise plan on Twitter as "one of the biggest gatherings in the history of Washington, D.C., on July 4th. It will be called 'A Salute to America' and will be held at the Lincoln Memorial. Major fireworks display, entertainment and an address by your favorite President, me!"[7] The president's speechwriters then crafted the speech, which he attempted to read in a way that was timed to the overflights.

At 6:00 p.m., as people across the land prepared for hometown fireworks and cookouts, rain started to fall on Donald Trump as he delivered his speech. With each approaching aircraft, he paused and turned from the crowd to look into the sky. With each passing minute, the plexiglass screen in front of the president became more fogged with moisture, and he became less sure of his words.

Much of Trump's speech was about American history, but he struggled even with the basics. In his telling, the Continental Army defeated a British general named "Cornwallis of Yorktown." In the War of 1812, "our Army manned the air, it rammed ramparts. It took over the airports. It did everything it had to do. And at Fort McHenry, under the rockets' red glare, it had nothing but victory."

For a commander in chief who was so eager to associate himself with the military to show such ignorance of its history was both shocking and a bit sad. Unfortunately, Trump had, through his own mocking ways, helped to train others to treat him mercilessly. Social media exploded with comments about the strange performance. Some posters created images of George Washington crossing the Delaware to arrive at an airport. Others wrote letters from soldiers complaining about missing their flights home from their fight against Cornwallis of Yorktown. However, the most biting comment may have come from Mick Jagger, who, like so many public figures, had been criticized by Trump in the past. Trump "made a very good point," Jagger said. "If only the British had held on to the airports, the whole thing might have gone differently for us."[8]

Not one to ever admit a mistake or laugh at himself, President Trump would offer a less-than-convincing excuse for his gaffes. Rain was the problem, he shouted out to reporters the next day over the whir of his helicopter on the White House lawn. "The teleprompter went out . . . right in the middle of that sentence it went out," he said. "I knew the speech very well so I was able to do it without a teleprompter."[9]

Having watched and heard the bully-boy president humiliate himself and then lie about what happened, many House Democrats indulged in a chuckle before returning to their worries about Robert Mueller and how they should confront the president's behavior. David Cicilline feared the House had waited too long for a formal move to impeachment. Jamie Raskin worried that Mueller would be unable to explain Trump's obstruction in a way the public could grasp. He began working more intently on the issue of emoluments—an arcane-sounding term that was deceptively simple.

Emoluments had never been a serious issue before. When the Marquis de Lafayette sent a painting of the Bastille to George Washington, the president only took possession and brought it home to Mount Vernon after his term of office. When the king of Siam offered to send elephants to Washington, Abraham Lincoln penned a polite rejection, noting, "Our laws forbid the President from receiving these rich presents as personal treasures."[10]

In contrast with Washington and Lincoln, Donald Trump had not only accepted but had also courted emoluments in the form of reservations at his hotels and resorts. His Trump International Hotel in Washington, which occupied the former post office a few blocks down Pennsylvania Avenue from the White House, accommodated businesspeople, lobbyists, and officials of foreign governments. "We've identified 24 countries," said Raskin, "United Arab Emirates, Saudi Arabia, Turkey, Egypt among them. He's paid $350,000 into the Treasury on what he calls the profits from foreign government payments. But the Constitution doesn't ban the collection of profits from foreign governments. It bans the collection of any payments at all. And you can't accept any of it without the consent of Congress. So, he's in direct violation of the Constitution."

At Trump Tower in New York, ten foreign governments paid for space, including China, which held a $2 million annual lease for space used by the Industrial and Commercial Bank of China. Although it wasn't a thing of value paid to the president, China also approved valuable trademarks for his daughter's retail businesses. Raskin considered all these payments and approvals emoluments and grounds for impeachment.[11]

For her part, Pelosi was struggling against the more aggressive members of her caucus. She had not shifted in her opinion since March, when she argued that Trump did not merit impeachment. Not that she was giving Trump a pass. When four Democratic women of color in Congress—Alexandria Ocasio-Cortez, Rashida Tlaib, Ayanna Pressley, and Ilhan Omar—condemned Trump's most recent racist remarks, the president countered by saying they should "go back [to] the totally broken and crime-infested places from which they came." Pelosi spoke out against Trump on the House floor, unrepentant though chastised for violating a House rule for doing so explicitly: "Every single member of this institution—Democratic and Republican—should join us in condemning the President's racist tweets. To do anything less would be a shocking rejection of our values and a shameful abdication of our oath of office to protect the American people."[12]

July 20, 2019 — Number of House members in favor of impeaching the president: 87

22

MUELLER IN THE HOUSE

Why didn't Robert Mueller & his band of 18 Angry Democrats spend any time investigating Crooked Hillary Clinton, Lyin' & Leakin' James Comey, Lisa Page and her Psycho lover, Peter S, Andy McCabe, the beautiful Ohr family, Fusion GPS, and many more, including HIMSELF & Andrew W?

—Donald Trump, president of United States, via Twitter, July 24, 2019

In the days prior to Robert Mueller's congressional testimony, speculation raged over what he might say. Nothing reported indicated that he would offer much beyond his written report, but among critics of the president, many hoped that he would repeat or even read some of his more significant findings and that his voice would reach the American people in a way his thick volumes did not. This hope rested on the belief that performance mattered as much as substance and that somehow Mueller would be willing and able to make a compelling presentation.

Given the special counsel's personality and reluctance, any thought that his words or demeanor might resonate was not supported by the evidence. In fact, as those with connections to the special counsel and his people pressed for information, official Washington began to temper expectations. Days before the hearing, Representative Jamie Raskin, who would question Mueller as a member of the Judiciary Committee, said the best he could hope for was "that Mueller expresses and the public perceives a few key ideas. One is that there was in fact ample collusive activity taking place between the Trump campaign and Russian nationals. The second idea is that the president repeatedly, consistently and in an obvious way, obstructed justice by tampering with witnesses and by threatening prosecutors and doing whatever he could to block the investigation. Anybody else would be prosecuted for this conduct." Raskin wasn't confident this would happen, in part because "the Republicans are going to be on a rampage against Mueller because of their completely fantastical and paranoid deep state conspiracy theory."

In fact, on the fringe of the GOP caucus, Representative Louie Gohmert of Texas, who had written a pamphlet called *Robert Mueller Unmasked,* claimed the special counsel had been "leading the effort to railroad President Donald J. Trump through whatever manufactured charge he can allege." He said Mueller had been willing to "threaten, harass, prosecute or bankrupt to get someone to be willing to allege something—anything—about our current president." Because of this, he believed Mueller "has got a lot of explaining to do," and he intended to use his time as a Judiciary Committee member to force him to do so. Other Republicans were more moderate in their tone and promised to limit their rhetoric. Privately, they talked about the possibility that the special counsel was not as capable as he had once been and might not do well.[1]

When July 24 arrived, the hallways on the first floor of the Rayburn House Office Building were crowded with people hoping to be admitted to the hearing. (By the time staff and members of the press were accommodated, fewer than one hundred seats would be available.) Mueller appeared at 8:30 a.m., was escorted around the metal detectors, and followed a phalanx of House staff and Capitol Police, who cleared a path in the crowded hallway. He wore essentially the same outfit from his May press conference—white button-down shirt, dark chalk stripe, dark tie with a pattern of white squares. The difference was that in May, he wore a tie with white checks on black. In July, the checks were cast on a blue background.[2]

Inside the hearing room, Mueller shook hands with some staffers and committee members before making his way to a witness table, where he would look up at the twenty-four Democrats and seventeen Republicans of the committee who occupied big swivel chairs arranged on two platforms that filled the entire width of the room. The chairman, Jerrold Nadler, sat in the center of this scene, with gold-colored curtains directly behind him. With a ceiling more than twenty-four feet above the floor and massive portraits of past committee chairs staring down from the walls, the room was intimidating, and that was before anyone asked any questions.[3]

Mueller had testified in this room dozens of times and had never shown signs of anxiety or indecision. However, more than five years had passed since he had appeared before any committee, and in his long career, he had never answered questions about such a substantial controversy in a proceeding that would be broadcast on national television. Scheduled to meet with the Judiciary Committee in the morning and the House Intelligence Committee in the afternoon, Mueller would likely answer questions for more than seven hours, and in this, he would be heard by tens of millions of people. The mandates of the committees required that judiciary focus on volume 2 of the report and obstruction of justice charges. In the afternoon, the Intelligence Committee would focus on volume 1, which covered Russia's election interference and its operatives' contacts with the Trump campaign in 2016.

As sometimes happens, the start of the hearing was delayed by a public demonstration. In this case, a bearded man wearing a long brown and white scarf leaped into the aisle close to the public entrance, shouting several times, "Kushner and Manafort downloaded encrypted apps on the day of the Trump Tower meeting!"

After the demonstrator was removed, Mueller clapped his hands together, sat at the table, and waited for Chairman Nadler and his Republican counterpart Doug Collins to offer their takes on Mueller's work and what they expected to hear. Nadler summarized the most troubling of Mueller's findings, often quoting from the report directly. "Among the most shocking of these incidents," he said while reciting obstructive acts, "President Trump ordered his White House counsel to have you fired, and then to—to lie and deny that it had happened, he ordered his former campaign manager to convince the recused attorney general to step in and limit your work, and he attempted to prevent witnesses from cooperating with your investigation."

Collins matched Nadler's serious tone but expressed a completely opposite view. He saw in Mueller's work an "extended, unhampered investigation" that yielded no troubling evidence about the president's behavior. Setting aside the part of the report the committee was to examine, Collins dipped into volume 1, which addressed Russia's election hack, to note that no Trump-Russia conspiracy had been proven, then turned to the old talking points about collusion, which had never been one of Mueller's subjects. "Collusion, we were told, was in plain sight even if the special counsel's team didn't find it," said Collins.

With the partisan expectations hanging in the air, Mueller announced that he wouldn't rise to any bait. "I do not intend to summarize or describe the results of our work in a different way in the course of my testimony today. As I said on May 29: the report is my testimony. And I will stay within that text."[4]

As the committee began to question Mueller, the man whom many expected to hear—the Marine Corps Vietnam veteran, a thirty-five-year veteran of government service, the respected former FBI director—seemed to be missing. Out of practice, and perhaps a little hard of hearing, he sometimes seemed unable to identify who was speaking and asked for questions to be repeated. His effort to be careful, coupled with moments when he struggled to recall details, made him seem detached. When given an opportunity to read from his report, which would relieve him of the work of composing responses to questions, he resisted. As the day wore on, he would deflect more than 190 queries by saying, "I'm not going to get into that," or "I can't respond," and "I leave that to you."[5]

When Mueller was questioned by Representative Collins, who was famous and parodied for his rapid-fire speech, Mueller could not keep up. "Is it also true that you issued over 2,800 subpoenas, executed nearly 500 search warrants, obtained more than 230 orders for communication records and 50 pen registers?" Collins asked.

"That went a little fast for me," said Mueller.

Later, Collins was able to get Mueller to agree to one of his party's talking points as he asked, "Is it true, the evidence gathered during your investigation—given the questions that you've just answered, is it true the evidence gathered during your investigation did not establish that the president was involved in the underlying crime related to Russian election interference as stated in Volume 1, page 7?"

"We found insufficient evidence of the president's culpability," Mueller answered.

Collins's reference was incorrect. Page 7 said no such thing, although it was true that Mueller had found insufficient evidence to prove a crime had been committed. What neither man said, however, was that the report also noted, "The investigation established that several individuals affiliated with the Trump Campaign lied to the Office, and to Congress, about their interactions with Russian-affiliated individuals and related matters. Those lies materially impaired the investigation of Russian election interference."

Although Collins had gotten Mueller to say something beneficial to the president, which could then be broadcast on television, others failed in this effort. One, Representative Gohmert, failed miserably. Gohmert was the kind of partisan whom even allies struggled to stomach. Days before the hearing, he had told an interviewer that Mueller was "an anal opening." On hearing day, he announced that he was submitting his *Robert Mueller Unmasked* pamphlet for the record and then commenced to badger Mueller about his relationship with James Comey and about a member of his team, Peter Strzok, who had criticized the president. Mueller had removed him when his statements about Trump were revealed.

Having argued that Mueller's proximity to Comey and his hiring of Strzok made him unfit for the special counsel's role, Gohmert then tried to say that Mueller himself was antagonistic toward Trump. His proof was the claim that Mueller had visited the White House to ask the president for the job of FBI director, but was passed over. This was a story the president had told and was popular among his followers. In fact, on May 30, Trump had made this case in one of his White House lawn Chopper Talks with reporters:

> Look, Robert Mueller should've never been chosen because he wanted the FBI job and he didn't get it. And the next day, he was picked as special counsel. So you tell somebody, "I'm sorry, you can't have the job." And then, after you say that, he's going to make a ruling on you? It doesn't work that way. Plus, we had a business dispute. Plus, his relationship with [former FBI Director James B.] Comey was extraordinary.[6]

No evidence had ever been offered to suggest Mueller wanted the FBI director job. He had held the post under other presidents for twelve years, and colleagues couldn't imagine he wanted to go back just as President Trump had demonstrated, by firing Comey, that the position would be subject to extraordinary political interference. Indeed, as White House staffers had told the special counsel's investigative team, they had urged the president to stop offering this complaint about Mueller being sore about not getting the post, because it wasn't true. Nevertheless, it was a good talking point, and Gohmert pressed it until Mueller said that he had indeed gone to see the president but "not as a candidate" for the job.[7]

With Gohmert and the others, Mueller was respectful if reticent. In another moment or setting, he might have been forgiven for what seemed to be foibles of age. But too much had depended on Mueller. It was safe to say that fully half the country had wanted him to say, plainly, that the president had obstructed justice. The other half likely wanted him to declare his work had been unnecessary. He did neither, choosing instead to say repeatedly, "It's in the report," or "I refer you to the report," and little more.

Instead of making his findings vivid, Mueller-in-the-flesh made them seem less powerful than they were on paper. He seemed less powerful personally, too. During the first break in the hearing, committee Democrats retreated to a small room behind the dais. There they first exchanged worried glances and then quietly acknowledged among themselves that Mueller's performance was not just underwhelming but also concerning. To some he seemed to have a hearing problem. To others he seemed a bit confused, perhaps due to a lack of preparation. Most agreed that expectations had been too high. The buildup for the hearing, epitomized by Robert De Niro's *Saturday Night Live* performances and newspaper column, had backfired as Mueller proved himself to be not a TV version of a veteran prosecutor but a real man who had demonstrated that in his lifelong devotion to the law, he had failed to develop the ability to play himself for the cameras. In the media age, where the pathway to the presidency had carried Donald Trump from *Lifestyles of the Rich and Famous* to *The Apprentice* and finally the White House, this deficiency was glaring.[8]

With Mueller failing as a television performer, Democrats could still encourage him to testify well as a witness in a serious proceeding. Representative Ted Deutch, a Democrat who represented a district on South Florida's Atlantic coast, showed how this could be done with painstaking effort devoted to just a single question. He began by calling Mueller's attention to page 90 of volume 2, where he read a quote: "News of the obstruction investigation prompted the President to call McGahn and seek to have the Special Counsel removed." Deutch then had the following exchange with Mueller:

DEUTCH: And then in your report you wrote about multiple calls from the President to White House Counsel Don McGahn. And regarding the second call, you wrote, and I quote, "McGahn recalled that the President was more direct, saying something like, 'Call Rod, tell Rod that Mueller has conflicts and can't be Special—can't be the Special Counsel.' McGahn recalled the President telling him Mueller has to go and call me back when you do it." Director Mueller, did McGahn understand what the President was ordering him to do?

MUELLER: I direct you to the—what we've written in the report in terms of characterizing his feelings.

DEUTCH: And in the report it says quote "McGahn understood the President to be saying that the Special Counsel had to be removed."

You also said on page 86 that quote "McGahn considered the President's request to be an inflection point and he wanted to hit the brakes and he felt trapped and McGahn decided he had to resign." McGahn took action to prepare to resign, isn't that correct?

MUELLER: I direct you again to the report.

DEUTCH: And in—in fact, that very day he went to the White House and quoting your report, you said quote "he then drove to the office to pack his belongings and submit his resignation letter," close quote.

MUELLER: That is—that is directly from the report.

DEUTCH: It is. And before he resigned, however, he called the President's Chief of Staff, Reince Priebus, and he called the President's senior advisor, Steve Bannon. Do you recall what McGahn told them?

MUELLER: I—whatever he—was—was said will—will appear in the report.

DEUTCH: It is, it is, and it says on page 87, quote "Priebus recalled that McGahn said that the President asked him to do crazy expletive." In other words, crazy stuff. The White House Counsel thought that the President's request was completely out of bounds. He said the President asked him to do something crazy, it was wrong, and he was prepared to resign over it. Now these are extraordinarily troubling events but you found White House Counsel McGahn to be a credible witness, isn't that correct?

MUELLER: Correct.

DEUTCH: Director Mueller, the most important question I have for you today is why? Director Mueller, why did the President of the United States want you fired?

MUELLER: I can't answer that question.

Mueller would not speak to the president's frame of mind because it was not described in his report. But then moments later, Deutch said, "You found evidence, as you lay out in your report, that the President wanted to fire you because you were investigating him for obstruction of justice. Isn't that correct?" Here Mueller felt comfortable saying, "That's what it—it says in the report, yes, and I go—I stand by what's in the report."

The point, obvious to all, was that the president had tried to obstruct justice by firing the man investigating him for obstruction of justice. Attempted obstruction is every bit as criminal as obstruction that succeeds, so Mueller's team had in fact caught the president violating the law. However as president, he enjoyed certain immunity from immediate prosecution, and this was what prevented Mueller from recommending he be charged.

"But the president did it anyway," said Deutch. "He did it anyway. Anyone else who blatantly interfered with a criminal investigation, like yours, would be investigated and indicted on charges of obstruction of justice. Director Mueller, you determined that you were barred from indicting a sitting president. We've already talked about that today. That is exactly why this committee must hold the president accountable."

Having exhausted the time he was given to question Mueller, Deutch would be satisfied with highlighting what was perhaps the most salient point in the Mueller report. The president had apparently committed the crime of attempted obstruction but, thanks to his special status, could not be charged. For its part, the House of Representatives could charge him in an impeachment proceeding where attempted obstruction would surely fit the notion of a high crime or misdemeanor as referenced in the Constitution.

•   •   •

Before Mueller had even finished his morning testimony before the Judiciary Committee, the president's allies in Congress and the media had declared him, and his report, practically dead and buried.

At 10:08 a.m., it was Senator Lindsey Graham, practicing what was called *concern trolling*, by observing, "Mueller hearing becoming very confusing and sad." And then, attorney David Wohl, whose pro-Trump son was blogging and apparently fabricating attempts to smear Mueller, wrote, "Mueller is coming off as a semi-senile old goat who doesn't have a clue what he's doing or talking about." One of the most exaggerated comments was issued by a blogger who, while a favorite among Trump boosters, was infamous for boosting conspiracy theories: "WOW! Robert Mueller FALLS

APART! Caught off Guard, Stuttering, Confused, Doddering, Nervous—
COMPLETELY LOST."⁹

Mueller's detractors were joined by some of his most ardent supporters, including Harvard law professor Laurence Tribe, who had once called his report
a road map for impeachment. After Mueller's morning testimony, Tribe announced, "Much as I hate to say it . . . Far from breathing life into his damning report, the tired Robert Mueller sucked the life out of it. The effort to save
democracy and the rule of law from this lawless president has been set back,
not advanced."

Although there were many declarations of Mueller's failure creating a
lasting impression—just like William Barr's distortion about the report—
they were premature. The Judiciary Committee, which was filled with extreme partisans, had delivered a Punch-and-Judy version of a congressional
hearing. In the afternoon session with the House Intelligence Committee,
led by Adam Schiff, more sober questioning permitted Mueller to offer more
helpful testimony. Allowed to be more thoughtful, he was able to emphasize
the most important finding of his volume 1, saying, "Over the course of my
career, I've seen a number of challenges to our democracy. The Russian government's effort to interfere in our election is among the most serious. As I
said on May 29, this deserves the attention of every American."

As the dust settled, more considered views described mixed results from
Mueller Day. Mueller had not done well in the moments when members of
Congress acted like combative radio talk show hosts and tried to get him to engage in debates he refused to join. However, as he confirmed the findings in his
report and offered careful additional views, Mueller had emerged as the perfect
example of someone whose character and values contrasted with the president's.
He would not say things he couldn't support with facts, and he would not stray
from his mandate.

In his Intelligence Committee appearance, Mueller was guided skillfully
by Chairman Schiff, who cited the report to move the special counsel through
facts that showed that the Trump team had welcomed Russia's sweeping effort
to aid his election and that the president had lied about his past dealings with
the Russians. The power of this calm back-and-forth can be seen in the hearing transcript.

SCHIFF: In fact, the [Trump] campaign welcomed the Russian help,
did they not?

MUELLER: I think we have—we report in our—in the report indications that that occurred, yes.

SCHIFF: The president's son said when he was approached about dirt on Hillary Clinton that the Trump campaign would love it?

MUELLER: That is generally what was said, yes.

SCHIFF: The president himself called on the Russians to hack Hillary's emails?

MUELLER: There was a statement by the president in those general lines.

SCHIFF: Numerous times during the campaign the president praised the releases of the Russian-hacked emails through WikiLeaks?

MUELLER: That did occur.

SCHIFF: Your report found that the Trump campaign planned, quote, "a press strategy, communications campaign, and messaging," unquote, based on that Russian assistance?

MUELLER: I am not familiar with that.

SCHIFF: That language comes from Volume 1, page 54. Apart from the Russians wanting to help Trump win, several individuals associated with the Trump campaign were also trying to make money during the campaign and transition. Is that correct?

MUELLER: That is true.

SCHIFF: Paul Manafort was trying to make money or achieve debt forgiveness from a Russian oligarch?

MUELLER: Generally that is accurate.

SCHIFF: Michael Flynn was trying to make money from Turkey?

MUELLER: True.

SCHIFF: Donald Trump was trying to make millions from a real estate deal in Moscow?

MUELLER: To the extent you're talking about the hotel in Moscow?

SCHIFF: Yes.

MUELLER: Yes.

SCHIFF: When your investigation looked into these matters, numerous Trump associates lied to your team, the grand jury, and to Congress?

MUELLER: A number of persons that we interviewed in our investigation turns out did lie.

SCHIFF: Mike Flynn lied?

MUELLER: He was convicted of lying, yes.

SCHIFF: George Papadopoulos was convicted of lying?

MUELLER: True.

SCHIFF: Paul Manafort was convicted of lying?

MUELLER: True.

SCHIFF: Paul Manafort was—in fact, went so far as to encourage other people to lie?

MUELLER: That is accurate.

SCHIFF: Manafort's deputy, Rick Gates, lied?

MUELLER: That is accurate.

SCHIFF: Michael Cohen, the president's lawyer, was indicted for lying?

MUELLER: True.

SCHIFF: He lied to stay on message with the president?

MUELLER: Allegedly by him.

SCHIFF: And when Donald Trump called your investigation a witch hunt, that was also false, was it not?

MUELLER: I'd like to think so, yes.

The contrast between Schiff's evocation of the damning elements of Mueller's volume 2 was obvious to serious observers who stayed with events to the end. They would have noticed, too, that Mueller was a different man in the Intelligence Committee, which is small, compared with the Judiciary Committee, and works under a tradition of greater collegiality and mutual respect.

As the hearing ended, committee member Denny Heck made a point to seek out Mueller for a private post-hearing chat. He came away with the impression that a hearing difficulty had made it hard for Mueller to determine who had addressed him—"it gave him a deer in the headlights look"—but that as the day wore on, he got better at it. "In a one-on-one conversation he was completely present and very acutely aware of everything and conversational in a way that he didn't always present himself during testimony." The problem was, Heck allowed, "that first impressions do matter." In this case, Americans watching Mueller on TV did not get a favorable first impression.

In the immediate aftermath of the two hearings, officials and ordinary citizens alike tended to apply a ball game style of analysis to events. Those who tuned in to Fox News, which was the home team broadcaster for Donald Trump, got the message that Mueller had failed miserably and the GOP proved that he was a witch-hunter. Those who watched the left-leaning MSNBC would have heard stronger support for Mueller but also concern that his findings had been overwhelmed by theatrics.

Among House Democrats, many felt frustrated that Mueller had not clarified the matter of impeachment. The firebrands, who thought Trump was committing impeachable offenses every day, still wanted to move against him. But Pelosi and the moderates saw no change—Mueller was a dud, and public sentiment was against impeachment. Americans still wanted improvements in health care and education and a better shake from the tax code. They expected the Democrats to get something done on these and other issues.

Little noticed in the aftermath was a shift among Democrats when it came to their thinking about how impeachment would proceed if it ever came to that. For months, it had seemed that the Judiciary Committee, led by Nadler, had first claim to impeachment. This was because the impeachment process was a judicial one and because the most damning elements of the Mueller report revolved around the obstruction of justice. However, during the seven hours Mueller had spent on Capitol Hill, Nadler's stock had fallen while Schiff's had risen. If the day had produced a star, he was it.[10]

The president, of course, considered himself the hero of the day and devoted ample time to assessing Mueller's showmanship and declaring himself victorious. "I think Robert Mueller did a horrible job, both today and with respect to the investigation," he told reporters during yet another Chopper Talk interlude. "Obviously he did very poorly today. I don't think there's anybody—even among the fakers—I don't think there's anybody that would say he did well."

"This was a devastating day for the Democrats," Mr. Trump said, adding: "The answer is very simple. Nothing was done wrong. This was all a big hoax. And if you look at it today, nothing was done wrong."[11]

July 30, 2019 — Number of House members in favor of impeaching the president: 102

PART III

HIGH CRIMES

23

A PROFILE IN ARROGANCE

Wow, Corey Lewandowski, my campaign manager and a very decent man, was just charged with assaulting a reporter. Look at tapes–nothing there!

—Donald Trump, then Republican candidate for president of the United States, via Twitter, March 29, 2016

When last seen in a starring role on the national political stage, Corey Lewandowski was the Trump presidential campaign manager who was caught grabbing a female reporter by the arm and spinning her around. Michelle Fields, a reporter for pro-Trump Breitbart News, was chasing candidate Trump to ask him a question. Caught midstride, she stumbled and then recovered her balance. When a few tears fell from her eyes, Ben Terris, a reporter from *The Washington Post*, noticed. He also saw finger-shaped bruises on her arm. As he wrote, she told him, "I'm just a little spooked. No one has grabbed me like that before."

In the days after the incident, video of the incident was broadcast on television, and the local police filed assault charges against Lewandowski. (They would be dropped in a few weeks.) Trump stated that Lewandowski was, in his estimation, "a very decent man." In fact, Lewandowski was characterized even in conservative circles as a "thuggish hothead" whose coarse language and manner alienated coworkers and who, like the candidate, resisted accountability. (He dismissed Fields as an "attention-seeker.") As a young man he acknowledged in an interview with one potential employer that he had a tendency to "piss people off." He also got caught carrying a pistol and ammunition into a congressional office building. Despite his professions of admiration, Trump would dismiss Lewandowski from his campaign.[1]

Three and a half years later, in September 2019, Lewandowski was back in the spotlight, testifying before the House Committee on the Judiciary as part of what Chairman Jerrold Nadler had announced was an *impeachment inquiry*. "I am an open book," Lewandowski explained when he agreed to appear. "I want to go and remind the American people that these guys are on a witch hunt." He was surely motivated, as well, by the attention he would attract as he considered challenging New Hampshire senator Jeanne Shaheen, a Democrat, in the next election.

In the days between Lewandowski's announcement that he would testify and the moment when he swore to tell the truth, the president's ever-changing political condition had changed yet again. Although Trump's camp believed he had been delivered from peril by Mueller's July 24 testimony, they were not yet aware of the fact that on the very next day, when he was more unencumbered by controversy than at any time in his presidency, Trump had picked up the phone and attempted to leverage military aid for Ukraine for his own political benefit.[2]

Alert observers would have first noticed something strange going on with Ukraine and the Trump administration on August 28, when *Politico* revealed that a hold was placed on hundreds of millions of dollars that would have helped pay for Kiev's fight against Russia. Although the public was not yet aware, Trump's phone call was the subject of a formal whistelblower complaint. Word went from Inspector General Michael Atkinson and the director of national intelligence to the White House and to certain members of the Intelligence Committees on Capitol Hill. In a matter of days, the wall of secrecy that concealed the long-running scheme to manipulate Ukraine for Donald Trump's benefit would begin to collapse like an undermined dam. A flood of revelations would wash over Washington, depositing in public view a vast number of creatures, including Paul Manafort, Rudy Giuliani, Lev Parnas, Igor Fruman, the Three Amigos, John Solomon, and various oligarchs and operatives.[3]

While those few who understood what was to come watched from a distance, Corey Lewandowski offered a virtuoso, if oblivious, performance of mockery and disrespect that made him seem even more like the president than the bright red Trump-style necktie he had selected for the day. From her seat in the first row of committee spots, facing Lewandowski, Representative Debbie Mucarsel-Powell worried that Nadler, who was comfortable with normal kinds of political conflict and was polite in an old-school way, would have a hard time adjusting if Lewandowski behaved in the thuggish manner she knew was part of his repertoire.

Nadler began with a typical chairman's opening statement—carefully worded to create context and convey seriousness—that treated Lewandowski with grace. He recited the witness's biography, noting his education and achievements. Before administering the oath, he said, "We welcome Mr. Lewandowski and we thank him for participating in today's hearing."

After a few glowing statements about Donald Trump's campaign, which began with a "ride down the golden escalator" at Trump Tower, Lewandowski launched into a diatribe filled with the reliable shiny object the president and his backers waved to distract from the seriousness of the Russian election interference, which the Trump campaign had welcomed. He falsely claimed that "as a special counsel determined, there was no conspiracy or collusion between the Trump campaign and any foreign government" and noted that thanks to the Mueller report, "the fake Russia collusion narrative has fallen apart."

Reading quickly, his eyes focused on the pages of his statement, Lewandowski referred to the "harassment" of the president and to "Trump haters" who wanted to destroy him. He finished with a lecture for the committee. "We as a nation would be better served if elected officials like yourself concentrated your efforts to combat the true crises facing our country as opposed to going down rabbit holes like this hearing. Instead of focusing on petty and personal politics, the committee focused on solving the challenges of this generation. Imagine how many people we could help or how many lives we could save."

Altogether, Lewandowski's opening statement was one part love letter and one part roaring defense offered with just one person in mind. That person, watching Lewandowski on a television aboard Air Force One, tapped out a message for his tens of millions of Twitter followers. "Such a beautiful Opening Statement by Corey Lewandowski! Thank you Corey! @CLewandowski."

What followed the statement that won the president's heart was a long exercise in which Democrats on the committee, followed by staff lawyers, tried to learn more about some of the more than one hundred mentions of Lewandowski in the Mueller report. He tried to parry many of them with claims of executive branch confidentiality rights. These were, as the legal writer Harry Litman observed, "make-believe" rights, "because Lewandowski never even worked in the White House or the executive branch." Nevertheless, the witness would refuse to answer questions based on this pretend right. He also used questions and complaints to drag out the proceedings as if he were a U.S. senator using a filibuster to kill a piece of legislation.[4]

Typical of the method, and a true signal of what was to come, was the exchange that ensued after Chairman Nadler posed the first question, which was about a very specific paragraph in the Mueller report. The paragraph referenced a one-on-one meeting between the president and Lewandowski on July 19, 2017, in which Trump asked his former campaign manager to take a message to Attorney General Jeff Sessions. (Trump, seeking to obstruct the government's Russia investigation, had been berating Sessions in public and in private, but he had been warned that firing him himself would be too much for even Republicans in Congress to accept.) As Mueller wrote, the president dictated a message that directed Sessions to curtail the scope of the special counsel's investigation. The message also said Sessions should publicly announce that Mueller's investigation was "very unfair" to the president, that the president had done nothing wrong. This information had been given to Mueller by Lewandowski and was in the public realm. The chairman wanted to discuss it with the witness and began by referencing this meeting. What ensued was a display of disrespect unusual even in the Trump era:

> **NADLER:** Mr. Lewandowski, is it correct as reported in the Mueller report on June 19, 2017, you met alone in the Oval Office with the president?
>
> **LEWANDOWSKI:** Is there a book and page number you can reference me to, please? I don't have a copy of the report in front of me.
>
> **NADLER:** Volume two, page 90. But I simply ask you is it correct that as reported in the Mueller report on June 19, 2017, you met alone in the Oval Office with the president?
>
> **LEWANDOWSKI:** Could you read the exact language of the report, sir? I don't have it available to me.
>
> **NADLER:** I don't think I need to do that and I have limited time. Did you meet alone with the president on that date?
>
> **LEWANDOWSKI:** Congressman, I'd like you to refresh my memory by providing a copy of the report so I can follow along.

NADLER: You don't have a copy with you?

LEWANDOWSKI: I don't have a copy of the report, Congressman.

After Nadler requested that a timer that limits committee members' statement be stopped, the witness asked again about the page number. When Nadler directed him to "Page—page 90, volume two," the witness said, "OK, and which paragraph, sir?"

NADLER: I don't have it in front of me.

LEWANDOWSKI: I'd like a reference, sir, so I can follow along in what you're asking.

NADLER: Do you not have an independent recollection of whether you met with the president on that date?

LEWANDOWSKI: Congressman, I'm just trying to find in the Mueller report where it states that.

And so it went, with Lewandowski performing like the wise guy in a junior high school classroom. He was soon aided by requests for adjournment voiced by GOP members of the committee. With rules permitting such requests and additional demands of roll call votes, the clerk or the committee would labor through calling dozens of names while the members of the committee fell into party-line exercises that always ended with the call for adjournment defeated but the proceedings delayed.

On and on it went with the Democrats on the committee attempting to get one or two straight answers from Lewandowski as he deflected them with questions about their questions and then reciting a letter from the White House advising him to decline to answer any questions about contacts with people in the executive branch.

It took more than half an hour before Lewandowski finally acknowledged that, as Mueller reported, he and Trump had spoken. Mueller had reported that "Lewandowski did not want to deliver the President's message personally, so he asked senior White House official Rick Dearborn to deliver it to Sessions. Dearborn was uncomfortable with the task and did not follow through."

Nadler noted that the committee had subpoenaed Dearborn to testify alongside Lewandowski. He refused based on a White House declaration that everyone surrounding Trump had "absolute immunity," which was ill-defined and a questionable argument in court. "We are considering all available options to enforce these subpoenas," Nadler said.

Among the options was a declaration of inherent contempt, which had not been employed by Congress since 1934. Under that procedure, Congress could order the House sergeant at arms to take up police powers to arrest an offender on contempt charges, bring that person to the Capitol, and even imprison him or her if he or she refused to cooperate. Congress also had the power to levy daily fines in almost any amount.

As Lewandowski proceeded to delay and even insult members of the committee, the Democrats began to whisper to each other about the spectacle and to discuss ways to deal with it. At one point, Representative David Cicilline of Rhode Island said, "Mr. Chairman, this witness continues to obstruct the work of this committee by refusing to answer questions. He's been ordered to do so by you. I ask that you judge him in contempt of these proceedings."

"I will take that under advisement," Nadler replied.

Nadler, who had consulted with Speaker Pelosi before the hearing, believed she did not want him to cite Lewandowski for contempt because such a move, she argued, might backfire politically. Instead, Nadler kept the hearing going by stopping the timer every time Lewandowski embarked on his antics. He also took opportunities to point out the game Lewandowski was playing. At one moment, he said, "You showed the American public in real time that the Trump administration will do anything and everything in its power to obstruct Congress's work. Make no mistake, we will hold President Trump accountable."

Finally, the House committee's counsel, Barry Berke, who had been seated to Nadler's right all the while, offering advice all along, finally had a chance to take over the questioning. But that was at around 6:00 p.m. eastern standard time. Americans still watching into the dinner hour were able to witness the finely honed techniques of one of the most proficient courtroom inquisitors in the United States.

In a thirty-minute barrage of questions, Berke got Lewandowski to confirm some facts that had eluded others, including that Lewandowski had lied on numerous occasions. Berke's questions were not related to anything

Lewandowski discussed with people at the White House, so he couldn't re-treat behind the imaginary privilege, and they dealt with statements made on the public record. Here, Lewandowski, his face drawn tauter than at any point during the day, showed he was fatigued but also annoyed.

When Berke asked why Lewandowski had told NBC's *Meet the Press* he had not given testimony for Mueller's investigation, the witness replied sarcas-tically, "Oh, I'm sorry. Nobody in front of Congress has ever lied to the public before. I'm sorry." A moment later, he added, "When under oath, I have always told the truth." This was not such a strange standard for someone so closely tied to a president whose lies and distortions had been counted at a rate of about five thousand per year, but it was remarkable coming from someone who was thinking for running for statewide public office.

After this lie was noted, Berke played a clip of an interview Lewandowski had done with TV newsman Ari Melber, in which he said, "I don't ever re-member the president ever asking me to get involved with Jeff Sessions or with the Department of Justice in any way, shape or form, ever."

Having pierced Lewandowski's defense, Berke's questions revealed the Orwellian nihilism of the Trump way. He, like the president, seemed to feel no obligation to basic morality and no need to respect other people or institu-tions created to nurture, serve, and protect society. If someone else somewhere had lied, then the president and Corey Lewandowski were under no obligation to tell the truth themselves. They also felt no compunction about then asking for the public trust in the form of high office.

•　•　•

Nothing before Lewandowski's performance—not William Barr's interception of the Mueller report or the special counsel's own difficult day in testimony—bothered House Democrats more than what they saw happen at the Judiciary Committee hearing. One of the longest-serving people in the House, Nadler was an avuncular figure who had helped many of them learn their way around when they first arrived. They saw his courtliness not as weakness but as a sign of his human decency. What Lewandowski had done, in their eyes, was equiv-alent to a daylong public mugging.

At the time when it occurred, the caucus was deeply divided on impeach-ment. Moderates from contested districts, like Max Rose, an Army Ranger from Staten Island, wanted the party to stick to its positive agenda. By fo-cusing too much on impeachment, the caucus risked "losing the trust of the American people," he said around this time. "I want to see this party—and I know it has it in it—get to work passing substantive infrastructure and health care bills by the end of the year."

Alexandria Ocasio-Cortez, whose Queens, New York, district was just eighteen miles from Rose's, held a view that was far more distant from her colleagues'. Her constituents included many immigrants and children of immigrants who had been appalled by President Trump's disparagement of people seeking refuge in the U.S. (Trump has also called their countries of origin "shithole" nations.) They had long passed the point where they had any doubt about the need for impeachment. AOC, as she was called, understood, too, that across the country, the president's behavior had turned many, if not most, against him. She said, "I want to see every Republican go on the record and knowingly vote against impeachment of this president, knowing his corruption, having it on the record so that they can have that stain on their careers for the rest of their lives."[5]

Looking at the Democrats from the outside, the president and his supporters, like Corey Lewandowski, may have overestimated the gulf between the likes of AOC and Max Rose. They may have also held in mind the famous Will Rogers quote—"I'm not a member of any organized political party, I am a Democrat"—which captured the quality that always seemed to make the Democrats incapable of moving decisively. However, insult and mockery tend to galvanize. After the hearing, Nancy Pelosi let it be known that she had been appalled by the nationally broadcast fiasco and concerned that Nadler had not been able to deal more effectively with a witness who had seized control. (It was not clear whether she had forgotten that she had told Chairman Nadler to tread lightly or if, perhaps, they had misunderstood each other.)

If Republicans considered what the Democrats were doing, rather than what they were saying, they would have noticed a shift. By designating his committee's work as an impeachment inquiry, Jerrold Nadler had signaled to the public, and any court that might consider a related complaint, that he was invoking Congress's impeachment authority. The move pushed the House closer to a constitutional conflict even as the Speaker of the House tried to manage the divisions in her caucus.

On a weekend back in his district, Representative Cicilline got an earful about Trump as he attended a variety of events, including a gathering for veterans, a school robotics fair, and a "clam boil" back in patriotic Bristol. In between events, he sorted out, in his mind, the state of play. "However you want to describe the work we're doing, some people call it an inquiry, some people call it a proceeding, some people call it an investigation. [But to] be clear, we are actively considering whether or not to recommend articles of impeachment to the full House. Let's stop all the semantic disagreements. We're doing this."

A member of Nadler's Judiciary Committee, Cicilline was one of the Democrats most determined to take up impeachment. He sympathized with those troubled by the pressure that he and others put on the Speaker but considered it part of a natural process. Pelosi was in charge, but this didn't mean she could manage the caucus like a military commander. Individual members and chairs of committees could act independently. This fact meant that sometimes House members seemed out of sync with the Speaker, but this could also be a useful way to test public opinion and even give her cover to explore options.

No matter what it was called, said Cicilline, "the committee is actively engaged in this determination [of whether to impeach the president] and we're going to hear from witnesses and we're going to continue to seek the production of documents and litigate where we have to." In Cicilline's view, the Speaker's fence-sitting contributed to the sense of struggle within the caucus. It also set up the possibility of a greater legislative drama. As he noted, articles of impeachment can be drafted and proposed by any member of Congress and can be offered in a way that requires a vote. "Eventually the local press [in members' districts] are going to figure this out," said Cicilline. "They'll say, 'This is all very nice that you respect Nancy Pelosi but why don't *you* file articles of impeachment?'"

August 31, 2019 — Number of House members in favor of impeaching the president: 119

24

WITCH HUNT GARBAGE

If that perfect phone call with the President of Ukraine Isn't considered appropriate, then no future President can EVER again speak to another foreign leader!

—Donald Trump, president of the United States, via Twitter,
September 27, 2019

On September 20, 2019, *The Wall Street Journal* reported that Donald Trump "in a July phone call repeatedly pressured the president of Ukraine to investigate Joe Biden's son" and had urged "Volodymyr Zelensky about eight times to work with Rudy Giuliani on a probe that could hamper Mr. Trump's potential 2020 opponent." The *Journal* also revealed the existence of the whistleblower complaint and the dispute that had delayed its transmittal to Congress.[1]

Joe Biden, the front-runner in the race for the Democratic presidential nomination, responded forcefully:

> If these reports are true, then there is truly no bottom to President Trump's willingness to abuse his power and abase our country. This behavior is particularly abhorrent because it exploits the foreign policy of our country and undermines our national security for political purposes. It means that he used the power and resources of the United States to pressure a sovereign nation—a partner that is still under direct assault from Russia—pushing Ukraine to subvert the rule of law in the express hope of extracting a political favor.[2]

Trump's aides convinced him he had to do something—so they released an edited version of what Trump had said to the Ukrainian president on July 25—one day after Mueller's limp appearance before the House Judiciary Committee. The details were damning, though Trump was selling the readout of the call as a "transcript," which it wasn't, and was saying that it was innocent, or in his words "perfect."

In fact, this was prima facie evidence of bribery, and Democrats immediately began using the term *quid pro quo*—Latin for "this for that." The term was too mild. Trump had not asked for a mere favor. He had conditioned lifesaving defensive weapons on Ukraine providing corrupt assistance to his reelection bid.

In addition to the substance of the perfect phone call, Speaker of the House Nancy Pelosi had been presented with the administration's effort to circumvent the whistleblower law and deny Congress notice of the complaint. Those who knew her background, like Representative Gerald Connolly, realized that the Speaker would surely change her mind on the question of whether Trump was now "worth" impeachment.

"She spent twenty-five years off and on as a member of the intelligence committee," said Connolly. "Each one of these committees have their own cultures, right? And she helped write the laws that govern whistleblowers and the reporting sequences that must be followed . . . the violation of law, she felt was clear by both the DNI [director of national intelligence] and the White House trying to block the whistleblower from coming to Congress, even though it's stipulated in law. So this one was for her crystal clear . . . this was right in her lane and she wasn't going to let it go."[3]

On September 24, Pelosi let it be known that an afternoon meeting of the caucus was going to be momentous, and afterward, she would have an announcement. These were unmistakable signals that big news was at hand. Still, some Democrats clung to the belief that impeachment would never happen. In his district for constituent work, Representative Bobby Scott of Virginia actually told a university class he visited that the impeachment question remained unresolved.

In fact, if Scott had read the morning paper, he would have known that change was afoot. Seven frontline freshman Democrats—precious to the Speaker's majority—had studied reports on the Ukraine phone call and the whistleblower complaint and published an article in which they said, "If these allegations are true, we believe these actions represent an impeachable offense." The seven—

Gil Cisneros, Jason Crow, Chrissy Houlahan, Elaine Luria, Mikie Sherrill, Elissa Slotkin, and Abigail Spanberger—had each worked in national security or defense and came to the topic with noteworthy credibility. They had each also been offended by Corey Lewandowski's treatment of Nadler and the Judiciary Committee.[4]

In the afternoon caucus meeting, the assembled Democrats were cheered to learn that their days of division were over. The Speaker was going to move ahead with impeachment. In a brief discussion of the process, some of the Security Seven pressed for the creation of a special committee. The House had created just such a committee during Watergate. It had streamlined things and made stars of those appointed to it. The Seven would be forgiven if they imagined taking positions on the 2019 version. More senior members of the House reminded them that Watergate had unspooled over the course of years and argued that between the Intelligence, Foreign Affairs, Government Oversight, and Judiciary Committees, the matter was well in hand.

As scheduled, Pelosi left the caucus for a news conference in a room that had been decorated with American flags. She wore a blue dress, which presented a contrast with all the red and white stripes of Old Glory. An American flag pin—another patriotic note—completed her outfit.

> Good afternoon. Last Tuesday, we observed the anniversary of the adoption of the Constitution on September 17. Sadly, on that day, the intelligence community inspector general formally notified the Congress that the administration was forbidding him from turning in a whistleblower complaint. On Constitution day. This is a violation of the law. Shortly thereafter, press reports began to break of a phone call by the President of the United States calling upon a foreign power to intervene in his election. This is a breach of his Constitutional responsibilities.
>
> The actions of the Trump presidency reveal dishonorable facts of the president's betrayal of his oath of office, betrayal of our national security, and betrayal of the integrity of our election. Therefore, today, I'm announcing the House of Representatives is moving forward with an official impeachment inquiry . . . [t]he president must be held accountable.
>
> No one is above the law.

When she finished speaking, Pelosi simply turned to her left and walked off. She would not respond to questions.

Two hundred twenty-five miles away, President Trump, who was in New York for the United Nations General Assembly, posted a message on Twitter:

Witch Hunt Garbage. So bad for our country.[5]

At the UN, where Trump was to deliver an annual speech, delegates remembered how in the previous year he had provoked laughter as he declared that he had achieved more in his first two years in office "than any administration had achieved before in history." But while they were poised to hear something funny, what they got instead was a dour rejection of international cooperation. "For decades, the international trading system has been easily exploited by nations acting in bad faith," Trump said hoarsely. Then he added a line lifted from his campaign stump speeches. "I will not accept a bad deal for the American people."

That top American officials might find themselves uncomfortably engaged with world events as domestic scandals raged was a fact of life. Although President Trump had done much to diminish the nation's global role, America remained the most important superpower on earth, and wherever its top diplomatic, trade, or defense officials traveled, they rightly garnered attention. A week after Trump's UN speech, Secretary of State Mike Pompeo arrived in Italy for public talks on trade and, he hoped, the possibility of "meeting all my cousins" during some private time. His first stop was a photo op with Prime Minister Giuseppe Conte at the stately sixteenth-century Quirinal Palace, the official seat of the Italian executive branch. With the cameras rolling, Pompeo walked briskly into a reception room, smiling broadly. As he reached out to shake hands with Prime Minister Conte, a well-known TV personality named Alice Martinelli joined the two men.

A "reporter" for the news parody program *La Iene* (*The Hyena*), Martinelli dashed onto the red carpet and gave Pompeo a large wedge of Parmesan cheese wrapped in plastic, telling him in accented English, "This is what we make best in Italy. . . . Take it to Mr. Trump, please, and tell [him] that we make it with our hearts, please."

Conte, embarrassed, shooed Martinelli away. Pompeo, confused, then handed the cheese to Conte, who passed it in turn to an aide, assuring the secretary of state, "It's a good one!" Pompeo replied, "I have no doubt," and patted his ample stomach.[6]

Pompeo's second day in Rome was not any easier. Questions from reporters at a joint news conference, this time with the Italian foreign minister, focused on Ukraine. Pompeo had previously tried to distance himself from Trump's July 25 talk with Volodymyr Zelensky but now finally acknowledged, "As for the phone call, I was on the phone call." He swallowed hard and continued. "I guess I've been secretary of state coming on a year and a half. I know precisely what the American policy is with regard to Ukraine. It's been remarkably consistent and we will continue to drive those set of outcomes. Even while all this noise is going on."[7]

Much of the noise emanated from the president. On the same Wednesday morning when Pompeo found himself holding the cheese, Trump was tweeting early, during the time of day he typically reserved for long periods of watching the news as reported by *Fox & Friends*. He wrote: "The Do Nothing Democrats should be focused on building up our Country, not wasting everyone's time and energy on BULLSHIT, which is what they have been doing ever since I got overwhelmingly elected in 2016."[8]

Trump's apparent rage was provoked by a House process led, primarily, by Adam Schiff. Among the leaders of the Democratic Caucus, the Intelligence Committee chairman had a strong claim to issues related to the Zelensky call. More importantly, he had also won the contest for Pelosi's confidence. In fact, when a letter was sent to the White House demanding that the administration provide information about the Zelensky call and make certain officials available for testimony, it was signed by Schiff, Elijah Cummings of Government Oversight, and Eliot Engel of the Foreign Relations Committee. Nadler's name was notably absent.[9]

After some delay, Pompeo said that he would comply with any lawful requests for documents and witnesses. House Democrats prepared a long list of people they might want to hear from, including State Department officials, but also White House staff and one outlier at the center of the Ukraine controversy, Rudolph Giuliani. As the president's personal lawyer, Giuliani would resist a summons because of attorney-client privilege. However, he had also acted as if he represented American interests as a kind of freelance foreign policy actor. His actions in this role would be subject to oversight. When asked about the possibility he might testify before the House he said he would not and that he "can't imagine" anyone in the administration would. Previously

Giuliani had called for Schiff to be removed from his position and replaced by some "neutral" person.

Schiff's new prominence bothered those who saw him as a more assertive and talented interrogator. As he negotiated to protect early witnesses' testimony by hearing it in closed sessions at an underground Sensitive Compartmented Information Facility (SCIF), right-wing commentators began to warn of an invisible "coup." The president referred to the Intelligence Committee chairman with derogatory nicknames, including "little Adam Schiff," and, true to his propensity for vulgarity, even indulged in calling him "little Adam Schitt."

Trump's most puerile comments about Schiff came after the chairman mixed parody into a public statement describing the president's call with Zelensky. Veering from the actual description of the readout released by the White House, Schiff said that in "essence" the president had acted like a mobster. Imitating what he imagined Trump had said, Schiff said, "I hear what you want. I have a favor I want from you, though. And I'm going to say this only seven times, so you better listen good. I want you to make up dirt on my political opponent. Understand? Lots of it, on this and on that."

A careful listener would understand Schiff's mockery, but it fell flat and gave Trump and his defenders an opportunity to lodge pearl-clutching complaints. In the weeks that followed, GOP members of the House would demand that Schiff resign and sought to have him censured. Neither of these notions was reasonable, nor did they lead to censure, but the incident reminded Schiff to avoid such attempts at humor again.[10]

Fortunately for Schiff, the Ukraine scandal was marked by so many absurd moments and figures that his parody would pale in comparison. For example, a few days after Schiff's stumble, Lev Parnas and Igor Fruman were arrested at Dulles Airport outside Washington as they were about to board a flight to Vienna where Dmytro Firtash still lived. The two, who possessed one-way tickets, were charged with violating campaign finance laws. News accounts reminded the public of their links to Trump and Rudy Giuliani. Parnas would commence a series of public statements revealing his role in the Ukraine affair. Fruman would keep silent. Federal courts scheduled their trials for after the 2020 election.[11]

•   •   •

On October 8, the White House finally issued a blanket response to the House leadership's request for information, written by White House counsel Pat

Cipollone. Cipollone contended that the decision to conduct an impeachment inquiry was somehow unconstitutional, but Trump had nevertheless "taken the unprecedented step of providing the public transparency by declassifying and releasing the record of his call with President Zelensky of Ukraine. The record clearly established that the call was completely appropriate and that there is no basis for your inquiry."[12]

Pelosi fired back the same day, rejecting the claim that they could not and need not conduct their inquiry as "the latest attempt to cover up his betrayal of our democracy, and to insist that the President is above the law." She said there was growing evidence that Trump had abused his oath of office. "Mr. President," she said. "You will be held accountable."[13]

Cipollone's letter in many ways laid out the White House game plan in dealing with the Democratic impeachment drive—attack the process and the players, rather than dealing with the evidence. First of all, the very fact that Cipollone himself was writing the letter gave pause—as a government official, the role of White House counsel was to protect the office of the presidency, not the particular occupant. Yet Cipollone ranged into politics by claiming that Democrats sought to overturn the 2016 elections, one popular Trump talking point. He also repeated a conspiracy theory voiced by Trump and his supporters that Schiff had coordinated the Ukraine whistleblower and lied about it.

Walter Shaub, who had resigned his post as director of the Office of Government Ethics in protest, said, "Cipollone's letter isn't so much a legal challenge as a press release. The letter is undignified and borderline hysterical [and] the points he raised are based on political bluster, not law." He added, "Its underlying assumption, that the executive must consent to an impeachment inquiry, mistakes Trump for a king."

Gregg Nunziata, a former Justice Department official and onetime counsel to Senator Marco Rubio, was more succinct. "This letter is bananas . . . a middle finger to Congress and its oversight responsibilities."[14]

October 9, 2019 — Number of House members in favor of impeaching the president: 215

25

"PRAY FOR THE PRESIDENT"

After defeating 100% of the ISIS Caliphate, I largely moved our troops out of Syria. Let Syria and Assad protect the Kurds and fight Turkey for their own land. I said to my Generals, why should we be fighting for Syria and Assad to protect the land of our enemy? Anyone who wants to assist Syria in protecting the Kurds is good with me, whether it is Russia, China, or Napoleon Bonaparte. I hope they all do great, we are 7,000 miles away!

—Donald Trump, president of the United States, via Twitter, October 14, 2019

No one in American politics was better than Donald Trump when it came to changing the subject of national concern. He had it done with a variety of methods, including a White House display of tractor trailer trucks to boost plans for building highways and multiple efforts to denigrate National Football League players who knelt during the national anthem to bring attention to racism. "Wouldn't you love to see one of these NFL owners, when somebody disrespects our flag, to say, 'Get that son of a bitch off the field right now. Out! He's fired. He's fired!'"[1]

Rarely did the president's distractions come with lethal potential, but on Sunday, October 6, 2019, less than two weeks after the Speaker of the House announced a formal impeachment inquiry, he began one that did, in fact, cost lives. After a telephone call with Turkey's strongman president, Recep Erdoğan, Trump had the White House press office issue a statement saying that Turkey's long-planned invasion of northern Syria would soon commence and that American troops "will no longer be in the immediate area."[2]

The statement, which surprised the Pentagon, did not note that northern

Syria was home to a large community of ethnic Kurds whose paramilitary had done most of the fighting and dying in the U.S.-sponsored war against the terrorist organization known as ISIS. Nor did it acknowledge that these same Kurds, who had long fought for self-rule in Turkey, would be overrun, and perhaps slaughtered, by Turkish forces who considered them to be the real terrorists in the region.

As Trump removed their protection, the Kurds were hit with air strikes and cannon fire. On October 8, though, as the Turkish infantry advanced, forcing three hundred thousand civilians to flee to nearby Iraq, Trump said it wasn't happening. He tweeted on October 8: "We may be in the process of leaving Syria, but in no way have we Abandoned the Kurds. We are helping the Kurds financially/weapons!" Over eight days, as many as one thousand Kurdish fighters and five hundred civilians would be killed.

The body count and sudden loss of American influence and prestige infuriated even Trump's allies in Congress. A written statement by Senate majority leader Mitch McConnell stung the president with the note that "American interests are best served by leadership, not by retreat or withdrawal." Worse was that from Senator Lindsey Graham, who invaded Trump's comfort zone on the Fox News TV network to criticize an "impulsive decision by the president [that] has undone all the gains we've made, thrown the region into further chaos."

Already besieged by the House impeachment proceedings, Trump's sudden move in Syria had backfired. Instead of getting credit for boldly moving U.S. troops out of harm's way, he was getting attacked from all sides. Many noted an article written by George Conway, a conservative attorney who happened to be the husband of Trump's advisor Kellyanne Conway. He wrote, "No president in recent memory—and likely no president ever—has prompted more discussion about his mental stability and connection with reality." After the Syria decision, Conway went further. He called on Trump's advisors to quit "if you can't have a positive effect on him, and I don't think anybody can."[3]

On October 16, the House condemned the Syria withdrawal in a bipartisan vote. Trump considered his action a success and was angry about the rebuke. Word went out to members of both parties to join the president for a meeting at the White House. The invitation set off an alarm at the office of New Jersey senator Bob Menendez, who had gotten support from Senate Republicans for a companion resolution he introduced to match the House measure. The ranking Democrat on the Foreign Relations Committee, he had received such invitations before only to discover he might end up being the only member of his party in attendance. Menendez was unwilling to trust what might happen, especially after Trump had tried to co-opt FBI director James Comey at a private dinner. "Nobody was going to corner me," he would later recall. "That wasn't going to work."

Menendez had his staff contact others in Congress to see if they, too, had been invited. Aides to minority leader Chuck Schumer, Speaker of the House Nancy Pelosi, and House majority leader Steny Hoyer all said yes. Persuaded that a serious discussion was planned, even in the midst of the bitter battle about impeachment, he joined the group who trooped to the White House in the afternoon and were ushered toward the Cabinet Room in the West Wing.

The Cabinet Room, with its eighteen-foot ceiling and view of the Rose Garden, is accessed through a door that opens onto a hallway that in turn leads to the Oval Office. As Pelosi, Schumer, and the others entered, they encountered the massive mahogany table, a gift from Richard Nixon, that dominates the space. Twenty leather chairs encircled the table. A similar number lined the walls.

For decades, Americans had seen commanders in chief in action at this table. It was here, for example, that George Bush gathered his team on September 12, 2001, to plan a response to the terror attacks of the prior day. In the Trump years, the room was most famous for a bizarre display of abject loyalty, which the president seemed to demand of his cabinet members in June of 2017. One by one, they offered praise to the boss, some eagerly larding on the flattery. Mike Pence, seeming to forget his roles as husband and father, announced, "The greatest privilege of my life is to serve as vice president to the president who's keeping his word to the American people." Menendez thought about Trump and his conduct and believed there was no telling what he would do.

"I've been through five presidents now," said Menendez days after the meeting. "You know every time a president comes into a meeting like that, he goes around the table, shakes everybody's hand, and then sits down." Not this time, added Menendez. "Trump walks in, you could see from his face, angry. He had a bunch of files in his hand. He slammed the files down on the table, that big old table."

Trump pulled a letter out of his document pile and directed that it be passed around the table. Dated two days after he had announced America's withdrawal from the region, it was addressed to Erdoğan. It began:

Dear Mr. President:

Let's work out a good deal! You don't want to be responsible for slaughtering thousands of people, and I don't want to be responsible for destroying the Turkish economy—and I will.

Trump asked Erdoğan to consider talks with his Kurdish enemies and to seize the opportunity to act with the caution that would win him the world's admiration. Trump concluded with these words, "Don't be a tough guy. Don't be a Fool! I will call you later. Sincerely, Donald J. Trump."[4]

As the lawmakers at the table absorbed one of history's strangest presidential documents, some had to struggle to keep a straight face. Congressman Mike Quigley, a Democratic member of the Intelligence Committee, wondered if it might be a gag, an icebreaker intended to reduce the tension. Menendez, however, recognized that the letter was real.

"All right!" Trump said. "You all wanted this meeting, which I reluctantly agreed to. So what do you want to talk about?"

It was at this moment when Menendez heard Nancy Pelosi speak for the first time in the session. From her seat, which was directly across from Trump's, she said, "With all due respect, Mr. President, we didn't ask for the meeting."

Trump didn't seem to know that he had sent the invitations, or perhaps he was playing some sort of boardroom game from the old days at Trump Tower. Either way, no one else indicated any doubt that the president had called everyone together.

"All right, that's it," he said, his voice rising. "No reason to have the meeting, let's end it."

Pelosi, who was the one person in Washington who could get under Trump's skin without seeming to try, spoke again. The moment was burned in Menendez's memory. As he recalled it, Pelosi began by saying: "What we *did* ask for was a briefing by the secretary of defense, secretary of state, and Gina Haspel, the CIA director, to understand, you know, the nature of the consequences of your decisions as this evolves."

"Then you don't need your meeting here," Trump responded.

"*You called the meeting*," replied Pelosi. "So if you don't want to have the meeting, okay, we were all invited by you. But while we're here, it's my obligation as Speaker of the House to tell you the House voted a little earlier, voted 354 to 60 to disagree with your decisions on Syria, to disagree with you on Syria."

Trump called the House resolution on Syria "nothing more than a hit job on the Republicans." A classic of the Trump lexicon, *hit job* is a term he has used to describe almost any action or statement he finds disagreeable.

"Mr. President, we [the Democrats] don't have 354 votes in the House," said Pelosi. "Two-thirds of the Republican caucus in the House voted alongside the Democrats because they feel this is such an important issue."

At this point, Pelosi's voice was, like Trump's, a little loud. Menendez looked around the room. Many of the attendees were looking down at the table. General Mark A. Milley, the chairman of the Joint Chiefs of Staff, who was seated just to Trump's right, gazed at his fisted hand. After Chuck Schumer mentioned Trump's former defense secretary James Mattis's criticism of the Syria pullout, Trump called Mattis "the world's most overrated general." He then announced, "I hate ISIS more than you do."

"You don't know that," answered Pelosi.

"You're just a politician," said Trump.

Schumer interjected, saying that name-calling was unnecessary.

"Was that a bad name, Chuck?" Trump replied, then he turned back to Pelosi to say, "You're nothing but a third-rate politician, Nancy."

"Madam Speaker to you."

At this point, Menendez felt the tension in his gut. He imagined everyone else did, too. Pelosi continued, saying, "I don't have a problem being called a politician. I wish you were. Maybe the country would be better off."

"Nah, you wouldn't want me as a politician, because look at all you politicians, all you Democrats. The reason you love the Kurds is just because they're all communists."

"Mr. President, do not, do not call us communists."

"Yeah, you love the Kurds and they're all communists. And that's why you're fighting by the Kurds."

Schumer interrupted again, noting that the Kurds had been guarding more than eleven thousand ISIS detainees, many of whom would return to terrorism were they to escape. With Turkey overrunning their bases, no one could be certain of what might happen to them.[5]

"They're all contained," said Trump, even though hundreds of terrorists had already escaped. When the president noted the ISIS fighters were seven thousand miles away, a Republican, Representative Liz Cheney of Wyoming and the former vice president's daughter, finally spoke up, saying, "Mr. President, they traveled 7,000 miles away on September 11th and we had one of the worst tragedies in U.S. history."

Trump did not respond to Cheney, but went on to describe his plan going forward. The plan, Trump said, was "to keep the American people safe."
Schumer answered, "That's not a plan. That's a goal."[6]

Pelosi then stood up to make the main point she sought to press home:
Russia was already moving to take over U.S. bases that had been abandoned.
This itself was a victory for Vladimir Putin, who "has always wanted a foot-
hold in the Middle East." Why would Trump do such a thing? Pelosi asked.
She then offered her own answer: "With you, all roads lead to Putin."

As Pelosi sat down, Hoyer, who occupied the chair to her left, spoke up.
"This is not useful," he said. As he rose, so did Pelosi and Schumer. Together,
they abruptly departed.

"Goodbye. See you at the polls," Trump shouted after them. "See you at
the polls."

Although the top Democrats had departed, the meeting continued. The
group discussed the opening America's withdrawal might provide to Iran as
well as Russia and the threat posed to Israel. When it was noted that Turkey
was bound to draw closer to Russia, Trump insisted this wouldn't happen. In
fact, Turkey had just purchased $2 billion in Russian-made antiaircraft mis-
siles. If Turkey, a member of NATO, was buying missiles designed to shoot
down American F-35 fighter jets, something was truly amiss.[7]

None of the risk seemed to matter to the president. He said, "The biggest
applause line I get at my rallies is when I say I'm going to bring the troops
home." General Milley clearly heard Trump say that, but looked down once
more to avoid eye contact with anyone else.

•   •   •

Even before the meeting was over, Pelosi, Schumer, and Hoyer were outside
on the White House driveway, talking to reporters breathlessly and describing
the bizarre confrontation. "What we witnessed on the part of the president
was a meltdown," Pelosi said. Schumer recounted key parts of the encounter,
including Trump's crude criticism of the Speaker as a "third-rate politician,"
which effectively caused their walkout. Back at the Capitol, they continued to
answer questions about Trump's behavior. "He was insulting, particularly to the
Speaker. She kept her cool completely," Schumer said. "I mean, this was not a
dialogue. It was sort of a diatribe—a nasty diatribe not focused on the facts,
particularly the fact of how to curtail ISIS, a terrorist organization that aims to
hurt the United States in our homeland."

"I have served under six presidents," added Hoyer. "Never have I seen a president treat so disrespectfully a co-equal branch of the government of the United States."[8]

Pelosi mentioned Trump's "meltdown" again at a news conference and said it might have been a result of anger about the number of Republicans who joined Democrats in condemning his action on Syria. "I pray for the president all the time and I tell him that," Pelosi said. "Now we have to pray for his health, because this was a very serious meltdown on the part of the president."

Predictably, this generated a new round of irate comments and tweets from Trump. By late afternoon, he was already tossing verbal jibes, posting a photo of Pelosi pointing at him across the table with the title: "Nervous Nancy's unhinged meltdown!"—reminiscent of his retort to Hillary Clinton during the 2016 campaign, "I'm not the puppet, you're the puppet."[9]

26

THE PIZZA PROTEST

As I learn more and more each day, I am coming to the conclusion that what is taking place is not an impeachment, it is a COUP, intended to take away the Power of the People, their VOTE, their Freedoms, their Second Amendment, Religion, Military, Border Wall, and their God-given rights as a Citizen of The United States of America!

—Donald Trump, president of the United States, via Twitter, October 13, 2019[1]

Trump's anger did not abate. For the next week, he continued to rage at the growing Democratic investigation into his Ukraine call, with Pelosi and Schiff the usual targets. Trump defended his actions with the repeated phrase "It was a perfect call" and accused anyone denying that of buying into a Democratic hoax and the "fake news" presented by his enemies in the media. This, in turn, heated up criticism of the Democratic inquiry on Fox News and among his allies in Congress. The following Monday, October 21, Trump said that his allies needed to do more to defend him against the Democrats. Dutifully, Steve Scalise, the number-two Republican in the House, tweeted that "Adam Schiff must be held accountable for his lies" and introduced a motion to censure Schiff, which was roundly rejected along party lines.

Less than two hours later, Trump spoke to Sean Hannity on his prime-time Fox News program, continuing to question the impeachment. "You know, it's one thing if you commit a real crime," Trump told Hannity. "This was a conversation. It wasn't even a big deal. Hey, how you doing, blah, blah, blah. This is a conversation. It was so perfect."[2]

With Trump heating up his rhetoric, the House GOP cooked up a stunt, focused on Schiff and the closed-door hearings. No matter to Trump and the

Republicans that the sessions were held in secret to protect national security information, nor did they acknowledge the fact that the sessions were hardly exclusive. Democrats and Republicans alike on the House Intelligence, Oversight, and Foreign Affairs committees, and their staffs, could attend, depose witnesses, and view evidence during the hearings.

Those members of Congress who tried to be present for most of the meetings found the work was a grind that extended through the weekends. Trips home to distant districts were canceled. Family functions were rescheduled. Even the aides, who weren't themselves attending the SCIF sessions, felt the stress. On one Saturday, Jamie Raskin dismissed his staff and drove himself to the Capitol from his home in Takoma Park. Along the way, he used pauses at stoplights to tie his tie and relied on a hands-free phone connection to talk about work.

For the first time, members of Congress were hearing about all the scheming that led up to the July 25 phone call, and the breadth of it came as a shock. As Raskin said at the time, "The July 25th phone call was really just the tip of the iceberg of an entire plan by Trump, and Mulvaney and Giuliani and others, to subvert the normal foreign policy apparatus in order to perpetrate their various political and financial schemes."

As distressed as Raskin was about the scandalous aspect of the tale, he was encouraged by the character of the witnesses who came to the hearings. Among the witnesses were Marie Yovanovitch, the ousted U.S. ambassador to Ukraine; William Taylor, who had followed her in that role; Fiona Hill, a U.S. National Security Council member specializing in Russian and European affairs; Lieutenant Colonel Alexander Vindman, director for European Affairs at the National Security Council; and Laura Cooper, deputy assistant secretary of defense for Russia, Ukraine, and Eurasia. Raskin found them all "pretty admirable and noble in their ways. [Many had] conservative assumptions about the world," he said, "but they value reason and evidence and they object to the government being used for consciously corrupt purposes."

Raskin and others were recognizing that the central episode of the scandal was the effort by Giuliani and others—he called them "the gang that couldn't shoot straight"—to remove Ambassador Yovanovitch. Her testimony, corroborated by many others, described a shocking intervention by nongovernment actors to subvert the State Department and ruin a well-respected diplomat. In fact, her demeanor, and that of the others, stood in such contrast with what members of Congress knew of Rudy Giuliani that it was easy to credit their accounts.

For Republicans who attended the sessions and then saw the unredacted portions of witness statements made public, the passing days became sheer misery. Never had a president been the subject of such a torrent of negative information, they complained, and Schiff was acting as if he were presenting a case to a grand jury. The tactic, predictably, brought charges from Republicans that he was conducting a secret inquisition. Before a hearing, Representative Doug Lamborn, an ardent Trump Republican from Colorado Springs, showed up at the SCIF and was barred from entry by Capitol Police because he was not a member of the three investigating committees. He tweeted out a message of shock and outrage: "Today, I was denied access to read the testimony of Kurt Volker in the SCIF. As a member of Congress, I demand access to review documentation that is vital to the process of impeachment. The secret hearings of Adam Schiff are unacceptable and a stain on our democracy." In his complaint, he conveniently avoided the fact that he was no more or no less able to attend or read documents than were Democrats who, like him, were not on the three committees.

There was little GOP representatives could do to change the course of events outside the SCIF. Inside, what they did attempt, over and over again, was to force into public view the name of the anonymous whistleblower who revealed the Trump-Zelensky call. Several witnesses, including Alexander Vindman, were pressed on the question of whether they were the whistleblower. And at various points, names were actually uttered so they might be placed on some record. (They were not.) In right-wing media outlets, pundits made guesses, but none was confirmed to be true.

For the House members who, like Raskin, tried to attend most of the sessions, the experiences in the windowless room juxtaposed with their normal routines—office work, committee duties, interactions with friends and family—made life seem a bit surreal. Representative Joaquin Castro, a Texas Democrat on the Intelligence Committee, held to his usual schedule as much as possible, making calls home at regular times and holding to his habits for exercise and meals. On October 23, weeks into this process, he rose early and got to his Capitol Hill office, where he wanted to get some work done before the staff arrived. Along the way, he went to a House cafeteria where he had breakfast—cereal and Coca-Cola—not quite what a nutritionist would recommend.

Breakfast choices aside, Castro was a serious man who thought deeply about the implications of impeachment and was not happy that Congress was reaching this moment. "I know that Republicans often think that Democrats are giddy about getting Donald Trump but really everybody's been very sober. Nobody ran for office saying, 'I'm running for office because I want to go to Washington to impeach the president.'" However, as he had listened to the testimony, Castro had become firm in his thinking that "Donald Trump's behavior has been overwhelming in terms of his violations of the law and his abuse of power."[3]

On October 23, the SCIF was quiet as Laura Cooper of the Defense Department arrived to testify. Members of the committee began arriving. Outside, in an upper-level hallway, a group of Republicans were gathered to stage a theatrical demonstration—some of the Republican protesters were authorized and could have just walked into the closed hearing. Reporters and photographers, notified that something dramatic was in store, encircled the group. When about two dozen were present, they marched down a spiral staircase to the basement. There, Representative Matt Gaetz, a fiery Trump supporter from Florida, spoke for his GOP colleagues.

"Behind those doors," he said, gesturing at the SCIF, "they intend to overthrow the results of an American presidential election. We want to know what's going on. We're going to go . . . let's see if we can get in." (As a member of the Judiciary Committee, Gaetz had clearance to enter the room freely.)

At about 10:45 a.m., the Republicans barged past the guards and through three doors, each of which was marked with a large red-and-white warning sign: "Restricted Area. No public or media access. Cameras and recording devices prohibited without prior authorization."

"Let us in!" shouted some. Others used their phones to record what was happening and posted photos and snippets of video on social media as they went inside the SCIF. Schiff, who could have ordered the House sergeant at arms to expel or even arrest the Republican protesters, called a recess and walked out. As he left, one of the protesters, Representative Bradley Byrne of Alabama, followed him, shouting his complaints. Some of the Democrats appealed for calm; others stood up and prepared themselves for a physical confrontation.[4]

For Democrats inside, it felt like a mob action. Gaetz was yelling about secrecy. Representative Val Demings, a former police chief of Orlando, Florida, shouted back. Louie Gohmert and Demings argued heatedly for several minutes.

"They were quite intimidating by shouting and screaming," said Representative Gerald Connolly, a Democrat on the committee. "It was actually very threatening to be there. I was frankly worried about where this was going to head."[5]

As members who were authorized to be present left, the interlopers settled in. Pizza was ordered for both the marauders and the press. The members of Congress got their seventeen pies from the best place in town—We the Pizza—where the pizzas start at $20 each. The journalists got Domino's pizzas that were priced at $5.99 each.[6]

Televised live in some moments, the attack on the SCIF was intended, in large part, to demonstrate the Trumpiness of those who participated. In this way, it was similar to the behavior of those Republicans who, in the SCIF sessions, made a show of trying to name the whistleblower or delay proceedings. Representatives Lee Zeldin of New York and Jim Jordan of Ohio, who led this effort, often seemed to be most intent on making sure that, when it was printed, the record of the sessions would show them behaving in a way that while obnoxious would be appreciated by the president.

Just as Donald Trump had, through his crude and profane statements and tweets, brought politics to a baser level, the Republicans' behavior in the SCIF demonstrated that many in the party had embraced the style as a way to signify their identity. Real men and women of the Trump GOP didn't obey rules, even when they related to national security, or respect others, even when they were colleagues. It was a strange turn for those who also identified with conservatism, which, perhaps they had forgotten, elevated civilized behavior, the value of institutions, and the merit of working within systems for change.

Representative Denny Heck, a deeply religious man, said he expected much more from his colleagues, Republican or Democrat. He found the security breach an affront to decency. "To me the faith journey is about being the best person I can be. I know for a fact that there are conservatives who are really good people with whom I disagree. But if we're really good people or trying to be good people of good faith and goodwill, then it will enable a constructive process. Who would have ever anticipated they would do something so shockingly inappropriate as storming the SCIF with their cell phones? That's so completely outside the realm of thinkability."

The Republican invaders finally left after occupying the SCIF for four hours. Security aides needed time to scan the room for electronics and reset systems that helped keep the space safe. The Intelligence Committee then resumed work.

27

ANGELS

Nervous Nancy Pelosi is doing everything possible to destroy the Repub-lican Party. Our Polls show that it is going to be just the opposite. The Do Nothing Dems will lose many seats in 2020. They have a Death Wish, led by a corrupt politician, Adam Schiff!

Donald Trump, president of the United States, via Twitter,
October 28, 2019

In great contrast to the unruly circus the day before, the Capitol Rotunda had been converted on Thursday, October 24, 2019, into a hallowed hall of remembrance as official Washington mourned Elijah Cummings, who had died a week earlier. In the week since his death, Cummings's most famous words already were his epitaph: "When we're dancing with the angels, the question will be asked: In 2019, what did we do to make sure we kept our democracy intact?"

Elijah Cummings had, in what he said and how he lived, always rejected Donald Trump's values and his way of politics. In his death, he united Democrats and Republicans in grief. Their coming together was a thing little seen in these days of rancor. The comity wasn't so great that anyone expressed contrition for the unruly protest of the day before. However, people did smile and greet each other warmly. Some even embraced.[1]

Cummings was eulogized best not by a fellow Democrat but by a man who appeared to share so little with him. Mark Meadows was one of the most conservative pro-Trump Republicans in Congress, a man who had opposed almost every legislative proposal that Cummings ever backed. And yet he was shaken with emotion. "Some have classified it as an unexpected friendship," Meadows said, his voice cracking. "But for those of us who know Elijah, it's not unexpected or surprising," Meadows said, bowing his head, choking away emotion before he could continue. "Perhaps this place would be better served by a few more unexpected friendships. I know I've been blessed by one."[2]

Nancy Pelosi and Chuck Schumer, sitting on each side of Mitch McConnell, acknowledged Meadows's words with sad smiles that seemed to telegraph the sentiment widely felt: Could they bottle the shared emotion of the moment to serve the task that lay ahead?

Cummings, said Pelosi, was "our North Star . . . a leader of towering character and integrity . . . the perfect testament to his commitment to restoring honesty and honor to government, and leaves a powerful legacy for years to come."[3]

No essence of Elijah Cummings was available to help the Congress. As soon as the memorial services ended, partisan rancor returned. However, the executive department officials who dutifully came to testify on Capitol Hill, many of whom would be regarded by the president as operatives of the sinister Deep State, proved that expertise, character, and devotion still counted for something in Washington. Representative Ted Deutch of Florida considered all the effort made to obscure the facts and said, "It hasn't worked because the State Department and the Defense Department are full of patriotic Americans who are committed to our national security, the reputation of the United States and the rule of law. And that's why we've seen this steady stream of witnesses come in to tell us the truth."

This truth telling was often interrupted by Republicans who wanted to know if this witness had some ulterior political motive for testifying or that one was friendly with a Democrat or two. One witness actually burst out laughing when it was suggested that diplomats and elected public officials had cooked up a conspiracy to hurt Donald Trump. How they might do this in the context that included the activities of Parnas, Fruman, Giuliani, the Three Amigos, and Trump's phone call with Zelensky was truly impossible to imagine.

Amid the silliness, witnesses like Ambassador Marie Yovanovitch nevertheless labored to help members of Congress understand what had happened and why it was so serious. "It was not surprising that when our anti-corruption efforts got in the way of a desire for profit or power, Ukrainians who preferred to play by the old corrupt rules sought to remove me," she said.

> What continues to amaze me is that they found Americans willing to
> partner with them, and working together, they apparently succeeded
> in orchestrating the removal of a U.S. ambassador.

How could our system fail like this? How is it that foreign corrupt interests could manipulate our government? Which country's interests are served when the very corrupt behavior we have been criticizing is allowed to prevail? Such conduct undermines the U.S., exposes our friends and widens the playing field for autocrats like President Putin.

Against such profound concerns, Devin Nunes, the ranking Republican on the Intelligence Committee, kept offering the Biden conspiracy theory.

[Hunter] Biden is another witness who the Democrats are sparing from cross-examination, the securing of an extremely well paying job on the board of a corrupt Ukrainian company, Burisma, highlights the precise corruption problem in Ukraine that concerned not only President Trump, but all of the witnesses we've interviewed so far.

The Democrats have dismissed questions about Biden's role at Burisma as conspiracy theories, yet they're trying to impeach President Trump for having expressed concerns about the company.

If we could hear from Biden we could ask him how he got his position, what did he do to earn his lavish salary? And what light could he shed on corruption at this notorious company? But Biden would make an inconvenient witness for the Democrats, so they've blocked his testimony.

The talk of Hunter Biden was such a departure from the work the Intelligence Committee had undertaken that few Democrats even sought to engage in a conversation about it. Besides, what was being said by the witnesses inside the SCIF was so compelling that Democrats didn't have time to focus on silliness. For example, when Alexander Vindman made his closed-door statement, he told a long story that stitched together a series of shocking events and revealed how he came to realize something potentially illegal was happening.

Vindman said that in the spring, he had heard about "outside influencers" who were promoting a "false narrative" that was "inconsistent with consensus views of the interagency" intelligence community. In plain language, this meant that he had learned about Giuliani's crew and their efforts to rewrite the history of Ukraine's relationship with the United States as it was known by all the American intelligence agencies.

The timeline Vindman covered included the April 21 call Trump placed to congratulate Zelensky on his election. Vindman judged this a "positive" development. Vindman talked about his experience on the May visit to Zelensky's inauguration with Secretary of Energy Rick Perry, Kurt Volker, and Gordon Sondland. By the time of the July 25 "perfect" call, Vindman was alert to what he feared was a diplomatically perilous moment. He listened in from the White House Situation Room and became concerned because "I did not think it was proper to demand that a foreign government investigate a U.S. citizen, and I was worried about the implications to the U.S. Government's support of Ukraine. . . . I realized that if Ukraine pursued an investigation into the Bidens and Burisma, it would likely be interpreted as a partisan play, which would undoubtedly result in Ukraine losing the bipartisan support it has thus far maintained. This would all undermine U.S. national security."

As he testified, Vindman was occasionally interrupted by House Republicans who seemed to be trying to rattle him. He was pressed to reveal the identity of the whistleblower, but as Chairman Schiff said the question threatened the whistleblower's safety, Vindman hesitated. As he waited, arguments raged about whether GOP members of the House could ask him about which office the whistleblower worked in and some threw out names to see if they had guessed the person's identity. They even asked him to name every person he saw in the Situation Room during the Trump-Zelensky call. Amid the arguing, Vindman didn't break a sweat. He didn't even move very much.

After listening to Vindman in the SCIF, Congressman Gerry Connolly found himself feeling reassured that some administration officials remained loyal to their duty and not the man, Donald Trump. "So many have proved to be cowards in the face of Trump's bullying," Connolly told us, "but he [Vindman] was undaunted. And you ask yourself, 'How did he manage to pull that off?' You know, I mean, he's a Purple Heart recipient. He fought in Iraq. He has a twin brother who also works in the NSC on the ethics desk. He is an immigrant from Ukraine. He was three when his family left and they settled here and he put on the uniform and sees himself as a proud American. And so in some ways he sort of, everything Trump doesn't like . . . unafraid to call something out when he thinks it's wrong and what, what he, what he heard on that phone conversation. And that was the other problem for the Republicans this week. They have heretofore argued that all this testimony is hearsay. He actually listened in to the phone conversation. He heard the whole thing."[4]

28

OPEN HEARINGS

I have been watching people making phone calls my entire life. My hearing is, and has been, great. Never have I been watching a person making a call, which was not on speakerphone, and been able to hear or understand a conversation. I've even tried, but to no avail. Try it live!

—Donald Trump, president of the United States, via Twitter,
November 21, 2019

As the impeachment proceedings moved from the quiet of the SCIF to the public venues in House committee rooms, the president and his allies understood that vast numbers of Americans who had not absorbed news accounts about the closed-door testimony would watch at least some of the nationally broadcast hearings. Not since Watergate, when John Dean and others became household names, had the public had the chance to see and hear history made by the players in such a profound drama. Marie Yovanovitch's face and voice would make her real, and as she became real—and known—it would be harder for many to accept that she was worthy of the scorn the president heaped upon her. This prospect came as a *Wall Street Journal* poll found nearly half of Americans believed Trump needed to be impeached *and* removed.[1]

Democrats on the House Intelligence Committee began to assemble for their first public session on impeachment before 8:00 a.m. on November 13. Adam Schiff was running late, and the Democrats milled about chatting in small groups. Denny Heck sat with Val Demings, who, feeling the weight of responsibility, reflected on her faith. She spoke about the bipartisan prayer breakfasts she attended, how important that was to her. Heck understood well; religion was also strong in his life. He appreciated her candor. "Some of the best conversations I ever had with my colleagues on that committee took place that morning," he would later explain.

Superficially, said Heck, the pre-hearing conversations weren't about the matter at hand. However, he felt like in their effort to talk about their reliance on prayer, their faith in God, and how they seemed to have reached a moment of great responsibility, they were talking about all they were about to experience. Short of wartime leadership, impeachment of a president was the most serious task an elected official could undertake, and there was no joy in it. In this moment Heck tried to remind himself that his faith could bring him through.

"We love to say they were naked and I clothed them. They were strangers, I took them in. And of course conservatives like to quote the most ridiculous book in the Bible, Leviticus, for all that crazy stuff, which is on the other end of the spectrum. And so I said, I don't really believe God's a partisan.

"My favorite scripture happens to be Micah 6:8, when Micah asked, 'What do you expect of me?' And he is told just this, 'That you love mercy, that you do justice and that you walk humbly with your Lord.'" The "walk humbly" part of the scripture led Heck to reject imposing his faith on others through legislation even as he felt the call to "do justice" meant that he must consider impeaching the president.

If the group gathered quietly before the hearing had one shared regret, it was that this duty had come at a time when they could expect none of their Republican colleagues to budge from their partisan positions. During Watergate, which was ignited by transgressions that were arguably less serious than Trump's, Republicans in the House like Howard Baker and William Cohen had been open to the facts and came to play important roles in holding the president accountable.

In 2019, no Republican in the House could be approached to even consider this option. This included even those who, like Will Hurd of Texas, had been critical of the president *and* announced they would soon retire. A young former CIA officer, Hurd was the only black Republican in the House of Representatives and the only one who represented a district on the border with Mexico. Given Trump's troubles with minority communities, these two factors should have emboldened him. However, he wasn't open to even discussing the impeachment cause.

One Democrat who tried said, "Well, it's uncomfortable. You don't ask them, 'Why, why do you support Trump when you know he lies?' You don't want to put them in that situation. You go around it, so, I haven't quite asked that question. Certainly not that way. I may have said to one or two of them,

'At what point is it no longer tenable for you to play along?' But that was usually when one of *them* brought up complaints about Trump."

•   •   •

On the day when Ambassador William Taylor finally got to appear in public
before the House Permanent Select Committee on Intelligence, public interest
in the business of Congress had reached a level not seen since the Clinton impeachment. Officials had reserved the Ways and Means Committee hearing
room, which is so large it had once served as a the House chamber when the
Capitol Building was being renovated, but even this space couldn't accommodate all who came to observe. In addition to the crush of people, the sense
of spectacle was amplified by the presence of a large contingent of reporters,
among them a very tall drag performer named Pissi Myles who represented an
online news site run by self-avowed amateur journalists. Prior to the start of the
hearing Myles's shimmering red minidress and huge blond hairdo riveted attention in the hearing room. In an era when a TV-show-host-turned-president
ran amok in the White House, it seemed almost fitting that spectators would
flock to have their photos taken with Myles even as the House considered the
sober business of impeachment.

Although the pre-hearing atmosphere was a bit heavy on showbiz, as he
testified, Taylor quickly changed the mood in the room. At age seventy-two,
his posture still suggested his service in the U.S. Army's 101st Airborne Division, where he was a decorated rifle company commander after graduating
from West Point in 1969. He left the military in 1975 for a career that brought
him to the Department of Energy, the United States Senate, and then the
Pentagon. He joined the diplomatic corps in the early 1990s and was ambassador to Ukraine from 2006 to 2009.

He had returned to his old post in Kiev, this time as acting ambassador, to
stabilize things after the firing of Ambassador Marie Yovanovitch. Although
it was a challenging assignment, he benefited from knowing most of the relevant players both in the State Department and in the Ukrainian bureaucracy.

In his testimony Taylor said he had arrived in Ukraine with no illusions.
As he told the committee, "Masha Yovanovitch had been treated poorly, caught
in a web of political machinations both in Kiev and in Washington. I feared
that those problems were still present. I consulted both my wife and a respected
former senior Republican official who has been a mentor. I will tell you that my
wife, in no uncertain terms, strongly opposed the idea. The mentor counseled:
if your country asks you to do something, you do it—if you can be effective."[2]

Taylor had considered it his mission to serve his country, and part of that service involved helping Ukraine, an ally, protect itself from Russian aggression. Anything else was secondary.

He was shocked to discover that through an "irregular channel" of policy that allowed Rudy Giuliani to access the White House and the State Department, relations between the two countries had been thrown into turmoil. Giuliani had worked with bad actors to develop a false narrative that could sabotage U.S. aid to Ukraine, he complained. He argued that holding back assistance had been a gift for the Russians. The Ukrainians did not "owe" President Trump anything, he told the hearing, and holding up security assistance for domestic political gain was "crazy."

Although Taylor testified in stark terms about the damage that Giuliani and others had done to American interests and how fully they had violated diplomatic norms, he could have shared much more about the ways the schemers worked against President Trump's supposed interest in fighting corruption. Taylor had written two highly valued papers about the oligarch system and the key figures in it. In one, he had explained the activities of billionaire Dmytro Firtash, whom Lev Parnas and Igor Fruman tried to cultivate for their energy business. Firtash was a dangerous man, well connected with the Kremlin, and little interested in the welfare of Ukraine. He had often operated more like a gang leader than a businessman. His presence in the Giuliani scheme was a red flag.

Firtash was also known by Taylor as a key player in the authoritarian wing of Ukrainian politics. He had bankrolled Viktor Yanukovych and the Party of Regions, which in turn employed Paul Manafort. The party had been dominated by Russian advisors, and its policies were distinctly pro-Russia. Had members of the committee thought to ask, Taylor would have explained how Firtash connected Russia with Manafort and ultimately Trump. Of course, all of this deep background might have only confused those who were trying to understand an already bizarrely convoluted scandal. Also, all this background wasn't necessary for anyone to understand how improper the Giuliani scheme had been.

"Ambassador Taylor," asked the Democratic lead counsel, Daniel Goldman, "in your decades of military service and diplomatic service representing the United States around the world, have you ever seen another example of foreign aid conditioned on the personal or political interests of the president of the United States?"[3]

"No, Mr. Goldman, I have not," Taylor replied.

• • •

After Taylor had explained how Trump's quid pro quo effort stood apart from the normal course of diplomacy, David Holmes, the embassy staffer who had overheard Gordon Sondland's cell phone chat with President Trump, brought a bit of color to the hearing as he talked about his experience of hearing the president through Sondland's phone.

Holmes said it was easy to hear Trump's distinctive voice, blaring over Sondland's cell phone, so loud that Sondland winced "and held the phone away from his ear." When Trump realized that Sondland was in Ukraine, he asked Sondland whether Zelensky was going to do the investigation Trump was demanding.

> **GOLDMAN:** So you heard President Trump ask Ambassador Sondland, is he going to do the investigation?
>
> **HOLMES:** Yes, sir.
>
> **GOLDMAN:** What was Ambassador Sondland's response?
>
> **HOLMES:** He said, oh, yes, he's going to do it. He'll do anything you ask.[4]

Perhaps the most striking testimony in the open hearings came from two women. One was Marie Yovanovitch, the seasoned American diplomat whom Rudy Giuliani targeted for removal from the embassy in Kiev. The other, Fiona Hill, was a veteran of U.S. intelligence and an expert on Russia. The drama of what they had to say was emphasized and enhanced by the fact that they were both immigrants who were grateful for the opportunities they had received in the United States and devoted to preserving American democracy.

"I'm an American by choice, having become a citizen in 2002," said Hill. "I was born in the northeast of England, in the same region where George Washington's ancestors came from. I can say with confidence that this country has offered me opportunities I never would have had in England." She then described in detail the role that people around her had played, wrongly, she believed, sacrificing U.S. policy to what she described as a "domestic political errand." But her testimony would be remembered by many for looking directly across the witness table and making a categorical statement that left the president's Ukraine conspiracy in shambles and defied Donald Trump without uttering his name.

Hill offered one of the more resonant quotes to come out of the entire impeachment process.

Based on questions and statements I've heard, some of you on this committee appear to believe that Russia and its security services did not conduct a campaign against our country and that perhaps somehow, for some reason, Ukraine did. This is a fictional narrative that is being perpetrated and propagated by the Russian security services themselves. The unfortunate truth is that Russia was the foreign power that systematically attacked our democratic institutions in 2016. This is the public conclusion of our intelligence agencies, confirmed in bipartisan congressional reports. It is beyond dispute, even if some of the underlying details must remain classified.

Delivered in a clipped accent that betrayed traces of her native Britain, Hill's statement left no doubt that the Ukraine-hacked-America theory promoted by the president and others was nonsense. She also left the House members with a warning about the risk in their devotion to a false narrative.

I say this not as an alarmist, but as a realist. I . . . Right now, Russia's security services and their proxies have geared up to repeat their interference in the 2020 election. We are running out of time to stop them. In the course of this investigation, I would ask that you please not promote politically driven falsehoods that so clearly advance Russian interests.[5]

Yovanovitch also opened her public testimony with a description of her arrival in the United States. "My mother's family escaped the USSR after the Bolshevik revolution, and she grew up stateless in Nazi Germany, before eventually making her way to the United States . . . I come before you as an American citizen, who has devoted the majority of my life, 33 years, to service to the country that all of us love. My service is an expression of gratitude for all that this country has given my family and me."[6]

Yovanovitch then described the intimidation she felt coming from Trump's private operatives in Ukraine, though she was the U.S. ambassador. "I do not understand Mr. Giuliani's motives for attacking me, nor can I offer an opinion on whether he believed the allegations he spread about me," she said. "What I can say is that Mr. Giuliani should have known those claims were suspect, coming as they reportedly did from individuals with questionable motives and with reason to believe that their political and financial ambitions would be stymied by our anti-corruption policy in Ukraine."[7]

The former ambassador said the most shocking moment of her recent experience came when she heard that Trump himself had mentioned her specifically during his July 25, 2019, conversation with Zelensky.

"I was shocked and devastated that I would feature in a phone call between two heads of state in such a manner, where President Trump said that I was 'bad news' to another head of state." The statement by Trump had continued: "She's going to go through some things." Yovanovitch said she felt personally threatened by Trump's remark.

"Prior to reading that call record, were you aware that President Trump had specifically made reference to you?" asked Goldman.

"No," the former ambassador replied.

"What was your reaction?"

"I was shocked, absolutely shocked and devastated."

Schiff interrupted the proceedings with information that elicited gasps in the room.

"As we sit here testifying, the president is attacking you on Twitter," Schiff said. "I'll read in part one of his tweets. 'Everywhere Marie Yovanovitch went turned bad. She started off in Somalia, how did that go?' The president implicitly in that call record threatened you. And now, the president in real time is attacking you. What effect to you think that has on other witnesses?"

Yovanovitch maintained her calm and nodded as she said, "Well, it's very intimidating."[8]

Democrats on the committee would later say that Trump's tweet was itself an impeachable offense. "It's witness intimidation—and innocent people don't intimidate witnesses," said Representative Eric Swalwell of California. "Intimidating a witness and tampering with witness testimony is an obstructive act." In a conversation after the hearing, Representative Denny Heck agreed, saying, "We know he's a misogynist. 'Going to go through some things?' That was an ominous threat [from] the most powerful man on the face of the earth."[9]

• • •

Before his public testimony, Gordon Sondland spoke to an old friend back home in Portland, Oregon. The friend, a lawyer, had called Sondland to warn him to tell the truth or face legal liability. "For what reason would he want to lie for the president, even if he did support him?" the friend later told us. "I told him simply, 'Tell exactly what happened, nothing more, nothing less.'"

The big question Sondland needed to clear up came from conflicts in his own prior statements. At different times, he had proffered opposing opinions about whether President Trump had sought a quid pro quo in his talk with Zelensky.

"I know that members of this committee frequently formulate these difficult questions in the form of a simple question: Was there a quid pro quo?" Sondland said.

> As I testified previously in regard to the requested White House call and the White House meeting, the answer is "yes."
>
> Mr. Giuliani conveyed to Secretary Perry, Ambassador Volker, and others that President Trump wanted a public statement from President Zelensky committing to investigations of Burisma and the 2016 election. Mr. Giuliani expressed those requests directly to the Ukrainians. Mr. Giuliani also expressed those requests directly to us. We all understood that these prerequisites for the White House call and White House meeting reflected President Trump's desires and requirements.
>
> Within my State Department e-mails, there is a July 19th e-mail. This e-mail was sent—this e-mail was sent to Secretary Pompeo; Secretary Perry; Brian McCormack, who was Secretary Perry's chief of staff at the time; Ms. Kenna, who is the acting— pardon me—who is the executive secretary for Secretary Pompeo; Chief of Staff Mulvaney; and, Mr. Mulvaney's Senior Advisor Rob Blair. A lot of senior officials. A lot of senior officials.
>
> Here is my exact quote from that e-mail: "I talked to Zelensky just now. He is prepared to receive POTUS' call. Will assure him that he intends to run a fully transparent investigation and will turn over every stone. He would greatly appreciate a call prior to Sunday so that he can put out some media about a 'friendly and productive call' (no details) prior to Ukraine election on Sunday."
>
> Chief of Staff Mulvaney responded, "I asked the NSC to set it up for tomorrow."
>
> Everyone was in the loop. It was no secret. Everyone was informed via e-mail on July 19th, days before the presidential call. As I communicated to the team, I told President Zelensky in advance that assurances to run a fully transparent investigation and turn over every stone were necessary in this call with President Trump.[10]

29

SCHOLARS IN WASHINGTON

It's going to go nowhere. They are going to impeach not because they have the evidence, but because they hate the president. I think the American people know that this is a waste of time, this is Democrats putting on a circus. @SenTedCruz interviewed by Sleepy Eyes Chuck Todd

—Donald Trump, president of the United States, via Twitter,
December 8, 2019

After Congress's Thanksgiving recess, the Judiciary Committee took up its role, which would be to consider the evidence gathered by the Intelligence Committee and others, to determine whether it supported articles of impeachment to send to the full House of Representatives. Their work would also include identifying which high crimes and misdemeanors the president had committed and then writing the texts of the articles.

As she announced this new phase in the process, Speaker Pelosi said, "The president's actions are a profound violation of the public trust. His wrongdoing strikes at the very heart of our Constitution. Today, I am asking our chairmen to proceed with articles of impeachment."[1]

In theory, the result of this process was in doubt. In truth, it was not. Democrats who constituted the majority on the committee knew they were going to approve the articles and that the House would soon receive them. It was also clear that the final articles would be focused on three possible categories of constitutional crime: abuse of power and bribery, obstruction of Congress, and obstruction of justice. It was still possible that other articles, including one based on emoluments, would be offered, but momentum was growing around the idea of limiting the charges.

With the Judiciary Committee getting the chance to take the lead, Jerrold Nadler decided it would be useful—educational, even—for the American people to hear from experts who might discuss and debate the meaning of impeachment, how it worked, and whether it was appropriate in this case. With this purpose in mind the committee invited four constitutional scholars to testify at a nationally televised hearing. One selected by the Republicans, Jonathan Turley of George Washington University Law School, had appeared before the Judiciary Committee twenty years earlier when the GOP held the House of Representatives. At that time, he had said that President Clinton's behavior demanded "an open and deliberative review under the conditions created for that purpose by the Framers" and that "the allegations against President Clinton go to the very heart of the legitimacy of his office and the integrity of the political system." He said then that Clinton had, by lying under oath about an extramarital affair, committed an offense worthy of impeachment. In the case of Donald Trump, Turley said that the president "could be impeached for abuse of power. You just have to prove it."[2]

In Turley's view, the Democrats had not proven Trump had abused his power. In his opening statement, he said the complaint against Trump was thin and so was the evidence. "This impeachment would stand out among modern impeachments as the shortest proceeding, with the thinnest evidentiary record, and the narrowest grounds ever used to impeach a president," Turley said. "That does not bode well for future presidents who are working in a country often sharply and, at times, bitterly divided."[3]

Turley then offered a line seemingly intended to produce a TV sound bite. "If you were going to make a case to George Washington that you could impeach over a conversation he had with another head of state—I expect his hair, his powdered hair, would catch on fire."

The other constitutional scholars on the witness list presented an opposite view. Among them, Noah Feldman, a professor at Harvard Law School, said he had come late to the decision that impeachment was warranted. "President Trump's conduct described in the testimony and evidence clearly constitutes an impeachable high crime and misdemeanor under the Constitution," he said. "President Trump abused his office by soliciting the president of Ukraine to investigate his political rivals in order to gain personal political advantage, including in the 2020 presidential election. . . . It embodies the framers' central worry that a sitting president would spare no efforts or means whatever to get himself re-elected."[4]

In an otherwise dry and academic hearing, a moment of drama emerged when Pamela Karlan, a professor at Stanford Law School, spoke ardently of impeachment, saying that Trump did not accept any limits to presidential power. But she overstepped by taking a needlessly snide turn in pursuit of her own version of a joke: "While the president can name his son Barron, he can't make him a baron."

Bringing up the president's child crossed a well-observed political line. Karlan heard the resulting outcry over lunch, but then issued only a half-hearted apology: "It was wrong of me to do that. I wish the president would apologize, obviously, for the things that he's done that are wrong."[5]

If the scholars proved anything, it was that constitutional law lectures are an acquired taste. In December of 2019, the Democrats on the Judiciary Committee were connoisseurs who wanted more. To satisfy their appetites, they invited Harvard's Laurence Tribe to a meeting that consumed an entire weekend.

Seventy-eight years old and nearing retirement, Tribe had been a clerk for Supreme Court Justice Potter Stewart before joining the Harvard faculty in 1968. His students had included a who's who of American jurisprudence, government, and politics. Among them were Supreme Court Justices John Roberts and Elena Kagan, President Barack Obama, and Senator Ted Cruz. He was the author of a leading textbook on constitutional law and had been one of the first legal experts to suggest Trump may have committed an impeachable offense. He made this observation when President Trump fired James Comey.

During the run-up to the public hearings, Tribe had spoken on the phone with committee members. He considered Raskin the leading constitutional scholar on Capitol Hill and one of the best in the country. They had consulted often on the emoluments issue. Tribe also talked with Nadler and Representative Eric Swalwell. He had a texting relationship with Nancy Pelosi, whom he considered one of the best legal minds in Congress, even though she had never studied law. Early in the Congress's work on impeachment, Tribe had discussed with her the challenge posed by Senate Republicans who, under the leadership of Mitch McConnell, would not serve as fair jurors. At that time they had discussed the possibility that the House could impeach the president but delay transmitting the articles and thus beginning the trial process.

As Tribe would recall, when he was invited to come to Washington to help the Judiciary Committee, "I stopped everything and went to D.C." To his surprise, the representatives decided to meet in the ornate old Ways and Means

Committee hearing room, and they set up their visit quite formally as if Tribe were a witness before them. He sat for hour upon hour as they peppered him with questions. They wanted his assessment of their work thus far and recommendations for their next steps. Did the evidence support some article of impeachment more than others? What direction would he take if it were his choice?

Much of the discussion revolved around the meaning of words that may have been understood differently when the Constitution was drafted. There was also great concern about whether proposed articles should reference crimes as they would be understood today. Among the questions Tribe recalled were: "What are the pros and cons of including or not including various things like bribery in the article?" and "What are the best ways of connecting the articles of impeachment to the patterns of misconduct in which the president engaged?"

Tribe did everything to encourage the Judiciary team. "I certainly had observed that in the face of an unprecedented refusal to let anyone testify they had managed nonetheless to put together a compelling and essentially airtight case." He also argued for limiting their charges to the Ukraine scandal, which had been so much in the news, "and not muddying the waters with any number of other things that are arguably impeachable, such as the violations of the emolument clauses and so on." Tribe's influence was probably sufficient to convince his former student Raskin to back away from emoluments, although he was a great proponent of using that standard to show that Trump was blatantly violating the Constitution.

In arguing for a limited scope in their articles, Tribe was urging the House Democrats toward an approach that would show the American people that they were focused and not simply throwing everything they could imagine at a president they didn't like. This idea likely appealed to Tribe's friend Pelosi, who knew that Trump would be protected from removal by the Republican Senate. Under these circumstances, the only way that Trump might be driven from office would be in the election of 2020. Democrats would have a harder time of reaching this goal if they overreached. Of course, the president was always going to claim he was victimized. This was his well-established habit. But why give him an extra reason, especially one based on a word—*emoluments*—most people don't understand, to make the claim?[6]

30

HOUSE RULES

It's not fair that I'm being Impeached when I've done absolutely nothing wrong! The Radical Left, Do Nothing Democrats have become the Party of Hate. They are so bad for our Country!

—Donald Trump, president of the United States, via Twitter,
December 13, 2019

One of the main complaints made by House Republicans who fought against the impeachment of Donald Trump related to timing. To be precise, they believed the process had been rushed. From start to finish, the closed and open hearings had consumed a little over ten weeks' time. This did seem like a short period, but in fact, it was longer than the GOP-controlled House had spent between declaring it had begun to work on impeachment and its vote to impeach Bill Clinton. Andrew Johnson, the only other president ever impeached, saw votes cast on the articles against him after just two days of consideration.[1]

As the Founders had anticipated when they wrote the Constitution, every impeachment circumstance is unique, and for this reason, the House was free to write its own rules, from scratch, every time. In this case, Robert Mueller's investigation of nearly two years' duration had contributed to the record, and House Democrats had to consider the imperative of the 2020 election. No one could doubt that if they delayed much longer, the Republicans would have then said, "You took too long! Election season is upon us! You can't impeach now!"

So it was that the Democrats had decided their Goldilocks moment had arrived and House Judiciary Committee Chairman Jerrold Nadler set aside two days for the process of reviewing the articles that House leaders had agreed would be offered. All legislation is produced in a similar fashion—generally called *markup*—in which details are debated, amendments can be offered, and committee votes determine what the full House would consider. It's rarely done in view of a national television audience. It's rarer still for the process to be done in the evening. However, on December 11, 2019, this Judiciary Committee began to mark up articles of impeachment against Donald Trump after most Americans had finished work and could tune in.

The first official words came from Nadler, who, after being abused by Corey Lewandowski and lapped in the race for impeachment leadership by Adam Schiff, still controlled a key part of the process. "Tonight, we begin consideration of two articles of impeachment against President Donald J. Trump," he said.

> The first article charges that the President used the powers of his public office to demand that a foreign government attack his political rivals.
>
> The second article charges that the President obstructed the congressional investigation into his conduct. Other Presidents have resisted congressional oversight, but President Trump's stonewall was complete, absolute, and without precedent in American history.
>
> Taken together, the two articles charge President Trump with placing his private, political interests above our national security, above our free and fair elections, and above our ability to hold public officials accountable. This Committee now owes it to the American people to give these articles close attention, and to describe their factual basis, meaning, and importance.

By offering just two articles, House Democrats had shown they would be restrained in their judgments, they would relieve the public from the chore of having to sift through too many issues, and they would limit the amount of time required for the House to act. No one wanted to be casting impeachment votes on Christmas Eve. A small number of articles would also limit the time the Senate would have to devote to a trial. Given how many senators feared Trump's wrath and how much Mitch McConnell wanted to hold on to his majority, there was no way that Trump would be convicted in a Senate trial, so there was no sense in letting one drag on and on.

At the markup hearing, Nadler used the rest of his statement to offer the equivalent of a trial lawyer's opening argument, running through what he deemed to be the unchallenged facts. He talked about the July 25 call in which Trump had demanded political help in the form of phony investigations and explained that he was holding up Ukraine's military aid. This was his abuse of power.

Next, Nadler discussed the ways that Trump had resisted Congress's effort to discover what happened. This was obstruction of Congress.

> When the House of Representatives opened an inquiry into the President's actions, President Trump did everything in his power to obstruct the investigation. He declared across-the-board resistance. He ordered every official in the federal government to defy all subpoenas related to the inquiry. At his command, the Administration also refused to produce a single document related to the inquiry. Not one.
>
> To put this obstruction into context, during the Watergate hearings, President Nixon turned over recordings of his conversations in the Oval Office; later, President Clinton handed over his DNA.

Summarizing, Nadler said Trump's obstruction had been absolute. "Those are the facts. They are overwhelming. There is no denying them," he continued. "If the President can first abuse his power and then stonewall all congressional requests for information, Congress cannot fulfill its duty to act as a check and balance against the Executive—and the President becomes a dictator."

Nadler then offered one other argument that went beyond the letter of the law toward the point that the Democrats would stress: what was the moral choice?

> I will close with a word to my Republican colleagues. I know you. I have worked with many of you for years. I consider you to be good and decent public servants . . .
>
> I know this moment must be difficult, but you still have a choice.
>
> I hope every member of this Committee will withstand the political pressures of the moment. I hope that none of us attempt to justify behavior that we know in our heart is wrong. I hope that we are able to work together to hold this President—or any President—accountable for breaking his most basic obligations to the country and to its citizens.[2]

Nadler's appeal for bipartisan action fell flat, as he must have known it would. His Republican counterpart on the committee, Doug Collins of Georgia, spoke next and rejected the articles as part of "the big lie."

"What's the big lie?" he said. "It's the one Democrats have told the American people for the last three years. The big lie is that the ends justify the means. The big lie is that a sham impeachment is OK because the threat is so great. The big lie is that political expedience is honorable and justifiable. History has shown that to be untrue and dangerous."

Louie Gohmert of Texas, one of the more volatile Republicans on the committee, said the Democrats had blocked a full inquiry. He and others repeatedly sought the appearance of the original whistleblower in the case, whom they and Trump had labeled a liar and a tool of the Democrats.[3]

No surprise, said Collins, "this day was inevitable. That is because, for House Democrats, the conclusion was never in doubt. Since the day President Trump was elected, Democrats have engaged in a crusade to impeach him, and the facts really do not matter."[4]

The markup now went into a second day, Thursday, December 12, twenty-two years to the day since the House Committee on the Judiciary had voted on articles of impeachment against Bill Clinton.

Florida Democrat Ted Deutch spoke in favor of the obstruction charge. While the Republicans claimed Trump had been railroaded, Deutch pointed to an opposite truth: Trump had blocked all testimony from his administration, amounting to a first in U.S. history. "My friends on the other side of the aisle cannot point to a single example where a president has said, 'I will not cooperate with you in any part of your work, period.' No president has ever, ever, ever obstructed Congress in the manner that we have seen from President Trump."[5]

Gohmert challenged Deutch on precedents. "We are told this is un-charted territory because no president has just completely refused," he said. "This *is* uncharted territory: never in the history of this country have we had an impeachment proceeding begun by lies . . . and not one person on the other side of the aisle is the least bit embarrassed."

Gohmert added, "Let me just say, this is a day that will live in infamy for the Judiciary Committee. This became a tool of the majority to try to de-feat—to use taxpayer funds to defeat a president."[6]

Representative Zoe Lofgren, Democrat of California, was one of the few members who had participated in the two other impeachment inquiries,

Nixon's in 1974 and Clinton's in 1998. She was exasperated and wondered if the endless markup would ever be over. "It seems," she said, "like we live in an alternate reality."

Tempers grew thin as Nadler kept the committee working. First, the Republicans sought and lost their chance to adjourn to attend Trump's Christmas party at the White House. Then, as they drew out the fourteen-hour meeting with objections and demands for roll call votes on doomed amendments, they tried to push the final vote on articles toward the early hours after midnight, when fewer TV viewers would see. Nadler had learned about the limits of even-handedness. Without warning, he abruptly declared the hearing adjourned.

The committee work was completed at just after 10:00 a.m. on Friday, December 13, as the members voted along party lines to approve the two articles. Nadler, having been run in circles by Corey Lewandowski, had redeemed himself through his management of the committee's final acts.

Over the weekend, David Cicilline went back to his Rhode Island district and found he couldn't get away from the impeachment issue. At a holiday party he noticed his host had displayed a Christmas card that said, "No quid pro ho ho ho." When he went shopping, constituents stopped to vent their anger over the tactics the president's allies had used to disrupt the Judiciary Committee. Cicilline was, himself, coming to believe that the committee Republicans were lost in a cult of personality.

"I always just thought they're doing what they think is right," said Cicilline. "But you know, having watched them now in this, the last, you know, three years, I don't actually think that anymore because I know these people, I know they can't possibly think this is okay. And so, you know, it's no longer that. I look at them and think, 'Oh, they're doing what they think is right for the country and for their constituents. And they represent that point of view.' I think they're making decisions about remaining in power, ignoring in a way that the president is a sick and dangerous and deeply, deeply ill person."

Democrats were not the only ones who thought the president's defenders were wrong. Fox News reported a poll that a majority of Americans of all parties supported impeachment. By a wide margin, the nation's newspaper editorial boards also approved of the action the House was pursuing. During the holiday weekend, the president went to the Army-Navy football game in Philadelphia. In between tweets about the game and the "Incredible young, strong and brilliant people" of the army and navy, he launched broadsides at his enemies and at the news media.

As the Judiciary Committee delivered its formal report on impeachment to the full House on Monday morning, senators anticipated their extraordinary proceeding, which would be both a judicial and political exercise. There was little doubt of the outcome. Yes, the Senate would conduct what was called a trial. Yes, they would each sign an oath to fairly consider the case. Even so, declared Republican senator Lindsey Graham of South Carolina, impeachment "will die a speedy death in the Senate."

Senate majority leader Mitch McConnell said he was not impartial and was coordinating his actions with the Trump White House. "I'm not an impartial juror. This is a political process," McConnell said. "There is not anything judicial about it. Impeachment is a political decision. The House made a partisan political decision to impeach. I would anticipate we will have a largely partisan outcome in the Senate. I'm not impartial about it at all."[7]

In the House, Val Demings said McConnell should recuse himself because he had declared his prejudice. Here again, the debate was framed in separate terms. McConnell had stressed politics. Demings wanted to apply a judicial standard. "No court in the country would allow a member of the jury to also serve as the accused's defense attorney," she said. "The moment Senator McConnell takes the oath of impartiality required by the Constitution, he will be in violation of that oath."[8]

The House Rules Committee would set the process. Nadler, who was to have been a witness as they carried out this work, could not appear. He had left Washington to be with his ailing wife, Joyce Miller, who had been diagnosed with pancreatic cancer. Jamie Raskin substituted for Nadler at the witness table.

"Given that an unrepentant President considers his behavior perfect," he said, "given that he thinks the Constitution empowers him to do whatever he wants, we can only ask what the 2020 election will be like or indeed what any future election in America will be like if we just let this misconduct go and authorize and license Presidents to coerce, cajole, pressure, and entice foreign powers to enter our election campaigns on behalf of the President. Who will be invited in next? The President's continuing course of conduct constitutes a clear and present danger to democracy in America."[9]

31

IMPEACHMENT DAY

IN CASE YOU WEREN'T LISTENING:

*SUCH ATROCIOUS LIES BY THE RADICAL LEFT, DO NOTH-
ING DEMOCRATS. THIS IS AN ASSAULT ON AMERICA, AND
AN ASSAULT ON THE REPUBLICAN PARTY!!!!*

—Donald Trump, president of the United States, via Twitter,
December 18, 2019

The House of Representatives began eight hours of debate on the articles of impeachment on the morning of December 18. The result appeared to be foretold,
yet impeachment of a president was an event so rarely seen, and so politically
traumatic, that it required full attention.

In 1868, Andrew Johnson had escaped the first impeachment trial of a
president when the Senate missed the required two-thirds needed for conviction by a single vote. More than one hundred years later, Richard Milhous
Nixon was on the verge of a House impeachment vote but resigned on August
9, 1974. William Jefferson Clinton was impeached by the House in 1998 for
lying about his sexual liaison with Monica Lewinsky but was not removed
from office by the Senate. Now Donald John Trump faced the same ignomini-
ous process for choosing, at the moment when he was clear of the long shadow
cast by the Mueller investigation, to plunge into scandalous behavior.

Nancy Pelosi, who personally presided throughout the day, wore a black
dress decorated with a gold, dagger-shaped pin placed over her heart. The pin
depicted the official Mace of the House, which was a symbol of congressional
power. Seen up close, the pin is not a dagger at all but thirteen rods—one for

each of the original states—bundled together and topped by the globe, and an American bald eagle. In wearing it on this day Pelosi recalled, symbolically, that she previously warned President Trump "not to characterize the strength that I bring."

"As Speaker of the House, I solemnly and sadly open the debate on the impeachment of the president of the United States. If we do not act now we would be derelict in our duty. It is tragic that the president's actions make impeachment necessary. He gave us no choice."

Pelosi said that the day's events would occur under the dome of what she called "the temple of democracy" and she stressed that impeachment was required by the oath members of Congress swear to defend the Constitution of the United States against all enemies, foreign and domestic. She noted that hundreds of legal scholars and prosecutors from different political backgrounds had concluded that the president had committed impeachable offenses and announced that she took her inspiration from figures as disparate as George Washington and the recently deceased Elijah Cummings. She quoted one of Cummings's last public statements, in which he said, "When the history books are written about this tumultuous era, I want them to show that I was among those in the House of Representatives who stood up to lawlessness and tyranny."

In the course of the day, all sides spoke of the historic moment but in starkly different terms. Republican Mike Kelly of Pennsylvania evoked the recent commemoration of the seventy-eighth anniversary of the Japanese attack on Pearl Harbor. "Today, Dec. 18, 2019, is another date that will live in infamy," Kelly said. "Just because you hate the president of the United States and you can find no other reason other than the fact that you're so blinded by your hate that you can't see straight, so you've decided the only way to make sure this president doesn't get elected again is to impeach him."[1]

Barry Loudermilk, a Georgia Republican, reached further back in history for his comparison. "I want you to keep this in mind [that] when Jesus was falsely accused of treason, Pontius Pilate gave Jesus the opportunity to face his accusers. During that sham trial, Pontius Pilate afforded more rights to Jesus than the Democrats have afforded this president in this process."[2]

A Republican from Utah named Chris Stewart saw some sort of class warfare at work: "This day is about one thing and one thing only. They hate this president. They hate those of us who voted for him. They think we are stupid. They think we made a mistake. They think Hillary Clinton should be the president and they want to fix that."

Less rational was Donald Trump, who tweeted up a storm while watching on TV. He had also written a letter to memorialize the event, which had been delivered to Speaker Pelosi the day before. In it, he called the impeachment proceedings an "illegal, partisan attempted coup." He charged he had been "deprived of basic Constitutional Due Process from the beginning of this impeachment scam right up until the present. . . . More due process was afforded to those accused in the Salem Witch Trials."[3]

Having lived by mockery, the president would, in this moment, die by it as the American people considered his self-pitying attempt at producing profound prose and found him sorely lacking. Snarky commentary flooded social media and news sites, but the most relevant observations came from the mayor of Salem, Massachusetts, where the witch trials actually had taken place in the 1690s. "Learn some history," said Mayor Kim Driscoll. In Salem, two dozen "powerless, innocent victims were hanged or pressed to death" without evidence, she wrote, while in Trump's case there was "ample evidence" and "admissions of wrongdoing."[4]

As the members of the House continued giving speeches, the chamber filled with men and women who felt compelled to be present. Very few were content to be silent on such a day, but time constraints meant that some received just a few minutes to be heard. Ted Lieu, a Democrat from California, stressed the impact of an impeachment that was sure to be followed by acquittal. "This impeachment is permanent," he said. "It will follow him around for the rest of his life and history books will record it. And the people will know why we impeached. It's all very simple. No one is above the law."

For Hank Johnson of Georgia, the moment was about the sanctity of elections, which was something that many black constituents knew could be impinged. In their state, GOP officials were closing polling places and creating bureaucratic barriers to voting that were obviously intended to limit their access to the polls because they tended to vote for Democrats. "If you think I exaggerate in warning that our elections can be undermined, I'd urge you to come down to Georgia, find a black man or woman of a certain age, and they'll tell you the danger is real."

Intelligence committee member Denny Heck, who had become what he called "soul weary" and had decided to retire in 2020, described impeachment as an obligation "to do our duty and defend our Constitution and the values underpinning it." His colleague on the committee, Joaquin Castro, reeled quickly through the timeline of the Ukraine scandal until the point where, he said, "the jig is up" and it was clear the president had tried to extort the Ukrainians. Although the military aid was sent to Kiev, he added, a crime had been committed. "Is attempted extortion and bribery a crime?" he asked. "Yes, it is." When the time for debate drew to a close, Steny Hoyer delivered an impassioned appeal to the Republicans, asking them to put their patriotic duty above party. He spoke wistfully of his thirty-eight years in the House under six administrations. "I've seen our two-party system work. And I've seen it break down," he said.

> Never in all my years of serving in this great institution that I love and the people of my district did I ever expect to encounter such an obvious wrongdoing by a president of the United States.
>
> The pages of our history are filled with Americans who had the courage to choose country over party or personality. But as President Kennedy wrote, the stories of past courage can teach. They can offer hope. They can provide inspiration. But they cannot supply courage itself. For this, President Kennedy said, each man, each woman must look into their own soul. I urge my fellow colleagues in the House and, yes, in the Senate to look into your soul. Summon the courage to vote for our constitution and our democracy. I understand we will all not see the same conclusion, but to do less betrays our oath and that of our founders who pledged their lives, their fortune and their sacred honor.[5]

Finally came the formality of the vote, which was tallied electronically. After ballots were cast on the first article of impeachment, Pelosi announced the result, reading from a card in her left hand. "The yeas are 230, the nays are 197, present is one," she declared. (The one vote of present was cast by Democrat Tulsi Gabbard of Hawaii, who was in the middle of a quixotic run for president.) Pelosi pursed her lips and wielding the gavel in her right hand, declared evenly: "Article one is adopted."

Before she could complete the sweep of the gavel, there was a sudden flurry of incipient cheers among Democrats to her right. She opened her eyes wide and waved off the cheers with a commanding gesture. It was emblematic of her stature and presence. The chamber went quiet. Justin Amash of Michigan, who denounced Trump and quit the Republican Party, had voted in favor of the resolutions as an independent.

The second article, obstruction of Congress, was adopted 229–198. Gabbard again abstained while Amash voted with the GOP minority. After the vote, Pelosi spoke briefly to the press. "The House has acted on a very sad day to protect the Constitution of the United States," she said. She then called the vote "appropriate and urgent."

•   •   •

As often was the case when he felt besieged, Donald Trump devoted much of his day to making comments on Twitter, issuing three dozen before the House even began to consider the articles. He complained that he had "DONE NOTHING WRONG" and insisted that Speaker Pelosi would "go down in history as worst Speaker." As evening approached Trump left Washington, choosing impeachment day to hold a rally where his spirits might be lifted. This time, he went to Battle Creek, Michigan, the home of his only overt GOP critic, Justin Amash. The event was held at the 6,200-seat Kellogg Arena, named for one of the nation's most-beloved brands, Kellogg's, the makers of Corn Flakes, Rice Krispies, Froot Loops, and a slew of other sugary breakfast foods. Michigan was of course a key battleground state, and Trump was itching to fire up the base and divert attention from the impeachment.

The staging was typical of Trump events. A select group of true believers was positioned behind his podium: adults wearing USA and MAKE AMERICA GREAT AGAIN hats; photogenic young people; the select few African Americans in the house.[6]

Brad Parscale, Trump's lanky, bearded reelection campaign manager, warmed up the crowd with a reference to the impeachment proceedings: "It is unbelievable how much they don't care about your voice here in Michigan," he told the crowd. "They want to erase your vote in 2016, and they don't even want to give you a chance in 2020."[7]

After Parscale, Mike Pence came to the stage, which was decorated with green-and-red trim and a lighted miniature fir tree for the season: "Well, hello Michigan," Pence bellowed out. "And Merry Christmas!" he added, perhaps a bit too forcefully, as if somehow saying that was a political statement. (In fact, Republicans had, for years, suggested that those who offer the less religious "Happy Holidays" greeting were somehow anti-religious and un-American.) "The president's going to be out in just a few minutes, but he wanted to wait to see that strong, unified Republican vote on the floor of the Congress tonight."

As Pence spoke, Trump could watch the final minutes of the House vote on a screen backstage. The TV networks were prepared to use a split screen, one side the House floor, the other with his speech, guaranteeing the best television ratings he could hope for. But the vice president finally ran out of things to say, gave a farewell wave, and walked off, leaving the stage empty to the incongruous sound of Mick Jagger and the Rolling Stones, including the line: "Don't play with me 'cause you're playing with fire." Jagger, it should be noted, was a vociferous Trump critic.

Though the final vote still had not taken place in Washington, Trump had no choice. He emerged like a rock star under a brick-painted archway sign that read "Merry Christmas!" He clapped as he acknowledged the crowd, then pumped one fist.

"I am the first person to ever get impeached and there is no crime," he told the crowd. "You know what they call it? Impeachment light."

He continued, "I just said to the First Lady, you're so lucky I took you on this fantastic journey—it's so much fun, they want to impeach you, they want to do worse than that."

He then unleashed a stream-of-consciousness attack on his best-known enemies, Hillary Clinton and the "hoax," *The Washington Post* and its tally of his deceptions, Nancy Pelosi and the "filth" of her district in San Francisco. He offered a special note of anger directed at a local member of Congress, Debbie Dingell, for having dared to vote for impeachment although she represented a swing district. Trump, who believed in transactional bargains, expected better from Dingell. After all, he had declared a day of mourning when her husband, John Dingell, died earlier in the year and implied that the popular longtime congressman had probably gone to hell. The free-form unscripted rant lasted almost two hours.[8]

32

THE WAITING GAME

The reason the Democrats don't want to submit the Articles of Impeachment to the Senate is that they don't want corrupt politician Adam Shifty Schiff to testify under oath, nor do they want the Whistleblower, the missing second Whistleblower, the informer, the Bidens, to testify!

—Donald Trump, president of the United States, via Twitter,
December 19, 2019

Shortly after 9:00 p.m. eastern standard time, moments after leaving the House floor, Speaker Nancy Pelosi and the Democratic leadership—Jerrold Nadler, Adam Schiff, and others—appeared before TV cameras to note the impeachment of Donald John Trump. Though Republicans had tried to find a way to delay the actual vote, they had failed, and the country had seen Congress act on a live television broadcast.

"December 18, a great day for the Constitution of the United States, a sad one for America, that the president's reckless activities necessitated us having to introduce articles of impeachment," said Pelosi. "We passed the two articles of impeachment, the president is impeached." Donald Trump had been marked for all time.

Pelosi's answers to reporters' questions were tellingly vague. She would not name which members would serve as House managers of the impeachment in the Senate until the Republican majority there negotiated terms for the trial with the Democrats. The subtext was this—she controlled the next course of events, and she would be making decisions—not Senate majority leader Mitch McConnell.

Reporters asked Pelosi several times whether she would withhold transmitting the articles of impeachment to the Senate, thereby delaying the process and leaving Trump's fate unresolved and denying him the right to claim he was not guilty as charged. McConnell had said he was not impartial; he was taking his cues from the White House.

Might Pelosi never send the articles to the Senate?

"We're not having that discussion," she said. "We have done what we have set out to do. The House has acted on a very sad day to protect and defend the Constitution of the United States," she continued. "We will make our decision on when we're going to send it when we see what they're doing on the Senate side."[1]

The question was repeated, but Pelosi would not be pinned down. However, her strategy had taken shape—a weak hand had been strengthened by waiting and doing absolutely nothing. Few had anticipated this choice, as Senate Republicans had talked about a trial involving witnesses related to the president's cause—bring in Joe Biden and his son!—and to his conspiracy theories.

The idea of withholding the articles of impeachment had been floated by Laurence Tribe in private conversations with Pelosi, but also publicly. "Where in the Constitution or in the history or theory of its interpretation is the House of Representatives required to deliver the articles of impeachment to the Senate?" he asked. "Holding off for the time being on transmitting them to the Senate. . . . As a tactical matter, it could strengthen Senate Minority Leader Charles E. Schumer's (D-NY) hand in bargaining over trial rules with McConnell because of McConnell's and Trump's urgent desire to get this whole business behind them."[2]

McConnell was taken aback when Pelosi first hinted at holding back the articles. "Looks like the prosecutors are getting cold feet," McConnell said. "They said impeachment was so urgent that it could not even wait for due process, but now they're content to sit on their hands. It is comical."[3]

"Oh pfft," Pelosi answered within hours. "Fear is never a word used with me. You should know right away, I'm never afraid and I'm rarely surprised."[4]

Besides putting McConnell, at least temporarily on the defensive, Pelosi's decision gave Trump more than two weeks to stew over the fact that he would forever be known as only the third president to be impeached. McConnell was under orders from Trump to make the trial quick. This would not happen. As in previous court cases, or with chances for full disclosure, Trump pretended that he wanted a full trial and an airing of the evidence. Few people believed that. McConnell said he was coordinating fully with Trump to make it short, but now Pelosi had made sure that would not necessarily be true.

In the interim, the Democrats' theory was that more damaging information might come out about Trump. Perhaps he would make more mistakes. Perhaps John Bolton would agree to speak up and galvanize public support for the president's removal. The idea seemed to work. On December 19, a day after the impeachment vote, an evangelical magazine, *Christianity Today*, published an editorial that agreed with the impeachment vote and called for Trump's removal from the presidency. This was a brutal blow—Trump depended on his evangelical base.

"None of the president's positives can balance the moral and political danger we face under a leader of such a grossly immoral character," wrote Mark Galli, the publication's editor in chief. The editorial also was a reminder that while Trump enjoyed broad evangelical support, buoyed by the presence of Vice President Mike Pence at his side, that support was not universal.

The editorial was worrisome. Lindsey Graham, for one, recommended that Trump avoid comment on the Christian magazine, which had been founded in 1956 by Rev. Billy Graham. But lying low was not the Trump way. He denounced the editorial and tried to recast the publication as "a far left magazine," which it was not. "No president has done more for the Evangelical community, and it's not even close," said Trump. "You'll not get anything from those Dems on stage. I won't be reading ET again!"[5] —confusing CT with ET, the extraterrestrial.

The Democrats sought other ways to appeal to the public. Chuck Schumer pressed for witnesses, noting that no fair trial was ever conducted without them. "Simply put," he said, "I told leader McConnell we would not accept a trial without witnesses and documents. What is a trial without witnesses and documents?"[6]

Schumer may have been right, but he had little leverage. In a telling interview with Rachel Maddow on December 19, Schumer was forthright in describing his weak hand. "I doubt we'll ever get McConnell [to change]. But all we need is four Republican Senators to side with us to get 51 votes [to call witnesses].

"You don't have very many powers as minority leader. But one power I do have is to force a vote and we will force a vote on all the witnesses and all the documents. And my guess is that those Republican colleagues do not want to vote against witnesses and documents. They know how bad it looks back home."

Also appearing on Maddow's show that night was Barbara Res, the former executive vice president of Trump's business enterprises, now a critic. "He's going around saying it shouldn't have happened and you let it happen," blaming everyone but himself, she said. "I think he's really out there."

But Trump would eventually skate out of trouble as he always has, she said. "Once he gets through this—and he probably will—[he will] exact revenge on a lot of people," she continued, shaking her head. "A lot of people."

Over the next two weeks, the confrontation generated by Pelosi's delay tactics gave voters the chance to reflect and pressure senators to remove the president. Could McConnell hold the line for Trump—and at what cost? Before the House impeachment vote, McConnell had been clear. His actions in the Senate trial would be "total coordination with the White House counsel's office and the people who are representing the president in the well of the Senate. Everything I do during this I'm coordinating with the White House counsel. There will be no difference between the president's position and our position as to how to handle this."[7]

McConnell planned to prevent witnesses and evidence beyond the documents provided by the House managers. "We certainly do not need jurors to start brainstorming witness lists for the prosecution and demanding to lock them in before we've even heard opening arguments," McConnell said.[8]

Lindsey Graham echoed McConnell's position, with more vitriol. He said that the House impeachment was the work of a "mob" and made no pretense to impartiality. "I am trying to give a pretty clear signal I have made up my mind. I'm not trying to pretend to be a fair juror here," Graham said. "What I see coming, happening today is just a partisan nonsense." (Observing this from the other side of Capitol Hill, Representative Jamie Raskin, the constitutional law professor, noted that Graham was joining with McConnell to create "the most egregious case of jury nullification in history.")[9]

The only question that remained was whether Schumer could attract the four Republican votes he needed to take away McConnell's bargaining power. The likely Republican candidates to jump sides on the question of admitting witnesses and evidence were Susan Collins of Maine and Cory Gardner of Colorado, both of whom faced tough reelection challenges in 2020. Lisa Murkowski of Alaska and Lamar Alexander of Tennessee were not up for reelection (in fact, Alexander had announced his retirement in 2022), but they had problems with Trump on moral grounds. And then there was the separate matter of Mitt Romney of Utah, who in private told Democratic colleagues that he did not support Trump.

Murkowski was first to raise concerns, saying she was "troubled" that

McConnell would announce he was coordinating with the White House in a supposedly impartial trial.

"And in fairness, when I heard that I was disturbed," Murkowski said, because she expected Americans wanted to see a fair trial. "To me it means that we have to take that step back from being hand in glove with the defense, and so I heard what leader McConnell had said, I happened to think that that has further confused the process."[10]

Just before Christmas, McConnell struck a more moderate tone. He was not going to push for a one-day trial. "We haven't ruled out witnesses," McConnell said during the Christmas break in an interview with *Fox & Friends*. "We're at an impasse. We can't do anything until the speaker sends the papers over."

The witness question became a demarcation line for the Republicans. McConnell and Trump's allies knew well that witnesses could do major damage to the president and potentially lead to further erosions of Republican support in the House. Privately, many Republican senators had gripes about Trump, and some of those facing potentially tough election races in 2020 were looking for a reason to defect.

With the new year, Pelosi's decision to hold back the articles of impeachment seemed to be succeeding. A series of leaks and revelations were proving embarrassing to Trump's cause. *The New York Times* had published a comprehensive look at the extent of the Trump administration's attempt to withhold aid to Ukraine.[11]

Chuck Schumer, still looking for leverage with McConnell, portrayed the *Times* report of the arguments that occurred in the White House during the Ukraine schemes as a "game changer." He said, "This new reporting shows that there were serious concerns raised by Trump administration officials about the propriety and legality of what the president was doing."[12]

Schumer may have thought this was a game changer, but not enough Americans had tuned in. Polls were improving slightly in favor of the Democrats—one survey after the new year said 57 percent of Americans wanted the trial to include witnesses—but the partisan divide on whether to convict Trump had not changed. Republicans would not budge in their support for Trump, which meant McConnell could probably hold the line by making only cosmetic compromises with the Democrats.[13]

On January 7, McConnell was assured that he would be able to hold on to wavering members of his caucus against Pelosi, Schumer, and the rest of the

Democrats calling for witnesses. He announced that he would support what he called "the Clinton rules: in which a decision on possible witnesses would be made during the trial." He said, "What was good enough for President Clinton is good enough for President Trump."[14]

On January 10, three days later, Pelosi announced that she would send the articles of impeachment to the Senate, setting the trial in motion. If she had waited any longer, she would have faced popular backlash. Americans wanted to get the impeachment over.

"I have asked Judiciary Committee Chairman Jerry Nadler to be prepared to bring to the floor next week a resolution to appoint managers and transmit articles of impeachment to the Senate," Pelosi said. "I will be consulting with you at our Tuesday House Democratic Caucus meeting on how we proceed further."[15]

33

THE REAL ARTICLES

I JUST GOT IMPEACHED FOR MAKING A PERFECT PHONE CALL!

—Donald Trump, president of the United States, via Twitter,
January 16, 2020

Pelosi announced the appointment of House managers on January 15. There was no surprise that Schiff and Nadler, central to the impeachment inquiries, were the principals. Also named were Zoe Lofgren of California and Hakeem Jeffries of New York. Val Demings of Florida had served on both the Judiciary and Intelligence Committees and was unflappable.

Among House Democrats, who watched the selection for signs of the Speaker's favor, Jamie Raskin and Eric Swalwell seemed sure bets, but neither was chosen. (This surprised many in the caucus and though it would be bad form to say it, surely disappointed both men.) Instead, Pelosi made two surprise choices, Jason Crow of Colorado and Sylvia Garcia of Texas, in an evident attempt at diversity and broader representation. Both were freshman members of Congress. Crow was a retired army captain who had served in Afghanistan and Iraq. Garcia was a former Houston judge.

"We had an inkling," said one member a day after the announcement, "that the managers would be Nadler and Schiff, but we didn't know who the others were going to be. Everybody was pretty shocked that Jason Crow was chosen because he isn't in either committee. So a lot of us don't really know why that happened. If anything, you know, a few of us thought that Joe Neguse should have been there also because he's so good and he speaks really well." Neguse was an attorney and trailblazer, elected at age 34 as Colorado's first black congressman.

On the day they were appointed, the seven managers took the ceremonial walk across the Capitol Rotunda to the Senate side to deliver the articles. They were led by Paul D. Irving, the House sergeant at arms. That afternoon, a ceremonial committee of Republican and Democratic senators led Chief Justice John Roberts to the floor of the Senate so he could take his place according to the Constitution to preside over the third impeachment of a president in American history. In a series of pro forma events, Roberts shook hands with Senator Chuck Grassley, the president pro tempore of the Senate, who administered Roberts's oath of office. Roberts then administered the oath to the one hundred senators who now became jurors who would decide Trump's guilt or innocence on each of the two articles of impeachment.

To close the ceremonial portion of the impeachment trial, the Senate sergeant of arms, Michael Stenger, issued a proclamation steeped in tradition:

"Hear ye! Hear ye! Hear ye! All persons are commanded to keep silent, on pain of imprisonment, while the House of Representatives is exhibiting to the Senate of the United States articles of impeachment against Donald John Trump, President of the United States."

With the Martin Luther King Jr. holiday approaching, the Senate adjourned for a week, at which time House Democrats would begin their opening arguments.

By now, the White House had also announced its team that would defend Trump. It would be led by Pat Cipollone, the White House counsel, Jay Sekulow, Pam Bondi, Robert Ray, and Ken Starr. And then there was Alan Dershowitz, an iconoclastic, press-seeking advocate whose brash manner and predictable unpredictability made for riveting television.

It was a team made for prime time. Sekulow had been a popular radio host and was a constant presence on Fox News, and he had represented Trump throughout the Mueller investigation. Bondi was a former Florida attorney general. Robert Ray and Ken Starr were veteran Republican operatives, having both served as special counsels investigating then president Bill Clinton prior to his impeachment in 1998. As the trial proceeded, a team of key Republican Trump supporters from the House would also come in to bolster the defense: Doug Collins, Mike Johnson, Jim Jordan, Debbie Lesko, Mark Meadows, John Ratcliffe, Elise Stefanik, and Lee Zeldin.[1]

On Wednesday, January 22, the substance of the impeachment trial of Donald Trump began, the outcome largely predetermined. One wild card was John Bolton, who continued to make declarations that he would testify if subpoenaed. However, there would have to be a public groundswell to demand his testimony. There was no such groundswell. Americans were as divided as they had been throughout the Trump years.

The House managers presented a 111-page trial complaint. Led by Adam Schiff, the Democrats detailed why Trump should be removed from office. The opening arguments for the Democrats concluded with this summary statement by Nadler, which went about as far as—even further than—he could reasonably go. Trump, he said, "wants to be all powerful. He doesn't want to have to respect the Congress, he does not have to respect the representatives of the will of the people. Only his will goes . . . He is a dictator. This must not stand and that is another reason he must be removed from office."

The Republican defense document was a page shorter than the Democratic document, and the Trump defenders complained about House Democrats for being repetitive. The real problem, they said, was Joe Biden's relationship with Ukraine. They pushed the Trump conspiracy theory that had been rejected and debunked by a series of witnesses before the House who would likely never appear in the Senate. And if they were to appear, the Republicans sought to subpoena Joe and Hunter Biden. "We would prefer not to be discussing this," said Pam Bondi, defending Trump. "But the [Democratic] House managers have placed this squarely at issue. You've heard from the House managers. They do not believe that there was any concern to raise here, that all of this was baseless. And all that we are saying is that there was a basis to talk about this, to raise this issue."

After both sides completed opening arguments, the case went to two days of questions and answers, alternating from Democrats to Republicans. Senators did not pose questions themselves. Instead, they wrote them out and submitted for reading by the chief justice. The questions were a vehicle for both sides to bob, parry, and make points.

According to the rules, senators were required to remain in the chamber and maintain silence. Tempers did flare at one point between the Democrats and Trump's defenders. Chief Justice Roberts intervened, saying, "I think it is appropriate at this point for me to admonish both the House managers and president's counsel in equal terms to remember that they are addressing the world's greatest deliberative body. Those addressing the Senate should remember where they are."[2]

One unscripted moment was the result of a question written by Rand Paul, the junior senator from Kentucky. His question included the name of the alleged whistleblower who had complained about Trump's contact with Ukraine and provoked the impeachment process.

Roberts, wearing his reading glasses, glanced down at what was written and looked up again. "The presiding officer declines to read the question as submitted," Roberts said.

In a news conference after the question-and-answer session, Paul defended his question. "I don't know who the whistleblower is," he said. He then said that he understood that the man he had named was in contact with a staffer on the House Intelligence Committee.

"My question is about two people who are friends who worked together . . . who have been overheard talking about impeaching the president years in advance of a process that then was created to get the impeachment process going," Paul told reporters.[3]

Though facing defeat, the Democrats still sought elevated oratory and inspired appeals to morality that might erode Republican support for Trump. The Republicans focused on and challenged the process the Democrats had followed in their inquiry. Arguments were along familiar lines, and the rebuttal from the Republican side was equally expected. The evidence was clear and overwhelming, said the Democrats. Full overreach, an attempted coup, an effort to suborn the will of the electorate in 2016, said the Republicans.

The Senate sessions were not easy days. For one thing, the average age of the senators was sixty-five. Some were well into their seventies and eighties. It was hard to sit still, more so for the older senators. So an admonishment under the rules for the impeachment trial—stay put and do not wander—was not universally observed.

"I mean look," said one Democrat, "in fairness, a good number [of the Republicans] stayed in their seats, listened and were attentive. But I would say there would be anywhere between eight and 10 members who habitually got up and left the chambers. I mean, getting up is not the worst thing 'cause I understand some people could have back spasms or whatever it is to be honest with you.

"But no, several of them would leave the chambers for extended periods of time. And so they weren't even in the cloak room listening to stuff. They just went out. You can go to the cloak room on each side, directly from within the chamber. They were going out the doors that lead to the hallway or other places."

Whether or not the Republicans remained physically present for the duration, some doodled at their desks, whispered to one another, and at times even snickered. Perhaps this was to be expected. Only the most starry-eyed bystander could have expected anything but acquittal for Trump. Republicans were not going to flip and drive him from office, Democratic senators agreed. But there were points to be made, and eloquent declarations on principle, always with the same refrain: "No one is above the rule of law."

There remained one bit of suspense: How would the Republicans vote on the question of witnesses or on whether document evidence should be introduced, as it would be in any criminal trial? The swing Republicans still were a source of speculation. Mitt Romney had hinted he was uncomfortable with the proceedings. Though he would not say how he would vote on the impeachment articles themselves, he wanted exactly the things that McConnell was blocking—witnesses and evidence.

"I think it's very likely I'll be in favor of witnesses, but I haven't made a decision finally, yet, and I won't until the testimony is completed," he had said. "I would like to hear from John Bolton and other witnesses, but at the same time I'm comfortable with the Clinton impeachment model when we have opening arguments first and then we have a vote on whether to have witnesses."[4]

In the end, only Romney and Susan Collins sided with the Democrats on the question of witnesses—the vote was forty-nine in favor of witnesses, fifty-one against. Romney's vote was based on his long-standing concern about Trump's presidency, and was widely regarded as a matter of conscience. Collins, however, was apparently given a no-fault license by the Republican leadership to be the other, ultimately futile no vote. It might help her claim independence from Trump's influence during her reelection campaign in Maine, where polls had consistently showed that a majority of voters disapproved of the president.

The Democrats were puzzled most by Romney. He appeared to have a strong moral sense—he did not like illegality or subterfuge or the greed that characterized the Trumpian age. But he was not a leader. He had been the standard-bearer of the Republican Party in 2012, as its presidential candidate, yet the rank and file of the GOP hardly respected him. It was now the party of Trump. Democrats said that he had no influence on other Republican senators who were committed to a quick process that would reach a preordained conclusion. This led, naturally, to skepticism among the Democrats.

"What were they trying to hide?" asked Senator Sherrod Brown after the trial ended. "When they don't let people who were in the room talk about it, the human mind is going to jump to some conclusion."

First elected to the Senate by Ohio voters in 2006, Brown had recently published a book that looked at progressive politics through the lives of eight senators who had occupied the desk where he now sat. It had revealed him to be a keen observer of the Senate in action. Brown had taken note of how his Republican colleagues had committed to voting not guilty before the trial began and he marveled at their behavior during the proceedings. As he told us in an interview, "In the back row, a couple of the senators, when votes were coming and their names were called, laughed and were doing high fives."

Indeed, during the trial many senators violated rules that required them to be present throughout the debate and instead took frequent breaks to appear on television or make telephone calls. During meal breaks the din in a crowded room where food was put out reminded some of a noisy dinner party. The odors, from so many different dishes and so many weary bodies, drove others to flee.

Near the end of the trial, Dershowitz briefly stole the spotlight with the type of confused rhetoric not usually expected from a constitutional scholar. "If a president does something which he believes will help him get elected in the public interest, that cannot be the kind of quid pro quo that results in impeachment." In plain language, Dershowitz was asserting that all that is required for a president to justify an action—no matter what it is—is the belief that it is good for the country. The president, then, can deploy a whim to stand above the law.

Responding to Dershowitz, Schiff reminded senators that Richard Nixon, three years after he had resigned the presidency, said, "When the president does it, that means it is not illegal." It was this kind of inanity that had rendered Nixon irredeemable in many Americans' hearts. Dershowitz would later say his comment was being mischaracterized: "A president seeking re-election cannot do anything he wants," he would explain. "He is not above the law. He cannot commit crimes."

After three weeks of presentations from both sides—without witnesses, without documentary evidence—Schiff's closing statement brought silence to the chamber.

> The American people deserve a President they can count on to put their interests first, to put their interests first. Colonel Vindman said, "Here, right matters. Here, right matters." Well, let me tell you something, if right doesn't matter, if right doesn't matter, it doesn't matter how good the Constitution is. It doesn't matter how brilliant the framers were. Doesn't matter how good or bad our advocacy in this trial is. Doesn't matter how well written the Oath of Impartiality is. If right doesn't matter, we're lost.

If the truth doesn't matter, we're lost. Framers couldn't protect us from ourselves, if right and truth don't matter. And you know that what he did was not right. That's what they do in the old country, that Colonel Vindman's father came from. Or the old country that my great grandfather came from, or the old countries that your ancestors came from, or maybe you came from. But here, right is supposed to matter. It's what's made us the greatest nation on earth. No constitution can protect us, right doesn't matter anymore. And you know you can't trust this President to do what's right for this country. You can trust he will do what's right for Donald Trump. He'll do it now. He's done it before. He'll do it for the next several months. He'll do it in the election if he's allowed to. This is why if you find him guilty, you must find that he should be removed. Because right matters. Because right matters and the truth matters. Otherwise, we are lost.

The speech was poignant then and within weeks would resonate in ways no one had imagined.

As Schiff spoke, one of the Democrats in the Senate focused his attention on the body language of his colleagues across the aisle. Some wore masks of disinterest. But that was not the case of Cory Gardner of Colorado, said the senator. "He was in a world of hurt."

Elsewhere in the chamber, Lamar Alexander shifted in his seat uncomfortably. Perhaps it was only the hard chair. The Democrat could only wonder, how many of them truly were comfortable in the roles they were forced to play?

If Mitt Romney was comfortable, it was probably because he did not care how the president and his followers might react to his vote in favor of calling witnesses. The newest member of the Senate, Kelly Loeffler of Georgia, had tweeted against the former presidential candidate's decision:

My colleague @SenatorRomney wants to appease the left by calling witnesses who will slander the @realDonaldTrump during their 15 minutes of fame.

Loeffler's comment was bad form in the generally staid and genteel upper-legislative body, especially since she was an appointee and had served a matter of weeks in the Senate. Many noted that Loeffler and her husband, Jeffrey Sprecher, chairman of the New York Stock Exchange, had been

Romney donors. So much had changed in the age of Trump. Romney's former aide Stuart Stevens said Romney was not disturbed by the criticism. "I hope it makes them feel better because I can tell you that Mitt Romney does not care," Stevens said.[5]

Late in the day, Mitt Romney stood in the well of the Senate to make a historic declaration. Many of his Republican friends rose and left the chamber. They would not give him the respect of their presence.

> The allegations made in the articles of impeachment are very serious. As a Senator-juror, I swore an oath, before God, to exercise "impartial justice." I am a profoundly religious person. I take an oath before God as enormously consequential. I knew from the outset that being tasked with judging the president, the leader of my own party, would be the most difficult decision I have ever faced. I was not wrong.
>
> The House managers presented evidence supporting their case; the White House counsel disputed that case. In addition, the president's team presented three defenses: first, that there can be no impeachment without a statutory crime; second, that the Bidens' conduct justified the president's actions; and third that the judgment of the president's actions should be left to the voters. Let me first address each of those defenses.
>
> The historic meaning of the words "high crimes and misdemeanors," the writings of the Founders and my own reasoned judgment convince me that a president can indeed commit acts against the public trust that are so egregious that while they are not statutory crimes, they would demand removal from office. To maintain that the lack of a codified and comprehensive list of all the outrageous acts that a president might conceivably commit renders Congress powerless to remove a president defies reason. . . .
>
> The defense argues that the Senate should leave the impeachment decision to the voters. While that logic is appealing to our democratic instincts, it is inconsistent with the Constitution's requirement that the Senate, not the voters, try the president. Hamilton explained that the Founders' decision to invest senators with this obligation rather than leave it to voters was intended to minimize—to the extent possible—the partisan sentiments of the public.

This verdict is ours to render. The people will judge us for how well and faithfully we fulfilled our duty. The grave question the Constitution tasks senators to answer is whether the president committed an act so extreme and egregious that it rises to the level of a "high crime and misdemeanor."

Yes, he did.

The president asked a foreign government to investigate his political rival. The president withheld vital military funds from that government to press it to do so. The president delayed funds for an American ally at war with Russian invaders. The president's purpose was personal and political. Accordingly, the president is guilty of an appalling abuse of the public trust.

What he did was not "perfect." No, it was a flagrant assault on our electoral rights, our national security interests, and our fundamental values. Corrupting an election to keep oneself in office is perhaps the most abusive and destructive violation of one's oath of office that I can imagine. . . .

I acknowledge that my verdict will not remove the president from office. The results of this Senate court will in fact be appealed to a higher court: the judgment of the American people. Voters will make the final decision, just as the president's lawyers have implored. My vote will likely be in the minority in the Senate. But irrespective of these things, with my vote, I will tell my children and their children that I did my duty to the best of my ability, believing that my country expected it of me. I will only be one name among many, no more or less, to future generations of Americans who look at the record of this trial. They will note merely that I was among the senators who determined that what the president did was wrong, grievously wrong.[6]

The condemnation was swift. Representative Jim Jordan, the shirtsleeved attack dog for the Republicans during the impeachment hearings, called out, "Wrong, wrong, wrong move!" Romney's own niece Ronna McDaniel, the Republican National Committee chairwoman, could have held silent but spoke up. "This is not the first time I've disagreed with Mitt, and I imagine it will not be the last. The bottom line is President Trump did nothing wrong, and the Republican Party is more united than ever behind him. I, along with the GOP, stand with President Trump."[7]

When the final votes were cast on February 5, 2020, 1,111 days into the Trump presidency, Mitt Romney's stand on principle was a mere twinkle in the larger Trumpian universe. On article one only, the vote was 47 Democrats and one Republican to convict, 52 against. On the second article, obstruction of justice, Romney returned to the Republican side of a party line tally of 47–53. All one hundred senators were in the chamber now. Roberts read from the required script for both charges: "Two thirds of the Senators present not having pronounced him guilty, the Senate adjudges that the respondent, Donald John Trump, president of the United States, is not guilty as charged."

After the trial was over, Sherrod Brown sounded the kind of note—in time "they are going to be embarrassed by their cravenness"—offered by those who fail in what they believe is a noble cause. Brown also welcomed the way the impeachment verdict highlighted the difference between the parties. "Yes it showed the polarization, but it shined a light on the culprits," he said. "It shined a light on Trump and the cabal around him, in some cases the thugs around him. It shined a light on McConnell and how he runs this place. That's how things change, when the public sees, 'Oh yeah, this wasn't on the up and up.'"

Brown's Democratic colleague Sheldon Whitehouse could see Brown's point, which he described as a happier perspective on a disturbing historical moment. "The happy version is that in the same way that we went through Nothing-ism [The Know-Nothing Party of the 1800s], and in the same way that we went through McCarthyism, and in the same way that we went through the conflict that led to the Civil War, America has these times when we get out of sorts. There's a kind of general public rejection of the way in which we've gotten out of sorts and we returned to the better angels of our nature and to progress."

However, Whitehouse had spent years investigating shifts in the political game, especially the way in which, after the Supreme Court struck down most campaign funding laws, a few major donors came to fill GOP campaign coffers and demand lockstep loyalty from McConnell and others. "The unhappy version is that this thing has been grown so far and reaches into so many corners that there isn't really a precedent," said Whitehouse.

Without a precedent to consider, Whitehouse, like Brown, placed his hope in the American people who, with the power to elect who serves in Washington, would render the ultimate judgment in the impeachment of Donald Trump. As the election neared, Joe Biden would hold an advantage in national polls. Nancy Pelosi and the Democrats seemed well positioned to hold the House and Mitch McConnell faced the unexpected but very real prospect of losing the Senate. Corey Lewandowski went to see Trump to warn him that he was in danger of a big defeat in November and the president began sowing doubt about the reliability of the election system, setting the stage to deny the legitimacy of an outcome that didn't favor him.[8]

EPILOGUE

THIS IS WHAT AUTOCRACY LOOKS LIKE

The defendant wants to hide the truth because he's generally guilty. The defense attorney's job is to make sure the jury does not arrive at that truth.

—Alan Dershowitz in 1982

In the end, the crucial words of the impeachment trial had been uttered by eighty-one-year-old Alan Dershowitz, whose previous star turn had seen him help to win acquittal for football star O. J. Simpson, who had been charged in the bloody knife murder of his wife Nicole and her friend Ronald Goldman. According to the former Harvard law professor, a president should be immune from removal any time he or she believes an action is in the national interest. Extending the notion to its logical extreme, Dershowitz said that if a president believed that something as self-aggrandizing as his or her own reelection was in the national interest, almost anything done to achieve this goal would be a legitimate exercise of power. Dershowitz seemed to be entirely alone among scholars on this point, but when he offered it to the Senate, the trial outcome Mitch McConnell had planned was assured.[1]

Dershowitz was not among the lawyers and loyalists Trump gathered for what he called an acquittal "celebration" in the East Room of the White House on February 6. This affair wasn't so much a party as a command performance at which Trump waved a newspaper with the headline TRUMP ACQUITTED, aired his grievances at length, and thanked, by name, some of those who sat in the rows of chairs arrayed before the presidential podium.

The event, which evoked the kind of party a mob boss might throw upon a victory at a criminal trial, was like nothing the East Room had ever seen before. As always, Trump said he had been treated "unfairly" but this time he went a bit further, calling the impeachment process an "evil" enterprise aided by "dirty cops" and "leakers and liars." Trump declared, "Adam Schiff is a vicious, horrible person. Nancy Pelosi is a horrible person," and he summoned his daughter Ivanka to join him before the crowd for a big embrace. With this hug, she reprised the role of humanizing-beautiful-daughter, which she has played for many years.[2]

On the very next day, Friday, February 7, Trump fired Alexander Vindman and his brother, who also happened to work at the National Security Council. Vindman was guilty, it seemed, of doing his duty by responding to a legal request that he testify before Congress. Trump would call Lieutenant Colonel Vindman, a decorated Iraq war veteran with an unblemished record, "very insubordinate." His brother was guilty by association. Both were unceremoniously marched out of their offices by security officers. Hours later, Trump fired the ambassador to the European Union, Gordon Sondland, who had also testified. Sondland's dismissal occurred despite appeals from Republican senators who thought it would seem vindictive and petty.

The president would also resume his propaganda war, offering a false interpretation of congressional testimony in an effort to support his yearslong campaign to discredit the original probes of Russia's election interference and all that followed.

> FBI Director Christopher Wray just admitted that the FISA Warrants and Survailence [misspelling in original] of my campaign were illegal. So was the Fake Dossier. THEREFORE, THE WHOLE SCAM INVESTIGATION, THE MUELLER REPORT AND EVERYTHING ELSE FOR THREE YEARS, WAS A FIXED HOAX. WHO PAYS THE PRICE?[3]

•   •   •

On the day that Trump fired the Vindman brothers and thereby commenced his score-settling spree, the House of Representatives met to conduct its normal business. The one major bill approved by the members authorized $4.7 billion in aid to the U.S. territory of Puerto Rico, which was struggling to recover from hurricanes that struck in 2017 and from two earthquakes that had shaken the island at the start of 2020. The House acted because the president had been withholding previously approved aid on the grounds that Puerto Rico is "one of the most corrupt places on Earth." The island had endured more than its share of corruption over the years, but a recent scandal in the disaster relief effort had involved members of Trump's team, who had been arrested on federal fraud charges. The House action was almost certain to be killed in the Senate or vetoed by the president. And yet Speaker Pelosi was adamant about advancing the legislation to show where the House stood. She presided over the voting herself, even though she could have assigned anyone in her caucus to perform this duty.[4]

Pelosi's decision to occupy the Speaker's chair at the end of a gloomy week offered a symbolic signal to those who were discouraged by the Senate's actions and by Trump's triumphalism. Seated high on the rostrum, beneath the Stars and Stripes and flanked by bronze faces, she controlled the action much like a conductor controls an orchestra. But as much as Pelosi projected confidence, she was not entirely calm. As most of the members hustled off the floor of the chamber to begin weekends in their home districts, Representative David Cicilline waited for the Speaker to descend the three levels of the rostrum to the House floor. Cicilline had surely annoyed Pelosi by pushing hard for impeachment when she wanted to go slowly, but once she had set a course, he had supported her loyally. In this moment, he thought he saw that she needed a bit of commiseration.

"Hell of a week, wasn't it?" he said.

"I don't know what's happened to our country," she replied.

•   •   •

On Monday, February 10, 2020, Pelosi gathered her leadership team in the same conference room where, five months before, she had talked about her call with a president who had been desperate to avoid impeachment. Abraham Lincoln still looked upon the room from his place on the wall. The same water tumblers and glass bowls filled with chocolates waited on the table. But no sunlight streamed through the windows. Instead, the view of the Mall was obscured by rain and shadowed by lowering clouds.

In September, Pelosi had concluded that by soliciting foreign help in his bid for reelection and seeking to hide this abuse of power, Donald Trump had made his impeachment necessary. In the months that ensued, she had engaged in the ultimate form of political struggle as permitted by the Constitution. Although the impeachment had set in motion the trial to consider Trump's removal, this outcome had never been a possibility. Not with a Republican Senate immune to facts and determined to conduct a sham trial. The impeachment had been instead about the House fulfilling its constitutional obligation to respond to Trump's abuse. Secondarily, it had been about revealing the facts

of the president's misconduct so that the American people might recognize
what type of leader occupied the Oval Office.

Much of the country, like many House Democrats, felt traumatized if
not defeated by the trial process. The natural response, for many, had been to
revisit every choice that had been made and wonder: Should the House have
filed additional articles of impeachment?

Then there were all the offenses—one might call them high crimes
and misdemeanors—that were omitted from the articles of impeachment
approved by the House and transmitted to the Senate. In addition to both
seeking and accepting emoluments and the obstruction of justice identified
by Mueller, many Democrats would say Trump merited impeachment for:

- Committing perjury when he told Mueller's team, "I do not recall
  discussing WikiLeaks with [former advisor Roger Stone], nor do I
  recall being aware of Mr. Stone having discussed WikiLeaks with
  individuals associated with my campaign." Trump campaign aide
  Rick Gates testified that in fact Trump knew of Stone's activities.

- Abusing his powers when he declared a national emergency to divert funds for an anti-immigrant southern border wall. The president
  himself said, "I didn't need to do this. But I'd rather do it much
  faster."

- Violating his oath to protect the United States from enemies foreign
  and domestic when he divulged intelligence secrets to the Russian
  foreign minister and Russia's ambassador to Washington during an
  Oval Office visit.

- Committing the crime of witness intimidation against both Michael
  Cohen and Marie Yovanovitch when he criticized both of them as
  they were about to testify before Congress.

- Urging federal agencies to carry out political vendettas against media
  companies that had criticized him. This included trying to block the
  merger of AT&T and Time Warner to harm Time Warner's news
  network CNN and pushing the Postal Service to raise shipping rates
  paid by Amazon, whose founder owns *The Washington Post*.[5]

In addition to the crimes not charged, troubled Democrats worried about whether their side had been outplayed politically. Did the House, wary of being accused of dragging out the proceedings, move too quickly? Had the impeachment managers made Trump's corruption fully obvious to the American people? What would happen if new crimes or new evidence were revealed? Could a second impeachment be considered?

For days, Pelosi's troops had been asking these questions and more, and the Speaker, who was renowned for her ability to control her caucus, must have been aware of the turmoil. Though disgraced by impeachment, Trump had taken a victory lap after his acquittal, and it was easy to consider his boasting and preening and conclude that he had actually gained from the ordeal. Opinion polls did show an uptick for Trump, but overall, he still fell short of 50 percent approval. Less widely noted were polls that showed that the public had actually shared Pelosi's view on impeachment from the moment the Democrats took control of the House until the Senate verdict.

In early 2019, as the nation had waited for Mueller and as Pelosi resisted the drive toward impeachment, Americans were evenly split on the matter of impeachment, and neither side claimed more than 45 percent in the polls. In March, as the Mueller report was completed, Attorney General Barr had used spin to sell it as an exoneration of the president, and anti-impeachment sentiment grew. With the administration defying Congress's subpoenas and hearings that produced confusion, the Speaker's reticence seemed to be reflected across the country. A great many Americans suspected that Trump had committed impeachable offenses. However, support for impeachment didn't rise to a majority until the Ukraine scandal became evident and Pelosi changed her mind. From that point forward, pro-impeachment sentiment led—in early October, 15 percent of *Republicans* supported impeachment—and it actually increased after the House approved the articles. During the trial, one poll found that 75 percent of Americans wanted the Senate to hear from new witnesses and consider new documentary evidence.[6]

The numbers confirmed that, just as in Watergate, when public opinion didn't move decisively against Richard Nixon until after Congress began to act, Trump's impeachment gained support when House leaders mobilized to act. Nancy Pelosi hit her highest favorable poll numbers ever after the House impeachment vote. All this data suggested that the Speaker had gauged public opinion well and managed to move it in her direction once she decided to go for impeachment. If House Democrats harbored doubts about Pelosi's skill, the polls and the Speaker's leadership style discouraged them from giving voice to those concerns.

Public postmortems and second-guessing were not Pelosi's style, and the weekend of doubt was over. The only bit of impeachment business considered at the leadership meeting related to the problem of John Bolton's offer to testify. Some members of the House Judiciary Committee wanted to test the cagey Bolton by sending him a summons to appear and make good on his offer. But with Bolton's book scheduled for publication in less than six weeks, a delay seemed in order. With this matter set aside, Pelosi noted that in nine months' time, voters would go to the polls.[7]

The election loomed large, and at that moment, the Democrats were deeply divided over their choice of candidates. Indeed, the two with real momentum—Senator Bernie Sanders of Vermont and former New York mayor Mike Bloomberg—were barely Democrats at all. Bloomberg, whose $55 billion fortune made him one of the richest men on earth, had been a Republican during the time he ran New York City. Sanders had, for most of his life, identified himself as an independent "democratic socialist." If Democrats puzzled over these men, God only knew how people in general would react were one of them to face off against Trump. With this uncertainty in mind, Pelosi's hold-the-House focus made sense. So, too, did her emphasis on members in swing districts, where voters wouldn't tolerate rabid anti-Trumpism.

In her calculation, Pelosi didn't need to bend toward liberal Democrats in safe seats. They were going to win reelection no matter what. And if certain individuals were angry about losing debates over strategy or tactics, there were Democrats waiting back home to fill their seats. "She's strictly by the numbers," noted one leadership Democrat at the end of the impeachment trial. "The personalities, the people, do not matter to her. It sounds cruel, but it's actually smart. We hear it all the time. Like if it weren't for the frontliners we wouldn't be in the majority and without the majority, you're nowhere."

The frontline Democrats who had given the party control of the House in 2018 would need a return to the issues that had gotten them elected then. Health care, wages, housing, education, jobs—these would be the priorities moving forward. Individual House and Senate Democrats who wanted to run against Trumpism were free to follow this strategy and could pick from vast amounts of evidence and testimony pointing to Trump's guilt. So much drama and struggle had been packed into the short time between the investigation and the trial travesty that no one could reliably recall it all. However, the highlights created a startling picture of Trump's drive to use power in a way no president had used it before. Among the key events were:

- Ambassador Gordon Sondland's confirmation that the president had frozen military aid to Ukraine in order to extract a personal political quid pro quo from the government in Kiev.

- Lieutenant Colonel Alexander Vindman's testimony about efforts by the president and others to embroil Ukraine in domestic politics in a way that would "undermine U.S. security."

- Ambassador Marie Yovanovitch's public description of a smear campaign conducted by the president's lawyer and others who considered her an impediment to their scheme.

- Ambassador William Taylor's confirmation that the Trump administration had, contrary to U.S. policy, conditioned authorized war aid for Ukraine on the announcement of investigations into the son of the president's rival and into a conspiracy theory about 2016 election interference.

- Pentagon official Laura Cooper's testimony refuting White House claims that since Ukrainian officials did not know of the hold on aid, they had not been pressured to fulfill the president's corrupt request.

Amid the effort to reveal and punish the president's abuse of power had come many episodes that could be regarded as either ridiculous distractions or ominous demonstrations of authoritarian impulse. The prime example of the ridiculous came as dozens of Republican representatives had noisily stormed a secure facility to protest the secrecy of the proceedings. In fact, the secrecy was required to protect national security information, and more than one hundred members of their party were welcomed to participate. The stunt only called attention to the stormers' disrespect for their colleagues and the truth. The lasting image from this silliness had been of the arrival of takeout pizza for the suit-and-tie protesters.

More ominous were the attempts made to name the whistleblower whose confidential report had revealed the president's bribery attempt to Congress.

In both the House and the Senate, Republicans had publicly stated the name of the person they suspected had made the report. In typical fashion, the president had repeated the name on social media. Clearly intended to intimidate anyone who might think to report misconduct in the administration, these actions had violated the spirit if not the letter of the law that protects whistleblowers and placed the named person—who had not been confirmed as the whistleblower—in danger.

For the individuals most affected by threats of exposure, and many other Americans, the outcome of the impeachment trial brought feelings of anxiety and even fear. The president's actions immediately after his acquittal indicated that this fear was warranted. In swift authoritarian style, he used his pardon and commutation powers to help release or wipe clean the records of eleven convicted criminals who were either old acquaintances or friends of his associates. One, a former New York City police commissioner convicted of corruption, had been Rudy Giuliani's driver. Another, the notorious Wall Street criminal Michael Milken, benefited from the intervention of the president's son-in-law, Jared Kushner. No president in modern times had used his pardon power to show such brazen favoritism. As Trump did so, he went around the Justice Department office that screens applications for clemency and showed he would not be bound by the standards of propriety and justice other presidents honored. He would wield power not on behalf of the American people but to benefit himself and his friends.

The pardons underscored Trump's drive to bring the Justice Department, which has long operated at arm's length from the president, under his personal control. In this endeavor, he could count on Attorney General William Barr, who was devoted to increasing the power of the presidency and dismantling the checks that might be imposed by Congress or the courts. Barr made his view clear in the anti-Mueller memo he distributed as a kind of job application in the summer of 2018. The key passage, which he wrote in italics, said that "the Constitution vests *all Federal law enforcement power,* and hence prosecutorial discretion, in the President." Then, in a twist worthy of *Catch-22* author Joseph Heller, he concluded that under the Constitution there could be "no limit on the President's authority to act [even] on matters which concern him or his own conduct." In other words the president was, in fact, like an elected monarch, which was precisely what the authors of the Constitution intended to avoid as they created the American system of democracy.[8]

Barr's reasoning led to the spectacle of a Justice Department where the president's conspiracy theories caused him to launch investigations of investigators. Add Trump's acquittal in the Senate trial, and you get a president who sensed he was free to act as if no limit could be imposed on his executive power. In the days after the trial ended, Trump took note of his longtime friend Roger Stone's conviction and sentencing and hinted, very broadly, about acting to keep him out of prison. When prosecutors followed Justice Department policy to recommend Stone receive a maximum sentence for his seven felonies, Barr intervened to withdraw the sentencing memo and recommend, instead, a prison term "far less" than the maximum.[9]

The living embodiment of all that was wrong with modern politics, Stone had capped his long career of lies, dirty tricks, and nasty rhetoric with a scheme to maximize the impact of the WikiLeaks release of stolen documents that aided Trump in 2016. These activities had made Stone a man of interest for both Congress and the Mueller team. Stone obstructed justice as he lied to Congress and prosecutors and threatened another witness. The evidence included an email Stone sent to the witness that included the sentence: "Prepare to die cocksucker."

Based on the facts, it would be hard to imagine a white-collar criminal less deserving of special treatment than Roger Stone. However, he was Donald Trump's pal, and so the Justice Department urged leniency, and the president publicly complained about the jurors and the prosecutors. "Everything having to do with this fraudulent investigation is badly tainted and, in my opinion, should be thrown out," he said.

By the time Stone appeared in court for his sentencing, the public outcry from the legal profession—more than 2,500 former Justice Department officials called for Barr's resignation—had prompted the department to back away from its call for leniency. Replacement prosecutors informed the judge that the department would rely on her judgment. The new lead lawyer said, "The Department of Justice and the U.S. Attorney's Office is committed to enforcing the law without fear, or favor, or political interference."

As one player in this drama whom Trump could not control, Judge Amy Berman Jackson devoted much of the hearing to debunking the complaints emanating from the Oval Office and Trump allies. Of Stone, she said, "He was not prosecuted, as some have complained, for standing up for the President. He was prosecuted for covering up for the President." Jackson had, in the course of the case, become a target of harassment by Stone himself—on social media, he posted a picture of her beside an image of the crosshairs in a gun sight—and by legions of right-wing media figures and their followers. Many of their statements suggested that Stone was charged and tried for behavior that was inconsequential. The judge boiled this argument, and the defense offered by Stone's lawyers, down to the phrase, *So what?*

"Of all the circumstances in this case, that may be the most pernicious," said Jackson. "The truth still exists. The truth still matters. Roger Stone's insistence that it doesn't, his belligerence, his pride in his own lies are a threat to our most fundamental institutions, to the very foundation of our democracy." The judge then announced that she would not be influenced by the circus around the case. Sticking to her usual practice, she sentenced Stone to serve a prison term of forty months, which fell in the low range for the crimes he committed.[10]

One could replace the name *Stone* with the name *Trump* and Judge Jackson's words would accurately describe much of the president's conduct since he campaigned for and won the White House. But while a judge could deal with a mini-Trump figure like Stone, no person or institution could keep in check a president who believed that by possessing certain power he was justified in using it. On the very day that Stone was sentenced, Trump shocked Washington with the sudden firing of Director of National Intelligence Joseph Maguire. Though far from an anti-Trumper, Maguire had followed the law in the case of the Ukraine whistleblower and threatened to resign if the White House blocked him from testifying before Congress.[11]

Already on the president's bad side, Maguire was targeted for firing when he sent a top aide—a plain-speaking intelligence veteran named Shelby Pierson—to brief congressional committees on a new Russian election interference campaign that was targeting Democrats in order to aid the president's reelection effort. According to Pierson, the 2020 variation of Russian interference would include online propaganda aimed at both the primary and general elections, with the main goal of reelecting Trump. At the briefing, several Republicans who were fully aligned with Trump on the matter of Russia and 2016 argued with the intelligence assessment as if they were in a partisan debate. However, the evidence was solid, and the dispute didn't change the facts.

Though it was hardly a surprise that Russia would again organize an online effort to help Trump, it was strange that the president and his allies weren't prepared to handle the intelligence findings more smoothly. Instead of fighting with the experts, who were employed for the purpose of tracking this kind of information, they could have welcomed the warning and called for the country to be alert to foreign manipulations. In choosing to contest the facts, they returned national attention to the scandal-plagued process that brought Trump to the presidency in the first place. For the better part of four years, Trump had paid little heed to the Russian threat and labored hard to replace the established facts about 2016 with his false narrative about Ukraine and others. Now it seemed that he and the country were going to plunge into a rerun of that story, and to make matters worse, his nemesis Adam Schiff was among the officials informed of the new intelligence.

According to *The Washington Post*, Trump was enraged to learn of the briefing from Intelligence Committee member Devin Nunes, and he initially believed that Schiff was the only person given the information. He berated Maguire in an Oval Office meeting and fired him days later. He then installed the ambassador to Germany, Richard Grenell, as acting director of national intelligence. Grenell was a devoted Trump loyalist, but with no intelligence experience, he didn't meet the statutory requirement set for the position and would only serve temporarily. Trump also appointed a former aide to Nunes named Kash Patel to a position in Grenell's office. Patel had played a major role in a Republican effort to attack and discredit intelligence findings on the 2016 election. His appointment signaled that Trump would continue to fight with the professionals in the intelligence communities over the evidence of Russian interference. The Kremlin, watching from afar, came down squarely in Trump's camp, as a spokesman said of the briefing, "These are more paranoid announcements which, to our regret, will multiply as we get closer to the [U.S.] election. They have nothing to do with the truth."

Ever ready to double down on his decisions, when Trump replaced the "acting" Grenell with a permanent director of national intelligence he selected Representative John Ratcliffe for the job. Ratcliffe had little if any experience in intelligence or foreign affairs but had been a rabid attacker when Robert Mueller testified before the House Judiciary Committee. This performance had certified that he possessed the one trait—abject loyalty—most appreciated by the president.[12]

The president's campaign of retribution included the firing of Ambassador to the European Union Gordon Sondland, and the withdrawal of Elaine McCusker's nomination to be comptroller of the Pentagon. (She would soon resign.) A host of inspectors general, beginning with Intelligence Community inspector general Michael Atkinson were also dismissed as Trump demonstrated what would happen to supposedly independent watchdogs who did their jobs. Trump would begin to extend his autocratic approach to governing by permitting the dismissal of the inspectors general of the departments of transportation and health and human services, where they were investigating potential scandals. Then he allowed the removal of the State Department inspector general, Steve A. Linick. News reports said that Linick had been investigating potential wrongdoing by Secretary of State Mike Pompeo. Trump later told reporters he did not know Linick but dismissed him at Pompeo's request. This move prompted bipartisan criticism and calls for an investigation in Congress.

In a continuing flourish of unchecked power, Trump then turned to undoing court action conducted during the Russia investigation that began at the start of his administration. The Justice Department under William Barr told a federal district judge in May that it wanted to drop the prosecution of former national security advisor Michael Flynn, who had already pleaded guilty to lying to the FBI. This petition meant that the government wanted to free a man who had twice pleaded guilty to felony charges and hold him blameless for lies told to investigators. The court appointed a retired judge to review the petition. His report concluded that the Justice Department was attempting a "gross abuse of prosecutorial power." While awaiting the court's decision, Flynn published an essay in which he declared that Satan was trying to corrupt America but he was putting his faith in God. "The power of hell, while strong, is limited," he wrote. "God is the ultimate judge and decision maker. His anointed providence is our country, the United States of America."[13]

After William Barr acted to keep Mike Flynn out of prison, President Trump himself acted to reassure his longtime friend and convicted felon Roger Stone, who was set to start serving prison time. Taking to Twitter where, an early press secretary had said, Trump's posts were official White House statements, the president signaled that a pardon was in the offing. "Roger was a victim of a corrupt and illegal Witch Hunt, one which will go down as the greatest political crime in history," he wrote. "He can sleep well at night!"[14] If Stone did rest easy, it was probably because he knew some of the president's secrets. On July 10, he told journalist Howard Fineman, "He [Trump] knows I was under enormous pressure to turn on him. It would have eased my situation considerably. But I didn't." This was, of course, mobster logic worthy of the TV series *The Sopranos*. Stone in the past had spoken in such terms, once referring to a former Trump aide as a "rat" and a "Stoolie." He was not going to be a rat, at least not if Trump protected him. Stone also told Fineman he would prefer commutation of his sentence rather than a pardon, because a pardon would imply guilt and could force him in the future to testify before a new grand jury. As if on cue, within hours, and only days before Stone was to begin his prison sentence, the White House announced the commutation that Stone had foretold. Among the few Republicans willing to speak against this abuse of presidential power was Senator Mitt Romney. Taking to Twitter, he wrote, "Unprecedented, historic corruption: an American president commutes the sentence of a person convicted by a jury of lying to shield that very president."

The Federal Bureau of Prisons, meanwhile, furloughed Trump loyalist Paul Manafort from federal prison, allowing him to complete a seven-year sentence on Russia-related crimes at home because of the coronavirus epidemic. Manafort did not meet guidelines set during the epidemic to be released. Michael Cohen, who had testified against Trump before Congress, was released some days later because of the outbreak, but then was sent back to jail in July on charges he had violated his furlough. He was serving a three-year sentence for campaign violations and for lying to Congress.

With Russian internet activists reprising their 2016 roles in America's election, Trump, now in possession of the power of the presidency, was again pushing back on the very idea that Moscow might try to tip the scale in his favor. If he had learned anything in his first term and from the disgrace of impeachment, it wasn't that he should trust others, respect the rule of law, and lead with the intent of creating a stable society. He had learned, instead, that through force of will, he could reshape the Republican Party in his own image, control a Senate impeachment trial, and use the power of the Justice Department in new and dangerous ways.

Always willing to do what was required to prevail, Trump was on his way to becoming the first American autocrat, and Republicans in the Senate were poised to help him by conducting public hearings on how investigations into Russia's interference were begun. Scheduled for the summer, these proceedings would drag the country back to the beginning of the 2016 election scandal when Paul Manafort was trying to help Russia by changing the GOP platform and Moscow's hackers had busied themselves in the cause of Trump's campaign.

True to a strategy often deployed by dictators, who never give up on rewriting history, Trump had refused to accept the ample proof that federal authorities had properly opened investigations into the Russian effort to aid him in 2016. In May 2020, the president began repeating the term "Obamagate," a play on "Watergate," to suggest that the investigations had illegal origins.

Once again he raised the idea that officials from the prior administration be imprisoned, saying, "people should be going to jail for this stuff" and "this was all [Barack] Obama; this was all Biden. These people were corrupt." When asked to offer specifics about the "stuff" he mentioned, Trump replied to Phil Rucker of *The Washington Post*, "You know what the crime is. . . . The crime is very obvious to everybody." All that was obvious, of course, was that the president of the United States was trying to smear Biden and Obama.

Writing in *The New York Times*, Michael Tomasky noted that Trump's history-defying lies made a mockery of society's need for the shared truths that make nationhood possible. "[Trump] doesn't care if he's caught, because he has no regard for the democratic limits," wrote Tomasky. "His only real purposes are holding on to power by any means necessary and relentlessly reinventing himself to keep his reality show on the air for as long as possible."[15]

The Senate Intelligence Committee, led by Republican Richard Burr, had previously confirmed that the federal government had acted properly, but this finding conflicted with the president's desire to cast doubt on the origins of his Russia troubles. So it was that his chief enabler in the Senate, Judiciary Committee chairman Lindsey Graham, decided to issue subpoenas calling for testimony from a number of current and former intelligence officials.

Graham's effort violated many unwritten rules of Washington, including one that restrains senators from insulting their colleagues by trampling on the territory they had already covered and another that prohibits subjecting retired officials to unnecessary grilling. In this case Graham was willing to insult chairman Burr and grill three men Trump regarded as enemies—former FBI director James Comey, former CIA director John Brennan, and former director of National Intelligence James Clapper. However, Graham did stop short of giving President Trump a prize he really wanted: Barack Obama, under subpoena, answering the committee's questions.[16]

As Graham diligently continued his effort to rewrite the record to suit Donald Trump, others added to the evidence of the president's corruption and impunity. In June 2020, former national security advisor John Bolton reported in a new memoir that Trump had all but begged President Xi Jinping to help him win reelection by increasing Chinese imports of American farm products. (This would improve Trump's standing with rural voters.) According to Bolton's book, for which he was paid a $2 million advance, President Trump sought Xi's political help in June 2019 as he was also pressuring Ukrainian officials to go after his rival Joe Biden.

Overall, Bolton described President Trump as an ignorant man who thought Finland might be part of Russia and didn't know that the United Kingdom was a nuclear power. According to Bolton, Vladimir Putin had little trouble manipulating Trump who, in turn, put special effort into helping autocrats like Erdoğan of Turkey. Bolton added substantially to the weight of evidence that would have favored Trump's conviction at the impeachment trial. House Democrats noted Bolton's refusal to testify before their committees when he could have affected events in a real way. "Bolton may be an author but he's no patriot," said Adam Schiff on Twitter.[17]

•   •   •

In a previous season, Senator Graham might have reasonably expected that his planned hearings would succeed in shoring up support for the president as the political parties had their conventions and began the general election campaign in earnest. However, as of June 2020, when Graham issued his subpoenas, Donald Trump and his GOP allies found themselves swamped by unexpected events that promised to dampen the effect of their efforts to revive public interest in 2016 by hauling former officials to Capitol Hill and subjecting them to intense questions.

The enormous and obvious challenge to this plan to capture attention was the devastating pandemic that arose in China at the end of 2019 and quickly spread around the world. The novel coronavirus, which caused a disease named Covid-19, for Corona Virus Disease 2019, was highly infectious, and more deadly than ordinary flu viruses. Because it was a brand-new pathogen, no one on Earth was naturally immune to it from previous exposure, and scientists would have to begin the work of devising a vaccine from scratch. Immunologists estimated this task would take at least eighteen months. In the meantime, the coronavirus would spread along the pathways that infected people traveled, causing an illness that could kill in many different ways.

As the virus swept from community to community it made vast numbers of people sick and overwhelmed health care systems. Public officials could only respond by limiting travel, to slow the geographic progress of the outbreak, asking people to confine themselves to their homes, and requiring that face masks and other precautions be used in public settings. By the spring of 2020, the pandemic cast every aspect of daily life in shadow, overwhelmed every other concern, and, in America, revealed the president's fatal incompetence as his prediction that the virus would disappear was met with thousands upon thousands of deaths.

The president's response to the pandemic was hampered by a sense of denial within his administration and by drastic prior cuts that he had made to funding for the office responsible for monitoring and responding to disease outbreaks. In early January, Dr. Rick Bright, an official at the Department of Health and Human Services, sought emergency action to prevent a deadly pandemic. At high-level meetings his alarms met resistance until, as he would recall, "I was told that my urgings were causing a commotion and I was removed from those meetings."[18]

While Dr. Bright tried to get attention for the looming health crisis, the president focused on his impeachment troubles and on his long-standing practice of mocking his supposed enemies. At a big rally in Toledo, Ohio, he declared that he was more popular than Abraham Lincoln. He bad-mouthed Adam Schiff, invited the crowd to chant "Lock her up!" about Hillary Clinton, and said Nancy Pelosi was "crazy." Two days later he was resting at his Mar-a-Lago resort when he received a call from Alex Azar, the Health and Human Services secretary. The new virus was potentially a serious problem, Azar said. It could create a devastating global pandemic that would not spare the United States. Yet Trump said the pandemic was a minor problem that would quickly disappear.[19]

As experts warned of a wave of illness, the administration failed to ramp up the country's capacity for testing, and long-standing shortfalls in the national stockpile of equipment became evident. As the president predicted a minor and short-lived problem, coastal states with major international airports were overwhelmed with the sick and the dying. Shortages of equipment became so acute that, lacking federal coordination, states bid against each other for whatever supplies were available on a global market. Planes dispatched to China, the primary locus of production of masks and protective equipment, to pick up supplies were met at U.S. airports by news cameras and armed guards. Governors formed regional compacts to give each other the support they had hoped to receive from Washington. Doctors and nurses in less-affected communities flew to those that were hard hit and volunteered to help. In New York City, the American epicenter, morgues filled, and excess bodies were transferred to refrigerated trailers that were brought to hospital parking lots by trucks.

Many volumes will be written about President Trump's failed response to the pandemic that, within 90 days, killed more Americans than all the wars since the Second World War put together. With the death toll topping 150,000, the pandemic forced so many closures of schools, businesses, and communities that the country was thrown into recession and the president lost the argument that he should be reelected because he had aided the economy. At the same time, his performance at news conferences where he touted dangerous and unproven treatments and speculated about whether household cleaners could be ingested by sufferers made him seem incapable of leadership.

As it devastated Trump's presidency, the pandemic contributed decisively to Joe Biden's easy capture of the Democratic nomination for president, ensuring that the man whom Trump had tried to undermine with his Ukraine scheme would become his competitor without suffering the bruising that typically comes with heated primary contests. One sign of the sense of desperation felt by Team Trump came as his son Eric used a national television appearance to claim the pandemic was a hoax perpetrated by Democrats. "You watch, they'll milk it every single day between now and November 3," said Eric Trump. "And guess what, after November 3, coronavirus will magically, all of a sudden, go away and disappear and everybody will be able to reopen."

By July 17, 2020, while many other countries had weathered the first phase of the pandemic well, the United States was still in crisis and led the nations of the world in the number of Covid-19 cases, 3.5 million—and deaths— more than 140,000. The U.S. death rate per 100,000 people was third-worst in the world after the United Kingdom and Chile. This state of affairs was widely blamed on the administration's failures at the start of the pandemic, which deprived the country of an organized national response. Left to their own, many states refused to implement basic public health protections—stay-at-home recommendations and face masks during public activities—and the president, through his own actions, signaled that these practices weren't necessary. As Covid-19 spread to every state in the Union, Biden's long presence in national politics came to be seen as a reassuring alternative to the lurching, emotional style of President Trump. In polls of likely voters Biden opened a sizable lead.[20]

• • •

Revealed by the pandemic to be both incompetent and devoid of empathy, Trump was faced by another enormous challenge, which he was also unable to meet. The inciting incident was the killing of a Black man named George Floyd, who died at the hands of three white Minneapolis police officers, one of whom kept his knee on Floyd's neck for 8 minutes and 46 seconds. A video recording of this killing, which captured Floyd's desperate cries of "I can't breathe" and onlookers pleading for the police to remove the pressure, was immediately posted to the internet, where it was seen by millions of people.

George Floyd's death was all too familiar in a country that had seen similar killings of African American men who encountered white police officers, some of whom had uttered the same exact words: "I can't breathe." Street protests in Minnesota inspired similar actions elsewhere. In America, where tens of millions of people had spent weeks away from their jobs and without social contact due to the pandemic, neighborhoods erupted in spontaneous protests and people took their anger and frustration to the streets until, in every state, people of every race, ethnic group, age, and identity were marching together. For a tense ten days, some cities were affected by looters and arsonists who, taking advantage of the protests and the cover of night, caused millions of dollars in damage.

President Trump's response to the protests was straight out of the 1960s. In fact, he quoted a police chief of that era who had warned "when the looting starts, the shooting starts," and then used his unique authority in Washington, D.C., to order federal troops and police to clear demonstrators from a park near the White House. Widely aired, the scenes of chemicals and truncheons being used against peaceful citizens shocked the nation. When Trump then walked to a nearby Episcopal church, not to pray but to pose with a Bible, the shock turned to outrage for the local bishop who objected to the parish being used for political purposes.

As the president repeatedly posted the phrase "Law and Order" on social media, public sentiment shifted markedly in favor of the protests and polls indicated many Americans believed that the country suffered from systemic racism in many institutions. Support for the Black Lives Matter movement, long rejected by the president, rose sharply, and states began to revise laws to limit the ways police could restrain those under arrest. As congressional leaders in both parties voiced support for stripping the names of pro-slavery Civil War traitors from U.S. military facilities, the president came out squarely against the idea.[21]

Taken together, the Covid-19 pandemic and the civil rights protests exposed Donald Trump to be inadequate in profound and obvious ways. His impeachment, though just months in the past, seemed like it had occurred in some distant era. However, that trauma, like the one that followed, could be seen as the inevitable product of the dangerous experiment begun when a demagogue who had made corruption and impunity part of his public identity gained the presidency. What remained in doubt was whether Americans had seen and heard enough of Donald Trump to conclude that the experiment had failed.

ACKNOWLEDGMENTS

We began work on this book as the House Committee on the Judiciary received Special Counsel Robert Mueller's *Report on the Investigation into Russian Interference in the 2016 Presidential Election*. At that moment we considered Rudy Giuliani a secondary figure in the drama. We had not heard of Igor Fruman and Lev Parnas, and the "Three Amigos" conjured a comic film starring Martin Short, Chevy Chase, and Steve Martin.

Prior to the report's arrival at the committee, the manipulations practiced by Attorney General William Barr, who offered distortions of Mueller's findings to influence public opinion, foreshadowed the furious propaganda effort that was to come. Given President Trump's record of lying and evasion, we were expecting to be buffeted by these winds of rhetoric. What we could not imagine were the turns that would bring the nation into the byzantine scheme that found Giuliani, Fruman, Parnas, and the Three Amigos furiously trying to blackmail a war-ravaged Ukraine into joining a scheme to smear former U.S. vice president Joe Biden and rewrite the record of the 2016 election.

The revelations of new and ongoing White House scandals required us to make daily, and sometimes hourly, shifts in our focus. At St. Martin's Press our editors Thomas Dunne, Stephen Power, and Pronoy Sarkar stayed the course when others would have abandoned ship. Managing Editor Alan Bradshaw and copy editors Sara Lynn and Christopher Ensey stuck with us as our manuscript grew in size and complexity. It was no easy thing for them to deal with a text that presented so many figures in such far-flung places pursuing such complex schemes. Eric Rayman, who worked under the same conditions, provided a legal review that came with unexpected and welcome literary assistance.

Fortunately, a host of experts, witnesses, officials, and helpers were ready to aid us as we struggled to grasp what had occurred and was continuing to transpire. Always first among our collaborators, Toni Raiten-D'Antonio and

Musha Salinas Eisner served as reliable sounding boards and wise evaluators. Like us, they couldn't have guessed that a daunting task would grow so much more demanding, but they remained steadfast.

First among our guides in Washington was John Cavanagh, who helped us make early contact with key sources. In Kiev we received similar assistance from Maria Varenikova, whose deep understanding of her country's affairs helped us jump-start our own education. Marichka came to us on the recommendation of Andrew Kramer of the Moscow bureau of *The New York Times*. We are grateful to them and to Keith Darden, a Ukraine expert at American University, who was a good-natured tutor. Similar kind guidance was offered by Bill Press and Stan Greenberg, two men who know how things work.

Some of our sources in the Washington bureaucracy cannot be named here because they fear retribution from an administration that devotes much time and energy to punishing truth-tellers. They know we consider ourselves indebted to them. Among those who would never seek acknowledgment but deserve it we would count Jonathan Winer, Lawrence Wilkerson, Richard Luchette, Jamie Smith, Katherine Schneider, Bobby Mattina, Gautam Rhaghavan, Jason Atterman, Sally Tucker, Lisa Bianco, Rachael Hartford, Richard Davidson, and Meaghan McCabe. We received great help understanding whistleblowers and the law from Louis Clark, Tom Devine, David Seide, Andrew Harmon, Andrew Bakaj, and Mark Zaid.

Among the representatives and senators who gave us time they really didn't have we count Sherrod Brown, Joaquin Castro, David Cicilline, Gerry Connolly, Ted Deutch, Denny Heck, Pramila Jayapal, Robert Menendez, Debbie Mucarsel-Powell, Joe Neguse, Jamie Raskin, and Sheldon Whitehouse.

We benefited greatly from the work of daily journalists whose work established both an accurate record of events and set important points on our compasses. Reporters, editors, and commentators at CNN, *The Washington Post*, *The New York Times*, and other news outlets made it possible for us to find the threads of the narratives that are entwined in this book. Some day someone will describe the long, consistent, and highly disciplined way that the press responded to the chaotic, frenetic, and dishonest style of President Trump, his aides, and his allies. With mere tweets, which could be concocted in minutes or less, they produced an endless stream of provocations and falsities. Knocked off balance by the way that the president and so many others abandoned the truth, journalists had to get used to examining every utterance and noting how they veered from the facts. Since this work required far more effort than was expended by those who made false statements and claims, they also had to develop a sense of detachment (being alarmed is distracting) and stamina. By the time the president had his fateful call with the president of Ukraine, the press was both ready to recognize that he was capable of such deceit and in the right condition to pursue the truth wherever it led.

Our observations about the news media could also be applied to members of the United States House of Representatives and the Senate. In both these bodies, lawmakers and their aides have been required to adapt to an unprecedented level of confusion and resistance as the president and much of the executive branch sought to obscure their behaviors and avoid accountability. The level of insult and stonewalling that lawmakers faced as they sought to perform their constitutional duties required them to act with tenacity, care, precision, and seriousness even as they were confronted with endless absurdities. After watching at close range we came away feeling that Congress was able to function more effectively than critics across the political spectrum would allow.

In our work with freelancers and others who came to our aid when the scope of this project seemed too great, we learned a similar lesson about the sense of mission that comes to the fore when people are asked to help. Stony Brook University's Barbara Selvin's intern crew of Kimberly Brown, Maya Brown, Cecilia Fuentes, Mike Gaisser, and Sherin Samuel ably assembled background information on the key players in the impeachment process and kept updating files as developments came at a breakneck pace.

Finally, we acknowledge the great work of our two key researchers, Lydia Carey and Victoria deSilverio, who built timelines, managed the Donald Trump "tweetpile," chased facts, and organized source notes. They raced into the night on many occasions, always professional, always persistent, and never failed to offer insights along with information, which helped us to understand the complex story as it unfolded and to see what it revealed about the character of the individuals we had under examination and of the nation that some abused and others defended.

NOTES

All interviews quoted in this text took place between May 1, 2019, and April 15, 2020.

INTRODUCTION

1 Representative Gerald Connolly, interviews with authors; Chris Baynes, "Trump Called Pelosi to Ask If They Could 'Work Something Out' Before Impeachment Launched, Report Says," *Independent*, September 25, 2019, https://www .independent.co.uk/news/world/americas/us-politics/trump-impeachment-news -pelosi-call-ukraine-whistleblower-a9119426.html.

2 U.S. House of Representatives Committee for Foreign Relations, "Three House Committees Launch Wide-Ranging Investigation into Trump-Giuliani Ukraine Scheme," press release, September 9, 2019, https://foreignaffairs.house .gov/press-releases?ID=D365D32B-D9D1-4A68-B07E-28B95DA593B0; Caitlin Emma and Connor O'Brien, "Trump Holds Up Ukraine Military Aid Meant to Confront Russia," *Politico*, August 28, 2019, https://www.politico.com/story/2019 /08/28/trump-ukraine-military-aid-russia-1689531.

3 Martin Pengelly and Victoria Bekiempis, "Trump Goes on Offensive over Biden and Ukraine as Schiff Ponders Impeachment," *Guardian*, September 22, 2019, https://www.theguardian.com/us-news/2019/sep/22/donald-trump-rudy-giuliani -joe-biden-ukraine.

4 Marshall Cohen, "Lewandowski Stonewalls and Frustrates Democrats in Contentious Capitol Hill Hearing," CNN, September 17, 2019, https://edition.cnn .com/2019/09/17/politics/corey-lewandowski-testifies-house-judiciary-committee /index.html.

5 Sheryl Gay Stolberg, "Pelosi and Her No. 2 Go Back 50 Years. But They're Not Quite Friends," *New York Times*, December 13, 2018, https://www.nytimes.com /2018/12/13/us/politics/pelosi-hoyer-house-whip-democrats.html.

6 MSNBC (@MSNBC), Twitter, September 24, 2019, 5:55 p.m., https:// twitter.com/MSNBC/status/1176631193279913985; Lindsey McPherson, "Pelosi

Announces Formal Impeachment Inquiry, but Leaves Some Questions," *Roll Call*, September 24, 2019, https://www.rollcall.com/2019/09/24/pelosi-announces-formal -impeachment-inquiry-but-leaves-some-questions/; Sheryl Gay Stolberg, "Pelosi Tells Trump: 'You Have Come into My Wheelhouse,'" *New York Times*, September 25, 2019, https://www.nytimes.com/2019/09/25/us/politics/pelosi-intelligence -impeachment.html.

7   McPherson, "Pelosi Announces Formal Impeachment Inquiry."

8   "Nancy Pelosi's Public and Private Remarks on Trump Impeachment," NBC News, September 24, 2019, https://www.nbcnews.com/politics/trump-impeachment -inquiry/transcript-nancy-pelosi-s-speech-trump-impeachment-n1058351.

9   "Trump: 'I Have an Article 2 Where I Have the Right to Do Whatever I Want as President,'" *Week*, July 23, 2019, https://theweek.com/speedreads/854487 /trump-have-article-2-where-have-right-whatever-want-president.

10   Britta L. Jewell and Nicholas P. Jewell, "The Huge Cost of Waiting to Contain the Pandemic," *New York Times*, April 14, 2020, https://www.nytimes.com /2020/04/14/opinion/covid-social-distancing.html; Jessica Snouwaert, "2 Medical Experts Estimate 90% of Coronavirus Deaths in the US Could Have Been Avoided If Everyone Started Social Distancing on March 2," *Business Insider*, April 15, 2020, https://www.businessinsider.com/coronavirus-deaths-us-could-avoided-by-social -distancing-sooner-experts-2020-4.

11   *For Donald Trump's lifelong record of self-promotion and mythmaking, see:* Harry Hurt III, *The Lost Tycoon* (Brattleboro, VT: Echo Points Books & Media, 2018); Gwenda Blair, *The Trumps: Three Generations That Built an Empire* (New York: Simon and Schuster, 2000); Tim O'Brien, *TrumpNation: The Art of Being the Donald* (New York: Warner, 2005); David Cay Johnston, *The Making of Donald Trump* (Brooklyn, NY: Melville House, 2016); Michael D'Antonio, *Never Enough: Donald Trump and the Pursuit of Success* (New York: St. Martin's Press, 2015); Michael Kranish and Marc Fisher, *Trump Revealed: The Definitive Biography of the 45th President* (New York: Scribner, 2016).

CHAPTER 1: INTERNATIONAL MAN OF MYSTERY

1   William Manchester, *The Last Lion* (New York: Bantam, 2013), 87.

2   "Killing Pavel," YouTube video, 49:30, posted by Organized Crime and Corruption Reporting Project, May 10, 2017, https://www.youtube.com/watch?v =liSa5OFCkf4; Christopher Miller, "Thousands Stand in Line to Mourn Slain Journalist Pavel Sheremet in Kyiv," Radio Free Europe, July 22, 2016, https://www.rferl .org/a/ukraine-sheremet-memorial-car-bomb/27873620.html.

3   Michael Kranish and Tom Hamburger, "Paul Manafort's 'Lavish Lifestyle' Highlighted in Indictment," *Washington Post*, October 30, 2017, https://

www.washingtonpost.com/politics/paul-manaforts-lavish-lifestyle-highlighted-in
-indictment/2017/10/30/23615680-bd8f-11e7-8444-a0d4f04b89eb_story.html;
Benjamin Oreskes, "Where in Beverly Hills Did Paul Manafort Spend $500,000 on
Suits?," *Los Angeles Times,* October 31, 2017.

4   "Paul Manafort Reacts to 'Speechgate,' RNC," YouTube video, 4:03, posted
by ABC News, July 20, 2016, https://www.youtube.com/watch?v=6k2cGilGg0g.

5   Hadas Gold, "Trump Campaign Manager Gets Rough with Breitbart Reporter," *Politico,* March 6, 2016, https://www.politico.com/blogs/on-media/2016/03
/trump-campaign-manager-breitbart-reporter-220472.

6   Pamela Brogan, "THE TORTURERS' LOBBY: How Human Rights-
Abusing Nations Are Represented in Washington," Center for Public Integrity,
1992, https://cloudfront-files-1.publicintegrity.org/legacy_projects/pdf_reports
/THETORTURERSLOBBY.pdf.

7   Josh Rogin, "The Trump Campaign Guts GOP Anti-Russia Stance on
Ukraine," *Washington Post,* July 18, 2016, https://www.washingtonpost.com/opinions
/global-opinions/trump-campaign-guts-gops-anti-russia-stance-on-ukraine/2016
/07/18/98adb3b0-4cf3-11e6-a7d8-13d06b37f256_story.html; Sally Bronston,
"Trump Chairman Denies Any Role in Platform Change," NBC News, July 31,
2016, https://www.nbcnews.com/meet-the-press/trump-chairman-denies-any-role
-platform-change-ukraine-n620511.

8   *For Putin and the oligarchs, see:* Fiona Hill and Glifford G. Gaddy, *Mr. Putin:
Operative in the Kremlin* (Washington, DC: Brookings Institution Press, 2013); Ellen
Barry, "Putin Plays Sheriff for Cowboy Capitalists," *New York Times,* June 4, 2009;
Anders Aslund, "Vladimir Putin Is Russia's Biggest Oligarch," *Washington Post,* June
5, 2019; *for oligarch system, see:* Hill and Gaddy, *Mr. Putin,* 203–209; *for Deripaska, see:*
Hill and Gaddy, *Mr. Putin,* 133–134, 196; Franklin Foer, "Paul Manafort, American Hustler," *Atlantic,* March 2018; Cristina Maza, "Trump Lawyer Rudy Giuliani's
Mysterious Ties to Russia and Former Soviet Union Go Back Decades, Experts Argue," *Newsweek,* November 16, 2018, https://www.newsweek.com/giuliani-mysterious
-ties-russia-former-soviet-union-decades-1215349; Peter Beinart, "The U.S. Needs to
Face Up to Its Long History of Election Meddling," *Atlantic,* July 22, 2018, https://
www.theatlantic.com/ideas/archive/2018/07/the-us-has-a-long-history-of-election
-meddling/565538/; Sandra Tan, "The Radical Adventures of Conservative Radio
Host Mike Caputo," *Buffalo News,* March 5, 2016, https://buffalonews.com/2016
/03/05/the-radical-adventures-of-conservative-radio-host-mike-caputo; "Can a New
Russia Emerge from the Rubble of Its Past?," *Chicago Tribune,* October 6, 1993, https://
www.chicagotribune.com/news/ct-xpm-1993-10-06-9310060157-story.html.

9   Edward Lucas, "Don't Be Fooled by Her Angelic Looks, She's as Ruth-
less as She's Corrupt: A Withering Portrait of Ukraine's 'Saviour' by EDWARD

LUCAS, a Russia Expert Who Knows Her Well," *Daily Mail,* February 23, 2014, https://www.dailymail.co.uk/news/article-2566299/Dont-fooled-angelic-looks-shes-ruthless-shes-corrupt-A-withering-portrait-Ukraines-saviour-EDWARD-LUCAS-Russia-expert-knows-well.html; Julia Ioffe, "Kiev Chameleon," *New Republic,* January 4, 2010, https://newrepublic.com/article/72252/kiev-chameleon.

10   "Ukraine: Firtash Makes His Case to the USG," WikiLeaks, December 10, 2008, https://wikileaks.org/plusd/cables/08KYIV2414_a.html.

11   Cristina Maza, "Paul Manafort's 'Russian Brain,' Konstantin Kilimnik, Is a Key Part of Robert Mueller's Russia Investigation, Court Documents Reveal," *Newsweek,* January 16, 2019, https://www.newsweek.com/konstantin-kilimnik-paul-manafort-mueller-russia-1293712.

12   Jeff Horwitz and Chad Day, "AP Exclusive: Before Trump Job, Manafort Worked to Aid Putin," Associated Press, March 22, 2017, https://apnews.com/12 2ae0b5848345faa88108a03de40c5a/AP-Exclusive:-Before-Trump-job,-Manafort-w orked-to-aid-Putin; Foer, "Paul Manafort"; Stephanie Baker and Daryna Krasno-lutska, "Paul Manafort's Lucrative Ukraine Years Are Central to the Russia Probe," *Bloomberg,* May 22, 2017, https://www.bloomberg.com/news/features/2017-05-22 /paul-manafort-s-lucrative-ukraine-years-are-central-to-the-russia-probe; Anton Troianovski, "'Whatever He Wants': Inside the Region Russian Oligarch Oleg Deripaska Runs Like a Personal Fiefdom," *Washington Post,* February 15, 2019, https://www.washingtonpost.com/world/europe/whatever-he-wants-inside-the-region russian-oligarch-oleg-deripaska-runs-like-a-personal-fiefdom/2019/02/15 /c00f7e10-1e61-11e9-a759-2b8541bbbe20_story.html; Tom Philpott, "The Rise and Fall of Ukraine's Fertilizer King," *Mother Jones,* December 1, 2019, https://www .motherjones.com/politics/2019/12/dmitry-firtash-trump-giuliani-ukraine-fertilizer -natural-gas-oligarch-ukraine/; Taras Kuzio and Paul D'Anieri, "The Soviet Origins of Russian Hybrid Warfare," E-International Relations, July 17, 2018, https://www.e .info/2018/06/17/the-soviet-origins-of-russian-hybrid-warfare/#_ftn27.

13   Shaunacy Ferro, "The Insane Opulence of the Ukrainian Presidential Palace," *Fast Company,* February 5, 2014, https://www.fastcompany.com/3027259 /the-insane-opulence-of-the-ukrainian-presidential-palace; Patrick Kingsley, "When Rebels Toured the Palace: How Does Ukraine's Presidential Compound Measure Up?," *Guardian,* February 24, 2014, https://www.theguardian.com /world/2014/feb/24/rebels-toured-palace-ukraine-presidential-compound-viktor -yanukovych; Sergii Leshchenko, "The True Story of Yanukovych's Black Ledger," *Kyiv Post,* November 24, 2019; Katya Gorchinskaya, "He Killed for the Maidan," *Foreign Policy,* February 26, 2016, https://foreignpolicy.com/2016/02/26/he-killed -for-the-maidan/.

14   Foer, "Paul Manafort"; Natasha Bertrand, "How a Russian Disinfo Op

Got Trump Impeached," *Politico*, January 22, 2020, https://www.politico.com/news/2020/01/22/ukraine-russia-disinformation-election-trump-101895.

15 Sonam Sheth, "Newly Unsealed Court Filing Shows Paul Manafort Was More Indebted to Putin Ally Oleg Deripaska Than Previously Known," *Business Insider*, June 27, 2018, https://www.businessinsider.com/court-document-shows-oleg-deripaska-loaned-paul-manafort-10-million-2018-6.

16 Gorchinskaya, "He Killed for the Maidan"; Chris Sommerfeldt, "Ukrainian Attorney Calls for Probe into Text Message Claims That Paul Manafort 'Knowingly' Had People Killed," New York *Daily News*, March 10, 2017. For all Manafort texts revealed, see https://emma.best/2018/07/20/a-note-on-the-manafort-texts/.

17 Laurens Cerulus, "How Ukraine Became a Test Bed for Cyberweaponry," *Politico EU*, February 14, 2019, https://www.politico.eu/article/ukraine-cyber-war-frontline-russia-malware-attacks/; Kim Zetter, "Inside the Cunning, Unprecedented Hack of Ukraine's Power Grid," *Wired*, March 3, 2016, https://www.wired.com/2016/03/inside-cunning-unprecedented-hack-ukraines-power-grid/; transcript, Manafort text messages, https://ia803108.us.archive.org/5/items/ManafortTextMessages/Manafort%20text%20transcript.pdf; Benjamin Fearnow, "Paul Manafort's Daughter Files to Legally Change Her Name," *Newsweek*, September 2, 2018, https://www.newsweek.com/paul-manafort-jessica-manafort-daughter-name-change-jessica-bond-manhattan-1101480.

18 "Who Is Viktor Trepak, Ukraine's New Deputy Prosecutor General?," *Hromadske International*, October 9, 2019, https://en.hromadske.ua/posts/who-is-viktor-trepak-ukraines-new-deputy-prosecutor-general.

19 Tom Hamburger, Rosalind S. Helderman, Carol D. Leonnig, and Adam Entous, "Manafort Offered to Give Russian Billionaire 'Private Briefings' on 2016 Campaign," *Washington Post*, September 20, 2017, https://www.washingtonpost.com/politics/manafort-offered-to-give-russian-billionaire-private-briefings-on-2016-campaign/2017/09/20/399bba1a-9d48-11e7-8ea1-ed975285475e_story.html; Simon Shuster, "Exclusive: Russian Ex-Spy Pressured Manafort over Debts to an Oligarch," *Time*, December 28, 2019, https://time.com/5490169/paul-manafort-victor-boyarkin-debts/.

20 Devin Gannon, "Problems at 666 Fifth Avenue Tower Linked to Jared Kushner's White House Role," 6sqft, September 14, 2017, https://www.6sqft.com/problems-at-666-fifth-avenue-tower-linked-to-jared-kushners-white-house-role/.

21 Sharon LaFraniere, Kenneth P. Vogel, and Scott Shane, "In Closed Hearing, a Clue About 'the Heart' of Mueller's Russia Inquiry," *New York Times*, February 10, 2019; Peter Stone, "Is Oleg Deripaska the Missing Link in the Trump-Russia Investigation?," *Guardian*, January 29, 2019, https://www.theguardian.com/world/2019/jan/29/oleg-deripaska-paul-manafort-trump-russia-investigation; Rosalind

S. Helderman and Tom Hamburger, "How Manafort's 2016 Meeting with a Russian Employee at New York Cigar Club Goes to 'the Heart' of Mueller's Probe," *Washington Post*, February 12, 2019, https://www.washingtonpost.com/politics/how-manaforts-2016-meeting-with-a-russian-employee-at-new-york-cigar-club-goes-to-the-heart-of-muellers-probe/2019/02/12/655f84dc-2d67-11e9-8ad3-9a5b113ecd3c_story.html.

22 Jason Leopold, Zoe Tillman, Ellie Hall, Emma Loop, and Anthony Cormier, "The Mueller Report's Secret Memos," *BuzzFeed*, November 3, 2019, https://www.buzzfeednews.com/article/jasonleopold/mueller-report-secret-memos-1?ref=bfnsplash.

23 Matt Naham, "What Happened in the Grand Havana Room? Intriguing Connections Emerge from Mueller Probe Deep Dive," *Law & Crime*, February 12, 2019, https://lawandcrime.com/high-profile/what-happened-in-the-grand-havana-room-intriguing-connections-in-mueller-probe-deep-dive/; Greg Walters, "Alleged Spy Took a Russian Oligarch's Jet for Secret 2016 Meeting with Paul Manafort," *Vice*, November 12, 2018, https://www.vice.com/en_us/article/439vdn/alleged-spy-took-a-russian-oligarchs-jet-for-secret-2016-meeting-with-paul-manafort; ibid.

CHAPTER 2: WORLDS COLLIDE

1 "Trump Tower's Woes Continue Above and Below; Condo Sales Now at 2006 Levels," CityRealty, October 31, 2019, https://www.cityrealty.com/nyc/market-insight/features/great listings/trump-tower039s-woes-continue-above-below-condo-sales-2006-levels/32901; Kevin Wack, "Bank CEO's Fire-and-Rehire Maneuver Reaps Windfall at Taxpayer Expense," American Banker, https://www.americanbanker.com/news/bank-ceos-fire-and-rehire-maneuver-reaps-windfall-at-taxpayer-expense; Kevin Wack, "CEO Calk Conspired with Manafort to Defraud His Own Bank: Prosecutors," American Banker, August 13, 2018, https://www.americanbanker.com/news/ceo-calk-conspired-with-manafort-to-defraud-his-own-bank-prosecutor; "N.Y. Charges Against Manafort Involve a Relatively Low-Profile Chicago Banker," Chicago Business, March 13, 2019, https://www.chicagobusiness.com/finance-banking/ny-charges-against-manafort-involve-relatively-low-profile-chicago-banker.

2 Jack Gillum, Chad Day, and Jeff Horwitz, "AP Exclusive: Manafort Firm Received Ukraine Ledger Payout," Associated Press, April 12, 2017, https://apnews.com/20cfc75c82eb4a67b94e624e97207e23.

3 Bob Woodward, *Fear* (New York: Simon & Schuster, 2018), 21–23.

4 Andrew E. Kramer and Barry Meier, "Ukraine Releases More Details on Payments for Trump Aide, Paul Manafort," *New York Times*, August 18, 2016, https://www.nytimes.com/2016/08/19/us/ukraine-releases-more-details-on

-payments-for-trump-aide.html?searchResultPosition=2; Jeff Horwitz and Chad Day, "AP Exclusive: Before Trump Job, Manafort Worked to Aid Putin," Associated Press, March 22, 2017, https://apnews.com/122ae0b5848345faa88108a03de40 c5a/AP-Exclusive:-Before-Trump-job,-Manafort-worked-to-aid-Putin; Andrew E. Kramer, Mike McIntire, and Barry Meier, "Secret Ledger in Ukraine Lists Cash for Donald Trump's Campaign Chief," *New York Times*, August 14, 2016, https://www .nytimes.com/2016/08/15/us/politics/paul-manafort-ukraine-donald-trump.html ?searchResultPosition=4; Jonathan Martin, Jim Rutenberg, and Maggie Haberman, "Donald Trump Appoints Media Firebrand to Run Campaign," *New York Times*, August 17, 2016, https://www.nytimes.com/2016/08/18/us/politics/donald-trump -stephen-bannon-paul-manafort.html?searchResultPosition=7.

5   Rosalind S. Helderman and Spencer S. Hsu, "Internal Mueller Documents Show Trump Campaign Chief Pushed Unproven Theory Ukraine Hacked Democrats," *Washington Post*, November 2, 2019, https://www.washingtonpost .com/politics/internal-mueller-documents-show-trump-campaign-chief-suggested -ukraine-hacked-democrats-during-2016-campaign/2019/11/02/cc8e461c-fd90 -11e9-ac8c-8eced29ca6ef_story.html.

6   Peter Pomerantsev, "To Unreality—and Beyond," *JoDS*, October 23, 2019, https://jods.mitpress.mit.edu/pub/ic90uta1; Christopher Paul and Miriam Matthews, "The Russian 'Firehouse of Falsehood' Propaganda Machine," RAND Corporation, 2016, https://www.rand.org/content/dam/rand/pubs/perspectives /PE100/PE198/RAND_PE198.pdf.

7   Dana Priest, "The Disruptive Career of Michael Flynn, Trump's National-Security Adviser," *New Yorker*, November 23, 2016, https://www.newyorker.com/news /news-desk/the-disruptive-career-of-trumps-national-security-adviser; John Kruzel, "Timeline of Michael Flynn's Turn, from Trump Aide to Mueller Witness," PolitiFact, December 5, 2018, https://www.politifact.com/article/2018/dec/05/detailing-michael -flynns-turn-trump-mueller/; Dana Priest and Greg Miller, "He Was One of the Most Respected Intel Officers of His Generation. Now He's Leading 'Lock Her Up' Chants," *Washington Post*, August 15, 2016, https://www.washingtonpost.com/world /national-security/nearly-the-entire-national-security-establishment-has-rejected -trumpexcept-for-this-man/2016/08/15/d5072d96-5e4b-11e6-8e45-477372e89d78 _story.html.

8   Helderman and Hsu, "Internal Mueller Documents"; Josh Clinton and Carrie Roush, "Poll: Persistent Partisan Divide over 'Birther' Question," NBC News, August 10, 2016, https://www.nbcnews.com/politics/2016-election/poll-persistent -partisan-divide-over-birther-question-n627446; Tom Stafford, "How Liars Create the 'Illusion of Truth,'" BBC, October 26, 2016, https://www.bbc.com/future/article /20161026-how-liars-create-the-illusion-of-truth.

9   Nick Gass, "Trump: I Don't Trust U.S. Intelligence Information," *Politico*, August 17, 2016, https://www.politico.com/story/2016/08/trump-us-intelligence-briefing-227109.

10   Ken Dilanian, Robert Windrem, and William Arkin, "What Really Happened at Donald Trump's Intelligence Briefing," NBC News, September 8, 2016, https://www.nbcnews.com/politics/2016-election/u-s-official-donald-trump-s-body-language-claim-doesn-n644856; Alexander Griffing, "Remember When Donald Trump Appeared on Alex Jones' 'InfoWars,'" *Haaretz*, August 6, 2018, https://www.haaretz.com/us-news/remember-when-donald-trump-appeared-on-alex-jones-infowars-1.5443723; Oliver Willis, "The Alex Jones Influence: Trump's 'Deep State' Fears Come from His Conspiracy Theorist Ally and Adviser," *Salon*, March 10, 2017, https://www.salon.com/2017/03/09/the-alex-jones-influence-trumps-deep-state-fears-come-from-his-conspiracy-theorist-ally-and-adviser_partner/; Oliver Willis, "Totally Synced: How Donald Trump and Alex Jones' Conspiracy Theory Movement Speaks with One Voice," Media Matters for America, August 12, 2016, https://www.mediamatters.org/donald-trump/totally-synced-how-donald-trump-and-alex-jones-conspiracy-theory-movement-speaks-one?redirect_source=/blog/2016/08/12/totally-synced-how-donald-trump-and-alex-jones-conspiracy-theory-movement-speaks-one-voice/212362.

11   Rosalind S. Helderman, Josh Dawsey, Paul Sonne, and Tom Hamburger, "How Two Soviet-Born Emigres Made It into Elite Trump Circles—and the Center of the Impeachment Storm," *Washington Post*, October 12, 2019, https://www.washingtonpost.com/politics/how-two-soviet-born-emigres-made-it-into-elite-trump-circles—and-the-center-of-the-impeachment-storm/2019/10/12/9a3c03be-ec53-11e9-85c0-85a098e47b37_story.html.

12   Alex Daugherty, David Smiley, Nicholas Nehamas, and Kevin G. Hall, "Florida Businessmen with Giuliani, Ukraine Ties Arrested on Campaign Finance Charges," *Miami Herald*, October 10, 2019, https://www.miamiherald.com/news/politics-government/a rticle235903397.html; "Odessa's Regards to Trump: How Businessman Igor Fruman Found Himself in the Center of an American Scandal" (in Russian), NV.ua, November 9, 2019, https://nv.ua/ukraine/politics/impichment-prezidenta-trampa-pochemu-arestovali-frumana-novosti-mira-50052320.html; Tom Hamburger, Rosalind S. Helderman, and Dana Priest, "In 'Little Moscow,' Russians Helped Donald Trump's Brand Survive the Recession," *Washington Post*, November 4, 2016, https://www.washingtonpost.com/politics/in-little-moscow-russians-helped-donald-trumps-brand-survive-the-recession/2016/11/04/f9dbd38e-97cf-11e6-bb29-bf2701dbe0a3_story.html.

13   Jeff Ostrowski and Wayne Washington, "Lev Parnas in Palm Beach County: Unpaid Bills, Failed Business Deals," *Palm Beach Post*, October 24, 2019,

https://www.palmbeachpost.com/news/20191024/lev-parnas-in-palm-beach-county
-unpaid-bills-failed-business-deals; Jane Musgrave and John Pacenti, "Lev Parnas'
Life in Boca Raton: Suburban Dad Got His Start in Penny Stocks on 'Maggot
Mile,'" *Palm Beach Post,* January 24, 2020, https://www.palmbeachpost.com/news
/20200124/lev-parnasrsquo-life-in-boca-raton-suburban-dad-got-his-start-in
-penny-stocks-on-lsquomaggot-milersquo.

14   Ben Schreckinger, "2014 Photo Shows Earlier Ties Between Trump and
Indicted Giuliani Associate," *Politico,* October 12, 2019, https://www.politico.com
/news/2019/10/12/trump-lev-parnas-photo-giuliani-045137; Adam Entous, "How
Lev Parnas Became Part of the Trump Campaign's 'One Big Family,'" *New Yorker,*
October 15, 2019, https://www.newyorker.com/news/news-desk/why-lev-parnas
-worked-for-rudy-giuliani-and-donald-trump?verso=true; Shelby Holliday, "Private
Photos of Indicted Donor Depict Ties to Trump, Giuliani," *Wall Street Journal,* October 21, 2019, https://www.wsj.com/video/private-photos-of-indicted-donor-depict
-ties-to-trump-giuliani/7EED4946-5201-4D70-A8FF-0516DCC1488E.html.

CHAPTER 3: WHY NOT GET ALONG WITH RUSSIA?

1   "Donald Trump on Russia, Advice from Barack Obama and How He Will
Lead," *Time,* December 7, 2016, https://time.com/4591183/time-person-of-the
-year-2016-donald-trump-interview/; Robert Farley, "Trump Landslide? Nope,"
FactCheck.org, November 29, 2016, https://www.factcheck.org/2016/11/trump
-landslide-nope/.

2   Mara Gay and Felicia Schwartz, "Rudy Giuliani Lobbies to Be Secretary
of State," *Wall Street Journal,* November 25, 2016, https://www.wsj.com/articles/rudy
-giuliani-lobbies-to-be-secretary-of-state-1480029769; Bradley Olson, "Rex Tillerson, a Candidate for Secretary of State, Has Ties to Vladimir Putin," *Wall Street
Journal,* December 6, 2016, https://www.wsj.com/articles/donald-trump-candidate
-for-state-has-close-ties-to-vladimir-putin-1481033938.

3   Joint Analysis Report, "Grizzly Steppe: Russian Malicious Cyber Activity,"
Department of Homeland Security and Federal Bureau of Investigation, December
29, 2016.

4   "The Pence/Flynn Cover Story Continues to Unravel," Moscow Project,
December 6, 2018, https://themoscowproject.org/dispatch/the-pence-flynn-cover
-story-continues-to-unravel/.

5   Kenneth P. Vogel and David Stern, "Ukrainian Efforts to Sabotage Trump
Backfire," *Politico,* January 11, 2017, https://www.politico.com/story/2017/01/ukraine
-sabotage-trump-backfire-23344; David Corn, "A Veteran Spy Has Given the FBI
Information Alleging a Russian Operation to Cultivate Donald Trump," *Mother
Jones,* October 31, 2016, https://www.motherjones.com/politics/2016/10/veteran-spy

-gave-fbi-info-alleging-russian-operation-cultivate-donald-trump/; Ryan Broderick, "How a Viral Article on Facebook Convinced Trump's Inner Circle They Had Found Their Very Own Ukrainian 'Whistleblower,'" *BuzzFeed*, November 4, 2019, https:// www.buzzfeednews.com/article/ryanhatesthis/ukraine-whistleblower-politico-story -dnc-telizhenko.

6 Philip Bump, "Here Are the Times That We Know Lev Parnas Inter- acted with President Trump," *Washington Post*, January 30, 2020, https://www .washingtonpost.com/politics/2020/01/24/here-are-times-that-we-know-lev-parnas -met-president-trump/?utm_campaign=wp_main&utm_campaign=wp_main&utm _medium=social&utm_medium=social&utm_source=twitter&utm_source=twitter; "Donald Trump Rails Against 'American Carnage' in Populist Inaugural Speech," *Daily Beast*, January 20, 2017, https://www.thedailybeast.com/cheats/2017/01/20 /donald-trump-rails-against-american-carnage-in-populist-inaugural-speech; Don- ald Trump, "The Inaugural Address," January 20, 2017, https://www.whitehouse.gov /briefings-statements/the-inaugural-address/.

7 Carol E. Lee, Devlin Barrett, and Shane Harris, "U.S. Eyes Michael Flynn's Links to Russia," *Wall Street Journal*, January 22, 2017, https://www.wsj.com /articles/u-s-eyes-michael-flynns-links-to-russia-1485134942.

8 Mike Flynn, "Our Ally Turkey Is in Crisis and Needs Our Support," *Hill*, November 8, 2016; Matt Apuzzo and Emmarie Huetteman, "Sally Yates Tells Sena- tors She Warned Trump About Michael Flynn," *New York Times*, May 8, 2017, https:// www.nytimes.com/2017/05/08/us/politics/michael-flynn-sally-yates-hearing.html; Courtney Kube, "Flynn Delayed Anti-ISIS Plan That Turkey Opposed," NBC News, May 18, 2017, https://www.nbcnews.com/news/us-news/flynn-delayed-anti -isis-plan-turkey-opposed-n761656.

9 Adam Entous, Ellen Nakashima, and Philip Rucker, "Justice Department Warned White House That Flynn Could Be Vulnerable to Russian Blackmail, Of- ficials Say," *Washington Post*, February 13, 2017, https://www.washingtonpost.com /world/national-security/justice-department-warned-white-house-that-flynn-could -be-vulnerable-to-russian-blackmail-officials-say/2017/02/13/fc5dab88-f228-11e6 -8d72-263470bf0401_story.html; Murray Waas, "Mike Pence, Star Witness," *New York Review of Books*, September 9, 2018, https://www.nybooks.com/daily/2018/09 /25/mike-pence-star-witness/.

10 Eugene Kiely, "Michael Flynn's Russia Timeline," FactCheck.org, De- cember 1, 2017, https://www.factcheck.org/2017/12/michael-flynns-russia-timeline/.

11 Andrew Kent, Susan Hennessey, and Matthew Kahn, "Why Did Congress Set a Ten-Year Term for the FBI Director?," *Lawfare*, May 17, 2017, https://www .lawfareblog.com/why-did-congress-set-ten-year-term-fbi-director.

12 Barbara Campbell, "Ex-Trump Adviser Flynn Seeks Immunity Before

Testifying on Russia Contacts," NPR, March 30, 2017, https://www.npr.org/sections
/thetwo-way/2017/03/30/522093187/ex-trump-adviser-flynn-seeks-immunity
-before-testifying-on-russia-contacts.

13   Aaron Blake, "A Paul Manafort Court Filing Just Accidentally Connected
Some Big Dots Between the Trump Campaign and Russia," *Washington Post,* January
8, 2019, https://www.washingtonpost.com/politics/2019/01/08/paul-manaforts-lawyers
-just-accidentally-connected-some-big-dots-between-trump-campaign-russia/.

14   Andrew E. Kramer, "How a Ukrainian Hairdresser Became a Front
for Paul Manafort," *New York Times,* September 15, 2018, https://www.nytimes
.com/2018/09/15/world/europe/ukraine-paul-manafort.html; Sergii Leshchenko,
"Sergii Leshchenko: THE TRUE STORY of Yanukovych's Black Ledger," *Kyiv
Post,* November 24, 2019, https://www.kyivpost.com/article/opinion/op-ed/sergii
-leshchenko-the-true-story-of-yanukovychs-black-ledger.html; Cristina Cabrera,
"READ: Newly Released Memos on Mueller's Russia Probe, Including Witness
Interviews," *Talking Points Memo,* January 2, 2020, https://talkingpointsmemo.com
/news/read-newly-released-memos-on-muellers-russia-probe-including-witness
-interviews.

15   Donald Trump (@realDonaldTrump), Twitter, July 22, 2017, https://
twitter.com/realdonaldtrump/status/888724194820857857?lang=en.

CHAPTER 4: ALTERNATIVE FACTS AND DEZINFORMATSIYA

1   Chris Cillizza, "Sean Spicer Held a Press Conference. He Didn't Take
Questions. Or Tell the Whole Truth," *Washington Post,* January 21, 2017, https://
www.washingtonpost.com/news/the-fix/wp/2017/01/21/sean-spicer-held-a-press
-conference-he-didnt-take-questions-or-tell-the-whole-truth/; Aaron Blake, "Kellyanne Conway Says Donald Trump's Team Has 'Alternative Facts.' Which Pretty
Much Says It All," *Washington Post,* January 22, 2017, https://www.washingtonpost
.com/news/the-fix/wp/2017/01/22/kellyanne-conway-says-donald-trumps-team
-has-alternate-facts-which-pretty-much-says-it-all/.

2   Jeffrey Toobin, "The Dirty Trickster," *New Yorker,* June 2, 2008, https://
www.newyorker.com/magazine/2008/06/02/the-dirty-trickster.

3   Michael W. Ross, E. James Essien, and Isabel Torres, "Conspiracy Beliefs
About the Origin of HIV/AIDS in Four Racial/Ethnic Groups," *Journal of Acquired
Immune Deficiency Syndromes* 41, no. 3 (2006): 342–344, https://www.ncbi.nlm.nih
.gov/pmc/articles/PMC1405237/.

4   Laura Daniels, "Russian Active Measures in Germany and the United
States: Analog Lessons from the Cold War," *War on the Rocks,* September 27, 2017,
https://warontherocks.com/2017/09/russian-active-measures-in-germany-and-the
-united-states-analog-lessons-from-the-cold-war/.

5   Spencer Ackerman, "'The FBI Is Trumpland': Anti-Clinton Atmosphere Spurred Leaking, Sources Say," *Guardian*, November 3, 2016, https://www.theguardian.com/us-news/2016/nov/03/fbi-leaks-hillary-clinton-james-comey-donald-trump.

6   Shane Savitsky, "Comey Defends His Clinton Email October Surprise," *Axios*, May 3, 2017, https://www.axios.com/comey-defends-his-clinton-email-october-surprise-1513302029-7d0cfbb5-cd72-4012-8f9b-3baf61717563.html.

7   Josh Dawsey, "Behind Comey's Firing: An Enraged Trump, Fuming About Russia," *Politico*, May 10, 2017, https://www.politico.com/story/2017/05/10/comey-firing-trump-russia-238192.

8   Greg Miller and Greg Jaffe, "Trump Revealed Highly Classified Information to Russian Foreign Minister and Ambassador," *Washington Post*, May 15, 2017, https://www.washingtonpost.com/world/national-security/trump-revealed-highly-classified-information-to-russian-foreign-minister-and-ambassador/2017/05/15/530c172a-3960-11e7-9e48-c4f199710b69_story.html; Austin Wright, "Sessions and Rosenstein Discussed Firing Comey Last Winter," *Politico*, May 19, 2017, https://www.politico.com/story/2017/05/19/rod-rosenstein-jeff-sessions-firing-comey-238608.

9   Peter Pomerantsev, "To Unreality—and Beyond," *JoDS*, October 23, 2019, https://jods.mitpress.mit.edu/pub/ic90uta1.

10   "Report: Russian Hackers Had RNC Data but Didn't Release It," *Daily Beast*, December 10, 2016, https://www.thedailybeast.com/cheats/2016/1; "Transcript of AP Interview with Trump," Associated Press, April 23, 2017, https://apnews.com/c810d7de280a47e88848b0ac74690c83; D'Angelo Gore, Robert Farley, and Lori Robertson, "Trump Repeats False Ukraine Claims," FactCheck.org, November 22, 2019, https://www.factcheck.org/2019/11/trump-repeats-false-ukraine-claims/.

11   Shane Harris, Josh Dawsey, and Carol D. Leonnig, "Former White House Officials Say They Feared Putin Influenced the President's Views on Ukraine and 2016 Campaign," *Washington Post*, December 19, 2019, https://www.washingtonpost.com/national-security/former-white-house-officials-say-they-feared-putin-influenced-the-presidents-views-on-ukraine-and-2016-campaign/2019/12/19/af0fdbf6-20e9-11ea-bed5-880264cc91a9_story.html.

12   "Donald Trump's Statements on Putin/Russia/Fake News Media," *Lawfare*, https://www.lawfareblog.com/donald-trumps-statements-putinrussiafake-news-media.

13   Carol D. Leonnig, Tom Hamburger, and Rosalind S. Helderman, "FBI Conducted Raid of Former Trump Campaign Chairman Manafort's Home," *Washington Post*, August 9, 2017, https://www.washingtonpost.com/politics/fbi-conducted

-predawn-raid-of-former-trump-campaign-chairman-manaforts-home/2017/08/09
/5879fa9c-7c45-11e7-9d08-b79f191668ed_story.html.

14   Aruna Viswanatha, Rebecca Davis O'Brien, and Rebecca Ballhaus, "Federal Prosecutors Scrutinize Rudy Giuliani's Ukraine Business Dealings, Finances," *Wall Street Journal*, October 14, 2019, https://www.wsj.com/articles /federal-prosecutors-scrutinize-rudy-giuliani-s-ukraine-business-dealings-finances -11571092100; Kenneth P. Vogel, "Ukraine Role Focuses New Attention on Giuliani's Foreign Work," *New York Times*, June 30, 2019, https://www.nytimes.com /2019/06/30/us/politics/ukraine-giuliani-foreign-work.html; Dan Friedman, "Rudy Giuliani Has a Long, Shady History with Ukraine," *Mother Jones*, September 28, 2019, https://www.motherjones.com/politics/2019/09/rudy-giuliani-has-a-long -shady-history-with-ukraine/; Conor Friedersdorf, "To Drain the Swamp, Start with Rudy Giuliani," *Atlantic*, December 7, 2019, https://www.theatlantic.com/ideas /archive/2019/12/rudy-giuliani-swamp-creature/603187/; Yuras Karmanau and Angela Charlton, "Ex-Ukrainian President Petro Poroshenko Says He Discussed Investments with Rudy Giuliani in 2017," *Chicago Tribune*, October 2, 2019, https:// www.chicagotribune.com/nation-world/ct-nw-ukraine-trump-giuliani-20191002 -5rovudi6nraqbkz5jh24vtbz5u-story.html.

15   Transcript, "The Trump-Ukraine Impeachment Inquiry: Full Testimonies of Yovanovitch," October 11, 2019, 53–56; Will Jordan, "Oligarch Named in Al Jazeera Investigation Faces Questioning," Al Jazeera, July 30, 2018, https:// www.aljazeera.com/news/2018/07/oligarch-named-al-jazeera-investigation-faces -questioning-180730132437308.html; Kurt Eichenwald, "How the Trump Organization's Foreign Business Ties Could Upend U.S. National Security," *Newsweek*, September 14, 2016, https://www.newsweek.com/2016/09/23/donald-trump-foreign -business-deals-national-security-498081.html; Madeline Stone, "Meet the Big Shots Who Live at 15 Central Park West, the World's Most Powerful Address," *Business Insider*, November 28, 2017, https://www.businessinsider.com/15-central-park-west -residents-2016-1#robert-am-stern-the-architect-of-15-cpw-was-inspired-by-the -great-new-york-apartments-of-the-1920s-not-todays-glassy-towers-the-building -has-two-sections-with-201-units-in-total-as-well-as-a-formal-driveway-2; Kenneth P. Vogel, "A Foreigner Paid $200,000 for Tickets to Trump's Inaugural. Now He Says He Was Duped," *New York Times*, June 18, 2019, https://www.nytimes.com /2019/06/18/us/politics/trump-inaugural-lawsuit-pavel-fuks.html.

16   Andrew Roth, "Unravelling Rudolph Giuliani's Labyrinthine Ties to Ukraine," *Guardian*, October 30, 2019, https://www.theguardian.com/us-news/2019 /oct/30/unravelling-rudolph-giulianis-labyrinthine-ties-to-ukraine.

17   Ibid.; Jeff Ostrowski and Wayne Washington, "Lev Parnas in Palm Beach County: Unpaid Bills, Failed Business Deals," *Palm Beach Post*, October 24,

2019, https://www.palmbeachpost.com/news/20191024/lev-parnas-in-palm-beach
-county-unpaid-bills-failed-business-deals; Jane Musgrave and John Pacenti, "Lev
Parnas' Life in Boca Raton: Suburban Dad Got His Start in Penny Stocks on 'Maggot Mile,'" *Palm Beach Post*, January 24, 2020, https://www.palmbeachpost.com
/news/20200124/lev-parnasrsquo-life-in-boca-raton-suburban-dad-got-his-start-in
-penny-stocks-on-lsquomaggot-milersquo; Jonathan Chait, "Trump Personally Directed Mob-Linked Figure Tied to Ukraine Shakedown," *New York Magazine*, November 18, 2019, https://nymag.com/intelligencer/2019/11/trump-parnas-fruman
-giuliani-ukraine-scandal-impeachment.html.

18   Musgrave and Pacenti, "Lev Parnas' Life in Boca Raton."

CHAPTER 5: FORREST GUMPS OF THE GOP

1   Jeff Ostrowski and Wayne Washington, "Lev Parnas in Palm Beach
County: Unpaid Bills, Failed Business Deals," *Palm Beach Post*, October 24, 2019,
https://www.palmbeachpost.com/news/20191024/lev-parnas-in-palm-beach-county
-unpaid-bills-failed-business-deals.

2   Philip Bump, "How Ukraine's Top Prosecutor Went After Marie Yovanovitch,
Step by Step," *Washington Post*, January 15, 2020, https://www.washingtonpost.com
/politics/2020/01/15/how-ukraines-top-prosecutor-went-after-marie-yovanovitch
-step-by-step/; Adam Entous, "The Ukrainan Prosecutor Behind Trump's Impeachment," *New Yorker*, December 23, 2019, https://www.newyorker.com/magazine/2019
/12/23/the-ukrainian-prosecutor-behind-trumps-impeachment.

3   Lucy Morgan, "Meet Harry Sargeant, Florida Republican Money Man,"
Tampa Bay Times, February 28, 2013, https://www.tampabay.com/news/politics
/elections/meet-harry-sargeant-florida-republican-money-man/1276970/%7C/.

4   Karen Freifeld, "New York Lawyer Is Source of $500,000 Paid to Trump
Attorney Giuliani," Reuters, November 7, 2019, https://www.reuters.com/article/us
-usa-trump-impeachment-giuliani/new-york-lawyer-is-source-of-500000-paid-to
-trump-attorney-giuliani-idUSKBN1XH29L; Kevin Johnson, Kevin McCoy,
and Bart Jansen,"Two Giuliani Associates Involved in Trump-Ukraine Controversy Arrested on Campaign Finance Charges," *USA Today*, October 10, 2019,
https://www.usatoday.com/story/news/politics/2019/10/10/impeachment-inquiry
-lev-parnas-igor-fruman-witness-list/3866159002/.

5   Marcia Heroux Pounds, "Ex-JetSmarter President Arrested, Faces Ex-
tradition to California on Grand Theft Charges," *Sun Sentinel*, February 24, 2017,
https://www.miamiherald.com/news/business/article134829629.html; Robert I.
Friedman, *Red Mafiya: How the Russian Mob Has Invaded America* (New York:
Little, Brown, 2000), 188–193; Aruna Viswanatha, Rebecca Ballhaus, Sadie
Gurman, and Byron Tau, "Two Giuliani Associates Who Helped Him on Ukraine

Charged with Campaign-Finance Violations," *Wall Street Journal*, October 10, 2019, https://www.wsj.com/articles/two-foreign-born-men-who-helped-giuliani-on -ukraine-arrested-on-campaign-finance-charges-11570714188; Brendan Fischer, "New Wire Transfer Records Reveal Shady Foreign Ties to a Pro-Trump Super PAC," Advancing Democracy Through Law, June 21, 2019, https://campaignleggal .org/update/new-wire-transfer-records-reveal-shady-foreign-ties-pro-trump-super -pac.

6   Viswanatha et al., "Two Giuliani Associates"; Justin Miller, "How Pete Sessions Became 'Congressman-1,'" *Texas Observer*, October 24, 2019, https://www .texasobserver.org/pete-sessions-congressman-1/; Mike Debonis and Anu Narayan-swamy, "Ex-Rep. Livingston, Player in Clinton Impeachment, Emerges as Character in Inquiry of Trump," *Washington Post*, October 30, 2019.

7   Skyler Swisher, Aric Chokey, and Gray Rohrer, "Gov. Ron DeSan-tis to Return Campaign Cash from Indicted South Florida Businessmen with Giuliani Ties," *South Florida Sun Sentinel*, October 10, 2019, https://www.sun -sentinel.com/news/politics/fl-ne-campaign-finance-indictments-20191010 -jwao3r2q3vd4ff3jpsprrl5azu-story.html.

8   Alison Kaplan Somer, "Igor, Lev and How Trumpian Politics Hijacked a Leading Orthodox Jewish Group," *Haaretz*, January 6, 2020, https://www.haaretz .com/us-news/.premium-parnas-trump-jewish-group-investigation-1.8348357.

9   Kevin G. Hall, "A Group Faced Heat for Being Too Political. Then It Feted Giuliani's 'Florida Fixers,'" Impact 2020, October 4, 2019, https://www.mcclatchydc .com/news/investigations/article235776342.html; Katie Rogers and Kenneth P. Vogel, "Outside Trump Hotel, an Uproar. Inside, a Calm Sea of Conservative Cash," *New York Times*, June 20, 2018, https://www.nytimes.com/2018/06/20/us/politics /trump-donors-america-first.html; Aiden Pink, "The Jewish Gastroenterologist Who Worked as an Agent for an Arab Sheikdom," *Forward*, June 7, 2018, https:// forward.com/news/national/402247/the-jewish-gastroenterologist-who-worked -as-an-agent-for-an-arab-sheikdom/; Jake Turx, "Leadership in an Age of Terror & Tragedy // An Exclusive Interview with Mayor Rudy Giuliani," *Ami Magazine*, November 7, 2018, https://www.amimagazine.org/2018/11/07/leadership-in-an-age -of-terror-tragedy/.

10   Maggie Haberman and Michael S. Schmidt, "Giuliani to Join Trump's Legal Team," *New York Times*, April 19, 2018, https://www.nytimes.com/2018/04 /19/us/politics/giuliani-trump.html.

11   Jon Ralston, "Video Connects the Dots on Laxalt's Interaction with Indicted Giuliani Pals," *Nevada Independent*, October 21, 2019, https:// thenevadaindependent.com/article/video-connects-the-dots-on-laxalts-interaction -with-indicted-giuliani-pals; Joe Palazzolo and Rebecca Davis O'Brien, "Giuliani

Associate Left Trail of Troubled Businesses Before Ukraine Probe Push," *Wall Street Journal,* October 31, 2019, https://www.wsj.com/articles/giuliani-associate-left-trail -of-troubled-businesses-before-ukraine-probe-push-11572527608; Viswanatha et al., "Two Giuliani Associates"; Ari Shapiro, "How a Complicated Web Connects 2 Soviet-Born Businessmen with the Impeachment Inquiry," NPR, October 23, 2019, https://www.npr.org/2019/10/23/771849041/how-a-complicated-web-connects-2 -soviet-born-businessmen-with-the-impeachment-in.

12   "Manafort Plea Deal: Trump Ex-Campaign Chief to Help Mueller Inquiry," BBC, September 14, 2018, https://www.bbc.com/news/world-us-canada -45525325.

CHAPTER 6: MEN ON A (SECRET) MISSION

1   Adam Serwer, "There's No Coup Against Trump," *Atlantic,* September 6, 2018, https://www.theatlantic.com/ideas/archive/2018/09/theres-no-coup-against -trump/569482/; Yascha Mounk, "The Real Coup Plot Is Trump's," *New York Times,* December 20, 2017, https://www.nytimes.com/2017/12/20/opinion/trump -republican-coup.html?searchResultPosition=7.

2   Vicky Ward, "Exclusive: After Private White House Meeting, Giuliani Associate Lev Parnas Said He Was on a 'Secret Mission' for Trump, Sources Say," CNN, November 16, 2019, https://edition.cnn.com/2019/11/15/politics /parnas-trump-special-mission-ukraine/index.html; Cristina Cabrera, "Giuliani Showed Up to Bush's Funeral with Indicted Associate," *Talking Points Memo,* October 15, 2019, https://talkingpointsmemo.com/news/giuliani-bush-funeral -indicted-associate-lev-parna; Adam Entous, "How Lev Parnas Became Part of the Trump Campaign's 'One Big Family,'" *New Yorker,* October 15, 2019, https://www .newyorker.com/news/news-desk/why-lev-parnas-worked-for-rudy-giuliani-and -donald-trump.

3   Ryan Goodman and Viola Gienger, "Timeline: Rep. Devin Nunes and Ukraine Disinformation Efforts," *Just Security,* November 26, 2019, https://www .justsecurity.org/67480/timeline-rep-devin-nunes-and-ukraine-disinformation -efforts/; Marshall Cohen, "Trump Contradicts Past Denials, Admits Sending Giuliani to Ukraine," CNN, February 14, 2020, https://www.cnn.com/2020/02/13 /politics/trump-rudy-giuliani-ukraine-interview/index.html.

4   Courtney Subramanian, "Explainer: Biden, Allies Pushed Out Ukrainian Prosecutor Because He Didn't Pursue Corruption Cases," *USA Today,* October 3, 2019, https://www.usatoday.com/story/news/politics/2019/10/03/what-really -happened-when-biden-forced-out-ukraines-top-prosecutor/3785620002/; Aubrey Belford, Tania Kozyreva, Christopher Miller, and Andrew W. Lehren, "Newly Promoted Prosecutor Acted as Go-Between for Giuliani in Ukraine," NBC

News, October 24, 2019, https://www.nbcnews.com/politics/donald-trump/newly-promoted-prosecutor-acted-go-between-giuliani-ukraine-n1071501; Adam Entous, "The Ukrainan Prosecutor Behind Trump's Impeachment," *New Yorker,* December 23, 2019, https://www.newyorker.com/magazine/2019/12/23/the-ukrainian-prosecutor-behind-trumps-impeachment; Sanjana Karanth, "Rudy Giuliani Doubles Down on Anti-Semitic Attacks Against George Soros," *Huffington Post,* December 24, 2019, https://www.huffpost.com/entry/rudy-giuliani-doubles-down-antisemitic-attacks-george-soros_n_5e029713e4b0b2520d111912; Omri Nahmias, "Jewish Groups Slam Rudy Giuliani for Saying George Soros Is 'Hardly a Jew,'" *Jerusalem Post,* December 24, 2019, https://www.jpost.com/Diaspora/Antisemitism/Jewish-groups-slam-Rudy-Giuliani-for-saying-George-Soros-is-Hardly-a-Jew-611946; Veronika Melkozerova, "Lutsenko's Luxury Vacation in Seychelles Draws Criticism," *Kyiv Post,* January 31, 2018, https://www.kyivpost.com/ukraine-politics/lutsenkos-luxury-vacation-seychelles-draws-criticism.html.

5   Michael Daly, "The Roots of Giuliani and Biden's 35-Year Grudge Match," *Daily Beast,* October 5, 2019.

6   Entous, "The Ukrainian Prosecutor."

7   Ben Protess, William K. Rashbaum, and Michael Rothfeld, "Giuliani Pursued Business in Ukraine While Pushing for Inquiries for Trump," *New York Times,* November 27, 2019, https://www.nytimes.com/2019/11/27/nyregion/giuliani-ukraine-business-trump.html.

8   "Ukraine Bans 41 International Journalists and Bloggers," Committee to Protect Journalists, September 16, 2015; Matt Zapotosky and Josh Dawsey, "Giuliani Associates Pressed Past President of Ukraine to Announce Biden Investigation in Exchange for State Visit," *Washington Post,* November 8, 2019, https://www.washingtonpost.com/national-security/giuliani-associates-pressed-past-president-of-ukraine-to-announce-biden-investigation-in-exchange-for-state-visit/2019/11/08/193b69a4-0273-11ea-8bab-0fc209e065a8_story.html; Rebecca Ballhaus, Alan Cullison, and Brett Forrest, "Giuliani Associates Urged Ukraine's Prior President to Open Biden, Election Probes," *Wall Street Journal,* November 8, 2019, https://www.wsj.com/articles/giuliani-associates-urged-ukraines-prior-president-to-open-biden-election-probes-11573247707.

9   Brian Schwartz, "Trump Asked Top Political Advisors Whether He Should Worry About Running Against Joe Biden," CNBC, March 6, 2019, https://www.cnbc.com/2019/03/06/trump-asked-advisors-whether-he-should-worry-about-facing-joe-biden-in-2020.html.

10   Paul McLeary, "John Solomon Gives Us Less Than Meets the Eye—Again," *Columbia Journalism Review,* February 27, 2007, https://archives.cjr.org/politics/john_solomon_gives_us_less_tha.php; Mariah Blake, "Something

Fishy?," *Columbia Journalism Review,* July/August 2012, https://archives.cjr.org /feature/something_fishy.php; Jake Pearson, Mike Spies, and David McSwane, "How a Veteran Reporter Worked with Giuliani's Associates to Launch Ukraine Conspiracy," *ProPublica,* October 25, 2019, https://www.propublica.org/article /how-a-veteran-reporter-worked-with-giuliani-associates-to-launch-the-ukraine -conspiracy.

11   Pearson, Spies, and McSwane, "How a Veteran Reporter Worked"; Sidney Blumenthal, "A Dozen Questions for John Solomon," *Just Security,* November 5, 2019, https://www.justsecurity.org/66962/a-dozen-questions-for-john -solomon/.

12   Melinda Haring, "Is This Ukraine? Or Is It Russia? Facing Bogus Charges," *Newsweek,* January 31, 2018, https://www.newsweek.com/ukraine-or-it-russia-locked -bogus-charges-796330; Daria Kaleniuk, interview with the authors.

13   John Solomon, "US Embassy Pressed Ukraine to Drop Probe of George Soros Group During 2016 Election," *Hill,* March 26, 2019, https://thehill.com /opinion/campaign/435906-us-embassy-pressed-ukraine-to-drop-probe-of-george -soros-group-during-2016; "Top Ukrainian Justice Official Says US Ambassador Gave Him a Do Not Prosecute List," *Hill,* March 20, 2019, https://thehill.com /hilltv/rising/434875-top-ukrainian-justice-official-says-us-ambassador-gave-him-a -do-not-prosecute; Tom Porter, "The Ex-US Ambassador to Ukraine Said She Was Told to 'Go Big or Go Home' and Tweet Lavish Praise for Trump to Keep Her Job," *Business Insider,* November 5, 2019, https://www.businessinsider.com/ex-us-ukraine -ambassador-told-tweet-trump-praise-keep-job-2019-11.

14   Kate Brannen, "McMaster Fires Iran Hawk from NSC," *Foreign Policy,* July 27, 2017, https://foreignpolicy.com/2017/07/27/top-middle-east-advisor-out-on -the-national-security-council/.

15   Viola Gienger and Ryan Goodman, "Timeline: Trump, Giuliani, Biden, and Ukrainegate (Updated)," *Just Security,* January 31, 2020, https://www.justsecurity .org/66271/timeline-trump-giuliani-bidens-and-ukrainegate/; Austin Wright and Nolan D. McCaskill, "Nunes Apologizes for Going Directly to White House with Monitoring Claims," *Politico,* March 23, 2017, https://www.politico.com/story/2017 /03/nunes-apologizes-after-going-directly-to-white-house-with-monitoring-claims -236415; Ryan Goodman amd Viola Gienger, "Timeline: Rep. Devin Nunes and Ukraine Disinformation Efforts," *Just Security,* November 26, 2019, https://www .justsecurity.org/67480/timeline-rep-devin-nunes-and-ukraine-disinformation -efforts/.

16   Ryan Saavedra, "Calls Grow to Remove Obama's U.S. Ambassador to Ukraine," *Daily Wire,* March 24, 2019, https://www.dailywire.com/news/calls-grow -remove-obamas-us-ambassador-ukraine-ryan-saavedra; Patrick Reis and Andy

Kroll, "It Doesn't Take a Genius to Interfere in the U.S. Presidential Election," *Rolling Stone,* October 10, 2019, https://www.rollingstone.com/politics/politics-features/joe-biden-hunter-ukraine-trump-lutsenko-burisma-holdings-interference-897187/; Tom Hains, "John Solomon: As Russia Collusion Fades, Ukrainian Plot to Help Clinton Emerges," *RealClearPolitics,* March 21, 2019, https://www.realclearpolitics.com/video/2019/03/21/john_solomon_as_russia_collusion_fades_ukrainian_plot_to_help_clinton_emerges.html.

17   Josh Kovensky, "Parnas Texts Expose Ukrainian Prosecutor's Role in Impeachment Scandal," *Talking Points Memo,* January 15, 2020, https://talkingpointsmemo.com/muckraker/parnas-texts-expose-ukrainian-prosecutors-role-in-impeachment-scandal.

18   Justine Coleman, "Yovanovitch Calls for Investigation Following Evidence Released by Lawmakers," *Hill,* January 14, 2020, https://thehill.com/homenews/administration/478302-yovanovitch-calls-for-investigation-following-evidence-released-by.

19   Rebecca Davis O'Brien and Christopher M. Matthews, "Ukraine Energy Official Says Giuliani Associates Tried to Recruit Him," *Wall Street Journal,* November 24, 2019, https://www.wsj.com/articles/ukraine-energy-official-says-giuliani-associates-tried-to-recruit-him-11574652499; Desmond Butler and Michael Biesecker, "Giuliani Associates Leveraged GOP Access to Get Ukraine Gas Deal," PBS, December 23, 2019, https://www.pbs.org/newshour/nation/giuliani-associates-leveraged-gop-access-to-get-ukraine-gas-deal.

20   "Ukraine Prosecutor General Lutsenko Admits U.S. Ambassador Didn't Give Him a Do Not Prosecute List," *Unian,* April 18, 2019, https://www.unian.info/politics/10520715-ukraine-prosecutor-general-lutsenko-admits-u-s-ambassador-didn-t-give-him-a-do-not-prosecute-list.html.

21   Catie Edmondson, "Impeachment Bombshell That Wasn't: Mysterious Packet Sends Rumor Mill into Overdrive," *New York Times*, October 2, 2019, https://www.nytimes.com/2019/10/02/us/politics/impeachment-packet-ukraine.html; Jonathan Landay and Mark Hosenball, "Democrats Say Trump Administration Used Misinformation to Attack U.S. Diplomat," Reuters, October 2, 2019, https://www.reuters.com/article/us-usa-trump-whistleblower-state/democrats-say-trump-administration-used-misinformation-to-attack-u-s-diplomat-idUSKBN1WH1WA; Leigh Ann Caldwell, Kristen Welker, Heidi Przybyla, Josh Lederman, and Abigail Williams, "Giuliani Says State Dept Vowed to Investigate After He Gave Ukraine Docs to Pompeo," NBC News, October 3, 2019, https://www.nbcnews.com/politics/trump-impeachment-inquiry/giuliani-says-state-dept-vowed-investigate-after-he-gave-ukraine-n1061931; Kenneth P. Vogel, "Giuliani Provides Details of What Trump Knew About Ambassador's Removal," *New York Times,* December 16, 2019,

https://www.nytimes.com/2019/12/16/us/politics/giuliani-yovanovitch-ukraine
.html; Entous, "The Ukrainian Prosecutor."

22   John Bowden, "Lobbyist Turned Wine Blogger Vetting UN, State Personnel for Loyalty to Trump: Report," *Hill*, May 13, 2018, https://thehill.com
/homenews/administration/392074-lobbyist-turned-wine-blogger-vetting-un
-state-dept-personnel-for; Warren Rojas, "Wine Critic Turned White House Adviser Is Checking Employee Loyalty for Trump," *Eater*, June 13, 2018, https://dc
.eater.com/2018/6/13/17460416/mari-stull-state-department-loyalty-trump; Office of Inspector General, "Review of Allegations of Politicized and Other Improper Personnel Practices in the Bureau of International Organization Affairs,"
United States Department of State, August 2019, https://www.stateoig.gov/system
/files/esp-19-05.pdf.

23   Anthony Kao, "Ukraine's 'Servant of the People' Is a Hidden Gem of
Political Comedy," *Cinema Escapist*, June 6, 2017, https://www.cinemaescapist.com
/2017/06/ukraines-servant-people-hidden-gem-political-comedy/.

24   William Cummings, Nicholas Wu, and Deirdre Shesgreen, "'Mysterious' Packet of Ukraine Disinformation Arrives on Capitol Hill amid Trump Impeachment Inquiry," *USA Today*, October 2, 2019, https://www.usatoday.com/story
/news/politics/2019/10/02/state-department-inspector-general-urgent-ukraine
-briefing/3840218002/; "Ukraine Prosecutor General Lutsenko Admits U.S.
Ambassador Didn't Give Him a Do Not Prosecute List," *Unian*, April 18, 2019,
https://www.unian.info/politics/10520715 ukraine prosecutor-general-lutsenko
-admits-u-s-ambassador-didn-t-give-him-a-do-not-prosecute-list.html; Michael
Birnbaum, David L. Stern, and Natalie Gryvnyak, "Former Ukraine Prosecutor
Says Hunter Biden 'Did Not Violate Anything,'" *Washington Post*, September 26,
2019, https://www.washingtonpost.com/world/europe/former-ukraine-prosecutor
-says-hunter-biden-did-not-violate-anything/2019/09/26/48801f66-e068-11e9
-be7f-4cc85017c36f_story.html; Matthew Daly, "Records Show Numerous Calls
Between Nunes, Giuliani, Parnas," *Mercury News*, December 3, 2019, https://www
.mercurynews.com/2019/12/03/records-show-numerous-calls-between-nunes
-giuliani-parnas/.

CHAPTER 7: AMBASSADORS, OLIGARCHS, AND MENTAL MIDGETS

1   Anton Troianovski, "Comedian Volodymyr Zelensky Unseats Incumbent in
Ukraine's Presidential Election, Exit Poll Shows," *Washington Post*, April 21, 2019,
https://www.washingtonpost.com/world/as-ukraine-votes-in-presidential-runoff-a
-comedian-looks-to-unseat-the-incumbent/2019/04/21/b7d69a38-603f-11e9-bf24
-db4b9fb62aa2_story.html; Andrew Higgins and Iuliia Mendel, "Ukraine Election: Volodymyr Zelensky, TV Comedian, Trounces President," *New York Times*,

April 21, 2019, https://www.nytimes.com/2019/04/21/world/europe/Volodymyr-Zelensky-ukraine-elections.html.

2   Gregg Re, "Clinton-Ukraine Collusion Allegations 'Big' and 'Incredible,' Will Be Reviewed, Trump Says," Fox News, April 25, 2019, https://www.foxnews.com/politics/trump-barr-will-look-at-incredible-possibility-of-ukraine-clinton-collusion.

3   Christopher Miller, "Evangelical Christians Also Wanted to Get Rid of the US Ambassador to Ukraine," *BuzzFeed,* February 5, 2020, https://www.buzzfeednews.com/article/christopherm51/marie-yovanovitch-ukraine-mike-pompeo-dale-armstrong; Alan Cullison, "Ukraine's Secret Weapon, Feisty Oligarch Ihor Kolomoisky," *Wall Street Journal,* June 27, 2014, https://www.wsj.com/articles/ukraines-secret-weapon-feisty-oligarch-ihor-kolomoisky-1403886665; Jo Becker, Walt Bogdanich, Maggie Haberman, and Ben Protess, "Why Giuliani Singled Out 2 Ukrainian Oligarchs to Help Look for Dirt," *New York Times,* November 25, 2019, https://www.nytimes.com/2019/11/25/us/giuliani-ukraine-oligarchs.html; Betsy Swan, "The Allegedly Murderous Oligarch, the Duped CIA Chief, and the Trumpkin," *Daily Beast,* March 27, 2018, https://www.thedailybeast.com/the-allegedly-murderous-oligarch-the-duped-cia-chief-and-the-trumpkin; Julian Borger, "Kafka in Foggy Bottom: Impeachment Transcript Reveals Fear of Trump Tweets," *Guardian,* November 5, 2019, https://www.theguardian.com/us-news/2019/nov/05/impeachment-marie-yovanovitch-ukraine-transcript-reveals-fear-and-chaos-in-the-state-department.

4   Robbie Gramer, "State Department Misled Congress on Ouster of Ukraine Ambassador," *Foreign Policy,* November 25, 2019, https://foreignpolicy.com/2019/11/25/trump-impeachment-state-department-marie-yovanovitch-ukraine-democrats/.

5   Kenneth P. Vogel, "Rudy Giuliani Plans Ukraine Trip to Push for Inquiries That Could Help Trump," *New York Times,* May 9, 2019, https://www.nytimes.com/2019/05/09/us/politics/giuliani-ukraine-trump.html?searchResultPosition=2; Ursula Perano, "Trump Claims He Didn't Know About Giuliani Letter to Zelensky," *Axios,* January 16, 2020, https://www.axios.com/trump-giuliani-letter-zelensky-ukraine-parnas-405ba89d-8538-4d8a-902d-a6ad0c228522.html; Vogel, "Rudy Giuliani Plans Ukraine Trip"; Charles Creitz, "Giuliani Cancels Ukraine Trip, Says He'd Be 'Walking into a Group of People That Are Enemies of the US,'" Fox News, May 11, 2019, https://www.foxnews.com/politics/giuliani-i-am-not-going-to-ukraine-because-id-be-walking-into-a-group-of-people-that-are-enemies-of-the-us.

6   Adam Entous, "The Ukrainian Prosecutor Behind Trump's Impeachment," *New Yorker,* December 23, 2019, https://www.newyorker.com/magazine/2019/12/23/the-ukrainian-prosecutor-behind-trumps-impeachment; Daryna Krasnolutska, Kateryna Choursina, and Stephanie Baker, "Ukraine Prosecutor Says No Evidence

of Wrongdoing by Bidens," *Bloomberg,* May 16, 2019, https://www.bloomberg.com /news/articles/2019-05-16/ukraine-prosecutor-says-no-evidence-of-wrongdoing-by -bidens.

7   Philip Bump, "How Ukraine's Top Prosecutor Went After Marie Yovano-vitch, Step by Step," *Washington Post,* January 15, 2020, https://www.washingtonpost .com/politics/2020/01/15/how-ukraines-top-prosecutor-went-after-marie -yovanovitch-step-by-step/.

8   Entous, "The Ukrainian Prosecutor."

9   Adam Taylor, "Trump Has Spoken Privately with Putin at Least 16 Times. Here's What We Know About the Conversations," *Washington Post,* October 4, 2019, https://www.washingtonpost.com/world/2019/10/04/trump-has-spoken-privately -with-putin-least-times-heres-what-we-know-about-conversations/; Mark Landler, "Trump Says He Discussed the 'Russian Hoax' in a Phone Call with Putin," *New York Times,* May 3, 2019, https://www.nytimes.com/2019/05/03/us/politics/trump -putin-phone-call.html; Justin Sink, "Russia Says President Trump Initiated Long Phone Call with Putin," *Time,* May 4, 2019, https://time.com/5583327/trump -intiated-putin-long-phone-call/; Permanent Select Committee on Intelligence, Committee on Oversight and Reform, and the Committee on Foreign Affairs, U.S. House of Representatives, George Kent transcript, October 15, 2019, https://www .justsecurity.org/wp-content/uploads/2019/11/ukraine-clearinghouse-2019.10.15 .kent_transcript.pdf.

10   "Interview: Steve Hilton Interviews Donald Trump on Fox News' the Next Revolution," Factbase, May 19, 2019, https://factba.se/transcript/donald-trump -interview-steve-hilton-fox-telephone-may-19-2019; Dave Lawler, "Fact Check: What Joe and Hunter Biden Actually Did in Ukraine," *Axios,* October 2, 2019, https://www.axios.com/joe-hunter-biden-ukraine-corruption-trump-1b031c30 -3173-4a45-a6a7-2e551759063c.html.

CHAPTER 8: THE THREE AMIGOS

1   Lauren Frias, "Giuliani Associate Claims Pence Didn't Attend Ukrainian President's Inauguration Because Ukraine Didn't Announce an Investigation into the Bidens," *Business Insider,* January 15, 2020, https://www.businessinsider.com/lev -parnas-mike-pence-zelensky-inauguration-ukraine-biden-investigation-2020-1.

2   Rudy Giuliani (@RudyGiuliani), Twitter, May 18, 2019, https://twitter .com/rudygiuliani/status/1129756189707984898?lang=en.

3   Julia Manchester, "Giuliani Attacks Davis for Representing Indicted Ukrainian Figure," *Hill,* March 8, 2019, https://thehill.com/hilltv/rising/433224 -giuliani-attacks-davis-for-representing-indicted-Russian-figure; Rosalind S. Hel-derman, Tom Hamburger, Paul Sonne, and Josh Dawsey, "How Giuliani's Outreach

to Ukrainian Gas Tycoon Wanted in U.S. Shows Lengths He Took in His Hunt for Material to Bolster Trump," *Washington Post,* January 15, 2020, https://www .washingtonpost.com/politics/how-giulianis-outreach-to-ukrainian-gas-tycoon -wanted-in-us-shows-lengths-he-took-in-his-hunt-for-material-to-bolster-trump /2020/01/15/64c263ba-2e5f-11ea-bcb3-ac6482c4a92f_story.html; Rosalind Helderman and Paul Sonne, "'Once This Is Over, We'll Be Kings': How Lev Parnas Worked His Way into Trump's World—and Now Is Rattling It," MSN, January 19, 2020, https://www.msn.com/en-us/news/politics/once-this-is-over-well-be -kings-how-lev-parnas-worked-his-way-into-trumps-world-%E2%80%94-and -now-is-rattling-it/ar-BBZ6dVI; "It Was All [Fruman's] Contacts in Ukraine," *EmptyWheel,* January 17, 2020, https://www.emptywheel.net/2020/01/17/it-was -all-frumans-contacts-in-ukraine/?print=print; Helderman et al., "How Giuliani's Outreach"; Valentina Pop, "Fake-Passports Gangs Arrested in Europe," *Wall Street Journal,* May 31, 2016, https://www.wsj.com/articles/fake-passports-gangs-arrested -in-europe-1464702132.

4   Walt Bogdanich and Michael Forsythe, "'Exhibit A': How McKinsey Got Entangled in a Bribery Case," *New York Times,* December 30, 2018, https://www .nytimes.com/2018/12/30/world/mckinsey-bribes-boeing-firtash-extradition.html; Eric Lutz, "Giuliani Crony Lev Parnas Is Going Full Kamikaze on Ukraine," *Vanity Fair,* November 11, 2019, https://www.vanityfair.com/news/2019/11/giuliani-crony -lev-parnas-is-going-full-kamikaze-on-ukraine.

5   Anatevka, https://www.anatevka.com; Tom Porter, "Lev Parnas Claimed He and Trump's Allies Sought Help from a Ukrainian Oligarch Fighting US Extradition in Search for Dirt on Joe Biden," *Business Insider,* January 16, 2020, https://www.businessinsider.com/parnas-claims-sought-help-of-ukraine-oligarch -biden-dirt-search-2020-1; Christopher Miller et al., "There's a Village in Ukraine Where Rudy Giuliani Is the Honorary Mayor. That's Not the Weird Part of This Story," *BuzzFeed News,* October 26, 2019, https://www.buzzfeednews.com/article /christopherm51/fiddlers-on-the-roof-ukraine-impeachment; Sam Sokol and Anna Myroniuk, "Why Is Rudy Giuliani Close with This Hasidic Ukrainian Rabbi?," Jewish Telegraphic Agency, October 28, 2019, https://www.jta.org/2019/10/28/global/why -is-rudy-giuliani-close-with-this-hasidic-ukrainian-rabbi.

6   Vicky Ward and Marshall Cohen, "'I'm the Best-Paid Interpreter in the World': Indicted Giuliani Associate Lev Parnas Touted Windfall from Ukrainian Oligarch," CNN, November 1, 2019, https://edition.cnn.com/2019/11/01/politics /parnas-firtash-giuliani-ties/index.html.

7   Alexandra Ma, "Giuliani Associate Lev Parnas Trolled Trump by Threatening to Release a New Photo of Them Together Every Time the President Claims Not to Know Him," *Business Insider,* January 17, 2020, https://www.businessinsider

.com/lev-parnas-trump-claims-threatens-photos-receipts-2020-1; Ari Shapiro, "How a Complicated Web Connects 2 Soviet-Born Businessmen with the Impeachment Inquiry," NPR, October 23, 2019.

8   Richard Parker, "Rick Perry, American Caudillo," *Atlantic,* March 27, 2015, https://www.theatlantic.com/politics/archive/2015/03/rick-perry-american-caudillo /388294/.

9   Robert Kuttner, "The Sleazy Career of Kurt Volker," *American Prospect,* October 8, 2019, https://prospect.org/impeachment/sleazy-career-of-kurt-volker -ukraine-hungary/; "Opening Statement of Deputy Assistant Secretary of Defense Laura K. Cooper," *Just Security,* November 20, 2019, https://www.justsecurity.org /wp-content/uploads/2019/11/ukraine-clearinghouse-cooper_opening_statement -2019.11.20.pdf.

10   "Orange Alert," *Institutional Investor,* March 14, 2006, https://www .institutionalinvestor.com/article/b150nr17vncy2k/orange-alert.

11   Lesley Clarke, "Records Raise More Questions About Rick Perry, Ukraine Ties," *E&E News,* February 5, 2020, https://www.eenews.net/stories/1062267129; Justin Miller, "Rick Perry Exports His Pay-to-Play Politics to Ukraine," *Texas Observer,* November 13, 2019.

12   Reeve Hamilton, "A Lightning Rod on U.T. Board, Regent Is Not Deterred," *New York Times,* June 11, 2011, https://www.nytimes.com/2011/06/12 /us/12ttcranberg.html; J. T. Stepleton, "Alex Cranberg: In the Background of the Koch Network," *FollowTheMoney.org,* July 20, 2017, https://www.followthemoney .org/research/blog/alex-cranberg-in-the-background-of-the-koch-network; Mark Maremont and Neil King Jr., "Campaign to Pony Up for Flight Costs," *Wall Street Journal,* October 20, 2011, https://www.wsj.com/articles/SB1000142405297020375 26045766415103555155144.

13   Desmond Butler, Michael Biesecker, Stephen Braun, and Richard Lardner, "After Boost from Perry, Backers Got Huge Gas Deal in Ukraine," Associated Press, November 11, 2019, https://apnews.com/6d8ae551fb884371a2a592ed85a74426; Simon Shuster, "Exclusive: Lawsuit Raises Questions About Rick Perry's Role in Ukraine's Energy Sector," *Time,* December 16, 2019, https://time.com/5750669/exclusive -lawsuit-raises-questions-about-rick-perrys-role-in-ukraine-energy-sector/; Matthew Daly and Richard Lardner, "New Swamp: Ex-Perry Adviser Lobbies for Energy Firm Bailout," Associated Press, May 29, 2018, https://apnews.com/e620b 6cb527d41ebbb1c27974d771822/New-swamp:-Ex-Perry-adviser-lobbies-for-energy -firm-bailout.

14   Viola Gienger and Ryan Goodman,"Timeline: Trump, Giuliani, Biden, and Ukrainegate (Updated)," *Just Security,* September 24, 2019, https://www.justsecurity .org/66271/timeline-trump-giuliani-bidens-and-ukrainegate/; "Opening Statement

Gordon D. Sondland," House of Representatives Committee on Foreign Affairs, Permanent Select Committee on Intelligence, and Committee on Oversight and Government Reform, October 17, 2019, https://games-cdn.washingtonpost.com/notes /prod/default/documents/8397891d-d1bf-4a05-93e0-795f6d1b7048/note/5cd6785f -4de2-42d4-937d-39224c08bc2d.pdf#page=1; "Additional Text Messages Produced by Kurt Volker," House Permanent Select Committee on Intelligence, https:// intelligence.house.gov/uploadedfiles/20191105_-_volker_additional_texts_final.pdf.

15   "Opening Statement of Ambassador William B. Taylor," *Just Security,* October 22, 2019, https://www.justsecurity.org/wp-content/uploads/2019/11/ukraine -clearinghouse-2019.10.22.taylor-opening-statement.pdf; Paul Kane, Karoun Demirjian, and Rachael Bade, "White House Directed 'Three Amigos' to Run Ukraine Policy, Senior State Department Official Tells House Investigators," *Washington Post,* October 16, 2019, https://www.washingtonpost.com/politics/top-state -department-official-expected-to-face-questions-about-ukraine-and-giuliani/2019 /10/14/8ba23d18-eeca-11e9-b2da-606ba1ef30e3_story.html; Betsy Swan and Erin Banco, "Exclusive: Trump Letter Promised Zelensky 'Unwavering' Support," *Daily Beast,* November 6, 2019, https://www.thedailybeast.com/trump-letter-promised -zelensky-unwavering-support-invited-him-to-white-house.

CHAPTER 9: THE DRUG DEAL

1   "Toronto Ukraine Reform Conference Co-Chairs' Statement," Government of Canada, July 10, 2019, https://www.international.gc.ca/world-monde/issues _development-enjeux_developpement/human_rights-droits_homme/2019-07-02 -urc.aspx?lang=eng.

2   Ian Schwartz, "Full Trump Interview with Hannity: We're Investigating If Intel Agencies Spied, 'That Would Be the Ultimate,'" *RealClearPolitics,* June 19, 2019, https://www.realclearpolitics.com/video/2019/06/19/full_trump_interview _with_hannity_were_investigating_if_intel_agencies_spied_that_would_be_the _ultimate.html.

3   Russ Read, "Pentagon to Send $250M in Weapons to Ukraine," *Washington Examiner,* June 19, 2019, https://www.washingtonexaminer.com/policy /defense-national-security/pentagon-to-send-250m-in-weapons-to-ukraine; Eric Lipton, Maggie Haberman, and Mark Mazzetti, "Behind the Ukraine Aid Freeze: 84 Days of Conflict and Confusion," *New York Times,* December 29, 2019, https:// www.nytimes.com/2019/12/29/us/politics/trump-ukraine-military-aid.html?smid =nytcore-ios-share.

4   Philip Rucker and Robert Costa, "Bob Woodward's New Book Reveals a 'Nervous Breakdown' of Trump's Presidency," *Washington Post,* September 4, 2018, https://www.washingtonpost.com/politics/bob-woodwards-new-book-reveals-a

-nervous-breakdown-of-trumps-presidency/2018/09/04/b27a389e-ac60-11e8-a8d7
-0f63ab8b1370_story.html; Lipton, Haberman, and Mazzetti, "Behind the Ukraine
Aid Freeze."

5   Peter Baker, "Trump Says NATO Allies Don't Pay Their Share. Is That
True?," *New York Times,* May 26, 2017, https://www.nytimes.com/2017/05/26
/world/europe/nato-trump-spending.html; William Hartung, "Trump Policy and
Trends in U.S. Arms Sales," World Peace Foundation, June 21, 2019, https://sites
.tufts.edu/reinventingpeace/2019/06/21/trump-policy-and-trends-in-u-s-arms
-sales/; Elizabeth McLaughlin and Conor Finnegan, "The Truth About President
Trump's $110 Billion Saudi Arms Deal," ABC News, June 6, 2017, https://abcnews
.go.com/International/truth-president-trumps-110-billion-saudi-arms-deal/story?id
=47874726; Read, "The Pentagon to Send $250M."

6   Mike Levine, "Testimony and Texts: How the Trump-Ukraine Allegations Fit Together in a Timeline," ABC News, November 20, 2019, https://abcnews
.go.com/Politics/testimony-texts-trump-ukraine-allegations-fit-timeline/story?id
=67015714.

7   Greg Miller and Greg Jaffe, "At Least Four National Security Officials
Raised Alarms About Ukraine Policy Before and After Trump Call with Ukrainian
President," *Washington Post,* October 10, 2019, https://www.washingtonpost.com
/national-security/at-least-four-national-security-officials-raised-alarms-about
-ukraine-policy-before-and-after-trump-call-with-ukrainian-president/2019/10/10
/ffe0c88a-eb6d-11e9-9c6d-436a0df4f31d_story.html; "Чалый о встрече Зеленского
и Трампа: Это вопрос следующих месяцев," *Pravda,* July 9, 2019, https://www
.pravda.com.ua/rus/news/2019/07/9/7220376/; Eric Banco, "Top Ukraine Official: I Trusted Bolton More Than Anyone," *Daily Beast,* January 28, 2020, https://
www.thedailybeast.com/oleksandr-danylyuk-former-top-ukraine-official-says-he
-trusted-john-bolton-more-than-anyone?ref=scroll; transcript, Alexander Vindman deposition, House Permanent Select Committee on Intelligence, October 29,
2019, https://assets.documentcloud.org/documents/6543473/Alexander-Vindman
-Full-Deposition.pdf; Michael Donley, Cornelius O'Leary, and John Montgomery,
"Inside the White House Situation Room," CIA, June 27, 2008, https://www.cia
.gov/library/center-for-the-study-of-intelligence/csi-publications/csi-studies/studies
/97unclass/whithous.html.

8   Letter from Adam Schiff and Eliot Engel to House Members, October
3, 2019, https://foreignaffairs.house.gov/_cache/files/a/4/a4a91fab-99cd-4eb9-9c6c
-ec1c586494b9/621801458E982E9903839ABC7404A917.chairmen-letter-on-state
-departmnent-texts-10-03-19.pdf.

9   Kenneth Vogel and Andrew Kramer, "Giuliani Renews Push for Ukraine
to Investigate Trump's Political Opponents," *New York Times,* August 21, 2019,

https://www.nytimes.com/2019/08/21/us/politics/giuliani-ukraine.html; transcript, William B. Taylor deposition, House Permanent Select Committee on Intelligence, October 22, 2019, https://context-cdn.washingtonpost.com/notes/prod
/default/documents/e4536518-d47e-4e1d-ba11-7b530ed2f9ff/note/cda28fcb-f404
-4abf-a57d-0ca806c4fe84.pdf; Andrew E. Kramer, "Ukraine Knew of Aid Freeze in
July, Says Ex-Top Official in Kyiv," *New York Times,* December 3, 2019, https://www
.nytimes.com/2019/12/03/world/europe/ukraine-impeachment-military-aid.html;
Eliot Engel, Adam B. Schiff, and Elijah Cummings, letter to House colleagues, October 3, 2019, https://foreignaffairs.house.gov/_cache/files/a/4/a4a91fab-99cd-4eb9
-9c6c-ec1c586494b9/621801458E982E9903839ABC7404A917.chairmen-letter-on
-state-departmnent-texts-10-03-19.pdf.

   10   Eric Halliday, "Summary of Mark Sandy's Deposition Testimony," *Lawfare,* December 2, 2019, https://www.lawfareblog.com/summary-mark-sandys
-deposition-testimony; Michael D. Shear and Nicholas Fandos, "White House Budget Official Said 2 Aides Resigned amid Ukraine Aid Freeze," *New York Times,* November 26, 2019, https://www.nytimes.com/2019/11/26/us/politics/impeachment
-trump-hearing.html; Kramer, "Ukraine Knew of Aid Freeze."

CHAPTER 10: THE CALL

   1   "Watching Live Kill from the Situation Room," Cryptome, July 9, 2011,
http://cryptome.org/0004/kill-sitroom/kill-sitroom.htm.

   2   Tara McKelvey, "Who Listens in on a Presidential Phone Call?," BBC, September 27, 2019, https://www.bbc.com/news/world-us-canada-49858318; J. J. Greene,
"Anatomy of a Presidential Phone Call," WTOP, November 11, 2019, https://wtop
.com/j-j-green-national/2019/11/anatomy-of-a-presidential-phone-call/; Ayesha Ras-
coe, "Who Was on the Trump-Ukraine Call?," NPR, November 7, 2019, https://www
.npr.org/2019/11/07/775456663/who-was-on-the-trump-ukraine-call.

   3   Lori Robertson, "Trump Wrong on European Aid to Ukraine," FactCheck
.org, September 26, 2019, https://www.factcheck.org/2019/09/trump-wrong-on
-european-aid-to-ukraine/.

   4   Transcript, memorandum of telephone conversation with President Zelensky of Ukraine, White House, July 25, 2019, 9:03–9:33 a.m., https://www
.whitehouse.gov/wp-content/uploads/2019/09/Unclassified09.2019.pdf.

   5   Kate Brannen, "Exclusive: Unredacted Ukraine Documents Reveal Extent of Pentagon's Legal Concerns," *Just Security,* January 2, 2020, https://www
.justsecurity.org/67863/exclusive-unredacted-ukraine-documents-reveal-extent-of
-pentagons-legal-concerns/.

   6   Jacob Schulz, "Summary of Jennifer Williams's Deposition Testimony,"
Lawfare, November 20, 2019, https://www.lawfareblog.com/summary-jennifer

-williamss-deposition-testimony; Jim Tankersley, Jack Nicas, and Ana Swanson, "Trump Escalates Feud with Apple and Threatens Tariffs on France," *New York Times,* July 26, 2019, https://www.nytimes.com/2019/07/26/us/politics/trump-apple-tariffs .html?searchResultPosition=6;Andrew Desiderio and Kyle Cheney, "'Improper' and 'Unusual': White House Aides Criticize Trump's Ukraine Call," *Politico,* November 19, 2019, https://www.politico.com/news/2019/11/19/trump-ukraine-scrutiny -officials-testimony-071395; Ana Swanson, "Trump Presses World Trade Organization on China," *New York Times,* July 26, 2019, https://www.nytimes.com/2019 /07/26/us/politics/trump-wto-china.html?searchResultPosition=29; transcript, Alexander Vindman deposition, House Permanent Select Committee on Intelligence, October 29, 2019, https://assets.documentcloud.org/documents/6543473/Alexander -Vindman-Full-Deposition.pdf.

CHAPTER 11: *SHO?*

1   Whistleblower complaint, U.S. Select Committee on Intelligence, August 12, 2019, https://intelligence.house.gov/uploadedfiles/20190812_-_whistleblower _complaint_unclass.pdf; Vivian Salama, Rebecca Ballhaus, and Andrew Duehren, "Trump Didn't Deploy Note Takers at Putin Meeting," *Wall Street Journal,* January 13, 2019, https://www.wsj.com/articles/trump-didnt-deploy-note-takers-at-putin -meeting-11547419186.

2   "US Rapper A$AP Rocky Found Guilty of Sweden Assault," Al Jazeera, August 14, 2019, https://www.aljazeera.com/news/2019/08/rapper-aap-rocky-guilty -sweden-assault-190814161332075.html.

3   Kevin Breuninger, "Impeachment Witness David Holmes Explains How He Overheard Sondland Call with Trump About Ukraine," CNBC, November 21, 2019, https://www.cnbc.com/2019/11/21/impeachment-witness-explains-how-he -overheard-trump-call-with-sondland.html; Desmon Butler, Michael Biesecker, and Matthew Lee, "AP Source: Second US Official in Kyiv Heard Trump Call," Associated Press, November 14, 2019, https://apnews.com/6d318542e50b45dc9e1 d4d829ad36c96.

4   Betsy Swan and Asawin Suebsaeng, "Parnas Attended Giuliani's Madrid Meeting with Zelensky Aide," *Daily Beast,* November 21, 2019, https://www .thedailybeast.com/lev-parnas-attended-rudy-giulianis-madrid-meeting-with -zelensky-aide-andriy-yermak; "Chairman Letter on State Department Texts," NPR, October 3, 2019, https://apps.npr.org/documents/document.html?id=6466661-6218 01458E982E9903839ABC7404A917-Chairmen-Letter#document/p6/a529910.

5   Carlos Hernanz, "La 'Jet Set' Venezolana Se Queda con la Finca de Gerardo Díaz-Ferrán," *El Confidencial,* March 29, 2012, https://www.elconfidencial.com /economia/2012-03-29/la-jet-set-venezolana-se-queda-con-la-finca-de-gerardo-diaz

-ferran_248691/; Matt Naham, "Actual Giuliani Response to Lev Parnas Claim: 'It Was a Confidential Meeting—If It Did Happen,'" *Law & Crime,* January 22, 2020, https://lawandcrime.com/high-profile/actual-giuliani-response-to-lev-parnas -claim-it-was-a-confidential-meeting-if-it-did-happen/; Jane C. Timm, "Trump Is Pushing a Baseless Conspiracy About the Bidens and China. Here's What We Know," NBC News, October 7, 2019, https://www.nbcnews.com/politics/trump -impeachment-inquiry/trump-pushing-baseless-conspiracy-about-bidens-china-here -s-what-n1062551; Jay Weaver and Antonio Maria Delgado, "Venezuela's Business Elite Face Scrutiny in $1.2 Billion Money Laundering Case," *Miami Herald,* updated November 8, 2019, https://www.miamiherald.com/news/local/article236793383 .html; Orlando Avendaño, "Photo Confirm Guaidó's Father Visited 'Bolichico' Castle Residence," *Panam Post,* February 3, 2020, https://panampost.com/orlando-avendano /2020/02/03/photo-guaido-bolichico-residence/cn-reloaded=1; Viola Gienger and Ryan Goodman, "Timeline: Trump, Giuliani, Biden, and Ukrainegate (Updated)," *Just Security,* January 31, 2020, https://www.justsecurity.org/66271/timeline-trump -giuliani-bidens-and-ukrainegate/; Jerry Lambe, "While Giuliani Worked for Trump 'Pro Bono,' He Lobbied DOJ on Behalf of Wealthy Foreign Client," *Law & Crime,* November 26, 2019, https://lawandcrime.com/high-profile/while-giuliani-worked -for-trump-pro-bono-he-lobbied-doj-on-behalf-of-wealthy-foreign-client/.

6   Joshua Green, "Trump's Impeachment Saga Stems from a Political Hit Job Gone Bad," *Bloomberg Businessweek,* October 2, 2019, https://www.bloomberg .com/news/articles/2019-10-02/trump-s-impeachment-saga-stems-from-a-political -hit-job-gone-bad; Jane Mayer, "The Invention of the Conspiracy Theory on Biden and Ukraine," *New Yorker,* October 4, 2019, https://www.newyorker.com/news/news -desk/the-invention-of-the-conspiracy-theory-on-biden-and-ukraine.

7   Kate Brannen, "Exclusive: Unredacted Ukraine Documents Reveal Extent of Pentagon's Legal Concerns," *Just Security,* January 2, 2020, https://www .justsecurity.org/67863/exclusive-unredacted-ukraine-documents-reveal-extent -of-pentagons-legal-concerns/; Josh Dawsey and Karoun Demirjian, "White House Political Appointees Overrode Career Staffers Before Freezing Ukraine Aid," *Washington Post,* October 10, 2019, https://www.washingtonpost.com/world /national-security/white-house-political-appointees-overrode-career-staffers-before -freezing-ukraine-aid/2019/10/10/e27435e2-eba0-11e9-85c0-85a098e47b37_story .html.

8   Justin Sink, Jennifer Jacobs, and Elizabeth Rembert, "Trump's Hamptons Fundraisers Put High-Profile Donors in a Bind," *Bloomberg,* August 8, 2019, https:// www.bloomberg.com/news/articles/2019-08-08/trump-s-hamptons-fundraisers -put-high-profile-donors-in-a-bind; Jennifer Gould Keil and Emily Smith, "Trump Cracks Jokes About Equinox Scandal, Kamikaze Pilots, at Hamptons Fundraiser,"

New York Post, August 9, 2019, https://nypost.com/2019/08/09/trump-cracks-jokes -about-rent-control-kamikaze-pilots-at-hamptons-fundraiser/.

9   Charlie Savage and Josh Williams, "Read the Text Messages Between U.S. and Ukrainian Officials," *New York Times,* October 4, 2019, https://www.nytimes .com/interactive/2019/10/04/us/politics/ukraine-text-messages-volker.html.

10   D'Angelo Gore, Robert Farley, and Lori Robertson, "Trump Repeats False Ukraine Claims," FactCheck.org, November 22, 2019, https://www.factcheck.org /2019/11/trump-repeats-false-ukraine-claims/; Hope Yen and Calvin Woodward, "AP FACT CHECK: Trump, GOP Claims on Ukraine Corruption," Associated Press, November 21, 2019, https://apnews.com/92fd8a4743e8447a8f8a7ec301ebe993; Jon Greenberg, "Trump and Russia, Clinton and Ukraine: How Do They Compare?," PolitiFact, July 12, 2017, https://www.politifact.com/article/2017/jul/12/did-ukraine -try-help-clinton-way-russia-helped-tru/; Ted Cruz, "'Ukraine Blatantly Interfered in Our Election,'" PolitiFact, December 8, 2019, https://www.politifact.com/factchecks /2019/dec/12/ted-cruz/checking-ted-cruz-whether-ukraine-blatantly-interf/; Julian E. Barnes and Matthew Rosenberg, "Charges of Ukrainian Meddling? A Russian Operation, U.S. Intelligence Says," *New York Times,* November 26, 2019, https://www .nytimes.com/2019/11/22/us/politics/ukraine-russia-interference.html.

11   "Remarks by President Trump Before Marine One Departure," White House, August 9, 2019, https://www.whitehouse.gov/briefings-statements/remarks -president-trump-marine-one-departure-59/.

12   Glenn Kessler, Salvador Rizzo, and Meg Kelly, "President Trump Has Made 12,019 False or Misleading Claims over 928 Days," *Washington Post,* August 12, 2019, https://www.washingtonpost.com/politics/2019/08/12/president-trump -has-made-false-or-misleading-claims-over-days/.

13   Brannen, "Exclusive: Unredacted Ukraine Documents."

14   Kevin Sampier, "Pekin Woman Sings Praises of Latest Combat Vehicle," *State Journal Register,* September 30, 2007, https://www.sj-r.com/x428370762.

15   Brannen, "Exclusive: Unredacted Ukraine Documents."

16   Caitlin Emma and Connor O'Brien, "Trump Holds Up Ukraine Military Aid Meant to Confront Russia, " *Politico,* August 28, 2019, https://www.politico .com/story/2019/08/28/trump-ukraine-military-aid-russia-1689531; Veronica Strac-qualursi, "Trump Was the One Who Altered Dorian Trajectory Map with Sharpie," *CNN,* September 6, 2019, https://www.cnn.com/2019/09/06/politics/trump-sharpie -hurricane-dorian-alabama/index.html.

17   Brannen, "Exclusive: Unredacted Ukraine Documents."

18   Bruce Haring, "President Donald Trump Tweetstorm—the Sunday Edition," *Deadline,* September 1, 2019, https://deadline.com/2019/09/president -donald-trump-tweetstorm-the-sunday-edition-46-1202708962/; Katie Rogers,

"President Trump, Weatherman: Dorian Updates and at Least 122 Tweets," *New York Times*, September 3, 2019, https://www.nytimes.com/2019/09/02/us/politics /trump-dorian.html?searchResultPosition=33; John Schwartz, "New Rollback to Ease a Ban on Old Bulbs," *New York Times*, September 5, 2019, https://www.nytimes .com/2019/09/04/climate/trump-light-bulb-rollback.html?searchResultPosition =79; Emily Cochrane and Helene Cooper, "Pentagon Lists Projects That Will Be Delayed to Fund Border Wall," *New York Times*, September 4, 2019, https://www .nytimes.com/2019/09/04/us/politics/pentagon-projects-border-wall.html ?searchResultPosition=100.

CHAPTER 12: THE WHISTLEBLOWER

1   "50 U.S. Code § 3033. Inspector General of the Intelligence Community," Cornell Law School, https://www.law.cornell.edu/uscode/text/50/3033.

2   Olivia B. Waxman, "Before the Trump Impeachment Inquiry, These Were American History's Most Famous Whistle-Blowers," *Time*, September 26, 2019, https://time.com/5684536/whistleblower-history/.

3   Letter, whistleblower complaint, House Intelligence Committee, August 12, 2019, https://intelligence.house.gov/uploadedfiles/20190812_-_whistleblower _complaint_unclass.pdf; letter from Office of Inspector General of the Intelligence Community to Joseph Maguire, acting director of national intelligence, House Intelligence Committee, August 26, 2019, https://intelligence.house.gov/uploadedfiles /20190826_-_icig_letter_to_acting_dni_unclass.pdf.

4   *For letter to Intelligence Committee, see:* Inspector General of the Intelligence Community letter dated September 9, 2019, https://intelligence.house.gov /uploadedfiles/20190909_-_ic_ig_letter_to_hpsci_on_whistleblower.pdf.

5   Mark Joseph Stern, "An Unaccountable Office Crafted a Secret Law to Conceal the Whistleblower Complaint," *Slate*, September 23, 2019, https://slate.com /news-and-politics/2019/09/whistleblower-complaint-office-of-legal-counsel-secret -law.html.

6   Greg Miller, Ellen Nakashima, and Shane Harris, "Trump's Communications with Foreign Leader Are Part of Whistleblower Complaint That Spurred Standoff Between Spy Chief and Congress, Former Officials Say," *Washington Post*, September 18, 2019, https://www.washingtonpost.com/national-security/trumps -communications-with-foreign-leader-are-part-of-whistleblower-complaint-that -spurred-standoff-between-spy-chief-and-congress-former-officials-say/2019/09 /18/df651aa2-da60-11e9-bfb1-849887369476_story.html; "Remarks by President Trump and Prime Minister Morrison of Australia Before Bilateral Meeting," White House, September 20, 2019, https://www.whitehouse.gov/briefings-statements /remarks-president-trump-prime-minister-morrison-australia-bilateral-meeting/.

7   Peter Wade, "Trump Admits Talking About Biden in 'Absolutely Perfect' Phone Call with Ukraine President," *Rolling Stone*, September 22, 2019, https://www .rollingstone.com/politics/politics-news/trump-admits-biden-phone-call-ukraine -president-888203/.

CHAPTER 13: WAITING FOR MUELLER

1   Seung Min Kim, "Trump Taps Former Kavanaugh Clerk to Fill Vacancy on Powerful D.C. Appeals Court," *Washington Post*, April 3, 2020, https://www .washingtonpost.com/politics/trump-taps-former-kavanaugh-clerk-to-fill-vacancy-on -powerful-dc-appeals-court/2020/04/03/3ddb5e50-7446-11ea-ae50-7148009252e3 _story.html.

2   Bob Moser, "Mitch McConnell: The Man Who Sold America," *Rolling Stone*, September 17, 2019, https://www.rollingstone.com/politics/politics-features /mitch-mcconnell-man-who-sold-america-880799/; Tal Axelrod, "Poll: 33% of Kentucky Voters Approve of McConnell," *Hill*, February 21, 2019, https://thehill.com /homenews/campaign/431002-poll-33-of-kentucky-voters-approve-of-mcconnell; Jane Mayer, "How Mitch McConnell Became Trump's Enabler-in-Chief," *New Yorker*, April 12, 2020, https://www.newyorker.com/magazine/2020/04/20/how -mitch-mcconnell-became-trumps-enabler-in-chief; Steve Benen, "McConnell Urges Dems Not to Investigate Trump After Midterms," MSNBC, October 11, 2018, http://www.msnbc.com/rachel-maddow-show/mcconnell-urges-dems-not -investigate-trump-after-midterms.

3   Christian Fong, "How Nancy Pelosi Overcame Her Opposition and Became House Speaker. Again," *Washington Post*, January 4, 2019, https://www .washingtonpost.com/news/monkey-cage/wp/2019/01/04/this-explains-why-nancy -pelosi-became-house-speaker-again-despite-opposition/.

4   "Nancy Pelosi Vows 'Bipartisanship and Common Ground' After Democrats Take the House," CBS News, November 7, 2018, https://www.cbsnews.com /news/nancy-pelosi-house-minority-leader-news-conference-democrats-win-house -of-representatives-today-2018-11-07/; Fong, "How Nancy Pelosi Overcame."

5   John Wagner, "Trump Calls for Bipartisanship but Warns Against Democratic Investigations," *Washington Post*, November 7, 2018, https://www.washingtonpost .com/politics/2018/live-updates/midterms/midterm-election-updates/trump -calls-for-bipartisanship-but-warns-against-democratic-investigations/?arc404 =true.

6   Matthew Weaver and Erin Durkin, "BBC Cameraman Shoved and Abused at Trump Rally in El Paso," *Guardian*, February 13, 2019, https://www.theguardian .com/media/2019/feb/12/bbc-cameraman-shoved-and-abused-at-trump-rally-in-el -paso; Brianna Sacks, "A Trump Supporter Attacked Journalists After the President

Blasted the Media at His Texas Rally," *BuzzFeed*, February 12, 2019, https://www
.buzzfeednews.com/article/briannasacks/trump-supporter-shoved-journalists-el
-paso-rally.

7   Sheryl Gay Stolberg and Annie Karni, "Pelosi vs. Trump: 'Don't Characterize the Strength That I Bring,' She Says," *New York Times*, December 11,
2018, https://www.nytimes.com/2018/12/11/us/politics/nancy-pelosi-trump.html;
Megan McCluskey, "Nancy Pelosi Inevitably Becomes a Meme with Post–Oval
Office Meeting Sunglasses Moment," *Time*, December 12, 2018, https://time.com
/5477993/nancy-pelosi-sunglasses-meme/; "President Trump Meeting with Democratic Leaders," C-SPAN, December 11, 2018, https://www.c-span.org/video/
?455813-1/president-trump-democratic-leaders-clash-border-funding.

8   Chris Sommerfeldt, "Nancy Pelosi Mocks Trump's 'Manhood' After 'Wild'
Oval Office Meet, Says She Tried to 'Be the Mom,'" New York *Daily News*, December 11, 2018, https://www.nydailynews.com/news/politics/ny-pol-pelosi-trump
-manhood-oval-office-20181211-story.html; Megan Cassella, Nancy Cook, and
Gabby Orr, "What Can Get Done in a Divided Washington," *Politico*, November 7,
2018, https://www.politico.com/story/2018/11/06/2018-elections-house-democrats
-trump-relationship-930651.

9   David Leonhardt, "Three Impeachment Options," *New York Times*, January 23, 2019, https://www.nytimes.com/2019/01/23/opinion/trump-impeachment
-democrats-republicans.html?searchResultPosition=1.

10   "Join Us," YouTube video, 1:02, posted by Tom Steyer, October 19, 2017,
https://www.youtube.com/watch?v=GXl8vRmLeJk.

11   Cheyenne Haslett, "Nancy Pelosi Says Impeachment or Even Indictment
of President Trump Open Questions," ABC News, January 3, 2019, https://abcnews
.go.com/Politics/nancy-pelosi-impeachment-indictment-president-trump-open
-questions/story?id=60135980.

12   Luke O'Neil, "'We're Gonna Impeach the Motherfucker': The Democrats'
New Street Fighters," *Guardian*, January 4, 2019, https://www.theguardian.com/us
-news/2019/jan/04/democrats-congress-trump-impeach-rashida-tlaib.

13   Ian Schwartz, "Pelosi on Tlaib's 'Motherf*cker' Comment: 'I'm Not
in the Censorship Business,'" *RealClearPolitics*, January 5, 2019, https://www
.realclearpolitics.com/video/2019/01/05/pelosi_on_tlaibs_motherfcker_comment
_im_not_in_the_censorship_business.html.

14   Daniella Diaz, "Rep. Maxine Waters: Trump's Actions 'Leading Himself' to Impeachment," CNN, February 6, 2017, https://www.cnn.com/2017/02/06
/politics/maxine-waters-donald-trump-impeachment/index.html.

15   Bess Levin, "Dems Demand Info on Acting Attorney General's 'Masculine Toilet' Scam," *Vanity Fair*, November 13, 2018, https://www.vanityfair.com

/news/2018/11/democrats-demand-info-on-acting-attorney-general-matthew
-whitaker-masculine-toilet-scam.

16   Eric Lach, "Trump Fires Jeff Sessions, and Throws His Administration
Back into Chaos," *New Yorker*, November 7, 2018, https://www.newyorker.com
/news/current/trump-fires-jeff-sessions-and-throws-his-administration-back-into
-chaos.

17   Russell Berman, "The Complicated Friendship of Robert Mueller and
William Barr," *Atlantic*, April 28, 2019, https://www.theatlantic.com/politics
/archive/2019/04/mueller-barr-and-their-pre-trump-friendship/588151/; Andrew
Rice, "Trump's Other Lawyer," *Intelligencer*, December 5, 2019, https://nymag.com
/intelligencer/2019/12/attorney-general-william-barr-donald-trump-impeachment
-hearings.html?utm_source=nym_press.

18   Jordan Fabian and Morgan Chalfant, "Trump Picks William Barr as
Next Attorney General," *Hill*, December 7, 2018, https://thehill.com/homenews
/administration/420166-trump-picks-william-barr-as-next-attorney-general; Mae-
gan Vazquez and Kaitlan Collins, "Trump Nominates William Barr to Be His Next
Attorney General," CNN, December 7, 2018, https://www.cnn.com/2018/12/07
/politics/william-barr-attorney-general-nomination/index.html.

CHAPTER 14: ENTER WILLIAM BARR

1   Ellis Kim, "READ: Bill Barr's 19-Page Memo Ripping Mueller Probe,"
Law, December 20, 2018, https://www.law.com/nationallawjournal/2018/12/20
/read-bill-barrs-19-page-memo-ripping-mueller-probe/?slreturn=20200401131615.

2   William Barr, memo to DOJ Mueller obstruction, June 8, 2018, https://
www.documentcloud.org/documents/5638848-June-2018-Barr-Memo-to-DOJ
-Muellers-Obstruction.html; Devlin Barrett, "Attorney General Nominee Wrote
Memo Criticizing Mueller Obstruction Probe," *Washington Post*, December 20,
2018, https://www.washingtonpost.com/world/national-security/attorney-general
-nominee-wrote-memo-criticizing-mueller-obstruction-probe/2018/12/20
/72a01304-044b-11e9-b5df-5d3874f1ac36_story.html.

3   Michael Bowman, "Senators Hear Praise, Criticism of US Attorney General Nominee," *VOA News*, January 16, 2019, https://www.voanews.com/usa/senators
-hear-praise-criticism-us-attorney-general-nominee.

4   Joshua Eaton, "Trump's Attorney General Pick Reveals New Details of
White House Meeting About Mueller Investigation," Think Progress, January 15,
2019, https://thinkprogress.org/william-barr-trumps-attorney-general-pick-reveals
-new-details-of-meeting-with-him-about-mueller-investigation-f5527bfc629e/;
Debbie Lord, "Here Is William Barr's Opening Statement at His Senate Confirmation Hearing," WSB Radio, January 15, 2019, https://www.wsbradio.com/news

/national/here-william-barr-opening-statement-his-senate-confirmation-hearing /pQmsvM0NwGoBc8e2EM7y8N/.

5   William Barr, memo to DOJ Mueller obstruction, June 8, 2018, https:// int.nyt.com/data/documenthelper/549-june-2018-barr-memo-to-doj-mue /b4c05e39318dd2d136b3/optimized/full.pdf#page=1.

6   Quinta Jurecic, "Document: William Barr Memo on Obstruction Investigation," *Lawfare,* December 20, 2018, https://www.lawfareblog.com/document -william-barr-memo-obstruction-investigation.

7   Matt Zapotosky and Karoun Demirjian, "Senate Confirms William Barr as Attorney General in 54-to-45 Vote," *Washington Post*, February 14, 2019, https:// www.washingtonpost.com/world/national-security/william-barr-expected-to-be -confirmed-as-attorney-general-thursday/2019/02/13/f162e514-2f1a-11e9-813a -0ab2f17e305b_story.html.

8   Marie Brenner, "'I Had No Problem Being Politically Different': Young William Barr Among the Manhattan Liberals," *Vanity Fair,* October 7, 2019, https:// www.vanityfair.com/news/2019/10/the-untold-tale-of-young-william-barr.

9   Ibid.; Wolfgang Saxon, "Donald Barr, 82, Headmaster and Science Honors Educator," *New York Times,* February 10, 2004, https://www.nytimes.com/2004 /02/10/nyregion/donald-barr-82-headmaster-and-science-honors-educator.html; panel, Open Mind, "American Values and the College Generation," PBS, June 20, 1974, https://www.pbs.org/video/the-open-mind-american-values-and-the-college -generation/; Gene I. Maeroff, "Barr Quits Dalton School Post, Charging Trustees' Interference," *New York Times,* February 20, 1974, https://www.nytimes.com/1974 /02/20/archives/barr-quits-dalton-school-post-charging-trustees-interference.html. Jimmy Lohman, "What William Barr Isn't Telling His Questioners," *Florida Flambeau*, Tallahassee, November 18, 1991.

10   Philip Bump, "The 1989 Precedent That Raises Questions About How Barr Will Redact the Mueller Report," *Washington Post,* April 15, 2019, https://www.washingtonpost.com/politics/2019/04/15/precedent-that-raises -questions-about-how-barr-will-redact-mueller-report/; Alex Emmons, "William Barr Has Long Tried to Limit What a President Must Share with Congress. The Whistleblower Complaint Is No Exception," *Intercept,* September 20, 2019, https://theintercept.com/2019/09/20/william-barr-has-long-tried-to-limit -what-a-president-must-share-with-congress-the-whistleblower-complaint-is-no -exception/?comments=1.

11   David Johnston, "Bush Pardons 6 in Iran Affair, Aborting a Weinberger Trial; Prosecutor Assails 'Cover-Up,'" *New York Times,* December 25, 1992, https:// archive.nytimes.com/www.nytimes.com/books/97/06/29/reviews/iran-pardon.html ?_r=1&oref=slogin; Greg Walters, "William Barr's Been Accused of a Presidential

Cover-Up Before," *Vice*, April 17, 2019, https://www.vice.com/en_us/article/pajdb9
/william-barrs-been-accused-of-a-presidential-cover-up-before; report, *The Case
for More Incarceration*, U.S. Department of Justice, Office of Policy and Communications, Office of Policy Development, October 8, 1992, https://www.ncjrs.gov
/pdffiles1/Digitization/139583NCJRS.pdf.

12   Eliana Johnson, "The Real Reason Bill Barr Is Defending Trump," *Politico*, May 1, 2019, https://www.politico.com/story/2019/05/01/william-barr-donald
-trump-mueller-report-129527.

13   Joan Walsh, "William Barr Is Neck-Deep in Extremist Catholic Institutions," *Nation*, October 15, 2019, https://www.thenation.com/article/william-barr
-notre-dame-secularism/; Katherine Stewart and Caroline Fredrickson, "Bill Barr
Thinks America Is Going to Hell," *New York Times*, December 29, 2019, https://www
.nytimes.com/2019/12/29/opinion/william-barr-trump.html.

14   Editorial Board, "Editorial: Confirm William Barr, Even Though It Requires a Leap of Faith," *Los Angeles Times*, February 7, 2019, https://www.latimes
.com/opinion/editorials/la-ed-barr-justice-20190207-story.html.

15   "Attorney General William P. Barr Delivers Remarks to the Law School
and the de Nicola Center for Ethics and Culture at the University of Notre Dame,"
United States Department of Justice, October 11, 2019, https://www.justice.gov
/opa/speech/attorney-general-william-p-barr-delivers-remarks-law-school-and-de
-nicola-center-ethics.

16   Michael Tackett, "Five Takeaways from Cohen's Testimony to Congress," *New York Times*, February 27, 2019, https://www.nytimes.com/2019/02/27
/us/politics/cohen-testimony.html; Kevin Breuninger and Dan Mangan, "Michael
Cohen: 'I Fear' Trump Won't Peacefully Give Up the White House If He Loses the
2020 Election," CNBC News, February 27, 2019, https://www.cnbc.com/2019/02
/27/michael-cohen-i-fear-trump-wont-give-up-the-white-house-if-he-loses-in-2020
.htm; Garrett Epps, "Trump Is at War with the Whole Idea of an Independent Judiciary," *Atlantic*, March 4, 2020, https://www.theatlantic.com/ideas/archive/2020/03
/trump-independent-judiciary/607375/e.

CHAPTER 15: ROBERT MUELLER REPORTING

1   Katie Rogers and Katie Benner, "Where's the Mueller Report? Washington Barely Handled the Anticipation," *New York Times*, March 22, 2019, https://
www.nytimes.com/2019/03/22/us/politics/when-will-mueller-report-come-out
.html.

2   Grace Panetta, "What 3 Past Presidents Did When They Were Subpoenaed, and What Could Happen If Mueller Tries to Make Trump Testify," *Business
Insider*, September 1, 2018, https://www.businessinsider.com/can-mueller-subpoena

-trump-2018-8#what-could-happen-if-trump-were-subpoenaed-to-testify-before-a
-grand-jury-4.

3   Alexandra Petri, "President Trump Has One of the Greatest Memories of All Time," *Washington Post,* October 29, 2017, https://www.washingtonpost.com /blogs/compost/wp/2017/10/27/president-trump-has-one-of-the-greatest-memories -of-all-time/; Tessa Stuart, "29 Things Trump Couldn't Recall While Answering Mueller's Questions," *Rolling Stone,* April 18, 2019, https://www.rollingstone.com /politics/politics-news/mueller-trump-29-questions-824126/.

4   Thomas Burr, "Call Him Mr. No Comment," *Salt Lake Tribune,* April 13, 2018, https://www.sltrib.com/news/politics/2018/04/14/mr-no-comment-meet-the -utahn-who-speaks-for-the-special-counsels-russia-trump-probe-but-dont-expect -him-to-say-too-much/.

5   Jonathan Lemire, Michael Balsamo, and Mary Clare Jalonick, "In a Plain Envelope, a Monumental Message: Mueller's Done," Associated Press, March 23, 2019, https://apnews.com/cad1b2eb4c944176bba5cc3fa53f8a2b.

6   Allegra Kirkland, "Dem Leaders: Barr Must 'Make the Full Report Public,' WH Must Not 'Interfere,'" *Talking Points Memo,* March 22, 2019, https:// talkingpointsmemo.com/livewire/pelosi-schumer-make-full-mueller-report-public; "Read William Barr's Letter to Congress on the Mueller Report," *New York Times,* March 22, 2019, https://www.nytimes.com/2019/03/22/us/politics/barr-letter -mueller.html?searchResultPosition=6.

7   Olivia B. Waxman, "President Trump Invoked Executive Privilege. Here's the History of That Presidential Power," *Time,* June 13, 2019, https://time.com /5605930/executive-privilege-history/; Eliana Johnson, "The Real Reason Bill Barr Is Defending Trump," *Politico,* May 1, 2019, https://www.politico.com/story/2019/05 /01/william-barr-donald-trump-mueller-report-1295273.

8   Quinta Jurecic, "Document: Attorney General Barr Letter on Mueller Re-port," *Lawfare,* March 24, 2019, https://www.lawfareblog.com/document-attorney -general-barr-letter-mueller-report.

9   "Mueller Says Searches Yielded Evidence of Stone-WikiLeaks Communi-cations," Reuters, February 15, 2019, https://www.reuters.com/article/us-usa-trump -russia-stone-wikileaks/mueller-says-searches-yielded-evidence-of-stone-wikileaks -communications-idUSKCN1Q502Z.

10   Jamie Ross,"The Story Behind Trump's Infamous 'Best Sex I Ever Had' Headline," *Daily Beast,* April 12, 2018, https://www.thedailybeast.com/the-story -behind-trumps-infamous-1990-best-sex-i-ever-had-headline.

11   Alana Abramson, "How President Trump's Defense Went from 'No Col-lusion' with Russia to 'Collusion Is Not a Crime,'" *Time,* July 31, 2018, https://time .com/5352628/donald-trump-rudy-giuliani-collusion-crime/.

12   Ann E. Marimow, "Trump's Allies Celebrate 'No Collusion' Findings, While Democrats Call for Release of Full Report," *Washington Post*, March 24, 2019, https://www.washingtonpost.com/politics/trumps-allies-celebrate-no-collusion -findings-while-democrats-call-for-release-of-full-report/2019/03/24/9c7d1770 -4e66-11e9-a3f7-78b7525a8d5f_story.html.

13   Staff, "Read: Mueller's Letter to Barr," *Hill*, May 1, 2019, https://thehill .com/policy/national-security/441547-read-muellers-letter-to-barr.

14   "Justice Department Fiscal Year 2020 Budget Request," C-SPAN, April 10, 2019, https://www.c-span.org/video/?459640-1/attorney-general-barr-thinks -spying-occurred-trump-campaign&start=5803.

15   Matthew Nussbaum, "Justice Department: No Evidence Obama Wire-tapped Trump Tower," *Politico*, September 2, 2017, https://www.politico.com/story /2017/09/02/obama-trump-tower-wiretap-no-evidence-242284.

16   Tom McCarthy, "Rudy Giuliani Admits 'Spygate' Is Trump PR Tactic Against Robert Mueller," *Guardian*, May 27, 2018, https://www.theguardian.com/us -news/2018/may/27/rudy-giuliani-spygate-robert-mueller-donald-trump.

CHAPTER 16: "[NOT] FULL EXONERATION"

1   Rod Rosenstein, "Rosenstein Letter Appointing Mueller Special Counsel," Office of the Deputy Attorney General, May 17, 2019, https://www .documentcloud.org/documents/3726408-Rosenstein-letter-appointing-Mueller -special.html.

2   Rick Klein, "ANALYSIS: Mueller Report Makes Political Case Against Trump," ABC News, April 19, 2019, https://abcnews.go.com/Politics/mueller-report -makes-political-case-trump-analysis/story?id=62456722; Staff, "Mueller Report Highlights: Read the Top Moments from the 448-Page Report," ABC News, April 18, 2019, https://abcnews.go.com/Politics/justice-department-release-redacted -version-mueller-report/story?id=62201315.

3   Charlie Savage, "How Barr's Excerpts Compare to the Mueller Report's Findings," *New York Times*, April 20, 2019, https://www.nytimes.com/2019/04/19 /us/politics/mueller-report-william-barr-excerpts.html?searchResultPosition=32.

4   Aruna Viswanatha and Sadie Gurman, "Mueller Report Lays Out Trump's Attempts to Curtail Inquiry," *Wall Street Journal*, April 18, 2019, https://www .wsj.com/articles/mueller-report-release-11555590084?mod=article_inline&mod =livecoverage_web.

5   Pramila Jayapal, interviews with the authors.

6   Jonathan V. Last, "Portrait of the President as a Gangster," *Bulwark*, April 18, 2019, https://thebulwark.com/portrait-of-the-president-as-a-gangster/.

7   Tal Kopan, "Nancy Pelosi: Standoff with Trump Is a Constitutional Crisis,"

SFGate, May 24, 2019, https://www.sfgate.com/politics/article/Nancy-Pelosi
-Standoff-with-Trump-is-a-13832587.php.

8 "Speaker Pelosi: Dems Focusing on More Than Mueller Report," MSNBC,
April 17, 2019, https://www.msnbc.com/morning-joe/watch/speaker-pelosi-dems
-focusing-on-more-than-mueller-report-1496556611832.

9 *For more on Article II, see:* Frank O. Bowman III, *High Crimes and Misdemeanors: A History of Impeachment for the Age of Trump* (Cambridge: Cambridge
University Press, 2019).

10 Rachael Bade and Josh Dawsey, "Trump's Feud with Jerry Nadler Rooted
in Decades-Old New York Real Estate Project," *Washington Post*, April 8, 2019,
https://www.washingtonpost.com/politics/ive-been-battling-nadler-for-years-feud
-between-trump-democrat-rooted-in-decades-old-new-york-real-estate-project
/2019/04/08/1c848f7e-57af-11e9-a047-748657a0a9d1_story.html.

11 Allan Smith, "Michael Cohen Filings Renew Discussion of Trump's Impeachment," ABC News, December 9, 2018, https://www.nbcnews.com/politics
/white-house/michael-cohen-filings-renew-discussion-trump-s-impeachment
-n945781.

12 David Weigel and Sean Sullivan, "Ahead of State of the Union, Democrats Are United Against Trump—but Not on Impeachment," *Washington Post*,
January 29, 2018, https://www.washingtonpost.com/powerpost/ahead-of-state-of
-the-union-democrats-are-united-against-trump—but-not-on-impeachment/2018
/01/29/0aef316a-02ec-11e8-bb03-722769454f82_story.html.

CHAPTER 17: "YOU LIED, AND NOW WE KNOW"

1 Christina Pazzanese, "Parsing the Mueller Report," *Harvard Gazette*, April
18, 2019, https://news.harvard.edu/gazette/story/2019/04/harvard-professor-mueller
-found-substantial-evidence-of-obstruction-of-justice/.

2 "William Barr Testimony on Mueller Report: Updates and Analysis,"
New York Times, May 1, 2019, https://www.nytimes.com/interactive/2019/05/01/us
/politics/barr-mueller-report.html.

3 Andrew Prokop, "Michael Cohen's Claim That President Trump Is Threatening His Family, Explained," *Vox*, January 24, 2019, https://www.vox.com/2019
/1/23/18194719/trump-michael-cohen-father-in-law-threat; Daniel Hemel, "Mueller's Biggest Bombshell? Trump Told the White House Counsel to Lie," *Washington
Post*, April 19, 2019, https://www.washingtonpost.com/outlook/2019/04/19/muellers
-biggest-bombshell-trump-told-white-house-counsel-lie/; Michael S. Schmidt, Jo
Becker, Mark Mazzetti, Maggie Haberman, and Adam Goldman, "Trump's Lawyer Raised Prospect of Pardons for Flynn and Manafort," *New York Times*, March
28, 2019, https://www.nytimes.com/2018/03/28/us/politics/trump-pardon-michael

-flynn-paul-manafort-john-dowd.html; "William Barr Testimony on Mueller Report Before Senate Judiciary Committee," C-SPAN, May 1, 2019, https://www.c-span.org/video/?459922-1/william-barr-testimony-mueller-report-senate-judiciary-committee&playEvent.

4   Office of Nancy Pelosi, "Trump Administration Obstruction: Unprecedented, Unwarranted, Unconstitutional," *Politico*, https://www.politico.com/f/?id=0000016a-72b0-dca8-a1ff-7fb813f60001; Darren Samuelsohn and Josh Gerstein, "Who Got Tossed Under the Bill Barr Bus?," *Politico*, May 1, 2019, https://www.politico.com/story/2019/05/01/william-barr-hearing-blame-1296866; Staff, "Factbox: Courts Poke Holes in Trump's Stonewall of Congress," Reuters, May 28, 2019, https://www.reuters.com/article/us-usa-trump-congress-investigations-fac/factbox-courts-poke-holes-in-trumps-stonewall-of-congress-idUSKCN1SY0YC; Ella Nilsen, "William Barr Has Refused to Testify in Front of the House Judiciary Committee," *Vox*, May 1, 2019, https://www.vox.com/policy-and-politics/2019/5/1/18525537/william-barr-house-judiciary-committee.

CHAPTER 18: CONFLICT ESCALATION

1   Charlie Savage, "Trump Vows Stonewall of 'All' House Subpoenas, Setting Up Fight over Powers," *New York Times*, April 24, 2019, https://www.nytimes.com/2019/04/24/us/politics/donald-trump-subpoenas.html?module=inline; Sean Illing, "How Do We Know If We're in a Constitutional Crisis? 11 Experts Explain," *Vox*, May 16, 2019, https://www.vox.com/2019/5/16/18617661/donald-trump-congress-constitutional-crisis.

2   Paul Krugman, "Trump Is Abusing His Tariff Power, Too," *New York Times*, January 23, 2020, https://www.nytimes.com/2020/01/23/opinion/trump-auto-tariff.html; Mark Greenberg and Harry Litman, "Trump's Corrupt Use of the Pardon Power," *Lawfare*, June 19, 2018, https://www.lawfareblog.com/trumps-corrupt-use-pardon-power; Michael Tackett, "Another Day, Another 'Acting' Cabinet Secretary as Trump Skirts Senate," *New York Times*, April 8, 2019, https://www.nytimes.com/2019/04/08/us/politics/trump-acting-cabinet-secretaries.html; Matthew Callahan and Ruben Fischer-Baum, "Where the Trump Administration Is Thwarting House Oversight," *Washington Post*, October 11, 2019, https://www.washingtonpost.com/graphics/2019/politics/trump-blocking-congress/.

3   Scott Stossel, "Trump Versus the Judiciary," *Atlantic*, January 13, 2019, https://www.theatlantic.com/politics/archive/2019/01/chief-justice-roberts-corrects-president-trump/579997/.

4   Michael K. Ferber, "Involvement in the Vietnam War Resistance Movement and the 'Boston Five,'" https://www.michaelkferber.com/politics-public-affairs/the-boston-five; John T. Correll, "The Pentagon Papers," *Air Force Magazine*, February 1,

2007, https://www.airforcemag.com/article/0207pentagon/; Daniel Arkin, "Daniel Ellsberg: Nixon White House Wanted to 'Shut Me Up' with Assault," NBC News, June 19, 2017, https://www.nbcnews.com/politics/politics-news/daniel-ellsberg -nixon-white-house-wanted-shut-me-assault-n774376; Caroline Newman, "Lies, Leaks and Larceny," *UVAToday*, January 11, 2018, https://news.virginia.edu/content /blow-safe-and-get-it-listen-nixons-response-pentagon-papers; "Nixon Tapes: Nixon on Prosecuting Ellsberg," C-SPAN, June 29, 1971, https://www.c-span.org /video/?444767-1/nixon-tapes-nixon-prosecuting-ellsberg; Harrison Smith, "Egil Krogh, the Nixon 'Plumber' Who Approved Break-In Targeting Daniel Ellsberg, Dies at 80," *Seattle Times*, January 2020, https://www.seattletimes.com/nation-world /egil-krogh-the-nixon-plumber-who-approved-break-in-targeting-daniel-ellsberg -dies-at-80/; Sam Berger and Alex Tausanovitch, "Lessons from Watergate," Center for American Progress, July 30, 2018, https://www.americanprogress.org/issues /democracy/reports/2018/07/30/454058/lessons-from-watergate/.

5 Burgess Everett, "McConnell on Mueller Report: 'Case Closed,'" *Politico*, May 7, 2019, https://www.politico.com/story/2019/05/07/mcconnell-mueller-report -case-closed-1307390.

6 "Jamie Raskin (D-MD) Full Remarks," House Judiciary Committee, C-SPAN, May 10, 2019, https://www.c-span.org/video/?c4797071/jamie-raskin-full -remark; Raskin interviews with authors.

7 Mary Clarke Jalonik, Lisa Mascaro, and Jonathan Lemire, "House Panel Votes Barr in Contempt, Escalating Trump Dispute," Associated Press, May 8, 2019, https://apnews.com/d64338bc6606456d978c33f11d2cf2b4; Andrew Desiderio and Kyle Cheney, "Barr Held in Contempt by House Judiciary," *Politico*, May 8, 2019, https://www.politico.com/story/2019/05/08/trump-invokes-executive-privilege-to -block-release-of-unredacted-mueller-report-1311738.

8 "Speech: Donald Trump Holds a Political Rally in Panama City Beach, Florida—May 8, 2019," Factbase, May 8, 2019, https://factba.se/transcript/donald -trump-speech-maga-rally-panama-city-beach-florida-may-8-2019; Aaron Rupar, "Trump Turns Shooting Immigrants into a Punchline at Florida Rally," *Vox*, May 9, 2019, https://www.vox.com/2019/5/9/18538124/trump-panama-city-beach-rally -shooting-migrants; Aaron Blake, "Trump's Rambling, Deceptive Q&A with Reporters, Annotated," *Washington Post*, May 9, 2019, https://www.washingtonpost .com/politics/2019/05/09/trumps-very-deceptive-qa-with-reporters-annotated/.

CHAPTER 19: SELF-IMPEACHMENT

1 Caitlin Oprysko, "Trump on Impeachment, 'It's a Dirty, Filthy, Disgusting Word,'" *Politico*, May 30, 2019, https://www.politico.com/story/2019/05/30 /trump-impeachment-dirty-word-1347500; Felicia Sonmez, "Pelosi Says Trump

Is 'Becoming Self-Impeachable,'" *Washington Post*, May 8, 2019, https://www
.washingtonpost.com/politics/pelosi-says-trump-is-becoming-self-impeachable
/2019/05/08/87464a68-718c-11e9-9f06-5fc2ee80027a_story.html.

2   Cristina Marcos, "Pelosi: 'Trump Is Goading Us to Impeach Him,'"
Hill, May 7, 2019, https://thehill.com/homenews/house/442493-pelosi-trump
-is-goading-us-to-impeach-him; "Inside Congress with Speaker of the House
Nancy Pelosi," *CornellCast*, May 7, 2019, https://www.cornell.edu/video/inside
-congress-house-speaker-nancy-pelosi; Jonathan Tamari, "Reps. Mary Gay Scanlon, Madeleine Dean of Pa. Call for Trump Impeachment Inquiry," *Philadelphia
Inquirer*, May 21, 2019, https://www.politico.com/story/2019/05/21/nancy-pelosi
-impeachment-donald-trump-1337143; Greg Sargent, "A Top Democrat Warns:
If We Don't Confront Trump, He'll Grow More Lawless," *Washington Post*, May
21, 2019, https://www.washingtonpost.com/opinions/2019/05/21/top-democrat
-warns-if-we-dont-confront-trump-hell-grow-more-lawless/; Alex Rogers and
Manu Raju, "Pelosi Says Trump Is 'Engaged in a Cover-Up,'" CNN, May 22,
2019, https://edition.cnn.com/2019/05/22/politics/pelosi-trump-cover-up-caucus
-meeting/index.html.

3   George Packer, "The Demise of the Moderate Republican," *New Yorker*,
November 5, 2018, https://www.newyorker.com/magazine/2018/11/12/the-demise
-of-the-moderate-republican; Staff, "4 in 10 House Republicans in Office When
Trump Was Inaugurated Have Now Quit or Lost Their Seats," *Week*, September 23,
2019, https://theweek.com/speedreads/866990/4-10-house-republicans-office-when
-trump-inaugurated-have-now-quit-lost-seats.

4   Felicia Sonmez and Paul Kane, "Trump Calls Rep. Amash a 'Loser' for
Saying President Engaged in Impeachable Conduct," *Washington Post*, May 19,
2019, https://www.washingtonpost.com/politics/trump-calls-rep-amash-a-loser-for
-saying-president-engaged-in-impeachable-conduct/2019/05/19/dab51228-7a3e
-11e9-a5b3-34f3edf1351e_story.html.

5   Isaac Stanley-Becker and Felicia Sonmez, "Justin Amash, Tea Party Star,
Earns Primary Challenge for Backing Impeachment," *Washington Post*, May 20,
2019, https://www.washingtonpost.com/nation/2019/05/20/justin-amash-trump
-impeachment-jim-lower-primary-challenge/.

6   "Justin Amash Holds a Town Hall," YouTube video, 2:08:49, posted by
13 On Your Side, May 28, 2019, https://www.youtube.com/watch?v=FsDs2fTbj1I.

7   Ibid., minute 1:21.

8   "Saturday Night Live Season 43 Episode 20 on April 14, 2018, with Host
John Mulaney and Musical Guest Jack White," NBC, April 14, 2018, https://www
.nbc.com/saturday-night-live/season-43/episode/20-john-mulaney-with-jack-white
-294240.

9   Kate Lyons, "Alec Baldwin Tweets Back as Donald Trump Talks of 'Retribution' for SNL," *Guardian*, February 18, 2019, https://www.theguardian.com/us-news/2019/feb/18/donald-trump-talks-of-retribution-after-alec-baldwin-parody-on-snl.

10   "Full Transcript: Robert Mueller's Statement on the Russia Investigation," *Politico*, May 29, 2019, https://www.politico.com/story/2019/05/29/robert-mueller-statement-russia-investigation-text-transcript-1346453.

11   Robert S. Mueller III, *Report on the Investigation into Russian Interference in the 2016 Presidential Election*, vol. 1, March 2019, https://www.justice.gov/storage/report.pdf; "Trump's Russia Cover-Up by the Numbers—272 Contacts with Russia-Linked Operatives," Moscow Project, updated June 3, 2019, https://themoscowproject.org/explainers/trumps-russia-cover-up-by-the-numbers-70-contacts-with-russia-linked-operatives/.

12   "Full Transcript of Mueller's Statement on Russia Investigation," *New York Times*, May 29, 2019, https://www.nytimes.com/2019/05/29/us/politics/mueller-transcript.html; Scott Clement, Emily Guskin, and Kevin Uhrmacher, "Did Congress Read the Mueller Report? More Than a Quarter of These Key Lawmakers Won't Say," *Washington Post*, May 31, 2019, https://www.washingtonpost.com/graphics/2019/politics/who-read-the-mueller-report/; Darren Samuelsohn, "'What's the Point?' Lawmakers Fess Up to Not Fully Reading the Mueller Report," *Politico*, July 9, 2019, https://www.politico.com/story/2019/07/09/congress-read-mueller-report-1402232; Laura Miller, "The Straight Story," *Slate*, April 22, 2019, https://slate.com/culture/2019/04/mueller-report-book-review.html; Quinta Jurecic, "Look at the Mueller Report as a Detective Story. It Will Blow Your Mind," *New York Times*, August 2, 2019, https://www.nytimes.com/2019/08/02/opinion/mueller-report.html.

13   Robert De Niro, "Robert Mueller, We Need to Hear More," *New York Times*, May 29, 2019, https://www.nytimes.com/2019/05/29/opinion/robert-de-niro-robert-mueller-we-need-to-hear-more.html.

14   "Speaker Nancy Pelosi on Mueller Report & Impeaching Donald Trump," YouTube video, 14:01, posted by *Jimmy Kimmel Live*, May 31, 2019, https://www.youtube.com/watch?v=4DphC6e3Y5w.

CHAPTER 20: BARR'S PREDICATE

1   Sharon LaFraniere, Mark Mazzetti, and Matt Apuzzo, "How the Russia Inquiry Began: A Campaign Aide, Drinks and Talk of Political Dirt," *New York Times*, December 30, 2017, https://www.nytimes.com/2017/12/30/us/politics/how-fbi-russia-investigation-began-george-papadopoulos.html; Michael D. Shear, Katie Benner, and Nicholas Fandos, "Embracing Conspiracy Theory, Trump Escalates Attack on Bruce Ohr," *New York Times*, August 17, 2018, https://www.nytimes.com/2018/08/17/us/politics/trump-conspiracy-bruce-nellie-ohr.html.

2 Devlin Barrett, "FBI Director Tells Congress He Has No Evidence of 'Spying' on Trump Campaign," *Washington Post*, May 7, 2019, https://www.washingtonpost.com/world/national-security/fbi-director-tells-congress-he-has-no-evidence-of-spying-on-trump-campaign/2019/05/07/075e6f3a-70cc-11e9-9f06-5fc2ee80027a_story.html; Paula Reid, "Barr Has Team Reviewing Origins of Russia Investigation," CBS News, April 10, 2019, https://www.cbsnews.com/news/william-barr-has-team-reviewing-how-investigation-started-official-says/; Chris Strohm and Billy House, "Barr Forms Team to Review FBI's Actions in Trump Probe," *Bloomberg*, April 9, 2019, https://www.bloomberg.com/news/articles/2019-04-09/barr-said-to-form-team-to-review-fbi-s-actions-in-trump-probe; Adam Goldman, "F.B.I. Director Defends Bureau Against Spying Accusations: 'That's Not the Term I Would Use,'" *New York Times,* May 7, 2019, https://www.nytimes.com/2019/05/07/us/politics/christopher-wray-fbi-spying-accusations.html.

3 Editors, "Washington's Most Powerful, Least Famous People," *New Republic,* October 11, 2011, https://newrepublic.com/article/96131/washingtons-most-powerful-least-famous-people; Rich Phillips, "Rogue FBI Agent Sentenced to 40 Years in Mob Hit," CNN News, January 15, 2009, https://www.cnn.com/2009/CRIME/01/15/connolly.sentence/index.html; Spencer Ackerman, "CIA Exhales: 99 out of 101 Torture Cases Dropped," *Wired*, June 30, 2011, https://www.wired.com/2011/06/cia-exhales-99-out-of-101-torture-cases-dropped/; Dror Ladin, "There's So Much We Still Don't Know About the CIA's Torture Program. Here's How the Government Is Keeping the Full Story a Secret," *Time,* February 7, 2020, https://time.com/5779579/cia-torture-secrecy/; Karen DeYoung, "Torture of Al-Qaeda Suspect Described in 2002 Cables Sent by CIA Director Gina Haspel," *Washington Post*, August 10, 2018, https://www.washingtonpost.com/world/national-security/torture-of-al-qaeda-suspect-described-in-2002-cables-sent-by-cia-director-gina-haspel/2018/08/09/dfd79b5a-9c21-11e8-843b-36e177f3081c_story.html.

4 Staff, "Inaugurata a Roma la 'Langley' Italiana, la Nuova Sede dell'intelligence per Mille 007," *Rai News,* March 6, 2019, http://www.rainews.it/dl/rainews/articoli/Inaugurata-a-Roma-la-nuova-sede-intelligence-per-mille-007-94e6208b-f139-4bd0-acb3-445dd7e16000.html; Valerio Valentini, "E' un Paese per Vecchione," *Il Foglio,* October 3, 2019, https://www.ilfoglio.it/politica/2019/10/03/news/e-un-paese-per-vecchione-278126/; Anna Palmer and Jake Sherman, "POLITICO Playbook: Bill Barr's Coalition of the Willing," *Politico,* October 1, 2019, https://www.politico.com/newsletters/playbook/2019/10/01/bill-barrs-coalition-of-the-willing-483656.

5 Melissa Davey, "Donald Trump Wants Investigation into Australia's Role in 'Russian Hoax,'" *Guardian,* May 25, 2019, https://www.theguardian.com/us-news/2019/may/25/donald-trump-wants-investigation-into-australias-role-in-russian-hoax.

6   Anna Momigliano, "Italy Did Not Fuel U.S. Suspicion of Russian Meddling, Prime Minister Says," *New York Times,* October 23, 2019, https://www.nytimes.com/2019/10/23/world/europe/italy-trump-conspiracy-conte.html; Ben Riley-Smith, "Australian PM Scott Morrison Agreed to Help Donald Trump with Investigation into Russia Probe Origins," *Telegraph,* October 1, 2019, https://www.telegraph.co.uk/news/2019/09/30/donald-trump-suggests-democrat-leading-impeachment-inquiry-should/; Patrick Wintour and Luke Harding, "William Barr Discussed FBI Russia Inquiry with UK Intelligence," *Guardian,* October 1, 2019, https://www.theguardian.com/us-news/2019/oct/01/william-barr-us-attorney-general-discussed-mueller-inquiry-uk-intelligence; Matt Zapotosky, "Barr Undercuts Mueller Investigation as Trump Cheers Him On," *Washington Post,* May 9, 2020, https://www.washingtonpost.com/national-security/barr-undercuts-mueller-investigation-as-trump-cheers-him-on/2020/05/09/dc15316e-9169-11ea-a9c0-73b93422d691_story.html.

CHAPTER 21: A PARTISAN THING

1   Aaron Blake, "Trump's Playbook on 'Obamagate' Is Extremely—and Dubiously—Familiar," *Washington Post,* May 15, 2020, https://www.washingtonpost.com/politics/2020/05/15/trumps-playbook-obamagate-is-extremely-dubiously-familiar/.

2   Dareh Gregorian, "'Off the Charts': White House Turnover Is Breaking Records," NBC News, September 23, 2019, https://www.nbcnews.com/politics/white-house/charts-white-house-turnover-breaking-records-n1056101; David Leonhardt and Ian Prasad Philbrick, "Trump's Corruption: The Definitive List," *New York Times,* October 28, 2018, https://www.nytimes.com/2018/10/28/opinion/trump-administration-corruption-conflicts.html.

3   "Waiting for Mueller, with a Plea or Two," *New York Times,* July 23, 2019, https://www.nytimes.com/2019/07/23/opinion/letters/mueller-testimony-trump.html.

4   David Cicilline, interviews with the authors.

5   Nicholas Fandos and Eileen Sullivan, "Weeks of Talks Led a Reluctant Mueller to Testify," *New York Times,* June 26, 2019, https://www.nytimes.com/2019/06/26/us/politics/trump-mueller-testimony.html.

6   "Dates from Testimonies," documents released from State Department to American Oversight, https://docs.google.com/document/d/1RGNcn3SDd9Dg1LnHrvmzPYdJxZLKO9T1Ucv7s-IcupY/edit.

7   Devan Cole, "Trump Touts 4th of July Event, Says It Will Be 'One of the Biggest Gatherings in the History of Washington, D.C.,'" CNN, February 24, 2019, https://www.cnn.com/2019/02/24/politics/trump-july-4th-celebration/index.html.

8   Owen Daugherty, "Mick Jagger Mocks Trump's Revolutionary War Airport Gaffe," *Hill*, July 9, 2019, https://thehill.com/blogs/blog-briefing-room/news/452211 -mick-jagger-mocks-trumps-revolutionary-war-airport-gaffe.

9   "Trump on Fourth of July Speech: 'The Teleprompter Went Out,'" *Washington Post*, July 5, 2019, https://www.washingtonpost.com/video/politics/trump-on -fourth-of-july-speech-the-teleprompter-went-out/2019/07/05/a88a9ae9-1ecc-45d7 -95f1-d483b33e80cd_video.html.

10   "Lincoln Rejects the King of Siam's Offer of Elephants," American Battlefield Trust, February 3, 1862, https://www.battlefields.org/learn/primary-sources /lincoln-rejects-king-siams-offer-elephants.

11   "Blumenthal, et al. v. Trump," Constitutional Accountability Center, https://www.theusconstitution.org/litigation/trump-and-foreign-emoluments -clause/; Congress emoluments complaint, United States District Court for the District of Columbia, June 14, 2017, https://www.theusconstitution.org/wp-content /uploads/2018/01/Blumenthal_v_Trump_DDC_Original_Complaint_Final.pdf.

12   Julie Hirschfeld Davis, "House Condemns Trump's Attack on Four Congresswomen as Racist," *New York Times*, July 16, 2019, https://www.nytimes.com /2019/07/16/us/politics/trump-tweet-house-vote.html.

CHAPTER 22: MUELLER IN THE HOUSE

1   Louie Gohmert, "Robert Mueller: Unmasked," Hannity.com, March 2018, https://hannity.com/wp-content/uploads/2018/04/Gohmert_Mueller _UNMASKED.pdf; David Lightman, "Here's How House Republicans Plan to Handle the Mueller Hearings," *McClatchy DC*, July 23, 2019, https://www .mcclatchydc.com/news/politics-government/congress/article232570392.html.

2   "Robert Mueller Arrival on Capitol Hill," C-SPAN, July 24, 2019, https:// www.c-span.org/video/?462970-1/robert-mueller-arrives-capitol-hill.

3   "Robert Mueller Testifies Before House Judiciary Committee," C-SPAN, July 24, 2019, https://www.c-span.org/video/?462628-1/robert-mueller-congressional -testimony.

4   Brandon Carter, "READ: Robert Mueller's Opening Statements Before Congressional Hearings," NPR, July 24, 2019, https://www.npr.org/2019/07/24 /744174570/read-robert-muellers-opening-statement-before-congressional-hearings.

5   Nigel Chiwaya and Jiachuan Wu, "Mueller Deflected Questions 198 Times. We Tracked When He Did It," NBC News, July 24, 2019, https://www.nbcnews .com/politics/politics-news/robert-mueller-house-testimony-tracker-july-2019 -n1033166.

6   Emily Tillett, "Trump Says 'Mueller Should Have Never Been Chosen' as Special Counsel," CBS News, May 30, 2019, https://www.cbsnews.com/news/robert

-mueller-trump-mueller-should-have-never-been-chosen-as-special-counsel/; Colby Itkowitz, Josh Dawsey, and John Wagner, "Trump Uses Discredited Conflict-of-Interest Charges to Attack Mueller," *Washington Post*, May 30, 2019, https://www .washingtonpost.com/politics/trump-uses-discredited-conflict-of-interest-charges -to-attack-mueller/2019/05/30/2f7c7908-82f6-11e9-95a9-e2c830afe24f_story.html.

7   Chris Mills Rodrigo, "Gohmert Calls Mueller an 'Anal Opening' Ahead of Testimony," *Hill*, July 1, 2019, https://thehill.com/homenews/house/451209 -gohmert-calls-mueller-an-anal-opening-ahead-of-testimony; Chris Cillizza, "10 Key Takeaways from Robert Mueller's Testimony," CNN News, July 25, 2019, https://www.cnn.com/2019/07/24/politics/robert-mueller-testimony-highlights /index.html; Itkowitz, Dawsey, and Wagner, "Trump Uses Discredited Conflict-of-Interest Charges."

8   "Transcript of Robert S. Mueller III's Testimony Before the House Judiciary Committee," *Washington Post*, July 24, 2019, https://www.washingtonpost.com /politics/transcript-of-robert-s-mueller-iiis-testimony-before-the-house-judiciary -committee/2019/07/24/7164abfe-ad96-11e9-a0c9-6d2d7818f3da_story.html.

9   Natasha Bertrand, "Mueller Wants the FBI to Look at a Scheme to Discredit Him," *Atlantic*, October 30, 2019, https://www.theatlantic.com/politics /archive/2018/10/special-counsel-refers-scheme-targeting-mueller-to-fbi/574411/; Jay Willis, "MAGA Trolls' Efforts to Take Down Robert Mueller Flame Out in Hilarious and Spectacular Fashion," *GQ*, October 30, 2018, https://www.gq.com /story/the-lasts-tweets-of-jacob-wohl; Paul Farhi, "What Is Gateway Pundit, the Conspiracy-Hawking Site at the Center of the Bogus Florida 'Crisis Actors' Hype?," *Washington Post*, February 23, 2018, https://www.washingtonpost.com/lifestyle/style /what-is-gateway-pundit-the-conspiracy-hawking-site-at-the-center-of-the-bogus -florida-crisis-actors-hype/2018/02/23/dded562a-174e-11e8-b681-2d4d462a1921 _story.html; David Wohl tweet, February 8, 2019; Christine Hauser, "Jacob Wohl Is Charged with a Felony in California," *New York Times*, September 5, 2019, https:// www.nytimes.com/2019/09/05/us/jacob-wohl-charge.html.

10   Zack Beauchamp, "5 Losers and 0 Winners from Robert Mueller's Testimony to the House of Representatives," *Vox*, July 24, 2019, https://www.vox.com /policy-and-politics/2019/7/24/20708503/robert-mueller-testimony-winners-losers; Brian Flood, "Anti-Trump Harvard Law Prof Laurence Tribe Calls Mueller Hearing 'Disaster' That Helped the President," Fox News, July 24, 2019, https://www.foxnews .com/media/anti-trump-harvard-law-prof-laurence-tribe-calls-mueller-hearing -disaster-that-helped-the-president.

11   Michael D. Shear and Lola Fadulu, "Trump Says Mueller Was 'Horrible' and Republicans 'Had a Good Day,'" *New York Times*, July 24, 2019, https://www .nytimes.com/2019/07/24/us/politics/trump-mueller.html; "Remarks by President

Trump Before Marine One Departure," July 24, 2019, https://www.whitehouse.gov /briefings-statements/remarks-president-trump-marine-one-departure-54//.

CHAPTER 23: A PROFILE IN ARROGANCE

1   Karen Tumulty, "Who Is Corey Lewandowski? His Rise—and His Relationship with Donald Trump," *Washington Post*, March 30, 2016, https://www .washingtonpost.com/politics/trump-and-lewandowski-an-unlikely-pair-of -kindred-spirits/2016/03/30/d82a58ca-f511-11e5-8b23-538270a1ca31_story.html; Kenneth P. Vogel, Ben Schreckinger, and Hadas Gold, "Trump Campaign Manager's Behavior Prompted Staff Concerns," *Politico*, March 15, 2016, https://www .politico.com/story/2016/03/donald-trump-corey-lewandowski-220742; Andrew Kirell and Justin Miller, "Video Shows Trump Campaign Manager Corey Lewandowski Grabbing Reporter Michelle Fields," *Daily Beast*, March 11, 2016, https://www.thedailybeast.com/video-shows-trump-campaign-manager-corey -lewandowski-grabbing-reporter-michelle-fields; Ian Tuttle, "On Donald Trump and the Two-Bit Thugs Who Do His Bidding," *National Review*, March 29, 2016, https://www.nationalreview.com/2016/03/donald-trump-corey-lewandowski -thuggish-campaign/; Alex Gangitano, "Remember That Time Corey Lewandowski Brought a Gun to Capitol Hill," *Roll Call*, June 20, 2016, https://www .rollcall.com/2016/06/20/remember-that-time-corey-lewandowski-brought-a-gun -to-capitol-hill/.

2   John Wagner, "Lewandowski Says He'll Happily Appear Before Judiciary Next Month and Defend Trump," *Washington Post*, August 16, 2019, https:// www.washingtonpost.com/politics/lewandowski-says-hell-happily-appear-before -judiciary-panel-next-month-and-defend-trump/2019/08/16/4487433a-c047-11e9 -a5c6-1e74f7ec4a93_story.html.

3   Caitlin Emma and Connor O'Brien, "Trump Holds Up Ukraine Military Aid Meant to Confront Russia," *Politico*, August 28, 2019, https://www.politico.com /story/2019/08/28/trump-ukraine-military-aid-russia-1689531.

4   Harry Litman, "Corey Lewandowski Is the Perfect Model for a Sustained Trumpian Legacy," *Washington Post*, September 17, 2019, https://www .washingtonpost.com/opinions/2019/09/17/lewandowskis-behavior-fits-right-with -sycophancy-trumpism/.

5   Sarah Ferris, "Moderate Democrats Warn Pelosi of Impeachment Obsession," *Politico*, September 15, 2019, https://www.politico.com/story/2019/09/15 /moderate-democrats-pelosi-impeachment-1495832; Abigail Weinberg, "Alexandria Ocasio-Cortez to Republicans: History Will Remember You Backed Trump," *Mother Jones*, September 10, 2019, https://www.motherjones.com/politics/2019/09/alexandria -ocasio-cortez-to-republicans-history-will-remember-you-backed-trump/.

CHAPTER 24: WITCH HUNT GARBAGE

1   Alan Cullison, Rebecca Ballhaus, and Dustin Volz, "Trump Repeatedly Pressed Ukraine President to Investigate Biden's Son," *Wall Street Journal,* September 21, 2019, https://www.wsj.com/articles/trump-defends-conversation-with-ukraine -leader-11568993176.

2   Zachary Cohen and David Shortell, "Trump Pressured Ukraine's President to Investigate Biden's Son," CNN, September 20, 2019, https://www.cnn .com/2019/09/20/politics/wsj-trump-ukraine-calls-biden-investigation-giuliani /index.html.

3   Gerald Connolly, interview with the authors.

4   Benjamin Wallace-Wells, "The Political Education of the Security Democrats," *New Yorker,* December 21, 2019, https://www.newyorker.com/news/the -political-scene/the-political-education-of-the-security-democrats; Gil Cisneros, Jason Crow, Chrissy Houlahan, Elaine Luria, Mikie Sherrill, Elissa Slotkin, and Abigail Spanberger, "Seven Freshman Democrats: These Allegations Are a Threat to All We Have Sworn to Protect," *Washington Post,* September 23, 2019, https:// www.washingtonpost.com/opinions/2019/09/24/seven-freshman-democrats-these -allegations-are-threat-all-we-have-sworn-protect/.

5   Caitlin Oprysko, "'Witch Hunt Garbage': Trump Blasts News of Pelosi's Impeachment Inquiry," *Politico,* September 24, 2019, https://www.politico.com/news /2019/09/24/trump-reaction-impeachment-inquiry-000033.

6   Stefano Pitrelli and Siobhán O'Grady, "In Italy, Pompeo Was Handed Cheese. The Italian Prime Minister Wasn't Having It," *Washington Post,* October 1, 2019, https://www.washingtonpost.com/world/2019/10/01/italy-pompeo-was -handed-cheese-italian-prime-minister-wasnt-having-it/.

7   "Secretary Michael R. Pompeo and Italian Foreign Minister Luigi Di Maio at a Press Availability," Office of U.S. Consulates and Embassies in Italy, October 2, 2019, https://it.usembassy.gov/secretary-michael-r-pompeo-and-italian-foreign -minister-luigi-di-maio-at-a-press-availability.

8   Donald Trump (@realDonaldTrump), Twitter, October 2, 2019, https:// twitter.com/realDonaldTrump/status/1179422987684077568.

9   "Committees Ready Subpoena for White House After Ukraine Documents Withheld for Weeks," Committee on Foreign Affairs, October 2, 2019, https:// foreignaffairs.house.gov/2019/10/committees-ready-subpoena-for-white-house -after-ukraine-documents-withheld-for-weeks; Adam Edelman and Haley Talbot, "Pompeo Resists House Democrats' Efforts to Interview State Dept. Officials in Impeachment Inquiry," NBC News, October 1, 2019, https://www.nbcnews.com /politics/trump-impeachment-inquiry/pompeo-accuses-house-democrats-trying -bully-officials-testifying-impeachment-inquiry-n1060776.

10   Donald Trump (@realDonaldTrump), Twitter, November 18, 2018, https://twitter.com/realDonaldTrump/status/1064216956679716864; Felicia Sonmez, John Wagner, and Colby Itkowitz, "White House Says It Will Not Cooperate with House Impeachment Inquiry; Democrats Subpoena State Dept. Official," *Washington Post*, October 8, 2019; Ellen Cranley, "Giuliani Said He 'Wouldn't Cooperate' with Adam Schiff in the Ukraine Investigation," *Business Insider*, September 29, 2019; Benjamin Fearnow, "Rudy Giuliani Says He Won't Cooperate with Adam Schiff-Led Ukraine Investigation," *Newsweek*, September 29, 2019; Daniel Dales, "Fact Check: Breaking Down Adam Schiff's Account of Trump's Ukraine Call," CNN, September 27, 2019, https://www.cnn.com/2019/09/27/politics/fact-check-adam-schiff-trumps-ukraine-call/index.html.

11   Mark Mazzetti, Eileen Sullivan, Adam Goldman, and William K. Rashbaum, "2 Giuliani Associates Arrested with One-Way Tickets at U.S. Airport," *New York Times*, October 10, 2019.

12   PAC letter, White House, October 8, 2019, https://www.whitehouse.gov/wp-content/uploads/2019/10/PAC-Letter-10.08.2019.pdf.

13   Nancy Pelosi, "Pelosi Statement on Trump Administration Refusal to Comply with House Subpoenas," Speaker of the House, October 8, 2019, https://www.speaker.gov/newsroom/10819-0.

14   John T. Bennett, "Former Ethics Czar Warns Impeachment Letter 'Mistakes Trump for a King,'" *Roll Call*, October 10, 2019, https://www.rollcall.com/2019/10/09/former-ethics-czar-warns-impeachment-letter-mistakes-trump-for-a-king/; Gregg Nunziata (@greggnunziata), Twitter, October 8, 2019, https://twitter.com/greggnunziata/status/1181685021926662144.

CHAPTER 25: "PRAY FOR THE PRESIDENT"

1   Bryan Armen Graham, "Donald Trump Blasts NFL Anthem Protesters: 'Get That Son of a Bitch off the Field,'" *Guardian*, September 23, 2017, https://www.theguardian.com/sport/2017/sep/22/donald-trump-nfl-national-anthem-protests.

2   Statement from the U.S. Press Secretary, October 6, 2019.

3   George T. Conway III, "Unfit for Office," *Atlantic*, October 3, 2019, https://www.theatlantic.com/ideas/archive/2019/10/george-conway-trump-unfit-office/599128/; Quint Forgey, "George Conway Says White House Advisers Should Step Down," *Politico*, October 10, 2019, https://www.politico.com/news/2019/10/10/george-conway-trump-043814.

4   "'Don't Be a Tough Guy. Don't Be a Fool!': Read Trump's Letter to Turkish President," CNN, October 16, 2019, https://www.cnn.com/2019/10/16/politics/trump-erdogan-letter/index.html.

5   Charlie Savage, "The Kurds' Prisons and Detention Camps for ISIS Members,

Explained," *New York Times,* October 13, 2019, https://www.nytimes.com/2019/10/13/us/politics/isis-prisoners-kurds.html.

6   Mike DeBonis and Seung Min Kim, "'All Roads Lead to Putin': Pelosi Questions Trump's Loyalty in White House Clash," *Washington Post,* October 17, 2019, https://www.washingtonpost.com/powerpost/pelosi-recalls-clash-with-trump-says-she-was-probably-telling-him-that-all-roads-lead-to-putin/2019/10/17/fdbde8d2-f0f2-11e9-8693-f487c46784aa_story.html.

7   Tim Lister, "Turkey Bought Russian S-400 Missiles Designed to Down NATO Planes. For the US, That's a Problem," CNN, July 13, 2019, https://www.cnn.com/2019/07/13/europe/turkey-russia-missiles-nato-analysis-intl/index.html.

8   J. M. Rieger, "Who Was in the White House Photo of the 'Meltdown' Meeting, Annotated," *Washington Post,* October 17, 2019, https://www.washingtonpost.com/politics/2019/10/17/who-was-white-house-photo-meltdown-meeting-annotated/.

9   Donald Trump (@realDonaldTrump), Twitter, October 16, 2019, https://twitter.com/realDonaldTrump/status/1184597281808498688/photo/1.

CHAPTER 26: THE PIZZA PROTEST

1   Interview, https://www.temi.com/editor/t/-8EOqfg7tcgjNaH4S-avsY37OeUENFnqpdZrjJYndvkCn_1xbtrdE7UqVJ5LXCwOyJ4RuMMMMFc0CuwuJTAsZ8wBnHQ?loadFrom=Dashboard&openShareModal=False.

2   John Wagner, Brittany Shammas, and Michael Brice-Saddler, "House Rejects GOP Resolution to Censure Schiff for How He Has Handled the Impeachment Inquiry of Trump and the Mueller Probe," *Washington Post,* October 21, 2019, https://www.washingtonpost.com/politics/trump-impeachment-inquiry-live-updates/2019/10/21/c6630a30-f3e9-11e9-8cf0-4cc99f74d127_story.html.

3   Rachel Frazin, "Schiff Says Committees Will Eventually Make Impeachment Inquiry Transcripts Public," *Hill,* October 16, 2019, https://thehill.com/homenews/house/466197-schiff-says-committees-will-make-impeachment-inquiry-transcripts-public-when.

4   Brian Barrett, "Total SCIF Show: The GOP's Raid Puts National Security at Risk," *Wired,* October 23, 2019, https://www.wired.com/story/republicans-storm-scif-national-security-nightmare/.

5   Addy Baird, "Republicans Stormed into the Impeachment Investigation's Secure Room, and It Was Absolute Madness," *BuzzFeed,* October 23, 2019, https://www.buzzfeednews.com/article/addybaird/republicans-storm-scif-impeach-trump-pizza-phones.

6   Nicolas Wu and Bart Jansen, "GOP Protest Temporarily Halts House Democratic Impeachment Deposition of Defense Official Laura Cooper," *USA*

Today, October 23, 2019, https://www.usatoday.com/story/news/politics/2019/10/23 /impeachment-defense-official-laura-cooper-summoned-ukraine-aid/4064408002/.

CHAPTER 27: ANGELS

1   Brian Conlin, "Cummings Speaks of 'Perseverance' to Special Education Students at Hillcrest," *Baltimore Sun,* May 22, 2012, https://www.baltimoresun.com /ph-ca-cummings-hillcrest-0523-20120522-story.html.

2   "Mark Meadows Gives Emotional Tribute to Elijah Cummings," YouTube video, 2:52, posted by CBS News, October 24, 2019, https://www.youtube.com /watch?v=0Fp6ylSIe6Q.

3   Kim Bellware,"'A Giant of Integrity and Knowledge Has Fallen': Washington Reacts to the Death of Rep. Elijah Cummings," *Washington Post,* October 17, 2019, https://www.washingtonpost.com/politics/2019/10/17/elijah-cummings-death -reaction-statement.

4   "Full Transcript of Testimony of Lieutenant Colonel Alexander S. Vindman, White House Ukraine Expert," *Washington Post,* November 11, 2019, https:// www.washingtonpost.com/context/full-transcript-of-testimony-of-lieutenant -colonel-alexander-s-vindman-white-house-ukraine-expert/6c7d991c-1916-47a2 -a320-cfbbea54eb52/; Mikhaila Fogel, "Summary of Lt. Col. Alexander Vindman's Deposition Testimony," *Lawfare,* November 11, 2019, https://www.lawfareblog.com /summary-lt-col-alexander-vindmans-deposition-testimony; Gerald Connolly, from interview with the authors.

CHAPTER 28: OPEN HEARINGS

1   Daniel Politi, "Almost Half of Americans Support Impeaching Trump, Removing Him from Office," *Slate,* November 3, 2019, https://slate.com/news-and -politics/2019/11/almost-half-of-americans-support-impeaching-trump-nbc-wsj -poll.html.

2   "Read William Taylor's Prepared Opening Statement from the Impeachment Hearing," *New York Times,* November 13, 2019, https://www.nytimes.com /2019/11/13/us/politics/william-taylor-opening-statement-impeachment.html.

3   Michael D. Shear, "Key Moments from the First Public Impeachment Hearing," *New York Times,* November 13, 2019, https://www.nytimes.com/2019/11 /13/us/politics/impeachment-hearings.html.

4   "Transcript: Fiona Hill and David Holmes Testimony in Front of the House Intelligence Committee," *Washington Post,* November 21, 2019, https:// www.washingtonpost.com/politics/2019/11/21/transcript-fiona-hill-david-holmes -testimony-front-house-intelligence-committee/.

5   Christina Prignano and Martin Finucane, "Fiona Hill Condemns

'Partisan Rancor,' Urges Unity and Other Key Quotes from Her Testimony," *Boston Globe*, November 21, 2019, https://www.bostonglobe.com/news/politics /2019/11/21/the-five-most-compelling-quotes-from-fiona-hill-testimony /m2MtYZ42GEd0ZeBLCoyWaI/story.html.

6 "Marie Yovanovitch's Impeachment Hearing Opening Statement: Full Text," NBC News, November 15, 2019, https://www.nbcnews.com/politics/trump -impeachment-inquiry/marie-yovanovitch-s-impeachment-hearing-opening -statement-full-text-n1082806.

7 "Transcript: Marie Yovanovitch's Nov. 15 Testimony in Front of the House Intelligence Committee," *Washington Post*, November 16, 2019, https:// www.washingtonpost.com/politics/2019/11/16/transcript-marie-yovanovitchs-nov -testimony-front-house-intelligence-committee/.

8 Sheryl Gay Stolberg, "Ex-Envoy to Ukraine 'Devastated' as Trump Vilified Her," *New York Times*, November 15, 2019, https://www.nytimes.com/2019/11/15/us /politics/marie-yovanovitch-testimony.html.

9 Rachael Bade, Devlin Barrett, Seung Min Kim, and Mike DeBonis, "Democrats Call Trump's Tweets 'Witness Intimidation,' Contemplate Adding Charge to Impeachment Articles," *Washington Post*, November 15, 2019, https://www .washingtonpost.com/politics/even-for-trump-its-pretty-shocking-democrats-accuse -the-president-of-witness-intimidation—via-tweet/2019/11/15/6c20cc74-07d0-11ea -b388-434b5c1d7dd8_story.html.

10 "Read Gordon Sondland's Full Opening Testimony in the Trump Impeachment Hearing," PBS, November 20, 2019, https://www.pbs.org/newshour /politics/read-gordon-sondlands-full-opening-testimony-in-the-trump-impeachment -hearing; "Sondland: 'Was There a Quid Pro Quo? The Answer Is Yes,'" *Washington Post*, November 20, 2019, https://www.washingtonpost.com/video/politics/trump -impeachment-hearings/sondland-was-there-a-quid-pro-quo-the-answer-is-yes/2019 /11/20/ca6c5824-27e4-477b-a7d3-53c60c05c06e_video.html?

CHAPTER 29: SCHOLARS IN WASHINGTON

1 Andrew Prokop, "Pelosi Announces Democrats Will Draft Articles of Impeachment Against Trump," *Vox*, December 5, 2019, https://www.vox.com/policy -and-politics/2019/12/5/20995975/articles-of-impeachment-pelosi-trump.

2 Jonathan Turley, "Clinton Impeachment Testimony: House Judiciary Committee," August 20, 2007, https://jonathanturley.org/2007/08/20/clinton -impeachment-testimony-house-judiciary-committee/; Staff, "READ: Jonathan Turley Testimony," *Hill*, December 4, 2019, https://thehill.com/homenews/house /472947-read-jonathan-turley-testimony.

3 Staff, "READ: Jonathan Turley Testimony."

4   "Noah Feldman Statement," December 4, 2019, https://d3i6fh83elv35t
.cloudfront.net/static/2019/12/Feldman-Testimony.pdf.

5   Alyssa Rosenberg, "Pamela Karlan Told a Bad Joke. The One We're Playing on Ourselves Is Even Worse," *Washington Post,* December 5, 2019, https://www
.washingtonpost.com/opinions/2019/12/05/pamela-karlan-told-bad-joke-one-were
-playing-ourselves-is-even-worse/.

6   John Nichols, "At the Center of the Impeachment Debate Stands a Constitutional Scholar," *Nation,* December 13, 2019, https://www.thenation.com/article
/jamie-raskin-impeachment-scholar/; Prokop, "Pelosi Announces Democrats."

CHAPTER 30: HOUSE RULES

1   Staff, "Trump Impeachment: Analysis and News on the House Charges
and Senate Acquittal of the President," NBC News, January 21, 2020, https://www
.nbcnews.com/politics/trump-impeachment-inquiry/live-blog/trump-impeachment
-inquiry-live-updates-latest-news-n1065706/ncrd1100651#liveBlogHeader.

2   Nicholas Fandos and Michael D. Shear, "House Panel Debates Impeachment Articles in Bid to Complete Charges Against Trump," *New York Times,* December 11, 2019, https://www.nytimes.com/2019/12/11/us/politics/judiciary-committee
-impeachment-debate.html.

3   Katherine Faulders and Benjamin Siegel, "Democrats, Republicans Offer
Stark Contrasts as House Judiciary Committee Debates Articles of Impeachment,"
ABC News, December 11, 2019, https://abcnews.go.com/Politics/house-judiciary
-committee-debate-articles-impeachment-trump/story?id=67660049.

4   Staff, "Trump impeachment."

5   "House Judiciary Committee Articles of Impeachment Debate, Day 2 Part
2," C-SPAN, December 12, 2019, https://www.c-span.org/video/?467314-12/house
-judiciary-committee-articles-impeachment-debate-day-2-part-2.

6   Ibid.

7   Grace Segers, Stefan Becket, and Melissa Quinn, "House Committee Ap-
proves Rules for Impeachment Vote," CBS News, December 18, 2019, https://www
.cbsnews.com/live-updates/trump-impeachment-house-rules-committee-debate
-live-updates-live-stream-2019-12-17/.

8   Marty Johnson, "House Democrat Calls on McConnell to Recuse Himself
from Impeachment Trial," *Hill,* December 13, 2019, https://thehill.com/homenews
/house/474487-rep-demings-senator-mcconnell-violated-oath-must-recuse-himself.

9   "Congressman Raskin Statement to Rules Committee in Support of Articles of Impeachment Against President Donald J. Trump," House Committee on
the Judiciary, December 17, 2019, https://judiciary.house.gov/news/documentsingle
.aspx?DocumentID=2310.

CHAPTER 31: IMPEACHMENT DAY

1   Sheryl Gay Stolberg and Annie Karni, "Pelosi vs. Trump: 'Don't Characterize the Strength That I Bring,' She Says," *Washington Post*, December 11, 2018.

Juliegrace Brufke, "GOP Lawmaker Compares Impeachment to Pearl Harbor," *Hill*, December 18, 2019, https://thehill.com/homenews/house/475151-gop-representative-compares-impeachment-to-pearl-harbor; Bob Bauer, "Trump Is the Founders' Worst Nightmare," *New York Times*, December 2, 2019, https://www.nytimes.com/2019/12/02/opinion/trump-impeachment.html.

2   Eliza Relman, "A Republican Congressman Claims Jesus Was Treated More Fairly Before His Crucifixion Than Trump Was During Impeachment," *Business Insider*, December 18, 2019, https://www.businessinsider.com/gop-lawmaker-jesus-was-treated-more-fairly-than-trump-2019-12.

3   "Letter from President Donald J. Trump to the Speaker of the House of Representatives," White House, December 17, 2019, https://www.whitehouse.gov/briefings-statements/letter-president-donald-j-trump-speaker-house-representatives/.

4   William Cummings, "'Learn Some History': Salem Mayor Rips Trump for Comparing Impeachment to Witch Trials," *USA Today*, December 18, 2019, https://www.usatoday.com/story/news/politics/2019/12/18/salem-mayor-kim-driscoll-criticizes-trump-impeachment-comparision/2686485001/.

5   Sean Collins, "Rep. Steny Hoyer Made a Quiet, Powerful Case for Bipartisanship During the Impeachment Debate," *Vox*, December 18, 2019, https://www.vox.com/policy-and-politics/2019/12/18/21029136/house-impeachment-debate-steny-hoyer-closing-statement.

6   Lydia O'Connor, "Kellogg Is Latest Company to Pull Advertising from Breitbart," *Huffington Post*, November 29, 2016, https://www.huffpost.com/entry/kellogg-breitbart_n_583db639e4b04b66c01bde6a.

7   Eliza Relman, "Trump Ridiculed His Opponents and Touted the Economy at a Michigan Rally While the House Impeached Him at the Same Time," *Business Insider*, December 19, 2019, https://www.businessinsider.com/trump-rally-impeachment-live-updates.

8   Rachel Maddow, MSNBC, December 19, 2019.

CHAPTER 32: THE WAITING GAME

1   "Speaker Pelosi News Conference," C-SPAN, December 18, 2019, https://www.c-span.org/video/?467571-1/speaker-pelosi-impeachment-managers-senate-trial-process#.

2   Laurence H. Tribe, "Don't Let Mitch McConnell Conduct a Potemkin Impeachment Trial," *Washington Post*, December 16, 2019, https://www.washingtonpost

.com/opinions/dont-let-mitch-mcconnell-conduct-a-potemkin-impeachment-trial
/2019/12/16/71a81b30-202f-11ea-a153-dce4b94e4249_story.html.

3 Mariam Khan, "McConnell Says He and Democrats 'at an Impasse' over
Senate Impeachment Trial," ABC News, December 19, 2019, https://abcnews.go
.com/Politics/democrats-cold-feet-mcconnell-afraid-send-shoddy-impeachment
/story?id=67824205.

4 Heather Caygle and John Bresnahan, "'I'm Never Afraid and I'm Rarely
Surprised': Pelosi Emboldened," *Politico,* December 20, 2019, https://www.politico
.com/news/2019/12/20/nancy-pelosi-interview-088292?nname=playbook&nid
=0000014f-1646-d88f-a1cf-5f46b7bd0000&nrid=0000015d-ccf3-de22-abdf
-eff70b570000&nlid=630318.

5 Donald Trump (@realDonaldTrump), Twitter, December 20, 2019, https://
twitter.com/realDonaldTrump/status/1207997319821615105?ref_src=twsrc%5Et
fw%7Ctwcamp%5Etweetembed%7Ctwterm%5E1207997319821615105&ref_url
=https%3A%2F%2Fwww.washingtonpost.com%2Fopinions%2F2019%2F12%2F2
0%2Ftrumps-rage-christianity-today-gives-away-his-scam%2F.

6 Rachel Maddow, MSNBC, December 19, 2019.

7 Jordain Carney, "McConnell Says He'll Be in 'Total Coordination' with
White House on Impeachment Trial Strategy," *Hill,* December 12, 2019, https://
thehill.com/homenews/senate/474399-mcconnell-says-hell-be-in-total-coordination
-with-white-house-on-impeachment.

8 Seung Min Kim, Paul Kane, and Elise Viebeck, "Senate Leaders Battle
over Impeachment Trial After McConnell Rejects Democrats' Calls for Witnesses,"
Washington Post, December 17, 2019, https://www.washingtonpost.com/politics
/mcconnell-rejects-democrats-call-for-new-witnesses-in-senate-impeachment-trial
/2019/12/17/dbdc326a-20e9-11ea-bed5-880264cc91a9_story.html.

9 Veronica Stracqualursi, "'I'm Not Trying to Pretend to Be a Fair Juror Here':
Graham Predicts Trump Impeachment Will 'Die Quickly' in Senate," CNN, December 14, 2019, https://www.cnn.com/2019/12/14/politics/lindsey-graham-trump
-impeachment-trial/index.html.

10 Sean Maguire, "Murkowski 'Disturbed' by McConnell's Vow for 'Total
Coordination' with White House for Impeachment Trial," KTUU, December 24,
2019, https://www.ktuu.com/content/news/-Murkowski-disturbed-by-McConnells
-vow-for-total-coordination-with-White-House-for-impeachment-trial-566472361
.html.

11 Eric Lipton, Maggie Haberman, and Mark Mazzetti, "Behind the Ukraine
Aid Freeze: 84 Days of Conflict and Confusion," *New York Times,* December 29, 2019,
https://www.nytimes.com/2019/12/29/us/politics/trump-ukraine-military-aid.html.

12 Sarah Gray, "Top Democrat Says Bombshell Report About Withheld

Military Aid to Ukraine Is a 'Game Changer' Ahead of Senate Impeachment Trial," *Business Insider,* December 30, 2019, https://www.businessinsider.com/schumer-says -bombshell-nyt-report-game-changer-for-senate-trial-2019-12.

13   Aaron Bycoffe, Ella Koeze, and Nathaniel Rakich, "Did Americans Support Removing Trump From Office?," FiveThirtyEight, February 12, 2020, https:// projects.fivethirtyeight.com/impeachment-polls/.

14   Nicholas Fandos, "McConnell Says He Will Proceed on Impeachment Trial Without Witness Deal," *New York Times,* January 7, 2020, https://www.nytimes .com/2020/01/07/us/politics/impeachment-trial-witnesses.html.

15   Nicholas Fandos, "Pelosi Alerts House to Be Ready to Send Impeachment Articles Next Week," *New York Times,* January 10, 2020, https://www.nytimes.com /2020/01/10/us/politics/trump-impeachment-pelosi.html.

CHAPTER 33: THE REAL ARTICLES

1   Tom LoBianco, Drew Griffin, and Scott Zamost, "Florida AG Sought Donation Before Nixing Trump University Fraud Case," CNN, June 11, 2016, https://www .cnn.com/2016/06/10/politics/pam-bondi-donald-trump-donation/index.html.

2   Marianne Levine, "Chief Justice John Roberts Admonishes House Managers and White House Counsel," *Politico,* January 22, 2020, https://www.politico .com/news/2020/01/22/roberts-admonishes-house-managers-wh-counsel-101990.

3   Kyle Cheney, Burgess Everett, and Andrew Desiderio, "John Roberts Refuses Rand Paul's Whistleblower Question," *Politico,* January 30, 2020, https://www .politico.com/news/2020/01/30/john-roberts-rand-paul-whistleblower-109527.

4   Veronica Stracqualursi, "Romney Says 'Very Likely' He'll Be in Favor of Witnesses but Won't Decide Until After Opening Arguments," CNN, January 25, 2020, https://www.cnn.com/2020/01/25/politics/mitt-romney-witnesses -impeachment-trial/index.html.

5   Mark Leibovich, "Mitt Romney, a Man Alone," *New York Times,* January 30, 2020, https://www.nytimes.com/2020/01/30/us/politics/impeachment-romney .html.

6   "Mitt Romney's Full Speech on Why He's Voting to Convict Trump," *Los Angeles Times,* February 5, 2020, https://www.latimes.com/politics/story/2020-02 -05/mitt-romneys-full-speech-on-why-hes-voting-to-convict-trump; "Sen. Mitt Romney's Full Speech Announcing He Will Vote to Convict Trump," YouTube video, 8:23, posted by *The Washington Post,* February 5, 2020, https://www.youtube .com/watch?v=C5oPNG6HLgM.

7   Matt Stieb, "Trump World's Backlash Toward Mitt Romney Has Begun, and It Will Never End," *Intelligencer,* February 6, 2020, https://nymag.com/intelligencer /2020/02/trump-worlds-backlash-toward-mitt-romney-will-never-end.html.

8   Stan Greenberg, "Americans' Revulsion for Trump Is Underappreciated," *Atlantic*, March 24, 2020, https://www.theatlantic.com/ideas/archive/2020/03/the -democrats-dont-understand-their-own-strength/608611/; Alex Isenstadt, "Trump's 2016 Campaign Brass Warns He's in Trouble in 2020," *Politico*, May 24, 2020, https://www.politico.com/news/2020/05/26/trump-campaign-lewandowski-bossie -283089; Nic Cheeseman and Spencer Piston, "Four Ways Donald Trump Is Already Manipulating the U.S. Elections," *Washington Post*, June 16, 2020.

EPILOGUE

1   Quint Forgey, "Dershowitz Attempts to Clarify Controversial Argument About Presidential Powers," *Politico*, January 30, 2020, https://www.politico.com /news/2020/01/30/alan-dershowitz-presidential-powers-109474.

2   Ben Gittleson and Jordyn Phelps, "Trump Declares Victory over Impeachment: 'It Was Evil,'" ABC News, February 6, 2020, https://abcnews.go.com/Politics /trump-respond-senate-trial-acquittal-noon-remarks-white/story?id=68800473.

3   Peter Baker, Michael S. Schmidt, and Maggie Haberman, "Republican Senators Tried to Stop Trump from Firing Impeachment Witness," *New York Times*, February 8, 2020, https://www.nytimes.com/2020/02/08/us/politics/trump -vindman-sondland-fired.html; Helene Cooper and Catie Edmondson, "Trump, Returning to Retribution, Withdraws Pentagon Nomination, *New York Times*, March 2, 2020, https://www.nytimes.com/2020/03/02/us/politics/trump-pentagon-mccusker -nomination.html; Jen Kirby, "Trump's Purge of Inspectors General, Explained," *Vox*, May 29, 2020, https://www.vox.com/2020/5/28/21265799/inspectors-general -trump-linick-atkinson.

4   Patricia Mazzei and Frances Robles, "Former FEMA Official Accused of Taking Bribes in Hurricane Maria Recovery," *New York Times*, September 10, 2019, https://www.nytimes.com/2019/09/10/us/puerto-rico-fema-arrests-corruption.html.

5   Jane Mayer, "The Making of the Fox News White House," *New Yorker*, March 4, 2019, https://www.newyorker.com/magazine/2019/03/11/the-making-of -the-fox-news-white-house.

6   Patrick Murray, "Public Opinion on Impeachment: Lessons from Watergate," Monmouth University, June 12, 2017, https://www.monmouth.edu/polling -institute/2017/06/12/public-opinion-on-impeachment-lessons-from-watergate/; "75% of Voters Say Allow Witnesses in Senate Impeachment Trial, Quinnipiac University National Poll Finds; 53% Say President Trump Not Telling Truth About Ukraine," Quinnipiac University, January 28, 2020, https://poll.qu.edu/national /release-detail?ReleaseID=3654; Aaron Bycoffe, Ella Koeze, and Nathaniel Rakich, "Did Americans Support Removing Trump from Office?," FiveThirtyEight, February 12, 2020, https://projects.fivethirtyeight.com/impeachment-polls/.

7 "Congressional Favorability Ratings," Rasmussen Reports, February 17, 2020, https://www.rasmussenreports.com/public_content/politics/mood_of _america/congressional_faves_jan17.

8 Donald Ayer, "Why Bill Barr Is So Dangerous," *Atlantic*, June 30, 2019, https://www.theatlantic.com/ideas/archive/2019/06/bill-barrs-dangerous-pursuit -executive-power/592951/.

9 Peter Baker, J. David Goodman, Michael Rothfeld, and Elizabeth Williamson, "The 11 Criminals Granted Clemency by Trump Had One Thing in Common: Connections," *New York Times*, February 19, 2020, https://www.nytimes .com/2020/02/19/us/politics/trump-pardons.html?action=click&module=Top%20 Stories&pgtype=Homepage; "READ: Justice Department's Updated Sentencing Memo for Trump Ally Roger Stone," CNN News, February 11, 2020, https://www .cnn.com/2020/02/11/politics/roger-stone-sentencing-memo-updated/index.html.

10 Dan Berman and Katelyn Polantz, "'The American People Cared. And I Care.' Top Lines from Judge Amy Berman Jackson During the Roger Stone Sentencing," CNN, January 21, 2020, https://www.cnn.com/2020/02/20/politics/amy -berman-jackson-quotes/index.html; Jacqueline Thomsen and C. Ryan Barber, "'Flagrant Disregard for the Institutions of Government': Roger Stone Sentenced to over 3 Years in Prison," *Law*, February 20, 2020, https://www.law.com/nationallawjournal /2020/02/20/flagrant-disregard-for-the-institutions-of-government-roger-stone -sentenced-to-over-3-years-in-prison/.

11 Greg Miller, Shane Harris, and Karoun Demirjian, "Acting Director of National Intelligence Threatened to Resign If He Couldn't Speak Freely Before Congress on Whistleblower Complaint," *Washington Post*, September 25, 2019, https:// www.washingtonpost.com/national-security/acting-director-of-national-intelligence -threatened-to-resign-if-he-couldnt-speak-freely-before-congress/2019/09/25 /b1deb71e-dfbf-11e9-be96-6adb81821e90_story.html.

12 Ellen Nakashima, Shane Harris, Josh Dawsey, and Anne Gearan, "Senior Intelligence Official Told Lawmakers That Russia Wants to See Trump Reelected," *Washington Post*, February 21, 2020, https://www.washingtonpost.com /national-security/after-a-congressional-briefing-on-election-threats-trump-soured -on-acting-spy-chief/2020/02/20/1ed2b4ec-53f1-11ea-b119-4faabac6674f_story .html; Daniel Lippman, "NSC Aide Who Worked to Discredit Russia Probe Moves to Senior ODNI Post," *Politico*, February 20, 2020, https://www.politico.com/news /2020/02/20/kash-patel-odni-post-116546.

13 Charlie Savage and Adam Goldman, "Outsider Tapped in Flynn Case Calls Justice Dept. Reversal a 'Gross Abuse' of Power," *New York Times*, June 10, 2020; Michael Flynn, "Forces of Evil Want to Steal Our Freedom in the Dark of Night, but God Stands with Us," *Western Journal*, June 11, 2020.

14   Peter Wade, "Trump Signals Roger Stone Pardon: 'He Can Sleep Well at Night!,'" *Rolling Stone*, June 4, 2020; Factbox: "'Prepare to Die' – Most Colorful Alleged Threats by Trump Ally Stone," Reuters, January 25, 2019, https://www.reuters .com/article/us-usa-trump-russia-stone-factbox/factbox-prepare-to-die-most-colorful -alleged-threats-by-trump-ally-stone-idUSKCN1PJ1FS; Mitt Romney on Twitter, July 11, 2020.

15   Michael Tomasky, "Why Does Trump Lie?," *New York Times*, June 11, 2020, https://www.nytimes.com/2020/06/11/opinion/trump-lies.html; "Report of the Select Committee on Intelligence United States Senate on Russian Active Measures Campaigns and Interference in the 2016 U.S. Election Volume 4: Review of the Intelligence Community Assessment," https://www.intelligence.senate.gov/sites /default/files/documents/Report_Volume4.pdf; Andrew Desiderio, "Senate Republicans Authorize Subpoenas in Probe Targeting Trump Enemies," *Politico*, June 11, 2020, https://www.politico.com/news/2020/06/11/senate-republicans-authorize -subpoenas-in-probes-targeting-former-obama-officials-313123.

16   Aaron Blake, "Trump's Playbook on 'Obamagate' Is Extremely—and Dubiously—Familiar," *Washington Post*, May 15, 2020.

17   John Bolton, "The Scandal of Trump's China Policy," *Wall Street Journal*, June 17, 2020, https://www.wsj.com/articles/john-bolton-the-scandal-of-trumps -china-policy-11592419564; Peter Baker, "Five Takeaways from John Bolton's Memoir," *New York Times*, June 18, 2020, https://www.nytimes.com/2020/06/18 /us/politics/john-bolton-memoir-takeaways.html?searchResultPosition=1. *For Adam Schiff's post about Bolton's book, see:* https://twitter.com/RepAdamSchiff/status /1273347802026979328.

18   Marisa Fernandez, "Ousted Vaccine Chief: I Was Told My Pandemic Warnings Were 'Causing a Commotion,'" *Axios*, May 14, 2020, https://www.axios .com/rick-bright-testimony-coronavirus-response-d1362f5e-9033-481b-afb7 -5e1a716f52bc.html.

19   Aaron Rupar, "'You Little Pencil Neck': Trump's Taunts of Schiff in Toledo Were Like a Parody of a Playground Bully," *Vox*, January 10, 2020, https://www.vox .com/2020/1/10/21059771/trump-toledo-rally-schiff-soleimani.

20   Ryan Goodman and Danielle Schulkin, "Timeline of Coronavirus Pandemic and U.S. Response," *Just Security*, May 7, 2020, https://www.justsecurity.org /69650/timeline-of-the-coronavirus-pandemic-and-u-s-response/; Derrick Bryson Taylor, "How the Coronavirus Pandemic Unfolded: A Timeline," *New York Times*, June 9, 2020, https://news.yahoo.com/covid-case-spike-united-states-texas-arizona -north-carolina-coronavirus-201958682.html; "Tracking the Pandemic: Are Coronavirus Cases Rising or Falling in Your State?," NPR.org, June 12, 2020, https://www .npr.org/sections/health-shots/2020/03/16/816707182/map-tracking-the-spread-of

-the-coronavirus-in-the-u-s; "Coronavirus (COVID-19) Deaths Worldwide Per One Million Population as of June 12, 2020, by Country," Statista.com; "Mortality in the Most Affected Countries," Johns Hopkins University Medicine, Coronavirus Resource Center, July 21, 2020, https://coronavirus.jhu.edu/data/mortality; Jeffrey Skelley, "The Latest Swing State Polls Look Good for Biden," FiveThirtyEight, June 12, 2020, https://fivethirtyeight.com/features/the-latest-swing-state-polls-look -good-for-biden/.

21   Anna North, "White Americans Are Finally Talking About Racism. Will It Translate into Action?," *Vox*, June 11, 2020, https://www.vox.com/2020/6/11 /21286642/george-floyd-protests-white-people-police-racism; Nate Cohn and Kevin Quealy, "How Public Opinion Has Moved on Black Lives Matter," *New York Times*, June 10, 2020, https://www.nytimes.com/interactive/2020/06/10/upshot/black-lives -matter-attitudes.html.

INDEX